Minor Prophets
Major Themes

Daniel Berrigan

WIPF & STOCK · Eugene, Oregon

Wipf and Stock Publishers
199 W 8th Ave, Suite 3
Eugene, OR 97401

Minor Prophets, Major Themes
By Berrigan, Daniel
Copyright©1995 Catholic Worker
ISBN 13: 978-1-60608-634-6
Publication date 4/23/2009
Previously published by Fortcamp/RoseHill Catholic Worker, 1995

SERIES FOREWORD

Daniel Berrigan is one of the most influential American Catholics of the twentieth century. A Jesuit priest, poet, and peacemaker, he has inspired countless people of faith and conscience to pursue the gospel vision of a world without war or nuclear weapons. Born in 1921, he entered the Society of Jesus in 1939, was ordained in 1952, and in 1957 published his first book of poetry, *Time Without Number*, which won the prestigious Lamont Poetry Award.

Since then Daniel Berrigan, my friend and Jesuit brother, has published over fifty books, including the award-winning play, *The Trial of the Catonsville Nine* (1970); an autobiography, *To Dwell in Peace* (1987); and many journals, essays, poetry collections, and scripture commentaries. Dan maintained close friend friendships with Thomas Merton and Dorothy Day. He also co-founded the Catholic Peace Fellowship and Clergy and Laity Concerned about Vietnam. But because of his early peace work, church authorities banished him to Latin America in 1966 and 1967. In early 1968, he traveled to Hanoi with Howard Zinn to experience firsthand the horrors of U.S. war-making and to rescue three U.S. soldiers who had been captured.

On May 19, 1968, with his brother Philip and other friends, he burned military draft files using homemade napalm in Catonsville, Maryland—an action which galvanized millions against the Vietnam war. For this creative nonviolence, Dan was tried, convicted, and sentenced to years in prison. In April of 1970, however, he went underground, eluding the FBI, and continued to draw widespread attention to his antiwar message. He was finally arrested in August, and imprisoned in Danbury, Connecticut until February 1972.

He continued to write and speak against war and nuclear weapons throughout the 70s. On September 9, 1980, both he and Philip participated in the first Plowshares Action, a protest at the General Electric Plant at King of Prussia, Pennsylvania. He faced ten years in prison, but was eventually sentenced to time served.

Since the early 1970s, Dan has lived in New York City with his Jesuit community. He continues to give lectures, conduct retreats, publish books of poetry and scripture study—and get arrested for his protests against war, injustice, and nuclear weapons. He remains a clear voice of resistance to war, gospel nonviolence, and peace for humanity.

Throughout his faithful, peacemaking life, Daniel Berrigan has consistently said no to every war, injustice, and weapon of violence. And with every no he accepts the cost. And he does not give up. Nominated many times for the Nobel Peace Prize, Dan often finds himself with friends before some judge and sitting on ice in some dismal holding cell. Such is the mark of a prophet, the sign of an apostle of peace.

"We have assumed the name of peacemakers," Dan writes in *No Bars to Manhood*,

> but we have been, by and large, unwilling to pay any significant price. And because we want the peace with half a heart and half a life and will, the war, of course, continues, because the waging of war, by its nature, is total—but the waging of peace, by our own cowardice, is partial. There is no peace because there are no peacemakers. There are no makers of peace because the making of peace is at least as costly as the making of war, at least as exigent, at least as disruptive, at least as liable to bring disgrace and prison and death in its wake.

Foreword

"The only message I have to the world is: we are not allowed to kill innocent people," he told the court during his Plowshares Eight trial.

> We are not allowed to be complicit in murder. We are not allowed to be silent while preparations for mass murder proceed in our name, with our money, secretly. . . . It's terrible for me to live in a time where I have nothing to say to human beings except, 'Stop killing.' There are other beautiful things that I would love to be saying to people. There are other projects I could be very helpful at. And I can't do them. I cannot. Because everything is endangered. Everything is up for grabs. Ours is a kind of primitive situation, even though we would call ourselves sophisticated. Our plight is very primitive from a Christian point of view. We are back where we started. 'Thou shalt not kill'; we are not allowed to kill. Everything today comes down to that—everything.

I am very grateful to Wipf and Stock Publishers for republishing some of Dan's classic works in a series, books which influenced millions of people when they first appeared. I hope these books will be studied, passed around to friends and neighbors, and promoted far and wide. They still offer great hope, wisdom, and encouragement.

In the life and words of Daniel Berrigan we discover new faith in the God of peace and courage to pursue God's reign of peace. We see signs and guideposts for the path ahead, toward a new future of peace. And we find strength to take our own stand for justice and disarmament, to take another step forward on the road to peace and nonviolence. May these books inspire us to become, like Daniel Berrigan, peacemakers in a world of war.

—John Dear
Cerrillos, New Mexico
August 2007

CONTENTS

FOREWORD	i
INTRODUCTION	vii
HOSEA	1
JOEL	79
AMOS	119
OBADIAH	157
JONAH	173
MICAH	211
NAHUM	247
HABAKKUK	277
ZEPHANIAH	313
HAGGAI	319
ZECHARIAH	333
MALACHAI	385

FOREWORD

Prophecy is the voice that God gives to the silent agony, a voice to the plundered poor, to the profaned riches of the world. It is a form of living, a crossing point.... God is raging in the prophet's word.
                                                            Abraham Heschel

Let me begin quite personally. Twenty years ago I was a student at Union Seminary in New York City. The anti-war and civil rights movements had already left their form on my young politics. I was a seminarian, but expected to emerge some sort of community organizer with "a theological perspective." Most of what I then believed was little more than sociology.

I recall at the time a course in the Passion of Christ from an eminent scholar. We were treated, among other historically critical data, to the latest in archeological evidence for the method of crucifixion, how the ankles would be turned and the nails driven, the excruciating mechanics of death. The accuracy was impeccable, but the passion was at a safe remove: past tense and lukewarm.

As providence would have it (from my perspective like an intervention of the Word) Dan Berrigan just then walked out of Danbury Prison, where he had done time in consequence of the 1968 Catonsville action, and into that upper west side academic fortress.

With him came the scent of prison. The smells of the charnel house, of napalm and tiger cage tortures, were also in the wind. He stood before us and read the news with Jacques Ellul in one hand and the Revelation of John in the other. Present tense afire.

Never had I met any one who took The Book with such life and death seriousness. Who thought in its own idiom. Who read it from the inside out. Who expected to find therein the powers of this world demytholo-

FOREWORD

gized and exposed, and who took recourse to the scriptures in hopes of imagining the real world. Who thereby resisted the former and bet his life on the latter.

I got knocked off my horse. A tidy worldview crumbled. I do not exaggerate: I was struck dumb and wandered the seminary for a time more than a little lost. Berrigan noticed and one day called my name down a long basement hallway. Would I come up for Irish coffee? By and by: did I pray? Or read the Bible for any reason but a paper assigned? Had I ever seen these books: Merton on the Dessert Fathers or Dorothy Day on the Long Loneliness? What signposts in the landscape did I follow? I took up the questions, like signposts in the landscape, and made them my own.

I have seen him do this with others since, some virtually in the grip of despair or death. Don't die, he would say. Come along, we need you. Don't be a conscious integer in the empire's spiritual body count. He made it seem as if resurrection and discipleship were synonyms.

And lo and behold: among us at Union a community of faith and resistance coalesced at the edge of the fortress wall.

Now these meditations on the prophets minor provoke my conversion once again.

As I first read the following pages, yet another war was in the air with its ever perfected mechanics of death: cruise missiles, fuel air bombs, laser-guided et cetteras. Their shadows cross the page herein. Their victims cry out.

The drumbeat of war is not merely contextual background music, it is virtually the occasion of recourse. Who would have thought that meditating on Haggai or Zechariah during the Persian Gulf War could preserve one's moral sanity? Indeed prove the very act of sanity? Indeed prove the very act of sanity? That is Berrigan's claim, and this book stands behind it.

Here is a commentary which ought to be required reading in Old Testament seminars, though one suspects in some it would need to be snuck in the door. This is more than a commentary in the conventional sense. It jumps the track of passionless objectivity and moves readily across time, deftly implicating our lives and history.

This is not to suggest that conventional scholarship is preempted. The academics have been attended to and given their due. Berrigan defers to them and lets them speak, setting off their quotations to shade in background or an historical skyline, to provide a subtle insight, or even to serve

FOREWORD

an ironic foil which may typify ourselves, our culture-bound imaginations and judgments.

But then. The commentary cracks and breaks open the genre. More than a hermeneutic is commended: it partakes the prophetic method.

Even the style betrays an intuitive act of mimicry. These reflections are laid out on the page almost in fragments, with breaks or breaths or seams between. We are reminded how the prophetic utterances are gathered up (by the prophets themselves or mayhap their disciples) and stitched together — by their best light and inspirations — into more or less coherent books. The scholars, in their turn, never tire of reversing the process, sifting and separating the isolated "periscopes," even rearranging material according to their own lights. In any event, the seams are there to be recognized. You can feel them in the fits and leaps of reading. And in between, in the gaps and the cracks there is — what? sighs too deep for words? a silent agony? the wrestling with God or doubt or death? the movement of history? — all these and more.

This book has its own pre-history. One hears portions offered and refined in retreats where this or that prophet was commended for common consideration. One imagines passages circulated hand to hand in jail cells, where prisoners of conscience abide and take heart. Certain fragments were surely commended among those preparing for public witness at, let us guess, a faith and resistance gathering. These are reflections hammered out in common decision.

One hastens to recall the Plowshares movement (now flourishing a decade or more) and wonders: was Micah 4 the breaking and entry point for this book? Was it the way in, the door opening for Berrigan upon the whole rag-tag crew of the minor prophets?

A small irony: the minors were almost exclusively word prophets, but this commentary is shot through with present day deeds and symbolic actions — more after the fashion of Jeremiah's signs: crashing down the pots, donning the yoke of empire, burying the loincloth, or investing in the absurd real estate of return. The actions which Berrigan invokes — at Pentagon and nuclear installations, laboratories and bunkers, in the streets and on the road of return with Salvadoran campesinos — are invariably to the point. Across the time, by grounded imagination and faith, the word and the deed, the text and community, illuminate one another.

This book is stunning in its ability to evoke the humanity of the prophets. Why should that seem such a rarity? From one theological extreme their canonization sanctifies them beyond reach, or (another version of the same

FOREWORD

thing) renders them faceless and empty conduits for the Word. From another, more sophisticated, they are reduced to cultural ciphers, instruments of the social forces which engage in the literary production of texts. Here, however, they are granted life, summoned in all their humanity. The Word is their struggle with conscience, their burning tears, their prayer and choice. In that sense, their humanity provokes our own.

And a conversation begins. Having heard them in their full humanness (with all the foibles and confusions and blind spots and shortfalls entailed) Berrigan claims a freedom to disagree, to criticize, even to call these mentors to account before community and our God. Do they challenge our lives and hearts? Yes. But if we're in this thing together, then let us push back.

Their sexism comes to mind, with Hosea a flaming exemplar. Has he reduced his wife Gomer to a theological metaphor? Berrigan names this nothing less than abuse, and turns things back on the prophet with a Book of Gomer giving the silent nobody a voice. Is Hosea thereby written off and out? By no means. But in his exposure we are all made the better.

Or take Obadiah. How, Berrigan goes so far as to ponder, did this small-minded, rancorous prophet full of vengeful bitterness even make it into the canon? He supplants Yahweh with Mars, and sits smugly in the book. And yet: his humanity is so like our own in this very regard, as are his confusions. "Let Obadiah remind us of a long and bitter history of bellicose folly." Even then the prophet has flashes of insight: if he's wrong about God, his take on empire is clear seeing and lucid.

Herewith another astonishment: that the prophets should be so unanimous, so univocal, so collectively relentless in their complaint against empire in its manifold forms, near and far. Has Berrigan inflated or inflicted this on the texts, bringing along and imposing some politic of his own? Read the texts. They are uncompromising. Perhaps our amazement is evidence against us that the imperial spirit, near and far, has muted and suppressed these neglected voices too long from our hearing.

There is one thing which Berrigan does bring unapologetically to these conversations and reflections: the commitment to nonviolence. It functions like the plumbline of Amos. He holds it out to us, out to the prophets. Its line goes straight to the heart of earth, straight to the heart of Christ. Of course, beside it empires are crooked and top-heavy walls shown ready to collapse. But prophets too may be bent, even their ideas of God might suffer a twist.

Another way of saying this is that the gospels are never far from the page. The One who is the fullness of humanity, a prophet mighty in deed,

FOREWORD

steps from the wings now and again — not so much to speak as to show his wounds, to look the prophets in the eye and love them.

Echoing Dorothy Day's derision of being called a saint, William Stringfellow used to inveigh against those who labeled Dan Berrigan a prophet (or a poet) in order to write him off, beyond the realm of ordinary people, ordinary responsibility, normative and human action. I suppose it is not unlike the tactic of confining the Word of God only to a sacred book — in order to banish it safely from our scene, as though it were not everywhere and always to be recognized in common history and our lives.

The fact of the matter is that Dan Berrigan *is* both prophet and poet. This book confirms and verifies both vocations once again. But let none of us thereby be off the hook of mere Christianity's demands, nor fear to recognize, endure and enjoy, the Word wherever it may be found.

Bill Wylie-Kellermann

INTRODUCTION

'Minor' prophet is, of course, a relative term. Sometimes the term is even taken to imply the pejorative. It is as though such spirits as Nahum, Micah, Zephania, Habakkuk, Obadiah, Joel and others, were pushed to one side by the great ecstatics - Isaiah, Jeremiah, Ezekiel, Daniel.

In a sense the contention is accurate. The minor prophets are displaced by the major. Perhaps better than 'displaced,' they are given their rightful place. And this it must be insisted, is to the glory of each.

The lesser too has its proper splendor, its glow. Can one be allowed an image? The diamond, tiny though perfect, is not diminished by the noon sun — the jewel takes the great planet to heart, breaks its white light into a concentrated blazing spectrum.

Did the Hebrew Bible contain only the minor prophets, we would still have accounts of a faith lived to the hilt, by one, by many, amid storm and reversal. A faith of central moment to ourselves, faithfully recorded and intact.

More to the point for Christians, through the minor prophets the imagination of Jesus is nourished by images both godly and human.

One ventures a heartfelt bias. We lean toward the 'minors'; we are (to grant ourselves a large honor) at home in their company. Their stature is not overpowering. Nor are their epiphanies, whether they are granted visions of Jawe and the heavenly court, or not. Usually they walk by faith.

We feel cut to their cloth; they are kind toward our (average or less than average) stature — and this without distain.

INTRODUCTION

More, this company of minors do the 'diamond thing.' They offer, in less detail certainly, one or another of the central themes, godly or worldly as may be (or both), political, mystical, themes explored by the great ones. They too, the minors, must confront the great, overweening, invasive, evasive, dissolute, power-ridden kings. They scrutinize the worship of the tribe with a cold or hot eye: does worship submit before the God of justice, or is it all sham and show? They are relentless in pursuit of public integrity. Are the poor being succored? Are widow and orphan held in honor?

These prophets also speak the truth to power. They stand for something, in their eyes infinitely more precious than life itself: fidelity, the 'hesed' of God, in the betraying world. And they suffer the consequence, more often than not. They go into exile along with their people, and keep the spirit of covenant alight in dark times.

Major or minor voices, the message is the same, the style alike. And the most powerful theme unites all — major, minor — they serve and speak for the one God.

Apart from the likes of these, then and now, the world is a lunar madhouse.

As we know, if we know so much as our own name.

Imperial ego, invasions, seizure of slaves, mass executions, booty beyond imagining, the rise and fall of empire. And then something else — crime and accountability.

Here we pause, and are grateful. No tyrant has escaped the withering glance of judgment. The prophets and their writings gather no dust!

We cannot be reminded of this too often: Then or now, in the lifetime of the prophets or our own generation, the 'kings' must stand under judgment.

Scripture is written for our 'instruction,' for our 'comfort.' Which is to say, our strengthening.

Thus the prophets stand as correctives against the bowdlerizing chaos of imperial history, the perversion and suppression of truth, the pretense of immortality, the triumphant arches, the steles, the pyramids and royal tombs — the preposterous sham of the superhumans. Come down, come down, is the prophetic cry; we shall take your true measure!

Indeed according to this noble company, the history of empire is for the most part a bloody cliche. One after another, the tyrants and their sycophants assume power, kill, invade, conquer — and then fall, assassinat-

INTRODUCTION

ed, betrayed, replaced. As they have done unto others....

They are like a procession of iron figures issuing on the hour from a town clock. Each is ominous, stilted, empty. Each resembles the other, the one who follows, the one who precedes. Each is seen for a moment full face, strikes his gong, then turns abruptly and disappears, clanking along the track into darkness.

And what is learned, what has changed? Nothing. Except, it might be argued (and so is argued by Nahum and his like), for the worse.

Judgment is the pivot, the meaning conferred by the prophet on the otherwise meaningless charade of power. Accountability is demanded. Ironically, judgment is the sole dignity of the imperial ones. And irony of ironies, the dignity must be conferred by an outsider, an adversary in fact!

To be held accountable, to be summoned to the court of Jawe is an ironic distinction, but a genuine. Which is to say, this or that Great One, before whom the world fell prostrate, was after all — human. He too, like all his kind, stands within the ambit of the law. And yet, all his imperial life long, no one dared say so, neither subject nor courtier nor court prophet nor colonized slave. Other titles, honors, immunities, fawnings! Everything but the truth.

Apart from the truth (and the great ones passed their lives in pursuit of that power which is stranger or enemy of truth), what remains is for the most part despicable, tawdry, greedy, bloodshot.

All of which raises a point.

What shall we say of public life today, of those who hold authority, of their policies — more particularly of that rush to war in the Saudi desert? Into the chaos the United Nations was caught up, transformed for the first time into a signatory of war. It was all a horror, a shambles; in Nahum's terms a neo-Babylonian incursion.

Only a judgment against the bloody proceedings, feeble and unheard as it may be, confers a semblance of coherence. We must hold to that, as another thump of the war drum summons the old bloody imperial story, dusted off, feebly justified. Let the nations rush to war; the vocation of believers is to speak up. To stand somewhere. To judge that which purports to stand outside or above judgment. Jawe has spoken.

INTRODUCTION

Taking such events seriously is a political offering of great moment. We must continue to question our souls. What does such carnage portend? Does it diminish or deepen or destroy faith? And what of community; are we drawn closer one to another by catastrophic times, or do such days scatter us like a chaff?

Awful events wreak havoc within, as well as in the world at large. Emotions rise and fall bewilderingly; moods veer wildly. As public life grows more violent and chaotic, are we swept away by fear, hatred, anomie, appetite, despair? Do we join (even by silence) the common outcry for vengeance, or do we hold firmly to a word of forgiveness and forebearing? Does our emotional life, feverish or icy, become the only reality we attend to? Do questions of public injustice, racism, war, cease to trouble us? (Thus alas, many 'cope' with the times — by withdrawing from the fray.)

HOSEA

In this prophet we have an early version of another, later firebrand. Jesus will refer to one of His own, half humorously, as a 'son of thunder'; Hosea is violent and tender, both.

One does well to underscore from the start the greatness of his oracles, as well as their shortcomings.

In its early chapters, commentators assure us, the book of Hosea offers neither an allegory nor a vision; it tells of an actual marriage, with all the vicissitudes and consequences — ecstasy, betrayal, pain, anger, hope deferred, diminished and enlarged — implied therein.

The marriage is much to the point of the book — in a double sense. Hosea and his bride encounter rough tides; so, it is stated plainly, do Jawe and Jawe's bride, which is to say ourselves, we humans.

Shortly however, the student, reader, believer, whoever, runs before heavy seas. Which is to say that the book conveys, alas, a large measure of contempt and malfeasance toward women, manipulation of their image, near derision at their ill fortune.

A prophet takes a bride, we are told. And shortly the event assumes a kind of cosmic glow. We are reminded that across all time and place, we too are wedded (for better or worse!) to Jawe.

There is a consensus of experts; the marriage imagery is to be taken as relentlessly factual. We shall do so.

Hosea rides the rough ties of life and overcomes; we shall grant him that much. So does Hosea's God.

What outcome awaits the woman, and by implication all women, is another matter entirely.

The poet William Carlos Williams must have rejoiced in Hosea. "No poetry, except in things." And Gerard Manley Hopkins as well, with his passionate insistence on the 'inscape' of events and created beings as holy, self-revealing hints of a larger meaning lurking.

No vision, Hosea keeps implying, except in the things of this world, in desert and town, marriage and labor, in the corners we poke into (and what we discover there), in the hints and fits and starts of grace. And likewise in the quickening or numbing of hearts.

The taste and savor of creation is after all, a constant prophetic outlook (and inlook.) Our roots are in time, in this world. In our great ones, the roots hold fast.

We humans have nothing to offer of God, godly, except through creation, above all through one another. How else, from what other basis, shall one read aright the text of the heart and speak truthfully of where we stand in the world?

Marriage, in densely personal and social terms, is the vocation of Hosea. He tells the tale of a stormy union, tells it in detail, without concealment or cavil.

And under the canopy of that imagery he also speaks of Jawe and the people, of God and ourselves; of fidelity on God's part, infidelity on ours; of the unfaithful who are received back, forgiven, by the faithful One.

This is the crisis, the rhythm within life, the life that underlies (and underscores) the sexual.

He tells of a choice and then a second choice on the part of the faithful lover.

The spouse has betrayed the marriage vows. Yet Hosea is determined to forgive all. So a reconciliation occurs, a second exchange of vows. This is the recovered choice, the wounded choice, which despite all that has gone before, becomes a moment of healing.

We might be inclined to see in all this our own story, the human condition; ourselves uttering both alas and alleluia.

HOSEA

The reunion, the second marriage, far surpasses the first in its human quality. For the second is achieved in groans and tears, in the thorny garden of experience. It is wrung from, recovered from a wound that was all but mortal.

A marriage indeed, at long length, bearing triumphantly the stigmata of betrayal, healing and forgiveness.

So rare, so rare! Both passion and anguish are here, a drama of love, a man and a woman, Hosea and Gomer, (God and ourselves), in ecstasy and combat, loss and betrayal, wrung asunder, eventually reconciled. Hatred and love in contention. A passage from one garden to - another? In any case, the two must pass from spiritual adolescence, false expectation, thence to be thrust into the real world, at whose gate romance languishes and dies quickly.

In order that something splendid, wounded, upright, may be born.

Who is this God of Hosea? In asking, we imply another question: Who is Hosea? And yet another: Who is Gomer, his wife? And finally: Who are we, in light of (in dark of) this drama, this interplay, hankering, ravaging and tenderness, adultery, jealousy, fury, betrayal, forgiveness?

For the actors are also — ourselves.

Dare we include in the circle a gracious, indeed passionate Third Party? Hosea has done so.

God is self-invited to the wedding feast, has in a sense invaded the scene. God is that Other of the marriage, the vocation, lot, existence. Hosea, Gomer, God in the first instance.

The circle widens; the music bursts forth, the dance begins. And the dancers? They come to the wedding from all the world; all are caught up in the rhythm.

The words of the bridal chorale are passionate, audacious. We will not come on such language elsewhere in scripture, except perhaps in the Song of Songs. Hosea, Gomer, God, ourselves. Love gives eloquent tongue to the mystery. These are a few of its words: 'cherish,' 'seduce,' 'speak to the heart,' 'espousal,' 'gifts of love.'

Then the horror, the dark side of brightness: 'forgetting,' 'abandoning,' 'lying,' 'hating,' 'immersed in shame,' 'stripped, pursued.' And yes, 'give birth to bastards,' 'commit adultery,' 'prostitute.'

"The people, grown stupid, lunge toward ruin." (4:14)

Thus goes the thunderous summary of society in the time of Hosea, the eighth century before Christ. Foreign intrigue, domestic decadence and anarchy are the scorching themes. And we are struck by parallels with our own predicament; they require no rhetoric or forcing.

Beyond such generalities of social breakup, Hosea reveals few indications of place and time. One thing though is implied: a change of public mood. After a certain time, for reasons that are not forthcoming, Hosea no longer addresses his oracles to the crowds. Such exhortations as 'hear the word of the Lord' disappear.

Are we to conclude that as the public woe worsened and Hosea's judgments grew more fierce, only a few hearkened? It would seem so; again the parallel strikes hard.

The book is for the most part a kind of omnium-gatherum — we encounter prayers, sayings, apothegms, exhortations — fragments, one would think, of a larger message, an anthology perhaps, assembled by disciples.

Once the marriage analogy is completed, there is no developed theme or narration. We have a series of emotional explosions: indignation, anger, then an ecstatic reconciling.

In a sense, the marriage imagery governs the entire book, though the text itself is often a matter of surmise — and of surprise. It falters and fades and yields contrary readings like a fascinating, hardly legible Dead Sea Scroll.

The theme of the book is simple, as indicated. An 'ideal' marriage of prophet and spouse is consummated in the desert. There is a hint here, immediate, even inescapable, of another marriage, another desert: the wilderness of Exodus. The memory is idyllic. It is a time, really, before dawn, a pre-awakening. The covenant, whether of marriage or of God-and-people, is sealed. It is not as yet tested.

Then the mood darkens. Even before the people enter into a land of promise, other gods are available, and invoked. Adoration of Baal occurs; (9:10) betrayal is underway.

Hosea too, that artless spouse, will see and suffer — and resist the worst of the destructive consequence.

Later, in Exodus, the people cry out for a king. The ambiguous quest is granted. But from a bad start, what goodness can come? The royal line is tainted; it was never ordained of God; it was cloned from 'the nations,' an import stained with ambition and greed. How then could kings over Israel (or their subjects) be thought to serve God?

In the benighted northern kingdom, Hosea groans, curses, rattles his chains. He must exist under an impossible political contrivance, irremediably secular, at odds with itself, with the vocation of the people, with God.

Military power, alliances with violent entities, domestic injustice — all multiply. Behold the 'new' Israel, a nation among nations, in defiance of God and covenant. Old and bitter themes — and ever new.

And what of religion and its nouveau purveyors? According to Hosea, the priests are grown furtive and rapacious and encumbered with dead ritual, even taking to open brigandage on the roads. (6:9) Blind leaders mislead the blind. People are uninstructed in the ancient faith; they know not God.

O that prophetic soul! A tradition that lives in Hosea, marrow and blood and bone, is dying before his eyes.

Hosea borrows the older prophetic sarcasm: the 'dwellers on the earth' adore 'the works of their own hands.' The vogue is a syncretism of God and Baal; altars, steles, idols arise throughout the land. A welter of liturgical protestations mask a dark unease. We are 'God's people,' an old cry on the world's wind (and a new). And public conduct worsens, rife with death and duplicity.

Old terrain and new! Time and place too familiar to be easily shrugged off. We could make our way blindfolded through Hosea's scene and know it for our own — the night of the iguana, the day of the toad.

The scene is a blind show of prosperity and pomp; behind a noble arras knavery of every sort flourishes. Hosea speaks indignantly of fools and knaves ensconced in seats of power. And wickedness pullulates; like begets like. A new species of public officials, religious and secular, much resembling one another, springs up. One and all, they are skilled in trickery, oppression of the powerless, greed.

But God is God, that is the rub. A jealous lover brooks no interlopers, claimants, rivals.

What Hosea refers to as 'knowledge of God' resides only in a few; so be it. Few or many, Hosea and his like must bring that knowledge to bear upon politics, religion, the entire social scene; to invalidate, unmask, topple the gods. More, such knowledge alone could be thought to create and vitalize structures of justice in an unjust time.

A vain hope, lacking all evidence? Hosea hopes on.

The sanctuary, polluted or pure as may be, is the criterion and measure of public life. Everything depends on, flows from the people's worship. Is not the sanctuary the heart of the body? Is the heart sound, affectionate, well-ordered? Is the sanctuary a scene of worship 'in spirit and truth'? If it is, all will go well in public behavior.

A fountain of 'living waters' flows from thence, and returns. The people bathe, and are strengthened unto works of justice.

The secret form and infusion, flowing and returning, is 'hesed,' grace, intimacy, tenderness. It is the soul of the social compact, the very gift of God; it renders humans — human.

Hosea's glance turns to the world of the nations, a bloody scene to be sure, something known widely as the 'real world.' He need not look far afield to see the dolorous truth; the gift of God, 'hesed,' has been refused, denigrated, wasted. This is his plaint, burdened as he is with the gift, violated as he sees the gift.

And the general plight is by no means a remotely tragic thing. It is his own plight. Tragic, an arrow tipped with poison strikes home. Its prey is — his own marriage.

Here is the incongruence, the woe and falling asunder, the dissonance that makes of life a hellish cacophony. Hosea is a divided man in a chaos he cannot mitigate.

At best he can merely cope, keep his wits relatively intact. He is under siege.

As is his God.

One need not harp overlong on the astonishing timeliness of Hosea. (Indeed, we sigh, if only it were not quite so timely!)

Timely; the word is carefully chosen.

To speak of the political, economic, personal timeliness of the Word of God is simply to indulge in a tautology. That eternal Word strikes hard, strikes sparks against the adamant times, whether of Hosea or ourselves. If it did not, of what point the Word, why set it down, why grant it a hearing? If injustice, rapacity, national myth and ego, war, fraud, political chicanery are not to be unmasked and condemned by the Word spoken by Hosea and his noble line — why then the Word?

(O hideous Gulf slaughter and bloody aftermath, O rot and wrangling of the senate 'hearings!' Blind, deaf, dead to the Word.)

The Word is eternal. By the term we mean nothing platonic, icy, hidebound, timeless. Perhaps the closest we can come to it is a word dear to Hosea and the other seers: 'faithful.' The Word of God endures — us, our crimes, our infidelities. It is like a guardian seraph, all eyes. In standing over against us, judging us, the word in effect stands with us in a plenary, undeserved sense. Who has ever deserved an angel?

A mercy, though relentless, surgical. The Word is two-edged; the angel bears a sword.

There is a rather constant effort on the part of commentators, preachers, church bureaucrats and the like (let alone Christian generals and politicians) to reduce the Word to a whisper, lost on the mad winds of the age. They would have the Word of God in effect rendered harmless; summoning no one, no nation, no church, to judgment, to repentance, to a new start.

And then the great central themes of Hosea, the majestic vision of what humans might accomplish (what we are called to accomplish) whether in spirit or political life, what we might make of God's creation (what we are summoned to make), architects rather than wreckers — such grand themes, lofty hopes, secret and public beckonings, reproofs, threats, blandishments of love — who takes them seriously, sends them winging abroad, ponders and preaches them, joyously lives them?

The word of God in Hosea we have called timely. Which is by no means to say, easy, acceptable.

For example, in the welter of world change, the relation between the United States and Israel, as between Israelis and Palestinians, continues to vex and trouble and let innocent blood. Our generation is overtaxed with the tragedy of a failed vision; a people who have passed, in the most bizarre exodus conceivable, from victim to oppressor.

Not only that. In the birth of Israel, we noted a certain healthy, first generational independence, verve, imagination, the hope that arises from ashes and vivifies a new beginning. (Though the South Africa connection cast a shadow that was to lengthen ominously.) The word 'miracle' was commonly invoked — and with some reason.

The new nation gloried in its breathing space, its independence of the powers that had betrayed its people. Indeed, there was sound reasoning implied in the policy of distancing the new nation from the great powers. For awhile, a bitter memory counseled: keep your distance. Had not the 'allies' failed to protect the victims of Hitler, or to welcome them to their shores?

Alas, all is changed. Israeli leadership is lined up with other client states, cap in hand for its annual bristling military handout. Intransigent beyond belief, Israeli policy goes its way. The occupation is an international disgrace; it rivals Hosea's scorching analysis of the crimes of his time and place.

More, the Israelis pursue alliances which Hosea denounces as faithless, indeed tactically doomed: the flitting of leaders 'between Assyria and Egypt,' huckstering weapons on behalf of tyrants, taking sides in the cold war adventuring of the powers.

One need not invoke an ancient theocracy to justify the text of Hosea. The point is not that modern Israel must be a 'people under God.' There exists at least the possibility of secular virtue, whether civic or personal. The prophet dwells on these as evidence that a social fabric is intact and in place.

The characteristics should be visible, one would think, in whatever social or political structure, no matter the tradition or ideology: justice, compassion for the poor, forthrightness of speech, political accountability of leaders.

The diatribes of Hosea do not, of course, stop short with Israel. He holds no brief on behalf of 'the nations,' quite to the burning contrary. But his message is primarily to his own people. They are, politically speaking, to be 'over against' the others, 'vis a vis' in an altogether special way. A way that might be translated today as the political will of a small nation to be and become a sign, a David before the Goliaths, a pro-human entity. And in the determination, winning honor, even grudging honor from Gog and Magog. Respect out of all proportion to 'clout,' whether military or economic. A way, a light amid the dark wrestling of the powers.

Nothing of this did Hosea see occurring. Hence his anger, an emotion entirely apt to the heart of the just and compassionate, at a spectacle that offends daily: murder, jailings, beatings, denial of civil and human rights. Then, now.

Shall we call him — modern, one who owns our sensibility, our language — and our plight? He much resembles us, all said; for good and ill, we know him for blood brother.

See how his faith wavers and mourns under the impact of worldly blows.

He reminds us of Pascal, that irremediable modern. In our day, faith has little of the fierce cold clarity that lights the martyrs' path. For most, faith can hardly summon a resonant 'yes'; it is shadowed by 'maybe.'

Thus faith is haunted, all but overtaken by the evidence of non-faith; and this not only in the world, but also in the depths of the soul. One summons a shadowed 'yes,' a circling quest for God, for traces, hints, nuances of the One who seems perennially absent.

Finally, (whether graced or unlucky, few can tell) faith comes to be a wager laid on — the very existence of God.

Shall there be faith after Auschwitz? It is a question that surpasses Auschwitz. The world is now Auschwitz. The fire is grown to a wildfire.

It was kindled at Hiroshima, burned fiercely over Hanoi's children, over the innocents of Afghanistan, over Grenada. It was struck anew by the Stealth bombers, pulverizing the barrios of Panama City. In the mideast it has torched and trashed the intifada. And its plenary horror was unleashed over the children of Iraq.

God may be true God, all well and good. But to Hosea (to ourselves?) the truth is of small comfort. Hosea wavers and stammers and intemperately shatters the peace (a questionable peace to be sure) with his outcry. In the spiritual desert he must inhabit, God appears as a shadow, a mirage, a mood. A maybe.

The gods hold all the cards. Their realm is the tormented murderous kingdom of Macbeth: 'the world, the way it goes.'

What then on such a planet as ours? Is one to make of a King of Losers who, despite all, will not permit one to cut his losses, to bow out of the game?

Why cannot such as Hosea lead us in an easier direction, play the game like all the others — cheat and win, cheat and win?

As the prophet would put it (as God would put it to the prophet) — faith is a marriage. You take your chances. You join hands, make a pact. Better or worse, you place your substance, future, in the hands of another. Thenceforth, all may go well — or ill.

Hands joined, feet on the same path — as best two are able, they undertake a new life in the world.

And be warned; the world is voluble and promissory — and a cheat from day one. A great signer of covenants and treaties and pacts and concordats — and a great reneger on their keeping.

This chanciness and darkness as to outcome has a divine counterpart. Thus the daring imagery of Hosea. God too must cope, do his sorry best in the world. God so deals with us, takes a chance, joins with us hand to hand, walks our path.

('We,' according to the imagery, and Israel as our universal stand-in.)

Israeli conduct toward Palestinians — it is all one seamy rotten garment. It is ourselves in the world, wrapped in a shroud. Indeed, it is ourselves become the world. The holy commerce, the human deportment commended (indeed commanded), the justice that makes the marriage 'work,' where have these gone?

The marriage is insulted, held to scorn, walked away from, secretly adulterated, defamed. This is the larger picture, the historical one, the image of 'the fallen,' ourselves, discomfited and disgraced.

Hosea is hardly reassuring as to our anthropology, our ancestry, our behavior in the world; he is merely truthful.

A question has arisen and remains unanswered to this day. Is Hosea commending a nomadic life, urging us to follow the 'song lines' of a new creation? Is he equating the human with the wandering tribes of the earth? Would God's will lead us away from New York's granite and macadam to the Colorado high desert?

Probably not, though the implication of desert imagery, taken literally, is seductive indeed. But the desert seems, in context of the book, not so much a place as a state of soul, and a temporary one at that. The desert is darkness, dispossession, impoverishment. As in the opening drama of Christ's adult life, the desert is that 'stage' of life or marriage or social formation into which one (or two, or a people) must be led. There something new may come to pass, after a momentous painful prelude. Combat with demons, awakening of vocation.

The imagery of Hosea rises like the noon sun of a wedding day. Nature rejoices in the vesture of high summer. A wedding feast is spread. And music! It is as though Hosea has composed a jubilant song, a 'hymn for a million voices.'

The jubilant wedding music plays on and on. Jeremiah, Ezekiel, Isaiah take up the theme in counterpoint to his genius. We would never have done with this wedding, the feasting and rejoicing.

Or so it is assumed.

And then the sky darkens.

As to Hosea and his presence in our Christian testament, someone has calculated sixteen citations on the lips of Christ and in the letters of Paul and John.

Again and again one image recurs; the church is the spouse of Christ.

As has been stated, Hosea's marriage is a literal event. So each Christian enters by analogy into mystical union with the Beloved. Our God is friend, spouse, lover; and faithful in spite of all.

The horror of our bloodshot history, so piercingly analyzed under the 'Israel' imagery of Hosea, cancels nothing of this 'hesed,' this faithful, inexplicable love of God for us.

How convey the wonder of it? The integrity of the marriage bond does not depend on us; this is to say the very least. If it did, if God waited upon our good-will, our sense of justice, our decency, we have indeed lost everything. As we must know if we have even minimal access to our own hearts.

Under a supposition of strict quid pro quo, in this horrific and darkened world the covenant could not stand for an hour.

We fray the bond; we adventure and plunder; the milestones of our passage through time are idolatrous altars, steles, cenotaphs. We have lost the measure, the norm. We raven and kill and lie and deal double.

And all this is taken as normal; it is the daily order, both policy and presupposition. Under a vile agreement, murder cannot even be named for what it is. It is no longer a moral item in the political lexicon.

What is disallowed piously by the courts, and in these days often punished capitally, is just as piously granted to governments. A go-ahead for war, any and all wars. An open season on humans. And the polls crying huzzah! And the obscene flags challenging high heaven.

Beware, the empery of death.

We are in fact a two pact people. We are torn between the pact of Hosea-Jawe, which we cannot entirely negate or forget, and that other pact forged with the principalities.

Still, our betrayal apparent, is it possible that others are honoring the covenant for our sake, thus redeeming us, the recusants and violators? Can it be that in our day, a sublime mediation of the poor and victimized, of the stricken peoples of South Africa and Iraq and Salvador and Guatemala, that from these arises the form of God's 'hesed' in our midst?

But for these, the poor, the base communities, the disappeared and their mothers and spouses, the murdered Jesuits of El Salvador and those they stood with, but for Romero and the host of unknown heroes — but for these, the original pact, the biblical pact of Hosea and the prophets would long since have vanished on the winds of hell.

To this have we come; it is as though the imagery of Hosea were turned on its head. A pact of another order has displaced the holy image of God-and-us. The new 'pact of public weal' is highly secular, violent, greedy, world encompassing. Transcendent hope sinks and is lost in its vortex.

The new pact makes of us willing 'dwellers on the earth.' Inevitably, we are also idolaters, 'worshippers of the works of our hands.'

And the original pact, the godly one? Who honors it, keeps it intact? To put the same matter more crudely: Who pays up?

Let us pose the question closely. When in our own country people of faith act justly or compassionately, clumsily as may be, but nobly as the times allow, uttering a 'no' that would echo Hosea's, in favor of a 'yes' all but frittered away — such are judged as having violated the abnormal 'norm.' They must, in public estimate and courts of law, pay up, be scorned and punished.

(1:1 ff.) A few general reflections.

The vocation of Hosea opens with no vision, no prophetic call from on high. No transcendent symbols, no wheels of fire, burning coals, angelic attendants, ceremonies of purification. Nothing of anguish or sense of unworthiness or incapacity such as gave pause to other great spirits, summoned as they were to they knew not what.

We open the text of Hosea, we grant its venerable character. We are also alert to the fact that the first chapters are marked by a dangerous ambiguity.

Do we study the words in order, like the first parents, to eat of the tree of knowledge, to glimpse evil, to judge mysterious matters for ourselves,

HOSEA

even to grow indignant?

What, for instance, are we to make of the dialogue between Jawe and the prophet regarding the fate of a third party — the woman?

She dwells in shadow; she is never consulted as to her own life, her fate. Are we to accept without question proceedings in which a woman is simply disposed of; all in order, as we are told, to point a moral lesson? A lesson moreover to be proclaimed by a (male) prophet, instigated by a presumably male God? Among other questions, what of means and ends here?

It is difficult to imagine that women would read the book of Hosea without such questions arising. (Or men either, in the degree that tedious Bible study, macho church and culture, have not throttled their human sense.)

One such commentator, both clear of eye and courageous, is Walter Wink. Writing of a text in the first letter of Paul to Timothy (2:1-7), his reflection sheds light, backward in time, as it were, on certain images of women in Hosea.

"... we avoid this text [Timothy] ... because of its attitude toward women. Gone here is the radicalism of Jesus, who in every encounter with a woman in all four gospels, violated the mores of his time.... [In the present text] the talk is of reinserting women back into patriarchy....

"We cannot duck the issue. Here scripture violates itself. When scripture is not faithful to the gospel, the gospel can still be heard and proclaimed — by pointing out the truth.

"Those who were repatriachizing and domesticating the gospel have left their fingerprints all over the text. The gospel of Jesus exposes them as the apostates they were.

"We do not do honor to Jesus by defending as inspired, texts of terror that dehumanize women.... God speaks through such texts nonetheless — to denounce them as apostate.

"Even so, these texts can bear witness to the Word of God, who is not a book, but a Being."

It would seem profitable to set down a working principle. Its source is in biblical reflection as well as experience. To wit, no human should be presumed to exist merely to 'symbolize' something or someone else —

whether on behalf of public or private weal. Typology is a dangerous affair. It can venture too far, on too flimsy grounds. It plays with fire.

If we are to trust the experts, the opening scene of the book presents us with an historical event. Let us follow their counsel and see where it leads. (Where it leads, let it be added, few experts are willing to point.)

God, we learn, commands Hosea to take to himself as bride a prostitute previously unknown to the prophet. More, he is to have children by her. In due time the names of the progeny will be conferred, also symbolically, by God.

One can only fret; we start badly.

The chosen bride, as is evident in the instructions from on high, is hardly a figure who merits cultural or religious approval. Possibly, we are informed, she engages in fertility worship, a ritual prostitute given over to the worship of one or another Baal.

Then by order of Jawe, she is plucked from the cultural pit. She is chosen, in a manner of speaking.

But the 'choice' is bewildering, a parody of vocation.

From the text we imagine her, passive, spoken for. Shall we call the text, in all charity, unambiguously male, defaming?

This God is, to say the least, forthright: "Marry a prostitute, and have children who will be as bad as she...."

Neither in her shame nor in her future status (by presumption, greatly improved) is Gomer granted much. It cannot even be claimed, in justification of this divine intrigue, that God intends Hosea to make an 'honest woman' of her.

A morganatic marriage then? Not even that; the children of the bond, conceived under divine command, are positively contemned. They are considered not only of lower dignity than their father, they are 'as bad as she.' Evil seed. Stark reminders of the sin of their mother, their very names are forms of humiliation, taint, stigma.

The text sags under a spirit of exclusion and disdain. The bride brings to her wedding no dowry of 'innocence'; she has little to offer God or a 'man (sic) of God.'

Excuses, devices abound. The benefits accruing to this marriage are dwelt on; it is of advantage to her husband, to the people — to Jawe. But what of her? She seems destined only to a different servitude, hardly less onerous than the former.

As a prostitute, in the eyes of Jawe she had value only as a symbol. Inert, passive, she stood for social degradation. ("My people have abandoned me and are prostituting themselves.") Then as a bride, her old status, which might be thought religiously and culturally purged by marriage, is in no wise improved. She continues to 'stand for' something, someone else. A symbol, albeit an 'improved' one.

God speaks: "Israel, I will make you my wife." Talk about alienation, talk about disposing of someone!

The impression is inescapable. The woman is being shuffled about a chess board, one square to another, prostitute to bride to mother — to serve one or another invariably 'noble' (inevitably male) interest. Never to be blessed, to raise her head, to be heard from. Never an outcry, whether of grief or rage. Never to exist in her own right.

She is doubly put to silence: first in the text, then in the commentaries, which ignore even the possibility that she too has a story worth the telling and a right to tell it, even the minimal right to have it told by another.

(1:3) So, we are told laconically, Hosea "went off and took Gomer, who conceived and brought forth a son." The birth is the first of three such events. And in each case God is, so to speak, the sedulous god-parent hovering over the cradle.

God names each child, ominously: the first, Jezreel, 'Plain of Massacre'; then a daughter, 'Unloved'; finally another son, 'Not My People.'

With the birth and naming of the third child, the rupture between God and the covenant people is announced as complete.

(And *BJ* improves the occasion by declaring, "The conferring of symbolic names ... implies, with regard to the children, neither accusation nor blame.")

Those terrible names; what a legacy for the newborn!

Named — and of God.

The newborn, like their mother, are — symbols.

The people are grown corrupt, God is angered. In public life, awful events impend. The northern kingdom is doomed, the clash of arms sounds

on the air.
And they, poor children, are the small mewing portents of doom.

Verse 10 presents a much later text, we are told, and a different political and military climate. The doomsday tone of the earlier verses is lifted. Now a message of hope emerges.

Thus according to Hosea, Jawe undergoes a change of, not so much mind as, heart. We shall hear much of these emotional eruptions; Hosea's God is a volcanic Being indeed.

Forgotten now are the ominous names of the children of disaster, forgotten the transgressions of the mother. Forgotten, that is to say, as useful symbols of crime and punishment. We breathe easier; with regard to our moral default, Jawe is the holy Amnesiac par excellence, remembering only to forget.

Perhaps in the beauty of the outcome, we too can forget the more than somewhat unbeautiful opening instruction: 'Go, take a wife....'

Still we have learned something — and do well not to unlearn it. Jawe is to be taken at his (sic) word. And that word, as it lodges in Hosea and finds tongue in him, is beyond reasonable doubt, the word of a male. It signals a pact concluded (one almost thinks in collusion), male to male.

This might be thought tolerable, to a degree. The flashpoint of trouble is reached when the word of God, here recorded, is fused with cultural attitudes which hardly merit praise, in this instance, demeaning attitudes toward women.

Then the word becomes questionable. Can such images be thought a divinely inspired guide to conduct worthy of the name human?

We do well perhaps to invoke here, the 'analogy of faith.' A given text is placed beside other declarations, events, commands, ethical instructions so it can be weighed and questioned against a larger field of evidence. Is the text presented as a statement of God's will for us? Or is it to be understood as imperfect or partial or even distorted, reflecting the attitudes, prejudices, follies, of a given culture?

Word of God, word of God! A complex reality indeed. Not every word of God comes to us untouched, uncolored, out of this world — uncensored.

What then of certain portions of the text of Hosea? Are we to take them whole cloth, leaving our critical sense to one side? Shall we cut the pages to ribbons in scornful anger? Or is a middle way possible?

One such might lie in this direction: in admitting to our prayer, our Bible study, the hard won lessons of our own day, or of former days; in hearing from the dispossessed and suffering peoples of our world as they take the Bible in hand; in taking to heart the outcry of women in the church, borrowing their critical and skilled eyes as they bring to the text a woman's heart and mind.

In such wise, the best of what is purportedly 'of Jawe' might be salvaged, exposed, purified.

Would not a God of truth be thought to approve such an initiative? Women (and others) have perhaps endured enough: a species of preaching and teaching that suggests a certain kind of male history, an abusive stampede through the Bible, an open season declared against women (and others). With a view perhaps of keeping intact a very old system of control, or of settling ancient scores.

The text has already indicated control and humiliation; the imposed silence, the victimizing, all in absentia, of the bride of Hosea.

Implied is a domestic picture that falls short of bliss. No wonder, we think, that shortly the bride fled this God-driven husband and his all-seeing Mentor in favor of her former pursuits!

The female lacunae, the (male) hand placed over her mouth — surely such body language, such deliberate silencing must be averted if we are to require properly human conduct, even of God.

An integrity, be it noted, which the text both denies and invites us to restore.

We linger over the shadowy form of the bride Gomer. We long to know her, in half-shamed admiration of her courage. We dare, perhaps in secret, to applaud her flight. What has religion wreaked against her? In what has she offended? When will she gain a hearing?

We recognize her; her sisters are numberless through the ages, abused, anonymous, put to naught, their lives 'arranged' by authorities, fathers, husbands, laws, customs, torahs, scriptures, hierarchs — everyone, it would seem, and everything at odds with the heart's deep cry.

This woman, one concludes, has abandoned an intolerable life. In so doing, in trading suffocation for bare breathing space, in risking a further stigma, she reminds us that there are worse crimes than female prostitution. (In any case, crimes of whatever degree of heinousness are variously dealt with in various criminal codes — in accord, for the most part, with a polluted standard of 'justice.' In cases involving women defendants, laws are rigorously enforced. And charges against male defendants are as often airily dismissed. We shall leave it at that.)

The God of Hosea, given time, surpasses (to a degree) the male ethos, and breaks through.

(2:2) Thus the sexually charged diatribe of vengeance is not to be taken as a final sentence. There is vast relief in the reflection.

The 'people of God,' we are told, are recusant, their conduct idolatrous, criminal; there seems no end to their follies. And God is whirled about in a very cyclone of emotion, a welter of anger, reproach, threat, jealousy, even of rejoicing, as the divine thunderbolts are launched. Of double mind, to say the least.

How cope with these fractious humans? Is He to play judge, prosecutor, jury, executioner? Is the outcome to be lightnings from on high or a deluge or plague?

Or perhaps the unexpected — forgiveness, reconciliation?

We are to imagine a distressing time for Jawe, brows furrowed, angry, shamed at the spectacle of creation gone awry.

What will serve to bring the fractious ones to a better mind?

(2:5) Punishment! In an all too human way, Jawe determines on issuing a humiliating lesson.

And here we go once more. The backsliding people are equated with, compared to, imagined under the form of — woman.

The imagery is pushed hard for all its purported worth. 'Her children' are held to scorn. A prophet begat them, granted. But the dignity in no wise has improved their status. They are referred to with sublime destain,

HOSEA

as 'hers.'

The people are imagined as — a woman. They have sinned.
Their punishment, also under the image of woman, is decreed.
The punishment of a collective 'she,' a 'nation-woman,' is charged with sexual imagery.
With sadism? 'She' must be stripped naked 'as in the day of her birth.'
Words are put in 'her' mouth, an idolatrous voice. (2:8)
(The recusant tribe is, of course, half-male, but no matter.)

(2:6 ff.) The punishment proceeds. Presumably it is designed to bring conversion of heart. But there is little of the nuanced realism that if conceded, would raise a crucial question (as in the book of Revelation, again and again [Rev. 6:15-17; 9:6,20,21]).
I.e., does misfortune (here, punishment from on high) bring people to a better heart? May it not as easily bring on a worse?

Nonetheless, hope beats on. (If only one can ignore, or take in stride, the prior insults.) We are in awe of the stubborn, rough hewn longing, the hope of Jawe: "She will say, 'I will return to my first love; I was happier then than now.'"
There is a powerful instruction implicit in such hope, a naivete, proceeding from a heart untutored in the labyrinthine darkness of the human.
Or perhaps quite thoroughly instructed — and hoping on nonetheless?
The hope of God! Hope even for us.
(If God can so hope, against all evidence and history, then what of ourselves, confined as we are to partial knowledge of evil, that of our own lifetime and little beyond or before — how can we not keep faith, keep hope in one another?)

Still, the limitation, one-sidedness, cultural bias of the imagery!
Let us indulge in a game we shall call 'Fair Play.' We suppose for a bit, that we were here presented with an oracle entitled "The Book of Gomer." Further, that Jawe is presented as feminine and Israel as masculine. And

HOSEA

that Hosea stands in the role of Gomer. Let us suppose then, that this feminine Jawe has appointed as prophet, a woman, Gomer. She is commanded to take to herself as spouse a male prostitute from the temple corps. We are told his name, Hosea, and little else. Then the word comes, horrific, final. In a momentous matter, his impending marriage, he is offered no choice; he is simply put on notice, chosen for.

In our hypothetical text the episode is taken quite for granted. It is typical of an amazonic, warlike matriarchate. The male is hauled from the temple and led to the house of the bride.

Shortly, also in accord with instruction from on high, the prophetess conceives, and again and again, three times. The bridegroom's will in the matter is unknown. He is a kind of stud, fecund by decree.

Love, tender secret matters, trellises and tarryings by moonlight, decisions, choices, 'I Hosea take you Gomer?' Nothing of this. The man is — a symbol. He serves divine ends, greater than he can know. Then let him know nothing.

In due time the children are born. They are stigmatized by Jawe as 'his,' the unworthy father's, even though they were born of a holy prophetess. The parents are shortly informed; to demean and despise their offspring is quite in order — these are to be their names, odious indeed, and conferred from on high.

Then Hosea, for reasons which might be gleaned from the narrative (and would win the approval of men everywhere), abandons the marriage and returns to his former trade.

His departure may be said to send a message, or perhaps more than one. Hosea has retained a measure of his humanity. He is resentful, weary of being held in contempt. And since male prostitution is connected with religious rites, practice, belief, the abrupt flight may be taken as his way of implying: I shall worship other gods; with my body I honor those who honor me.

Whatever the message, (our suppositious story continues) it is hardly well received in heavenly places. A celestial outcry is raised: How dare he?

In the heavenly breast, we may imagine, multitudinous emotions are in contention. Threats are uttered, threnodies abound, themes of ingratitude, plaints, also words implying or stating — jealousy. Mother Jawe mourns and rages, "Denounce your father, denounce him. He is no longer husband to me, nor am I his wife. Plead with him to cease and desist this

HOSEA

abominable adultery and prostitution.... I will show no mercy to his children; they are the offspring of a shameless one. Did not he himself declare, 'I will go to my lovers — everything I have is from their hands....'"

Our altered story of Hosea, in sum, is told by others, on his behalf, presumably for his benefit. He is extrinsic to the tale, an outsider to his own life. Jawe has greater, wider concerns than he; and Hosea might be thought useful in illustrating these. He is, like it or not, a symbol. And to that degree in his own person he is a reduction just short of zero.

Is the day sunny? The human casts him, a shadow. But let the sun set, he disappears.

Perhaps with our fictive change of roles, a point is somewhat clarified: images and the destructive uses to which they are put.

Thus here. The story of one woman and her defaults is extended into a vast social, military, political parable. God (or someone) help the poor symbol!

Our story (the real one, the book of Hosea) continues. Gomer-Israel has fled her (sic) God. How then win her back?

At a certain point the woman, her life, her torment, her non-choices, her children, all but vanish from the text. If there remains a trace of the 'feminine,' a 'she,' the 'she' is transformed — into a nation, a people. In a kind of final abuse, an act of divine prestidigitation, Gomer has been subsumed. She has vanished into her metaphor.

She could even be thought, and has been so regarded and written of (invariably by male scholars), as a 'type.'

Now she will serve the future. Under this literary form the time frame is leveled off. For all the future she is to serve as a bleak illustration. In this larger sense, somewhat clouded and by no means complementary, she is presented as a 'type' of Israel, faithless, then redeemed.

We can only conclude that the more 'useful' she becomes, the more poor Gomer is dehumanized.

The power of chapter two depends finally on her disappearance.

Gomer never counted for much; shortly her imaginative usefulness ends. But her story, the 'lesson,' that is another matter.

She casts a great light, borrowed to be sure; she is a moon to the sun of Jawe. In such hands her story breaks in a spectrum, engenders nuances, flights of sublime fancy. Imagine! A new 'she' appears. Metaphors abound: land and season, sowing and harvest, altar and desert.

The marriage bond is hardly forgotten, nor the infidelity of a woman who dared bring a marriage made in heaven, to naught.

But not quite to naught; Gomer-Israel rises again from the shades; she is confabulated anew — but only to serve. This time as a counter symbol of renewed ecology and covenant strengthened.

To a close eye, means and ends have collided.

The end is a breathtaking poem, beautiful beyond praise. It concerns love and its violation, forgiveness and reconciling. We are not allowed for a moment, a strophe, to forget this: that Jawe does not forget us. Jawe ventures that hardest first step of all — in the direction of the human heart. So prone (our own heart) to forget, make light of, delay, deride — the Love who forgets not, casts not off.

As to the means, we have made bold to suggest their vexed, mixed quality. Of this no more need be said.

(2:18) We are transported once more, to a later time.

A new covenant is announced. It is sealed with all living beings 'for her sake.' All will be safe, all cherished and included. Let us rejoice and be glad. How wonderful!

And that is not all. '... I will destroy war and the bow and sword, and the people will sleep secure.' O long desired peace, immemorially delayed! The peaceable realm at last, warring factions reconciled, the lamb and lion in gentle concert. We can only cry out as the lurid infernal light exploded over Baghdad; come quickly, angel!

With verse 21 we note immediacy, urgency, a breakthrough. No longer is the word spoken 'about' us; a cry is raised — the I and thou of love. "I will wed you, my people for ever."

"I will wed you in justice and righteousness." We do well not to take the promise lightly. God is just. The justice of God is conferred on us, shines vastly on our tormented world, majestic as a ring of Saturn, a wedding ring. A reminder, a bond, a sign.

This is a venerable matter, and weighty, and not always taken with seriousness. The wedding symbol implies that the justice of God is henceforth our dowry, reserve and resource. God would see justice done in the wobbling world, and we the pivot. Justice, a matter of the heart, dwelling in ourselves, radiating from us into the tormented world. Thenceforth, the behavior is bonded with the gift.

What shall we call the gift? Grace? The graciousness, the courtesy of God? (2:19) The famous first step in our direction, even as our footfalls freeze in incapacity and numbing, the chance taken in despite of all, the risk, the leap of love, the held breath of God?

On that beckoning gesture depends the entire human trudge, our pilgrim's (or rake's) progress and outcome. (And along the way — fissures and valleys and crags and dizzying spaces, torrid high noon, and the heart of darkness.)

God, we are told, makes love to us. The image is intimate, secret, connubial, undoubtedly sexual. The act of love is consummated, in spite of everything; all our impeding and withholding — our adulteries.

(2:21-24) And what of those children of Hosea and Gomer, so ominously shamed and named, apparently bound for disaster?

Another time warp.

An eruption of love cancels the earlier names, conferred as they were in a storm of dismay and fury.

The infants, we are to imagine, are by now young adults. And they are named anew, and — lovingly. More, they are embraced, included in holy favor and affection.

How shall we live with this God and his changeful weathers of mood?

Thus we imagine the design. A creative hand weaves and shuttles from the outer edges of creation, inward, naming and renaming all things. Or it is all a dance, a circle that closes, breaks open, reassembles, bows, turns and turns about, an enclosure and disclosure, mutuality and response, lovely and busy and rhythmic, step and counter-step.

"In that day I will respond to the heavens, and they to the earth. And the earth shall respond to the grain, the wine and oil; and all shall respond to 'God sows.'"

'God sows'; Jezreel, the name of the first-born of Gomer and Hosea. As first conferred, the name was shot through and through with bloody ambiguity. The child was named for a northern plain of Palestine, the dwelling place of Jezabel and Ahab, scene also of an historic massacre. Did God choose to sow in such a place?

Now a new sense is conferred. The children are summoned to a world of plenty and peace, of 'grain, wine and oil.' The ethical ecology of humans is healed and so is the earth. For the two are in fact one.

The heavens await, God 'responds,' the healing rains fall. The heavens are clouded, pregnant, the time of rains has come. Then the parched earth signals, 'responds.' Come, sweet tempest.

The crops await the fertilized earth, they 'respond' a hundredfold.

Thus the circle is completed, the web, the dance. For the crops are signs of the divine will-to-bounty, 'God sows.' Thus the first child, and its vindication and blessing.

Then the second, named again, in dramatic wise: 'I Shall Love — the Unloved.'

And for the third, likewise a new name: "To 'Not My People' I shall say, 'You Are My People'"

And the New People answer wholeheartedly. Their voice is a trumpet blast: "You are our God!"

They too confer a new name on an old Reality, long dreaded. For generations like had created like to the benefit of neither. The people cowered and ignored and feared, fled from Jawe in favor of other, more benignant, promissory deities. Promises, promises! Need it be said, the word of the idols was brittle and broke in shards under the hammer of time and adversity?

It is our story, we and our gods.

Then, something different. The gods are foresworn.

And the former dread dispensation, like a wall of fire about a recusant camp, this is extinguished. The image of Jawe is altered. No longer judge, prosecutor, executioner, the Jovian hurler of thunders, the enraged violated One.

New names all around! The history of mis-naming, mis-directing, missing the point — is finished. Now: "You Are My God."

(3:1 ff.) Again a considerable passage of time is implied.

The briefest of chapters, and alas, the objectionable symbolism returns. The woman Gomer has fled; once more, she is a hierodule. And summarily the order comes to Hosea. She is to be recovered, 'bought back,' 'redeemed,' one supposes, in a religious (though also an economic) sense.

Her price, we are told, is roughly the ransom of a slave.

The seizure of the runaway bride repeats in quite remarkable fashion, the dynamic of the original marriage (chapter 1) — with a difference worthy of note.

In deciding upon the appropriate or expedient action, (whether against or on behalf of the delinquent, remains unclear), the two, Jawe and Hosea, are once more in close conjunction. The prophet is attentive and obedient. No tiresome mediators or witnesses are present. Jawe and his man converse regarding a third party; the talk leans heavily toward the working out of 'any and all means required.'

The woman, the prize, though accounted for, is absent. Indeed her presence could hardly be thought of as advantageous to the project. Nor, as far as one can judge, is she appraised of the goings on.

As for the difference between the original betrothal and the second act, the (forced?) return of the recidivist: In each instance, Gomer must be liberated from her sinful circumstance. In the second act, having defaulted, she must be bought back — for a price.

More, she is sentenced by her husband to a period of penance and abnegation; "For many days you will dwell here, neither playing the harlot nor giving yourself to another; so will I also conduct myself in your regard."

At least, one thinks, she is at last spoken to! Even punishment, one would think, is preferable to the conniving in corners that has preceded.

(4:1) The tale so lamentably introduced, proceeds to its point.

Hosea, to give him his plain due, is a genius of sorts. Like others of his line, he is a social critic of the highest order. Which is to imply many things. For a start, a geography of import.

Where does he dwell, whence his income? Though his antecedents and trade are uncertain and his prophecy brings an uncertain income, one fact can be taken as certain. Hosea is no hanger-on or sycophant; his name is on no official payroll.

Such independence implies its shortcomings. But it is also a great enabler. Like Daniel and others, Hosea holds his head high, a free and far-ranging spirit. He surpasses beyond compare the skills of academe, court and temple in defining the ills of the time.

Then to another topic: the humanism of Hosea. And with all due deference to our biblical betters, we had best proceed here in a somewhat minimalist fashion, and gingerly.

The text insists on the prophet's direct access to God. But we note with a measure of dismay, the limitations of the messages sent down. The deity for His (sic) part accepts without question a curious male supposition about women — even erects the hypothesis into a master (sic) metaphor.

We have seen its working and enlargement. The woman, according to this construct, will be serviceable, illustrating in her behavior the ills of an entire culture. More, in redeeming the delinquent woman from public disgrace, the personal and social magnanimity of the prophet (and of Jawe) are vindicated. Thus the reading of most commentators.

Is the word of Jawe designed only to quicken the beat of the cultural drum?

The metaphor we have found so vexing, be it noted once more (and no more after that), in the second verse of the first chapter — is it not Jawe who instigates the beat?

Seldom has a human been so disposed of, in an off-hand way, as mere after-thought. "Take for wife a prostitute, for this land commits prostitution...." The 'for' is a hinge; a great door has closed on Gomer. The door of a tomb?

The strengths of Hosea are mysteriously intermingled with moral cloudiness, as we have seen. Once his story finishes with the offensive bridal metaphor, his humanism burns brightly, a light beating back the darkness.

A resister of note! His passionate ethical sense stands squarely in conflict with a heinous culture — and this especially (and with grievous consequence) on questions of violated justice. One small voice; and what an echo across the centuries!

In this crucial area of justice, his world resembles nothing so much as a snarling bear pit. Tooth and claw, the powers rend the victims. Merciless, voracious!

In the matter of justice, violated interminably, vindicated so rarely, his spirit stands firmly in accord with the will of Jawe.

Indeed, a burning sense of justice is the touchstone and credential of his claim to speak for God.

And further, Hosea and the prophets understand that in this matter of justice, they touch closely on the character of Jawe himself. God wills justice. Justice is central to God's hope for the world, passionate, choleric, tireless as that hope is.

God must be named Justice itself. God is shown as the perennial, untiring witness, standing by, standing with, the victims — and those who speak for them.

But for Gomer.

In Hosea the frequently invoked term 'knowledge of God' is concrete, historical, consequential. Such knowledge cannot be imagined to lurk weightless in the back of the mind. Nor can it be expressed in weightless worship. It summons more than 'holocausts.' It touches on time; it must cope with the world.

The knowledge, a gift of God, comes to rest weightily, presses downward upon humans like the apex of a great pyramid reversed. There it touches the inflamed point of the worldly powers, pushing relentlessly upward from the earth.

If the latter are to flourish or indeed to survive, they must challenge such a God as well as those who speak on God's behalf. The challenge is invariably 'legal'; the law of the land is invoked like a magical chant. Then and now!

The prophet speaks; the king hails the prophet before a court for an accounting. And a consequence.

But first, through Hosea, Jawe will have his say. It is a furious outburst, a devastating social and cultural diagnosis, shall we say, of the human condition as such? At least in certain times and places, under certain political and religious arrangements.

For a start, Hosea presents the case for the prosecution. It goes like this: nothing in the land, no aspect of life, whether pursued by tribe or individual, in public or in secret — nothing flourishes, makes sense, makes good. The culture is folding in like a sour dough in an icy wind. People stand at an impasse — ethically, ecologically, religiously — humanly.

This is the situation, from what we may call a divine point of vantage. Hosea lays it bare, the bones of things.

There is little new here. We of later centuries have heard it all before, from the psalmist, Isaiah, Ezekiel, Jeremiah, Daniel. Indeed the analysis is devastatingly consistent. It is as though we placed an ear against the breast of creation, heard amplified there the faltering heartbeat of the human, ill unto death.

The word of Hosea strikes like a lightning. Is it a recognition scene? Presented is an utterly strange (and yet utterly familiar) commingling of ethical disarray and ecological disaster. This too is a biblical commonplace; the moral state of the community brings about, reveals, is the measure of, the flourishing or decline of all living beings. Choose well and all will be well, is the word. Choose ill, selfishly, greedily, without forethought or mindfulness — all goes under.

We are well advised to take note, to step softly on the earth. (But mindless we take little note. Memories are foreshortened. The poet says terribly: every generation ends with itself.)

Yet Hosea re-minds us, literally. He restores our minds, our sanity.

Nothing of the web of things is apart or disjointed; everything bespeaks, connects, goes beyond itself, lending light, life-giving.

And what of ourselves?

Creation, alas, is at odds with us, who are so bloodily at odds with one another. Out of joint as we are, out of kilter with the dance. It follows that Jawe, vis a vis ourselves, grows contentious, adversarial.

So we have a judgment scene, a court. And the case for the prosecution is underway.

(4:2 ff.) God surveys creation, discovers only — a void. He can hardly breathe there. A void and worse — a stench.

The self-knowledge of God, engaging the human heart, is made available, bountiful among us (hesed). We are thereby enabled to know and love the One who so piercingly knows us and loves beyond measure.

But this gift has been despised, wasted, frittered away, turned to naught. This is our plight; we neither know nor love God, nor greatly desire to do so.

And what of the defense? It comes to this: there is no biblical defense.

Let us, nonetheless, summon the arguments, pointless or frivolous as they are. (We have heard them before, the debased coin of the realm.)

One such goes like this: granted we humans are bereft of godly gifts. Still we are benignant, inoffensive, neutral, harmless to ourselves and others — and to the earth we walk.

Would it were so, would that we could worship our gods and do no harm in the world! Listen to Hosea; into the vacuum of non-hesed rush 'false oaths, lies, assassinations, thefts, adulteries, murder upon murder.'

And the consequences in nature are swift to follow. "The land is in mourning ... also the beasts of the field and the birds of the air; and even the fish are endangered in the sea." Need one say more?

Verse four says much concerning the source, whence the infection takes its start — in the priesthood.

This is the insupportable anomaly. Those consecrated to worship 'in spirit and in truth' have betrayed their charge. In their befouled wake they drag the people to ruin.

It is first of all 'true knowledge' that the priests have spurned.

We think of the unity God would establish between knowledge and love and action. Yet, through the delicts of a corrupt priesthood, the human is sundered from the human as limb from limb. The altar is closed off from life; the votaries are blind to their crimes as to the neglected good.

Worst of all, the sanctuary itself is sunk in confusion of mind. (4:19) What indeed is the point of a worship that leads nowhere? The teaching is morbid, lifeless.

(5:1) The assault on the priests continues without abatement. Among forms of authority responsible for the moral education of the people, theirs is crucial, if the truth were known. In this, the priesthood exceeds the king and assembly. Rightly then, in the retributive realm the priests must be named as chief defaulters. They are adulterers in fact; they prostitute the purity of God's word.

A corporation of self-interest and aggrandizement has seized control of temple offices and emoluments. Perhaps 'seized' is too vigorous a word; the priesthood has simply drifted along in the wake of imperialized culture, morally anonymous, spineless, complicit.

The arrangement, seductive and self-perpetuating, draws into its vortex the court prophets as well. They preen and pullulate and give public voice to unsteady thought. Thus priests and prophets, in chaotic unison, compound the plight of the people.

(5:8) The glory of God, hypostasized in the 'shekinah,' the cloud that led the demoralized slaves out of bondage into dawn, promise and land — this sign has vanished. The temple is the tomb of God.

The Glory is debased, the currency of an obscene exchange. Glory is exchanged for Shame, Disgrace (5:7); thus the worship of Baal is named by God. And the people are degraded to an image of the idol stamped on their currency. They are literally Shameful, captive to Shame.

'Things as they are' is a key phrase; it trips from the tongue of those who have most to gain from the status quo, most to lose from a shakeup. The phrase, especially when drawn into 'sacred' or temple discourse, takes on an weird aura of legitimacy. 'Ne tangas.' Touch not this quasi-sacred precinct!

In such an atmosphere, social or political (or personal) change is simply unthinkable. 'Things as they are' is one with the law of gravity, the coming of dawn or a new season.

Unhappily for most of us, the nature of these sacrosanct 'things' is left undefined. Let it only be understood that they are off-limits to the criticism of outsiders.

Let it be declared, with a roll of the eye and a minatory finger, 'the things' are primary evidence of God's will, irrefutable.

The subject detains us since 'things as they are' is not merely a form of warrant, a credential, a badge of office, a steely or scornful glance laid upon the demurring word. It underlies the rhetoric of whatever guardian of the status quo, whether such eminences be vested for the altar or decked in uniform and bristling with weapons. It is all the same. Each stands on posted turf, a police figure, a guardian spirit of sorts, appointed to protect the sacred (and very real) estate.

Moreover, each is convinced that 'benefits accruing' are not the issue here. The status quo is. Perquisites are beside the point — of guardianship. The issue is finally — spiritual; 'things as they are' has a divine weight and warrant. Has not St. Paul said as much? The authority that defines and vindicates public order is of divine origin. Therefore.

Shall scripture then be at war with scripture?

It all depends. Depends not so much on the conflicts within the text, as on the conflicts that rend our lives.

Perhaps a sorry inevitability is at work here. Though castigated by Jawe, the priests might be thought at peace amid the temple folderol. After all, their access to the king is intact, as is the larger easy-going assumption they both entertain and announce: that all is well in the realm.

They miss the nuances, the gaps, they hear no cries of distress, feel no tremors underfoot. What are slaves to them, or foul slave quarters, what the captives of war, the widows and children bereft?

Nothing. Everything the virtuous eye lights on is persuasive and reassuring; the world unrolls before these religious nabobs like a magic carpet.

Images of the eternal surround them. Sanctuary, royal court, marble, bronze, hewn stone — it all looks steady, deep-founded, lasting, secure. Sonorous liturgies, preaching, psalmody, regal favor, ample livelihood — everything in sum, makes sense. The walled enclosure, the world walled out, and they in.

Those priests of Hosea's time; a minuscule world lay like a scrim upon their eyes. There it impinged and impeded.

Obsession with liturgical punctilion and, in regard to the moral code, with jot and tittle.

The priests brought to the altar a perfectly sensible, prosperous, rational existence. They were temperate and mealy-mouthed, men of the golden mean.

They opened the scripture at worship. What occurred then can be inferred from the diatribes of the prophet. A cool eye comes to rest on the torrid word of God, mitigating, banking its fires.

Such priests were great levelers. They cooled the fury that boiled up in the history of covenant: sin, betrayal, martyrdom, prison, exile, slavery, the bloody price of truth-telling, the fury of God against folly and wickedness in high places. Leveling, cooling all that. Applying it elsewhere, elsewhen; relegating it to past event, past delict, to the others, the 'nations,' the 'kingdom of darkness.'

Never here, never now, never ourselves.

The method and habit is codified under the rubric of liturgical punctilio. A species of good housekeeping is insisted on. A plethora of rules serves adroitly, aptly to mask, distance, render remote and inapplicable certain great and awesome matters, matters one must think, of moment to God.

Such matters as are insistently dwelt on by Hosea and his like.

What slow reluctant learners we are! How the works of justice escape us, those modest, difficult arts named by Hosea: 'knowledge of God,' 'hesed' — the heart of God kindled in us, a divine light struck amid the darkness.

All this is perhaps a long way round a short matter. According to Hosea, the anger of Jawe rests on the waste and defamation of time.

Time, one's own time, urgent, untidy, bloodstained as may be. Time as it is — not as wistful and wishful god talk, uttered in a temple cloister (or a television tube). Time of the political predators. Time for religious jugglery, time to stroke the great, to cosmeticize and compromise the truth, all the while battening off the injustice that flourishes terribly around.

HOSEA

The indictment is God's insistence that the past, even a sacred past, is not to be invoked as an excusing cause. Nor the purported genesis from the great. Sons of Abraham? But ye are bastard sons!

Time to hem and haw, to bow, graceful, cowardly, a liturgical ballet of the blind, sweeping the dancers out of the torrid and icy world. Into — what?

That famous 'past,' so preferred, so invoked and praised and longed for — it too merits a closer look. Everything, anything is bearable, once it can be relegated to a mere matter of history, a clean text on a page, a sculpture on a pedestal. In that sense, everything, every crime, once past, is also redeemed, cleansed, forgiven.

The generals who orchestrated the slaughter in the Iraqi desert, whom Hosea would name simply war criminals, flourish, batten in our midst. They are heroes, ikons.

Crime, outrage, war — no matter. They prosper, they gain a monument.

Thus the priestly sense of time. The pharaohs are dead. They are off the scene, horrors that they were. Leave them to God. We have done with all that. And what of our own day? Why, things have changed, and indubitably for the better.

But the diatribe of Hosea is exactly and inescapably a judgment on — today. The day of these priests, of this king, of these injustices. Of this war, the Gulf war.

The words are a shout; they fall like a lightning bolt.

Then a crack appears, a thin line of ruin. Did not a supposition hum through the temple, a subdued psalmody: All is well?

Hosea offers a fierce counterpoint. A wail, a long drawn groan, a cry of outrage, a judgment.

An intrusion. A necessary break, wild, intemperate, destructive of purported 'good order,' of a fraudulent 'new world order.'

Also, as must be insisted, the diatribe is uttered for the sake of a debased priesthood. It offers an alternative. An only hope.

If things as they are, if liturgy as performed, if priesthood as sedulous and subdued, if the people follow suit — if these are the measure of the human — what then has life come to?

Hosea tells it. Life comes to this: Pharaoh, or the king, or the current political satraps — these have the last word in our regard. We belong to them; we belong where we are — in lockstep, in moral bondage, hostages to a politics of turpitude and dishonor.

"You do not!" thunders Jawe.

Thus the question is answered. And by the same token, the diatribe of Hosea is justified.

Let us, he implies, put our lives to the test; let us allow the scrutiny of Jawe to fall on us, scalding. God has spoken: "I have a case against you."

(6:1) Would we seek to undergo true conversion of heart? (For sight of a convert, we have only to look closely at Hosea — but perhaps that is too much, too soon.)

Let us then, under his tutelage, take a look, an ironic look indeed, at an ephemeral 'conversion,' a change — of sorts.

How easily the phrases are taken to lips, how elegantly they roll from the tongue. How beneficial to imagine a 'return to Jawe,' how easy to bring to pass!

(No great effort being required to summon the contemporary incarnations of these incantations.)

To have the ersatz thus presented invites a glance at the real thing — the fierce difficulty, the halting step-by-step progress, the constant harping upon unpleasant topics of ethical behavior, above all the neglected matter of justice.

Nothing of this in our vignette. Hosea is a master of mockery. He offers a parody of conversion, a ceremonious placation, a gentle stroking of the deific one.

Has the idol grown unaccountably angry? Surely he can be persuaded to turn and turn about, if only we come upon the correct phrases, the formal beguiling. There is even a timetable. (6:2) "After two days, he will revive us; on the third day he will raise us up."

And let us by all means be prudent, be clever, borrow to our favor the words Jawe has used against us. (As in 5:14, where he spoke like a lion of 'rending' us.) Surely, 'he has torn, but only that he might heal us.' Now that should please him!

Also a large matter has been made of 'knowledge' of God. Let us assure him of our diligence in this matter. (6:3) "Let us know, let us press on to know the Lord."

(But the knowledge, let it be noted, leaves the original accusation unaddressed; the knowledge is devoid of 'hesed,' of the solicitous love that includes and embraces sisters and brothers.)

The scene goes on, self-assured, cute. There are certainties aplenty and images of providence adroit and delicate as a fruit newly plucked — and as delicious. His coming, 'sure as dawn ... like the showers ... like the spring rains....'

Verses one to three are remarkable. We have here a perfectly straightforward, perfectly meaningless liturgy. All swagger and cadence, it promises nothing of substance, announces nothing new, neither admission of crime nor purpose of amendment. Compared with the 'case for the prosecution' outlined in chapter five, it is a pale defense at best.

More accurately, the ceremony simply by-passes the terrible indictment in favor of a mindless hum, an OM, low-pitched and cunning!

Praise of whom? A god of complicity?

Who is God and who are we? An authentic liturgy of repentance illumines both questions.

The questions are terrible. They imply that the universe, reality, the Creator and ourselves, are — an interrogation point. Why such a world, why suffering and innocence and early death, AIDS, torture, assassinations, disappearances? Why the death of children? Why Bush's wars, their price exacted in innocent blood?

But here the mark is missed. One can only think the arrow has gone wide — with malice aforethought.

HOSEA

In sum, the mocking liturgy proposed by Hosea is a cover. It is as though in the court procedure, Hosea were reading the hearts of the accused, exposing, expressing the moral darkness that engulfs them. They would deceive even God. Let the praises swell, the good times roll!

Conduct is in question here, as it invariably is when a community turns to worship. What spirit do we bring to the altar of God?

Addicted as Hosea's people are to an entirely satisfactory idolatry, they see no compelling reason to renounce or even to review their 'dolce vita.'

Indeed the gods are at our side; the flag flies high and mighty; the market is steady. By every token, God stands in our corner. And if here and there, some must pay dear, be plucked from life in their blood, why, too bad — the gods after all are fickle potentates!

We take note here of a momentous breakthrough. The kingship has been condemned before, indeed from its inception. But the idolatry of kings and kingdoms, rulers and subjects alike, has never been explored. Indeed, we have in Hosea the first prophetic attack on the idols.

Prodigiously, alone, Hosea has entered a cave, a crack in existence. It lies beneath the splendid temple, a dark sanctuary, a mine, a lost dark truth, a ghastly priesthood and its rites. Below ground, the truth; above, the decor and mick-mock.

Other noble spelunkers will follow: Jeremiah, Habakkuk, the author of Wisdom, Isaiah at great length.

The outcome of idolatry is stated flatly. (8:7) "They have sown the wind, they will reap the whirlwind." This indeed may well be the fate of the nations — and commonly is. But that it should be the fate of the people of covenant!

A squandered faith. A faith which, in a radical and sorrowful sense, has degenerated into bad faith. The surface of things is intact; the temple resonates; voices, instruments of worship drum and throb away. The drums are hollow. So are the hearts.

(8:8-10) Of benefit, the 'politic of security' has brought only — nothing, or near nothing; no harvest worth gathering. Out of the whirlwind comes a sterile grain, no meal. And even if there were a harvest, it would nourish only 'strangers.' Hypothetical as it is, the harvest is already lost, sold, frittered away.

As if that were not terrible enough. The 'harvest,' as the imagery develops, is the people themselves. People of God? They 'hire allies among the nations.'

(8:11-13) It would be a fond soul indeed who, arising in the midst of the people, would address such words to Israel today — or to the Jews of New York. Or to the Christian leaders of the U.S. Or to any synagogue or church — here, in Israel, anywhere.

The words move like a firestorm across the landscape of time. A furious judgment races and burns. Everything in its path, every supposition, every security, all we have considered proof against fire — is rendered combustible, twists about and falls to ash.

It is a question of God alone knowing who God is. It is a question of God revealing 'true knowledge' to those he will. A question of God grown jealous — of the truth and its consequence.

Such knowledge has all but vanished from the earth. The world is a universal madhouse, a wilderness of folly, obsession, fantasy, agitation, distraction.

It is as though God had taken a shocking form in our midst, a kind of John the Baptist, a hirsute, raving solitary in a desert place, an illegal presence, a voice shouting against prevailing winds. And no one to give heed. I am God, and who is accounted my equal?

No one gives ear. The winds are contrary. The 'people of God,' as they love to be known, love to tout themselves — they dwell upwind. They are most pitiable of all. Called to be vessels of the 'knowledge of God,' in Hosea's phrase, they move content, blind, deaf, among their squat idols.

In the high places, in the sanctuaries, the lair of the gods of death, flourishes a very forest of weapons and flags. The carven faces of the images, a pantheon of foreign gods, claims them, the 'people of the gods,' blood and bone. Claims them for war and conquest, a ferocious ghastly atavism.

A caveat is perhaps in order here. The contest between God and the gods is not to be understood as the gods (or their devotees) would have it. The contest is a simple corollary of the nature of God — which is to say, of the 'jealousy' of God.

The One who creates, holds creation at heart. The God whose self-knowledge is beyond our ken, yet would have a measure of 'knowledge of God' dwelling in us — the precious, the essence, avatar of the human. And our only hope.

We cannot conceive of a God (or can we?) who, like a deranged parent, abandons the 'work of God's hands,' who washes hands in effect, of the noble work of the Seven Days. Or more nearly to our point, a God on equal footing with the gods, one amid a pantheon. One who might be thought, according to this view, to enter a vexed contest as to primacy of place — the outcome being altogether uncertain.

The prize of which bizarre match is thought to be the hearts and minds of spectators, distracted and deranged as they are. And placing their bets on this contestant or that, morally indifferent (but financially 'committed') as to the outcome of a war of titans.

(7:8-12) There is yet another arena of offense: the people have aped the sorry behavior of the pagans.

The (former) believers are like an 'unturned cake,' burned on one side, scarcely baked on the other, worthless, savorless.

'Aliens devour their strength,' an interesting diagnosis, implying as it does the enervating effect of assimilation.

"Grey hairs are sprinkled on their head, and they know it not." They have gone from adolescence to decrepitude with no middle period of moral maturity; lassitude, numbness, ennui mark them.

The 'not knowing' sums up the judgment. In the common phrase, anything goes. A dead mediocrity is the norm. The norm, it must be added, is flexible and allows for heinous deviation — from moral indifference to vile crime.

Yet all is assumed to be in good order. Life is satisfactory for some, a slipstream bears the culture along. The people are 'like a silly, senseless dove,' riding the whirlwind. The leaders flit here and there in search of military alliances, shoring up an unsteady throne. Inevitably these eminences are victimized and despised by foreign allies. (8:8)

Any ploy, any tactic will do — if only the stalking holy Hunter can be evaded! All in vain: "I will spread my net over them, I will bring them down like birds of the air."

Moral blindness, inability to imagine one's true plight, one's need for succor, the nature of one's crime. Repentance? Return? As well persuade a school of fish to reject its watery element or birds to renounce the air that upbears them.

(7:11) They 'cling to Egypt, they approach Assyria.' Such being the tilt of policy, toward the imperial, toward kingship, toward the ideology of 'the nations,' toward domestic injustice and foreign wars, — it is futile to claim a place in the heart of Jawe.

Covenant of Sinai? A 'chosen' people? Granted they once were the very apple of that providential eye — the eye has turned wrathful. History is chaff in a whirlwind. The eye of Jawe smarts.

Dare we acknowledge that America is the Assyria, the Egypt? Today too the polity of Israel bows and scrapes before the imperium. The international and internal conduct of the 'chosen' is so close to the facts of Hosea's time, so akin to the predatory guile of the Assyria and/or Egypt of Hosea's time, as to make the seraphim weep.

(8:1 ff.) Hosea is appointed a 'sentinel of alarm.' Granted a hearing or no, he is to announce that the sin stops here, the wickedness in high places is to be brought low, the masks ripped off. Judgment is at hand.

Beyond doubt this is a sorry and tempestuous vocation; the name of Hosea stands for — trouble.

HOSEA

And yet, and yet. It is when all good things are in jeopardy, the covenant in tatters — then hope comes alive. It springs up in Hosea, in his courage, his translucent vocal soul.

There is a norm after all, a law, a covenant, a God who judges. The sentinel hovers above 'the house of the Lord, like a crying vulture.'

In the midst of moral disarray, the people are assured that all is well. So they call darkness light, midnight high noon. They stumble and fall and curse and wreak havoc all about and speak of 'normal' conduct. Tradition? Covenant? The ancient realties are shrugged off like an old garment, useless, worn out.

Not only do the people create gods to their image, they bring into being a 'new human' in the imperial image, the idolatrous image: voracious, cruel, duplicitous, predatory. And they name this havoc 'good.' (8:2) Jawe points to an insupportable irony: "They do well to cry out, We know you, God of Israel!"

But the vulture named Hosea is hardly blind; to the contrary, he sees well and widely. He dwells high above the welter and chaos; he is no 'dweller on the earth.' A bird of prey, his meat is — judgment. There is platonic calm and purity in his conclusion: "Israel has rejected the good, the enemy shall pursue him."

His moral insight is both gift and affliction. To see, to say aloud that one sees, to insist on the veracity of what one sees, to judge the human scene as — inhuman. In such times as his (and ours) this might well be accounted a crime. Toil and trouble!

(8:4 ff.) What follows is in many respects momentous. There is a subtle joining of two themes: the quest of the benighted people for a kingly line and the practice of idolatry.

It is almost as a matter of course (at least in the mind of Jawe), to be taken for granted. Hosea says it aloud: The two appetites are one. Together they spell a single disaster; the people are engorged by the structures and ethos of this world. (8:8) "Israel is swallowed up; already they are among the nations as a useless vessel."

Grown vain, have such a people not grown useless also to the nations, their light quenched? Fidelity is in desuetude. What then will the people offer others, this once burning light of 'knowledge of God,' this heart beating strong with 'hesed'?

Is there no alternative? Can the people come on no better way in the world? Must we be morally sinuous and selfish and our government rapacious forever? Can there not be a leaven, even in the midst of a mass grown sodden?

Once, the covenant spoke for another way than Caesar's, another way of imagining our lives. There was a common assumption, a movement. It was possible to live differently, to embody that other way.

And the possible became actual, visible. Such a community so lived and even thrived as though God existed, a God of justice and nonviolence. The community dealt with its neighbors in godly fashion, making peace where tumult had raged. It held its goods in common, lived modestly, coveted no one's possessions.

Were not such believers a burning hope, a light among the nations, a precious human and political alternative?

Hosea lived to see nothing of this. He must by main force, by prevailing grace, embody the covenant in his own person, together perhaps with a few of like mind. But in his lifetime there could be no thought of a great social and religious movement sweeping aside the debris of the centuries, renewing the face of the earth.

Like our own time, hardly to be accounted pentecostal! Here and there dwells an unknown, perhaps despised and persecuted Hosea, in whom the flame, hesitant but persistent, lives.

As for the public life of his times, subtly, then brutally, the tradition died. What once was vividly present, exigent, forceful, a living voice, a shekinah by day, a pillar of fire by night, a summons that spoke to the heart, angels at right hand and left, an ecstatic inner sense of purpose, design, distinction, the unrolling ages like a scroll of meaning and symbol — all was gone on the wind.

To such a people Jawe is a dead God. That admitted, a relief of sorts follows; at least the sorry truth is in the air.

Meantime, also according to Hosea, a charade continues. The covenant is honored in a remote taxidermic sense. It is part of common ancestry. The reigning ideology owes much to it; it helps sustain the myth of national virtue and preeminence in the world. Honoring it on occasion, referring to it sonorously whether in worship or secular gathering, these are helpful ploys.

It is like a document penned in a remote ancestral language. The scroll rests under glass in a national museum. There it is on view to the gaze of citizens or foreign dignitaries. A noble relic indeed, a 'something' that once mattered greatly to many. But to the living, high and low, it is dead, indecipherable, a hieroglyph.

Kings of covenant, kings over Israel? It once seemed a cruel oxymoron. But here they are, one after another, one worse than another, the 'kings' of the north, a ferocious line. They are heard from, they make great mischief in the world, alert to the main chance, vigorous, virulent.

And one after another like a succession of bloody Macbeths, they are murdered. Another seizes the moment, assumes the throne — and is assassinated in turn. The times are like a Grand Guignol; incursions, domestic strife, secret assignations.

For the kings, as for the kings' subjects, the covenant was hardly a matter of serious moment. How could it be? The covenant stipulated — no king but Jawe!

What mattered, what was of supreme moment? Consult the nations for that. Or consult Hosea and his diatribes against diplomacy, war, idolatry.

Undoubtedly the kings serve a necessary religious function. Whatever the temple arrangement and the glad-handing between priests and puppet-prophets, the kings are in charge. They are the chief priests, artificers, worshippers, placators and intercessors — of the idols.

Indeed, it might be said (and is seldom said), the kings are something more ominous than absolute monarchs. They are what the Bible calls principalities; they hold an ominous sway, surpassing the resources of humans. Egyptian art showed it forth masterfully; the majestic pharaohs are pictured holding in hand the key to the nether world.

There, as the images make clear, the contention between life and death is stilled. Death, as a matter of course, of common assumption and acceptance — prevails. This is the world of the idols, the world beyond and within the trappings of royalty or of whatever overbearing form of secular authority.

The Egyptian images rest on a simple assumption: the ruler holds sway over life and death. In his priestly function, the nether world is the sovereign image of the real world. Indeed the nether world and its images rule the ruler. They instruct the king as to right conduct of royal affairs in the world of time.

And the king obeys the images. He invokes, honors, adores the spirit of death. Thus he conducts the religious life of the nation and grants or bars access to eternity.

Meantime, in the empire, women and men are regarded as strictly instrumental. Their fate is governed by a nightmarish class system. Those are allowed to live who are deemed useful to the imperial arrangement.

There are the king's advisors who interpret the auspices and dreams and the course of planets. And the great merchants, active in the world markets. And those who wield the sword. Still others, at the bottom of the pyramid, keep the engines of empire humming away: the hoplites and slaves, the ant-like producers of goods and services.

Thus in many places and climes, in hot wars and cold, domestically and in the world at large, the king announces who is to flourish and who eke out life under the lash, who is to live and who die, who is to kill and with what justification and under whose ensign.

Thus too, the pharaoh wins approval from the gods. In death too, he rules; as he stood in this world at the apex of a great pyramid, in death he enters the nether world and is raised to godly estate.

We are considering the extraordinary words of a single verse (8:4), the quest for a king and the practice of idolatry. The two are set down side by side. The verse thus stands as a flat statement; no argument, no proof is adduced. In the word of God, idolatry is strictly consequent on a certain form of politics.

Let us speak of that long ago, when the people first sought a king. He was chosen and anointed and assumed a throne, newly set in place. Little matter that his holdings, compared with the great world powers, are puny indeed. Such matters are secondary, and subject to improvement.

He is king. The word says everything. In the minds of his subjects, he (and they) are on equal footing with the empires: Assyria and Egypt.

A mini-tyrant has arisen in the midst of the gigantic ones, a David uneasily seated between Gog and Magog.

In short order, urgent matters arise. This newly furbished potentate must secure his borders. Before, the question of armed force never arose; in the eyes of the mighty this tiny non-nation, an outpost, a peculiar tribe, was in every sense 'hors de combat.' But now!

Armies, wars, a nation among the nations, pride of place — the ruinous assimilation is underway.

And what of Jawe? Could his approval be thought to rest on such developments? By no lyric leap. "They have made kings, but not through me. They set up princes, but without my knowledge."

The spirit of the newborn monarchy is one of defiance and rebellion. The 'princes' for their part assume control of the military.

In practice, they instigate coups, assassinations. A pretty picture: bloody divisions, intrigues mortify the heart of the new empire.

But to that question of idols. God, according to Hosea, could hardly be thought to approve the witless clash of arms, the sanguinary adventuring that marks the royal 'progress.'

Alas, imperial dreams, delusions of grandeur possess the people. Divine approval, divine blessing — small matters now! Pride is in the saddle; there are other gods available.

After all, the 'nations' too are worshipful. This is the rule, always, everywhere. Religion confers the ultimate blessing on imperial conduct. What greater credential than 'the gods will it!'

The people who once knew only Jawe, import one or another Baal.

Now we shall have gods on our side! Gods and their war-horses and chariots, gods to whom wars are native, gods at peace with war!

Thus the connection is forged. Now we have gods that resemble us, gods of polity, gods that march with the armies, that whisper a code language of greed, that know nothing of objection against violence and duplicity. Quite to the contrary, these gods!

This 'baalization' has a long history; it is older even than the monarchy. It confronted Moses. At the moment of the sealing of covenant, the people erected a golden calf. They were thus infected with idolatry even before their entrance into Palestine. No wonder that later, Jeroboam will repeat the shame (1 Kings, 12: 28,32).

It is not as though the loss of 'knowledge of God' were without consequence, as though importing foreign idols would have no effect on the moral tone of a people, as though the gods offered a perfectly adequate version of the human.

One argues here simply from the facts of the case (Then? Now?) as presented by Hosea (as presented by Dr. King? Dorothy Day? In Israel or elsewhere, who shall play Hosea?).

Surely no one of us requires instruction in the decline of a human sense among our people, the adventuring in wars, the domestic injustice and pillage. Something that once held firm has fallen apart: a sense of one another, of our rightful place in the course of history. That 'sense' of how one lives and dies, consequent on a sense of God's hope.

One concludes that the effects of idolatry are drastic, lethal, among those once granted to know and follow the 'precepts of my law.'

(8:11-13) These few verses are hot with irony; it scorches the eyes as we scan. "Let them multiply the altars, they serve for nothing but sin." How can that be?

The altars are rendered terribly equivocal in view of the gifts that are borne to them as well as the gifts that are refused or withheld. In Hosea's time justice is reneged on, pillage and prey are multiplied. God is shunted to the edge of life; mammon is welcomed. The altars in effect are dedicated to — what, whom?

Let God declare it, that exiled one, the Lazarine figure at society's gate.

Compassion, 'hesed,' 'knowledge of God,' those troubling immemorial realities? Such as Hosea may, if it so please him, insist on their import. But another law has superseded. It governs a civilization most uncivilized.

Call their law the law of the jungle.

Let the ritual, the sacrifice proceed. They love the meats of the altar; let them eat their fill.

But be it known: I will have no part in this.

What could be more vivid as a metaphor of Jawe's transcendence, of self-understanding, of what might be called a covenant of honor binding the people? Despised, cast to one side, derided by humans, an irreplaceable spiritual hegemony is here ingathered to God. God enfolds himself head to foot in a garment of mourning. No more food in the wilderness; God calls the ravens home.

So matters comport.

And what response? In a time of vandalism, one salvages what one can. The scene calls to mind stories of another time and place.

One tale speaks of the ancient round towers of Ireland. These were raised stone by stone as places of concealment and protection; in them the monks, we are told, hid out in periods of chaos and the scorching of earth. The vandal armies approached. The monks closed the door of the tower and climbed the stair. They bore in hand only the Cup and the Book.

Eventually the invaders passed on, the monks descended once more. The tradition was secure, something had survived.

The book lay open, the cup was passed.

(9:1-6) The scene is a national festival, perhaps a harvest feast. It is celebrated, ironically enough, on the threshing floors of the countryside.

Hosea enlarges the irony. The nation has been 'threshing' its own people. More, the imperial mind pupates its depravity. It would, if only chariots and swords were numerous enough, thresh bloodily in the world at large, a harrowing of hell.

A national holiday, with the usual pseudo-religious overtones! And a stern 'volte-face' is commanded by Hosea: Thou shall not celebrate in the manner of the pagans.

Memorial Day? Fourth of July? Thanksgiving? victory parade? Let us say at least, we are commanded to scrutinize the meaning of the frenetic rejoicing, the symbols exposed on such days. To do so, is to 'celebrate not.'

Some years ago on July 4 a vast flotilla, assembled from around the world, was displayed in New York harbor. Ships ancient and new, sailing ships and nuclear warships, steamed forth, set proud sails through the harbor and up the Hudson River. The celebration marked the bicentennial of the United States. Millions watched, were enchanted. Power! Majesty!

On that day, discovering small reason to rejoice either in the history of our country or its present conduct, a few stayed indoors, prayed and fasted.

Christmas? New Year? Day of the Holy Innocents? Hiroshima Day? Believers are urged to declare holidays of their own, profoundly antisecular days, days of remembrance and mourning, of protest and resistance.

A further point. We humans do not exist like the angels, or as such exalted spirits are imagined by some to exist, airily in outer space.

To a saner view of ourselves as well as the angels, they and we are appointed guardians of the planet. With however a difference. Enjoined on us is right use of the earth, on the angels oversight of human conduct.

The theme of Hosea is of misuse and abuse of the earth. The violation of covenant cannot be correctly understood apart from the fate of the natural world. Indeed, as the prophets never tire of insisting, ecology as such is summed up in the moral ecology of the human community.

How are we conducting ourselves in the world? Is greed riding high? Have institutions become idolatrous? Are the poor neglected, and injustices multiplied? The answer to such questions sheds all the light we require concerning the prospering or decline of the natural world.

The general question comes to a point here, according to Hosea, in a harvest celebration, perhaps a Baalized Feast of Tents.

His condemnation ranges far. Pandering to Baal is to be understood not merely as a gross national orgy. The celebration inevitably tends toward idolatry. 'Hesed' and 'knowledge of God' have vanished. 'Threshing floor,' 'wine vat,' 'new wine ... shall not feed ... shall fail....' Life implies more than bread. By bread alone comes death.

The feast, as wantonly celebrated, holds up a sorry vision — bread only, wine only. Which is to say, given the ethos of those who celebrate, no gift of the earth grows transparent, beckons beyond itself to the Giver of bread and wine. Nothing sheds light on ourselves who till the earth and live off its fruits. Our labors grow slavish; we are the willful 'migrants' of creation.

Indeed, in such debased worship, loving knowledge and just conduct are despised. The quest is for bread alone. Or perhaps bread and circuses.

The motto of the 'Baals,' here excoriated, comes to this: Everything has its price. Baal is, among other things, a market god.

'Everything,' including humankind, exists only 'as priced.' Creation is a vast world flea market. Everything has its price. Indeed, the price tagged upon humans is their only reality.

Humans are on sale, precious as jewels or gold, their price inflated or reduced, remaindered, expendable as slave labor, to be discarded if unproductive — the disabled, the aged, dwellers in-utero, the condemned on death row.

Then comes an enormously brutal, necessary insight of the Bible: By bread alone — we die.

The theme is struck most vividly in the Book of Revelation. There, the merchants of the earth weep over the fall of Babylon, since 'no one buys their cargoes anymore.' And the vast wealth in the holds of merchant fleets is enumerated, item by item, a catalogue of appetitive luxury. The list is shocking; '... horses and chariots and slaves — that is, human souls.' (Rev. 18:11-13)

If everything has a price, and everyone, it follows that the price is — everyone and everything. The market subsumes creation, seizes on all reality: values, religion, fruit of the earth, humans themselves.

And to protect, secure and enlarge this empery, this mad Croesus obsession, war is necessary, inevitable.

At this point, property possesses its possessors; it has become simply idolatrous. And by the same token the human is devalued to the point of absolute contempt. Property and war! Those who wage war in defense of property also dispose of great numbers of non-combatants, the aged, women, children. These have become expendable. They are known to the sycophants of Mars as nothing more than 'collateral damage.'

These are clues as to the meaning of the verses: "You have set your heart on filthy lucre, upon every threshing floor," and "Nettles will inherit the precious silver; thorns will grow in the tents."

(9:7-9) But how is the word of God received? We are soon to be told.

Inserted artfully, even precipitously, is the flat account of the fate of the prophet. His news is bad news, 'a day of punishment ... of recompense....'

Does he dare interrupt the revelry? Then kill the messenger! Or failing that, deride him mercilessly.

Hosea is simply accounted — demented.

(Is the episode so painful that it must be inserted here, an interruption in the text? In any case, the episode is brief, and the main theme, the indictment by Jawe, resumes.)

Still, the matter remains unsettling. It is as though the prophet had stirred waters so thoroughly that they simply cannot be stilled.

The judgment of insanity seems curiously entailed, irresolute. The tag, the fool's cap, are conferred too quickly. Bad faith, guilt unassuaged? In any case, mad or sane, Hosea will not go away; his words lodge like a speck of radium in the blood.

Can it be that the tactic is a cover-up, that it conceals something both deep and dark? If insanity is the clue to the behavior of Hosea and his imprecations no more than the ravings of a madman, why then the hostility? Why are 'snares laid against him in the roads'? And yet more....

'... and in the house of the God of Hosea, hatred.' No need to pursue the point here, both obvious and often verified. Self-justified, vindictive, in control of the apparatus of salvation, the temple factions cannot tolerate a word of judgment. They stand firm, beyond critique; it is others like Hosea, interlopers, troublemakers, who are to be disposed of. And their

HOSEA

excellencies shortly see to the matter.

Deep waters indeed. They still run deep. Enter them at risk, who will.

(9:10-17) There follows a remarkable face-to-face dialogue between Jawe and Hosea.

Mad or cold sane, the prophetic indictment of the renegade people continues. The sin, we are told, is a matter as old as the hills of earth, as old as the memory of Jawe — quite a span indeed!

The memory rests like a healing hand upon a diseased part. There lies the trouble, the suppurating source, the infection.

In the beginning, many centuries ago, ancestors, slaves, shook off their chains. Ever so slowly and painfully, a people arose and became itself.

And something else, (Nb. 25:1-5) something doleful and diseased, also seized that great moment for itself. "At Gilgal I began to hate them." It was there Saul became king (I Sam. 11:15). The 'original sin' is underway (I Sam. 15:10-11). And to the time of Hosea, nothing is changed.

The capital event, the liberation from the pharaoh — let us take a close look. It is by no means to be understood as the spontaneous achievement of genius or heroism. An image of this people does not conjure up a Michangelesque giant in chains, casting off his bonds. Nothing of the kind.

If the liberator Moses appears, it is due to a divine intervention; simple as that. He came forward, a rather commonplace and violent man, a slave among slaves. And if thereafter, mighty pharaoh is thwarted and put to naught by this transformed one, we are witness to yet another episode of divine intervention. The God who began a good work, sees it through.

Surely it was a time of the shaking of thrones. Exodus tells the story; a sorry crew of men and women is beaten into the dust for generations. They are nameless and devalued, a throw-away people, exiles and slaves, in servitude to arrogant goyim. Their God (presuming such a One exists) is silent as a sealed tomb. No hope, no hint of respite or breakthrough.

And then — they inexplicably take heart, arise and walk toward freedom. There is a warp in time, an effect with no known cause. No one of them can tell what power set them marching on an utterly untrodden path, disoriented, victimized as they were. It is an event beyond human contriving, ingenuity or pride. As well explain the days of Genesis as the self-willing of all things into being!

Thus goes the story. Beyond doubt it is not set down as an isolated event, long past. It infers a hint, a parable of perennial helplessness, dispirited subservience.

We too are stuck. We cannot know our own hearts or move our lives. We cannot move toward God. We are destined to live as 'sojourners and strangers on earth'; a sorry lot indeed, unrelieved by any leader arising, any ransom paid.

This must be confessed, this helplessness.

A people was struck dead, as slaves are dead, are presumed so, pushed off the pages of recorded time, denied rights commonly honored among the civilized. Hardly to be accounted a people, turning and turning like animals, the slavish wheel of time.

And then? In the twinkling of an eye, as the millennia go, and inexplicably, the great exodus was underway. A word of love sounded like a gong, set history moving fast and vast on behalf of a shadowy people, a tribe without hope.

No longer the perpetually indentured, the wretched of the earth.

We have seen it in our lifetime. A stroke of lightning in a blank sky. A people is transformed, stands erect and marches. Suddenly confronting the oppressor, rattling the royal throne, announcing its ultimatum, walking with linked arms.

They breathe deep; they have grown conscious of their worth, those of ill favor, the underdogs. The word of God entered their ears, opened their eyes. The word poured into their being, a heady wine. They cried out like sentinels, like archangels. Cried, 'No More!' Cried, 'We Shall Overcome!'

They were not, then they were. To Jawe they were 'grapes in the desert;' in Hosea's wonderful phrase, 'the first fruits of a fig tree.' So loved, so savored.

And then, something else, an 'alas!' The good start is contaminated. At the gates of Palestine, with the scent of conquest and arrival in the air, they 'paid their vows to the Infamy.' They became 'detestable in the image of the thing they adored.'

It is irrational, beyond credence. There was a kind of poison unexpurgated, a social malice in the air, a pride that displaced the achievement, arrogated it in favor of other gods. What is solely due Jawe (in a double sense, Jawe source of benefit, to Jawe praises due), the gracious gift of Jawe — their survival in the years of slavery, the signal given and the long march undertaken, manna and water in barren places, the theophany and law of Sinai — these are squandered abroad.

And what of the slow and steady cohesion of spirit and symbol, flesh and bone, truth and consequence into — a people?

'They paid their vows to the Infamy.'

We have a disquieting illustration of something known elsewhere as original sin. The sin, ancient almost as the first step of humans on the earth, the sin that each generation makes its own, makes new, makes — original. New ways of pride, greed, deception, cunning, ferocity, willed hatred, justified war. Will there be no end of it? (There will be an end of it, as there was a beginning; but not yet.)

Hosea is the prophet of consequence, of the 'not yet,' and more — of the judgment here and now. "And their glory will vanish like a bird on the wing." The images of loss, touching the genetic heart of things, are multiplied. They deny a future to the renegade tribe; 'no birth, no pregnancy, no conception.'

And if children are born against all chance? They will come to ill, for in them ancestral violence seeds itself in the next mad furrow. Fathers will consign their sons 'to slaughter.'

No need here to invoke a gross fundamentalism, a punishing god, a good hater, a settler of accounts. To do so would be to summon yet another Baal.

No, the intent of Hosea is more modest, more concrete, merciful even. Let events, crimes, wars, speak for themselves. They will tell us who we are, for consequence follows the crime, as night the day.

We have no need of an avenging God to bring us to ruin! Left to ourselves ("Woe to them, if I depart from them!"), we grow pertinacious on the hour.

(The Gulf War. Let the countdown commence, let the vast invasive force gather! Glee and bombs, stealth and boldness, blood and resolution. Night and day, our demons are on call.)

If God speaks through a prophet, the words are not 'theological' at all, in an abstract sense, 'about God.' The words are about connections — a God of history and ourselves.

The prophet places a merciless lens against the heart of the human. The lens is a burning glass, the eye of God, as the word of Hosea is the word of God. What he sees there and tells of is a word of both corruption and hope.

The word is in the nature of vision and instruction in a crucial matter. Concerning each we know lamentably little and under the yoke of a larcenous culture, less and less. What it is to be human, what it is to be inhuman. Call it biblical anthropology, biblical psychology.

To paraphrase Hosea: This is what I see. If you could know yourselves, were you not perennially blinded (like those who went before you), this is what you might come to know — of yourselves.

He announces and denounces. He announces something at once terrifying, innate, modest, logical, biologically sound. Something of what might be called 'the nature of things.' And he denounces in God's name those who depart from a human way and yield before criminal blandishments.

Take it or leave, Hosea says God says. A murderous deviance lies deep in our nature. It goes thus far: that fathers send their sons to kill and to die.

Hosea's is a holy teaching, never more desperately needed, precious and ferocious at once. Who, taking thought, can deny it? This is what many have become, unnatural parents driven mad by frenzies, ideologies, cowardice, stonewalling, atavisms, lubricity, moral juggling, blind obedience, flags, anthems, ghastly mountebanks in white houses, the rockets' red glare blinding the heart.

On a thousand battlefields we have verified, approved, signed the declarations of war — again and again in our own lifetime. The misleaders compose the text in blood (never their own blood); the misled enlist, sign in their own blood as well as the blood of the enemy.

Decree the fathers: Let the sons kill and die, once more, yet once more! And count it all honor! 'Dulce et decorum,' the mad incantation rises.

Granted so stark an image of our past, our present, our all too probable future (or non-future, we have brought events to that horrid possibility), it is accounted preferable to many today, that 'wombs miscarry and breasts are dry.' Better no children, it is said in bitterness or moral torpor, than children consigned as sacrifice to Baal.

It bears repeating; it is not God who works havoc or utters the curse. The scripture is far more subtle. Hosea here brings to surface a commonly felt despair, the mood of multitudes who live in the shadow of war. Their lives darkened by prospect, many renounce parenthood utterly.

(9:15-17) And to speak of Gilgal, where the kingship was born, rancor persists in the memory of Jawe. That ancient betrayal!

The point is not a matter merely of a politics that challenges the supreme theocrat. The point of objection is this: the people have taken to themselves the ways of the world, have not 'listened.'

A king sits the throne. Once he is crowned, certain consequences follow, inexorably. A far different ethic is heard.

The people and their regent set out on an ancient well-trodden path. It was traced by armies, conquerors, colonizers, rapacious merchants. It is the way of 'the nations.'

Henceforth, the ethos leads the king — who misleads the people. Henceforth, the common direction is a kind of spiritual reversal and renunciation of the story of Exodus. Aping the nations, adopting foreign

HOSEA

gods, assembling armies and amassing wealth, David has become a great Goliath. The formerly 'chosen' henceforth loom big in secular history.

They all but disappear as God's people. They have become merely another imperial cliche.

Terrible crimes bring terrible reprisals: sterility, the violent death of the young.... We have heard it before and seen it with our own eyes.

The message of Hosea is intolerable. Subsequently, it is hinted, he is to be denied a public hearing. His words will be addressed to a few followers only — and preserved by them.

(10:1-15) If only the memory of Jawe could be obliterated, if only a people could dwell at peace in the welter of its proliferating idols! Alas, the memories lie too near, the relics of righteous history are too vivid. Torn between old ways and new, abandoning this and adopting that, the people are reduced to a scattering of uneasy bewildered ghosts.

In Hosea's time they mourn for the golden calf, handed over in payment of tribute to Assyria. 'Their hearts are divided' between placating Baal and worshipping Jawe; between toadying to Assyria and allying with Egypt; between a history of truthfulness and justice, and a present polluted with agitation of spirit, banality and greed.

The sorry game goes on. They would be a mini-Assyria, assimilated, amnesiac. But memory, Torah, temple, (dare we add, Hosea) these haunt the memory, a scourge by day and an avenging angel by night.

As for the pretentions, the petty mimicry of power, it is all 'words, words, words, false oaths, treaties.' Nothing of it avails to bring peace or unity.

Seldom, even in the greatest prophets, is so scornful a glance laid upon a sycophant people and its rulers: 'like a chip on the face of the waters,' frivolous and pitiful, bent on a deadly course.

"And they shall say to the mountains, 'Fall on us!' and to the hills, 'Cover us!'" Despair is the final clutch upon the heart of such a people. The words are borrowed by Jesus and the author of Revelation. Despair is the moral slag of the killing machine, the detritus cast off by the behemoth empire.

(10:13-15) The seeds of war are one with its fruits: 'wickedness ... injustice ... lies ... chariots ... warriors....' It is all one. It is all foretold. The chariots roll, the injustice multiplies. For generations beyond count, the blind lead the blind in one direction: toward the killing fields.

We note how Hosea forges the connection between spiritual malaise and armaments. And then the logic of the outcome: "Because you trusted in chariots and warriors ... therefore war shall arise among your people, and all your fortresses be destroyed."

Does such a people retain a measure of respect for the innocent, trapped in merciless cross fire? No. Wars are waged without mercy; no one is spared: "Mothers dashed in pieces with their children."

It is breathtaking, the wisdom. It stops the heart: the incapacity, the blind faces, helmeted, set like steel against the terror and truth of history. The terror of one's own lifetime.

Put out more flags!

The spring tightens. The blindness here mourned by Hosea afflicts a people who (so they were told) had been singled out, set free, a light to the unenlightened — a people into whose keeping the word of God was entrusted.

Wisdom? Light? Entrusted? Say rather, the ignorant lemmings rush to the sea, the warriors rush to the weapons — then and today. Oftener than not with Bible in hand. No intervention, no word of the nonviolent God avails to cool the murderous ardor.

The ardor builds the weapons. The weapons are 'defensive,' a code word. They are concocted in good faith; the makers are decent; the weapons will not be used first. Or so we are assured.

But the truth implied by Hosea is something other: 'defensive weapon' is a gross absurdity, an oxymoron. Every weapon built is in the strictest sense, offensive. It offends decency; it offends God. The gunsights are aimed at the heart of God.

The weaponry offends that within us which scripture has praised and blessed as decent, human, generous, compassionate. It mortally offends

HOSEA

the same qualities in others. It would have them and their goodness removed from the earth.

Thus the 'defensive' in theory becomes the 'offensive' in fact. Once the weapons are in place, everything changes. Normal intercourse comes to a halt, sociability is banished. In its place — isolation and contaminating fear. A bruising atmosphere grows, a seismic rumble of mistrust and resentment. Each side seeks an excuse, any excuse, to justify taking the fatal step.

And then, inevitably, a flash point.

And once again we are at war. It is the saddest, most sinful, horrid, banal, idolatrous, dreary, calamitous, constantly repeated aberration and alienation of humankind from its Godly vocation. In the wake of war, in its prospect, in its course, we crawl the earth in moral tatters, bereft of vocation, dignity, humanity.

(11:1-11) This God most human! The moods of Jawe swing in the wild winds. He is like a Lear on a blasted heath, driven to distraction by perfidy and betrayal. Shall God take revenge? Or shall he forgive, summoning once more a prodigal people to heart? Shall he wash hands of this bleak experiment gone wrong, this twisted creation?

Immutable, Omnipotent, this God?

There once flourished a family, there were children who gave respectful heed to a loving parent. All went well. The mother was wild with love and wonder. She held the little ones in her arms, dried their tears, bent to their need, fed them with her hands, led them gently into life. The bonds of compassion were strong and adamant.

The something changed. Indeed, everything, the entire usual world, the world whose center held — all grew slack, fell apart. "The more I called, the more they went from me ... they kept sacrificing to Baals, burning incense to idols...."

Mocked, despised, the old ways. Sons and daughters became wastrels, prodigal and selfish. And the parent's famed tenderness? It was drowned in spontaneous rage, a determination never again to intervene, protect or cherish.

The parent need not raise a hand or loose a thunderbolt. In time, wickedness and perversion bring a sorrowful closure to the story.

Divine love, persistent, patient, forgiving as it has shown itself, is spurned: This is the plaint of Jawe.

What then is to be done? Nothing. Or very little. Except by indirection, instruction in matters long neglected. And this is where Hosea enters.

The teaching must lie near the heart of life, if it is to offer healing — not only to the immediate defaulters, but to the unborn as well. (Paul tells us as much: scripture is 'for our instruction,' those who are born long after these events.)

Then speak it, write it down. The blind need not forever beget the blind; someday eyes may again see.

In the terrible meantime, "The sword shall rage against their cities, consume the bars of their gates, devour them in their fortresses."

And the summing up. Year after year, generation on generation, this people welcomed imperial fantasies by night and played them out by day. The nations were their model and obsession, Baal their god. And it all came to ruin — an ever renewed, gilded servitude. "So they are appointed to the yoke, and none shall remove it."

There is a scorching irony here. Where will a people go, who is to lead them out, when in contempt they turn against their own prophets, when the 'great law' is dead and the slavery self-forged, when the Pharaohs of the nations is extinguished in pure darkness?

No second Moses to confound with prophecy and plague the ruler, no showing forth of the power of Jawe.

What we are left with by way of hope, then and now is — Hosea and his God, a duet much despised, shunted to the edge of custom and estimate, outsiders both.

One recalls a scene from the Acts of the Apostles. Paul has arrived in Athens. (Acts 17:16) At that crossroad of the civilized world, he raises his voice. They hear him out, to a point. But the impact of his words is meager. With the amused puzzlement of light minds, they shrug and turn away.

What, in such a message as Paul uttered, might be thought native to mind and heart, apt for pondering, sweetly and strongly invitational, apt to induce a change of heart? And what is taken as foreign, bizarre, intractable?

In Hosea's situation, weighty matters have come upon hard times: Jawe, law, prophecy, worship in spirit and truth, flourishing of 'hesed' and 'knowledge of God' — these are an aposiopesis, an 'import.' They are utterly foreign, unendurable to conscience and conduct.

And what might be thought domestic, familiar, quotidian? Altars of Baal multiplied, hypocritical priest-craft, usury, injustice, war-making, larcenies, deception.

Scripture could hardly be thought to make matters clearer, or more terrifying, to conventional notions of the power (and the impeding) of memory.

We had thought perhaps that a religious tradition was self-perpetuating. Indeed that a title of its authenticity was precisely its power to perdure. And how mistaken we were! We underestimated the lethal counterforce of a culture, skilled in vitiating and destroying (and replacing) venerable symbols, values long esteemed, honorable behavior.

In the space of a night (or so it seemed, the dreadful fact foreshortens one's sense of time), all was brought down. The tradition faded, lost force. It was reduced to a kind of folklore, tedious, remote, weightless; a tale to be told of an evening around a fire.

There were stories of Jawe, of a covenant, a liberation. The children heard them out, variously entertained or bored. Then they raised their eyes. In pride of place the image of Baal stood in the house.

And what of moral instruction? The children were told more or less overtly, as occasion required, of the benefits accruing to greed, to the sword, to the main chance and the wary eye. Of the advantages of affluence and the impertinence implied in questioning the source or ethic of one's prospering. Of time as money. Of mammon, a jolly green giant. Of the gelt that multiplies wonderfully, if cherished above all else. Of eggs that must be broken if omelettes be eaten. Of the nine points of the law implied in possession and pride. And as to the sweats and chills of competition — be warned, for the devil tails and takes the hindmost.

Thus the world, and our place in it, according to the book of Baal.

The imperial culture, the diplomacy, the police and armies and weaponry and surveillance, the luxury and misery juxtaposed, the blood-letting justified before a neutered citizenry, the sweet-talk, religious-talk emanating from on high — all these come together like sixteen great winds colliding, a clap of thunder, a final closure. Irrefutable! This is the shape of things! Enlist, hearken, walk along, take part, yea say — and prosper!

And lonely Hosea (or Daniel or Amos or Jeremiah) and thrice lonely Jawe, the altars neglected or pulled down, Torah a dead letter.

And what of the riposte, the feeble word of resistance uttered against the thunder of those sixteen winds in one? How curmudgeonly it sounds, how intemperate the tirade of Hosea, how 'negative,' 'judgmental,' 'irrelevant.'

And how his 'NO' is drowned out and lost, save for a few nay-sayers, stubborn, isolated, stuck with a dead word, with an all but dead God!

That 'last word' uttered by imperial lips. Hosea keeps translating, transposing it. Outrageous.

From the throat of empire emerge promises, promises. The imperial soul is a veritable cornucopia, from it a very lava of beneficence, from it every good thing flowing our way.

Promises, promises! A future even grander than the present!

And Hosea responds: Untrue. Lie upon lie. You, the people, languish under a heavy yoke. Say it: the system. It is laid on you by your own leaders; they have neither will nor power to lift it.

With a great push, Hosea puts shoulder to the massive lie, casts it aside. It is like the shift of a boulder from the mouth of a cave.

We see within.

The grave is empty.

Life — the last word.

HOSEA

(12:1-15) A melange of texts comprises this chapter: adages, recollections, warnings, set down later we are informed, by disciples of Hosea. The sequence of thought and image is often difficult.

A few words may help anchor reflection.

Hosea cannot finish with the awful theme; the people, soi dit 'of God,' have joined in a sorry league. Their officials, he repeats scornfully, ricochet wildly on errands of diplomatic trade-off between Egypt and Assyria. So deception, double-talk become a stock in trade.

The nations build lethal armaments and presuppose their necessary use. But there are other weapons in the imperial armory: the wiles of diplomacy.

War or negotiation, it is all one baffling, apparently incurable spiritual illness, 'falsity,' 'lies' — the cult of Baal. The key word is 'spiritual.'

Such understanding is precious not only to Hosea. Such lethal nonsense continues in our own time: the national 'grand designs,' detentes, peace parleys, etc.

The insight of Hosea strikes with the force of a thunderbolt. Consistently in the prophets, but perhaps most strongly here, a truth is insisted on. The ordinary 'business' of empire, diplomacy, commerce, war — all on a grand scale, all enlisting the 'best minds' to the 'noblest ends,' all winning the huzzahs of a public eagerly footing after the flag — these are absolutely incompatible with worship of true God.

Hosea says it plain; so do the other hardy souls named prophetic.

The teaching is remarkably consistent and has no parallel elsewhere. To wit, all such maneuvering and machination as are the stock in trade of the 'nations' (as well as of their sedulous 'religious' apes) is evidence of the realm and sovereignty of Baal, the kingdom of necessity, the vain glory of a chief principality: terrifying, claimant, persuasive, overbearing, omnivorous. Name it 'death.'

Imperial conduct is also evidence of the truth of the Fall. Which is to say, of the rude and ready socializing of death — death in all its metaphors and methods.

Methods, metaphors — the idleness, passivity, indifference and numbing induced in the citizenry in face of their world gone mad; the research and deployment of armaments on a vast scale; the seizures and invasions; the wars normalized; wars reduced (or elevated as the case may be) to a 'matter of course'; wars declared virtuous, unavoidable, just; wars claiming every cranny of existence, every aspect of life, profession and attitude.

We exist in such a time. Hosea's oracles are so to the point as to be hardly bearable; 'lies and violence multiplied.'

(12:3-5) As to his own people. Hosea will not let them off easily. Their situation springs from a polluted history.

How often they have heard their own past glorified! (But not by Hosea.)

Now, the national heroes are held up to scrutiny; Hosea takes a close look at the conventional 'founding fathers.' He summons to judgment one of their 'great ones,' a patriarch, an honored ancestor of the line. And makes of him something else: the sorry forerunner of the deceit that kills.

We might think here of a kind of prophetic deconstruction; the task being to topple an heroic ancestral image. Upon such a one too much has depended. It is as though a great equestrian statue rested on a shoddy uneasy foundation. One heave and the image lies in the dust!

The quest is — a more truthful truth. Too much public folderol, too much religiosity, too many inflated paeans in the sanctuary, too many flags, too facile a myth!

We have in Genesis (c. 29) an entirely different interpretation of Jacob.

Hosea presents him in a sorry light. He is also a genetic clue as to present sorry events. Jacob's very name means 'Deception.' And according to Hosea he set out single-mindedly to dramatize the name, in moral sinuousities, pitfalls and by-ways, the sorry evidence accruing to his status as Ancestral Liar.

There might occur to us here a chastened reflection on national myths. Columbus rediscovered! The father of our country; the heroic early pioneers; the first Thanksgiving in rude weathers (and God invoked, manifestly on our side); the Native Americans, their fate settled by the settler-state in fire and sword, extermination, exile; the African slaves; the wars of conquest and consolidation — one following another like the tick of a bloody metronome — the nation battening on imperial dreams, the wrestling match for world commerce and international domination....

Taking our lead from Hosea in the search for the truth that saves, we follow one thread: the necromancy of diplomacy. Which is to say, deception, lies, double dealing, propaganda, covert murder, laundered money, perjury, fraud, evasion of the law, non- accountability — whether to holy covenant or national constitution.

Finally, Hosea insists — such crimes of mind and tongue, such collusion on the part of authority and conspiratorial silence on the part of the public, though it reap great plunder in the world and create a trumpery national myth — all this serves only to make of the nation a vast sanctuary of Baal, father of lies.

We resemble our ancestors; we resemble one another. The citizens resemble the leaders, the 'believers' are solid citizens. For generations the system, which is to say the fiction, stands intact. Out of the citizenry arise the leaders; they are clones one of the other.

High or low, all are stirred by like ambition, all undergo similar rites of passage, agree on like suppositions regarding war, economy, prestige, pride of place — together with the cost of all this and the will to exact, always of others, that cost.

Thus the achievement: a weird historical integrity, that of the Monumental Lie, is cast in bronze — father Columbus. 'Exegi monumentum aere perennius.' The Latin poet exults in his own genius, and rightly so. But the empire gives the lines a different, ominous twist.

And what of believers, what of us?

This is a lifelong passionate concern of Hosea and his like; their fiery outcry and its echo perdure across centuries. With different emphases and metaphors, be the national fate exile and slavery or a settled prosperous life, the prophetic word is the same: dire warning, insuperable hope.

(12:9) Even in this pit we have dug, a self-blinded self-serving age, there remains — hope. Hosea insists on it.

As a people there is little to commend us. And judgment, Hosea insists, is immanent. Pride, national frenzies, flags and wars, socialized injustice — these in sum are a monstrous zero traced by the finger of God in the dust.

The zero is warrant of no favor, only of judgment.

Yet the judgment is wonderfully patient. It lurks just across the borders, in camps of exiles, it smolders in the eyes of a murdered Iraqi child. And at home, beyond the economic pale set in place by greed, judgment lies like a stigma in the face of a homeless woman, wandering the alleys of our proud 'First World' atlas.

Domestically, all may appear to proceed prosperously. And the appearance of things is commonly taken for the substance.

But the likes of Hosea are gifted with a third eye. He sees flashes of lightning in a clear sky, he hears thunder on the left.

So he turns vulgar expectations and satisfactions on their head. The prosperity of the powerful is a dire sign, a curse. The hand of Jawe, the shadow of that hand, is raised upon the greedy and powerful. The hand will shortly fall.

What then of hope?

The God who judges, Hosea reminds us, is also merciful. Do we merit God's mercy, we who have all but banished goodness from the earth? We do not.

It comes to this, the elusive matter called hope. If humans consent to become inhuman, God has not become Baal. Death and the gods of death, over Jawe have no dominion. The God of life — lives.

Which is to say, God offers hope, a virtue utterly beyond the capacities of the gods — or of their votaries. (The best these gods and godlings can offer, as false worship proceeds and chimeric bounty and commerce swamping our humanity, is — optimism. Which is to say, a momentary feverish relief from a despair ever lurking. A distant pole, whether lying to south or north, of despair.)

(12:10 ff.) True hope takes form; it is visible and audible in our midst. "I will speak to the prophets, I will multiply visions."

And then the flick of the blade: 'and through the prophets, I will bring death.' We are stopped in our tracks. Why this strange linkage of hope and death?

The words sound in our ears like a clash of titanic forces, as in the Easter hymn: 'life and death in mortal combat.'

HOSEA

Whether to Hosea or Jeremiah or Isaiah or Ezekiel — or Christ — the call to speak the truth, as well as the command to obey the truth, comes as a terrifying vocation. A command: Speak the truth, as the truth is given you to speak. And no matter the outcome.

From the moment of his calling, Jeremiah must bear the burden of this hope of God (Jr. 1:10). Conferred on him is a strange form of 'authority.' It is breathtaking in its scope 'over nations and kingdoms.'

In the world's terms, the commission is meaningless, laughable. Either he or his God is a fool. The great ones smile. No great acuity is required to see that of a certainty he is — powerless, a laughing stock.

The message ventures further into a fantasy that can only be termed calamitous. He is to 'uproot and pull down, to destroy and overthrow, to build and to plant.'

It is as though in a mad charade, a corpse or leper were being raised from the dust, a Lazarus or a Job. The witless show goes on; a scepter and globe are placed in inert hands, a crown on the head. Judiciary, police, sycophants, diplomats, merchants, subjects, all surge forward, applauding.

It is pure and heartless mockery.

And yet, we are given pause. This Jeremiah is a classic mourner and doubter; his features resemble an aged Rembrandt. He is hapless, inward turned. He considers his vocation a sorrowful error, a mischance, himself a broken vessel.

And yet. In weakness is his very strength. Lowered expectation, a sense of having little or nothing to offer in an evil time — these cleanse the ground of the soul and allow place for the word of God.

It is this solitary one and no other, so emptied, dependent, 'irrelevant' as they say, self-distanced from imperial pomp — this one is chosen to speak, with finality, clarity, nobility, the word of God. And more than speak. Jeremiah is the embodiment of the hope of God.

In him the word is isolated, lucid, unmistakable, a jewel set in a cruel foil. Nothing, no noise or appetite or witness or credential, neither ego nor ambition or stake in this world — nothing of these impedes.

He is to have no illusions; the word that is bestowed upon him will be acceptable to no one. (Jr. 1:18-19) "Listen Jeremiah! Everyone in the land, the kings, the officials, the priests and the people — will be against you."

But because he is faithful, because the word lives in this forlorn Third World figure — that other word, the overbearing, claimant word of empire, the summoning clash of the arms of nations, has not entirely prevailed. "Today I am giving you the strength to resist them."

Jeremiah has joined the solitude of God, God the exile, thrust out of the world. This is his likeness, his greatness. Abandoned, despised, alone (yet not alone!), he offers an only hope.

What he is appointed to do for others, has first been done in him. His life has been 'uprooted and pulled down....' In him, God will 'build and plant.'

The story of Isaiah is similar; the word lives in him, his illusions have been exorcised. Then, his lips purified by the 'burning coal ... taken from the altar,' he is 'sent' to the people (Is. 6:7).

How, when, by what means shall hearts turn around? Through Isaiah God can only try.

The hope beats on. Despite all, Jawe refuses to give up, to abandon humans to their sorry impasse. In the preeminent time of illusion, the time of the headlong march of empire, the tone of the message entrusted to Isaiah is this: hope.

The word of Jawe to Isaiah is like a sidelong glance of sardonic irony, the black humor of God. (Is. 6:9) "Go, tell them this: No matter how much you listen, you will not understand. No matter how much you look, you will not know what is happening."

Which of the kings or officials or priests or presidents or juntas or corporate moguls or generals or secretaries of war, head on high, prosperous, overweening, stepping roughshod over an Hosea or Jeremiah or Isaiah, which of these would pause in his tracks, glance within his heart and see there and straightway confess to an appalling illness, a pathology of power?

Were a prophetic word uttered, diagnosing the spiritual malaise of these 'dwellers on the earth,' it would be received with supreme contempt, the muttering of a madman.

Isaiah in this much resembles Jeremiah. Each presents a public, humiliated, derided, absolutely crucial message, an only hope. They speak for a God, these courageous ones, a holy One who cannot, for deep heart's sake, give up on those who have contemptuously given up on God.

Ezekiel is another image of this surpassing, patient love. He is appointed watchman over the nation (Ezk. 3:17). The charge is strangely announced.

At the outset he is appointed to no political or social task. He is simply to act as guardian over individual lives and conduct, to intervene here and there, to interpret, to mediate, even to interrupt a questionable deed.

Eventually he will become a kind of guardian angel of the nation. But he must first learn the larger trade by safeguarding one or another life.

And his fate is linked with the one he is appointed to. It is terrifying; in contrast to perfidious Cain, he is appointed his brother's keeper.

Suppose one of his charges persists in evil. That one will die. Unless Ezekiel has warned the delinquent to change his ways, (Ezk. 3:18) "I will hold you responsible for his death."

Once more, hope wears a face of terror. God will not despair. And Ezekiel is God's sign, an intervening, warning, saving presence. Against all folly, moral meandering and squandering of spirit, the people may still come to walk in God's ways. But only if an Ezekiel is at hand, strengthened and 'sent.'

If the word of hope is consistent, so, in a bleak sense, is the response: rejection, contempt, persecution.

It comes to this: the prophets walk a savage gauntlet in the world. They offer no comfort, satisfy no one, are hearkened to by a pitiful few, are variously considered witless or downright criminal, are hailed before courts, disposed of with prompt, altogether spurious legality.

Thus the word to Hosea is fulfilled. "Through the prophets, I will bring death." When the truth is spoken, death is in the air; the truth is death-dealing as often as it bears life. It is two-edged, damascene; it cuts to 'the joining place of bone and spirit.'

Let the one who wields the truth be prepared also to be wounded for its sake.

(13:1-15) The images, whether of Jawe or the national leaders, grow ever more urgent, even savage. There is an ominous sense in Hosea — the end is near. The patience of God, like the blood of a slit vein, has run out. (13:9) "I will destroy you ... and who then will rescue you?"

The images are unprecedented. Jawe speaks (13:7,8).
"I will be to them like a lion ... like a leopard lurking beside the way.... I will fall on them like a bear robbed of her cubs, I will tear open their breast ... devour them like a lion, as a wild beast rend them."

The violence is by no means arbitrary. It is the dark side of love outraged, of hope contemned. Dante's inferno, Bosch's extravagant monsters, the livid lubricous canvases of Francis Bacon — such images yawn with horrific truthfulness. They recur in dreams, nightmares, lurk there, a warning or portent. They will not be banished.

Saul, Pilate's wife, Macbeth, all were so afflicted and warned. What the conscious mind would banish, would walk gingerly past, as though with face averted from a corpse, hurrying toward an only comfort, the light of day, companionship, human voices alive — these images regurgitate horrifically. See this, smell this, taste this! Recoil, vomit! Its name is crime, sin, damnation!

Assumed by Jawe, the images speak of something terribly amiss, whether in the world or the human soul — or both, the one interpenetrating and poisoning the other.

The prophets too suffer such nightmares. Wild beasts (in scripture, invariably images of empires) roam through the world, devouring whom they will. Such images shook the soul of Daniel in the worst years of exile (Dn. 7:4-6). John of Patmos suffers a like onslaught of images as he records for his afflicted community, images that rave, roam, prowl — and strangely heal.

Daniel's ancient nightmare (daymare?) seizes upon John of Patmos with monstrous talons. He sees three successive empires symbolized in one composite beast, a horrific being never seen on land or sea. It resembles a winged lion, symbol of Babylon. Also a ravening bear, symbol of the Medes. And finally a leopard, symbol of the Persian empire.

Nightmarish indeed, comprising and compacting all former empires in one; behold Rome, a monstrous killing machine loosed on the newborn community of Jesus.

To most, such images are simply bizarre; the beasts, we are assured, have been tamed long ago. We and our children may view them 'burning bright,' behind bars in zoos.

The tyrants too are tamed (and the citizens as well). Everything hums along like a well-known tune in a deep groove. A rut? The record turns and turns, the tune caresses our ears, purrs like a prospering cat.

Behold the intricate machine, the system. Behold, Admire! It is wonderfully punctual, progressive, productive, 'on target.'

Are many in misery, hungry, homeless? Is nature and our own soul wasted on mad armaments? Are we being cozened, lied to, betrayed by authorities? Are we denied a voice in our own future? Have we humans become the most endangered species of all?

The questions are never raised. Or if they are, the questioners are adroitly nudged aside, their voices drowned out in a cacophony of media or the thumbs-up of the latest poll. Sane politics, political maturity, compassion? They are gone with the wind, reduced to — getting and consuming.

An abbatoir.

As to the nightmare imagery, in Hosea two transpositions are implied. Rightly apprehended, the wild beasts are no longer to be thought of as images out of vivid or stressing dreams. They stalk about in the day — they invade the conscious mind.

And more important by far, these are images, not of the worldly powers, but of Jawe. Let us not confabulate; they are images of violence and death, of the divine will to destroy.

Untamed this God, this lion of Judah (this Jesus?). By no means domesticated, tamed, bribed, cozened, placated, sedated by empty liturgies, sonorous prayer, banal vows, sterile fasts or feasts.

And there is logic in the images — a logic wild, terrible, furious. They imply a crude quid pro quo, a righting of the scales, a bold illumination and rebuke of a certain history.

The lion image stalks meat, even human meat, with all deliberation. But not only the lion is predator; humans are also the great carnivores of the world, the first and worst. They consume one another. Rouault's etching says it: homo homini lupus. "Toward one another, humans are wild beasts."

Thus the images are by no means arbitrary. They veritably explode in Hosea (in Jawe); the holy One strikes like a prodigious battering ram against the deep-founded criminality of imperial (and would-be imperial) society.

Other times, other images. The choice here, the range, the aptness, the coincidence of oppositions, these witness to the scope of Hosea's genius, the furious dervish dance of his intuition.

Earlier, Hosea had described roughly the same period of national history as is recalled in our present chapters 13 and 14. The times are wicked and woeful indeed.

Yet it is striking that in the earlier chapters he offered utterly different images. We were told that God was displaced by foreign gods, rejected, contemned, his sanctuaries polluted. And the heart of Jawe was torn from his breast. The images that arose were like a veiled chorus of mourners, loud with longing, sorrow and loss, an epiphany of enduring, connubial love.

(13:9-11) When the leader becomes the misleader, wrote Bonhoeffer from prison, the led become the misled.

It is all too familiar.

A time of national elections nears. And yet once more, unto distraction and ennui, a (third rate) drama is cranked out in our midst. A new savior appears just over the horizon. The foolish images are refurbished, a kind of John Wayne saga resuscitated. Steamy rhetoric denounces predecessors or current rivals. The hero mouths promises and more promises: a new era, salvation, change, nirvana, a national cornucopia teeming with plenty for the votaries of empire.

Yet the tactics, the huckstering candidates, the dreary jugglery, hint at a kind of bastardized biblicism. There are no issues, only images. And these invariably tease and play and promise, invoke the realm of God, secular covenant, redemption.

We would be, above all else, a godly people — our candidates too. Would be, nay are, a new phenomenon on the stage of history, the first and only godly empire. No part in the sins of Babylon, Assyrian, Egypt, (Israel?), Rome.

The absurd pretention is as anti-biblical as it is publicly acceptable, warmly received, refurbished, cozened and blessed by the pieties of imperial religion, verified in idolatries surrounding the flag. Above all, the pretention is self-justified in wars hot, cold, invasive, pre-emptory.

We have suggested that in Hosea, as elsewhere in the prophetic books, the question raised is not one of a theocracy versus pagan empires with Jawe insisting on primacy, and now and again, like an Achilles distempered, on occasion of default from his will, retiring in dudgeon.

The question is not, 'Jawe or the gods,' as though Hosea were witness to a war in heaven, outside time and this world, disconnected from the behavior of mortals.

The meaning of Jawe's plaint and fury is quite simple — a battle for the soul and meaning of the human.

Let us assume for argument's sake that a godly people, a people of the gods, Assyrian or other, pursued political and religious life under a covenant with the Baals. This people, by supposition, was innately peaceable and just; they sought no other goods than their rightful ones, coveted no foreign soil, went their own way, artless or sophisticated as might be.

A dream indeed, and all unverified.

The people of Jawe were surrounded by no such tribe of innocents. In Hosea's time, the empires at the northern and southern borders pressed hard and fast; a sea of lances, a phalanx of troops, chariots beyond number. Wealth was amassed, world markets seized; fleets of commerce roved the seas. Savagery, violence, sophistication, arts, gods, slaves, colonies, greed, wealth, misery, all fell together in the vast teeming hodge-podge: the cargo of the whorish hold of Empire.

And then the enticement offered the people of covenant? It is to the gods, our Baals, that we owe all this. Why not be like us, and prosper?

But what has occurred within the souls of citizen-worshippers of Baal, what version of the human has perished, what version has won out? This would seem to touch close on the question raised by Hosea. Jawe's version of the human is in combat with the version of empire. And a choice impends.

It is in light of such reflections that verses 10 and 11 are to be understood. It is not this or that political form, one king or another, on whom the objection rests. The rub occurs when such authority, whatever form it takes, presumes to play God, to demand quasi-divine fealty, staking its claim upon human life (and death).

We have here, splendid and squalid, the panoply of idolatry. The Baals are images of a pseudo-divine seizure. The politics are hypostatized; the kings are raised to the empyrean; holy ikons, divine. Thus empire. Thus the subtle and not so subtle intertwining of worship-war-greed-injustice and the rest.

Thus too the 'new human,' worshipful, starry-eyed. Lost in wondering admiration. Lock stepping. Implacable. Unquestioning. Banal. Apt for the dealing of death, on command.

Possessed.

And then the contrast, the blessing offered by Hosea and his like.

They have preserved some hint and inkling of the 'human according to God.'

The human! That darling mind and heart emerging from clay under the hand of Jawe, the very apple of God's eye.

What does he look like, this marvel? Whom does she resemble?

This: just, compassionate, equable of mind, self-giving, word for warrant, promise and deed in close accord.

The 'kings' have another version in mind; it requires no enlarging here.

Appallingly, today the ancient imperial image of the human is conjoined with the national myth, homo-Americanus, at once stereotype and threat.

What form of religion this citizen takes? In what or whom does he trust? What weaponry is near to hand? What goods of the earth are required and amassed, and in whose despite? National style and behavior answer such questions day after day, in a monstrous body language, before an appalled or silenced (or bloodily subdued) world.

Of such style and behavior, Eduardo Galeano, author of *The Open Veins*

Of Latin America, is much to our point:

"The promise of politicians, the reasoning of technocrats, the fantasy of the unprotected, goes like this: the Third World will some day be like the First World, if it behaves itself and does what it is told without complaint.

"But what cannot be, cannot be. If the poor countries were to ascend to the level of production and waste of the rich countries, the planet would die.

"A few countries squander the resources of all. Here is the crime and delirium of the society of extravagance ... a North American consumes the equivalent of fifty Haitians.

"Clearly, the average does not define a black person in Harlem, nor Baby Doc Duvalier. But anyway, it is worth asking: what would happen if every Haitian suddenly consumed as much as fifty North Americans? What would happen if the immense population of the South could devour the world with the voracious impunity of the North?

"We would have to look for another planet.

"The precarious equilibrium of the world depends on the perpetuation of injustice. The misery of the many is necessary to make the waste of a few possible. For a few to continue to consume more, many must continue consuming less. And to make sure no one gets ahead of the few, the system multiplies weapons of war. Incapable of combating poverty, the dominant culture combats the poor and bless the violence of power."

"I have given you kings in my anger, and I have taken them away in my wrath." Indeed.

We are perhaps nearer an understanding of that wrath of God — the hot flare of love outraged. Outraged be it noted, in a most disinterested sense — because in us, beloved as we are, the divine fire is diminished and spent.

(14:1-10) So we near the end, not only of the book, but also of the kingdom of Israel, a recusant people that chose to create, to its ruin, an imperial state 'like the others.'

No need to press the contemporary issue. Nor indeed to restrict the diatribes of Hosea to the violent, sterile, settler-state of the mideast, as it persists in miming the diplomacy, military might and idolatries of Big Brother to the west.

To the west, believers and others are in a like predicament, of course. Universal, the illness diagnosed by Paul in his letter to the Roman Christians: "All, all have sinned and fallen from glory."

The sins spoken of by Hosea as mortal impediments to 'true understanding' and 'hesed' — these are thrust like nails into the body of humanity. Violence of ever sort, quixotic and self-consuming, idolatry, greed beyond satiation — these infect the heart of the human, even as they anger the heart of the divine.

Astonishing. No generation learns from a prior one, no military theorist or political scientist or historian is able to unveil a persuasive or useful critique of the imperial past with a view to amending current behavior.

In our own time, various versions, twists, applications, forays, trials and errors, all reek of the ancient methods: duplicity, murder on a grand scale, false worship.

The nails stand firm in living flesh. No skill draws them forth.

Yet the sorry fact is a source of realism, even of hope. At least biblical folk know whereon they stand with regard to secular assaults and claims, whether asserted against their God, their conscience, their community.

Hosea offers also a cold comfort, an assurance; this is a word of truth concerning political and ethical realities. The one who conveys the words is faithful and true to the One who inspired them.

What is to be done?

According to Hosea, the believers are to stand somewhere; this is the heart of the matter. It is the geography of the faithful that counts in the long run, sometimes even in the short.

This is the first offering. One is alert to the signs of the times, stands 'over against' wickedness in high places, its chills and fevers. Under God one is, so to speak, one's own first convert. From this capital event and mystery, much may follow.

Hosea's strictures look as well to the conversion of others; conversion of a certain kind to be sure.

He is contemptuous of personal pieties which leave some caged and resigned, others tending and guarding the cages — an image of public woe worsening. He would open the cages, discharge the guards, summon all to justice, peace and true worship.

He even composes an admirable prayer of reconciliation:

"Take away our iniquity, that we may once more prosper and render to you words of truthfulness."

The words implore a divine initiative, lost in the unsavory shuffle of power politics. Better, they indicate that the initiative sought has already been granted.

There indeed flourishes iniquity, and spiritual illness, and untruthful words in a flood; and who but a remnant has known or greatly cared?

No false or facile hopes inspire Hosea, no obsession with success or prevailing. He holds no expectation that the malaise of empire would be healed by his efforts.

His intent is otherwise. He would leave in God's name a legacy, a truthful account of the times. And a prayer, whose words suggest for powerful and the powerless alike, a better way.

For all, high and low, 'make alliances'; all construct and cheer on 'the chariots'; all 'say "My God" to the works of their hands.'

And all, in the telling conclusion of the prayer, are 'orphaned.'

The image is merciful. It favors the delinquent. An orphan is bereft of a parent; but the infant or child could hardly be accused of bringing about this great loss.

That the 'bereft' have earlier been scored again and again for blindness, cruelty, malice aforethought, injustice, warmongering, (a catalogue of the behavior not of children, not even of wayward children, but of adults gone berserk) — all this is now ignored. The crimes are out of sight, out of mind.

We are witnessing that great and noble 'forgetting' which is the glory of Jawe. And of Hosea.

The mood is one of a noble 'return.' The prayer is God's declaration of a new start. It is a rainbow after a flood; under a radiant arc the disastrous waters recede. We are lost (and found) in admiration.

There follows a very dervish dance of images. The imagination of Jawe strikes free. The arms of God, right and left, reach out and embrace the people. Then all are whirled away in an ecstasy of love.

Jawe is to them a refreshing dew. (14:6) Is to them a cypress ever green. (14:9) They will bear fruit only through Jawe. (More, a play on words: in the original the 'bearer of fruit' is one with the name Ephraim. Fecundity comes through Jawe.)

In that embrace, what images flourish! Jawe is intoxicated with joy, as the rhythms of the dance whirl the beloved through the vast round of the universe. The people, clothed in the glory of creation, are healed in that embrace.

(14:5-7) The human at last! The apotheosis and crown of creation: 'blossoming lily ... rooted poplar ... spreading shoots ... beauty of the olive ... fragrance of Lebanon ... flourishing garden ... blossoming vine ... wine of Lebanon.'

It is a marriage imagery, a return, after the most disastrous meanderings, to a garden of innocence.

And finally. (14:10) Caveat lector; let the reader be warned. If through Hosea God takes heart against all odds, to hearten and restore us — surely the grace continues, the river of grace reaches us; it has not been set flowing solely for the sake of an ancient people.

The oracles of Hosea are good news for us also; ghastly, barely endurable as the times are.

Hard too, hard as death — or birth.

JOEL

EVEN THE WILD ANIMALS CRY OUT TO YOU

"Woe and yet again woe!" he cries
nor ever ceases ranting -
and what, think you, fires his tongue,
what wrong, what gone amiss?

Behold, our worship duly wrought,
God's own we are, sealed
seared with his image,

'What ferocity then
fuels a woebegone soul
that into sixteen winds he shouts
lamentation, imprecation,
until the winds, icy, torrid,
aboutface turning,
affright and afflict -
and the locusts descend
like God's exterminating
blind eye, blotting the sun?

'What, why, whence?
is then the universe
so at odds, and we at odds,
as though all sweetness
 were wrung from the laden garden
and common weal and worship were
prelude only of woe?

JOEL

"'Grieve," he cries, "grieve
like the girl who mourns
lorn, her bridegroom's
corpse, and none to comfort!'"

'Grieve, and for what?'

"You, you, blind, besotted ones!"
(Thus Joel, fiery mouthpiece)
"The sun casts down its sword
stands blind, abated
and locusts swarm in madness
upon his blackened eye, a night
of contradiction upon the noon -

"Blind, blind, your priests
thrice blinded,
caricatures, clones,
lugubrious, mindless,
nothing caring, daring no jot
for justice, compassion, cherishing -
incanting from a cave
of self willed darkness,
'See, we see!'

"Blind, you stumble after
into that yawning cul-de-sac.
What then can prosper?
Nothing, you gods of nothing.

"Sweetly, gently all things
waft from My hand
like newborn birds' first essay
tentative, of wing upon air.

"They fall from air. All things
bountiful, beautiful, tender,
fail and fade upon your breath -
you winds of betrayal.
      Riding the winds
like rumor's hum and strum -
locusts! a terrible army

set in array -
image of yourselves, truth known,
you, swarming
predators storming the day.
"Earth groans and sickens,
My garden, your desert!
Open then the drama
the frenzied hordes -
I summon
you and you and you
for judgment, for chastisement!

"And yet - and yet -
judgement? punishment - ?
It were like
lashing the blind, the halt
to a finish line.
         Heart
leaps to my eyes in tears
Nolo prosequi !
      HESED be My name!

For your sake, in all despite
a tenderness unborn, half formed
(as in a woman's body
a wordless sightless child)
signals, (as though from unutterable
distance a star
swam into ken);
      'Remember
me, your darling, your flesh
forever - come what awful
mayhap of this.'

"I hearken, I hasten to
 the heart's sweet cheat.
Posthaste my Spirit
I bend, breathe, outpour
 upon you

"And you lost, lorn
wild, wilful progeny -

forsworn
to awful death's dominion -
death's NO I abrogate!
you shall be
shall be
twice born
of mothering Me."

At the start, as though to stake everything on what is to follow, the 'word of God' is invoked. That word, according to Joel, is an utterance that bears an altogether unique solemnity and weight.

A long history of 'the Word' in the prophets culminates in John's "In the beginning was the Word... and the Word was God." (Jn. 1:1)

To be without the word is to be without God.

One asks his soul as though lost in the night: What resource could one envision in such times as we endure, where to turn, what to think or say or stutter about God, creation, one another, the meaning of the human, the horrid violence that all but rides hope under — what would befall us were we deprived of this Word?

The question is both cruel and crucial. It touches on the mind's powers, the affective life, right understanding, conduct worthy (as well as basely unworthy) of humans.

And lately and lamentably, in our day the question touches on the fate of creation — our own fate included.

Words, words, words. Shakespeare mocks the futility and waste and ennui which perennially infect habits of speech.

We require no instruction today on the abuse of language. How commonly our precious thesaurus is narrowed, defamed, put to degraded use, bowdlerized, bent out of all semblance to the truth. We have been lied to, we are lied to, we shall be lied to. It is the sorry declension of our lives.

How cruelly prescient Orwell was! War is peace; misery is prosperity;

all pigs are equal, but some pigs....

The lie, amplified beyond bearing, seemingly irresistible, sounds in the ear like a final trump. With skill and persistence the Big Lie takes on the semblance, wide-eyed and innocent of the truth itself.

In order to wage war it is made clear that there is no need to declare war. Can this be in accord with the constitution of the land? The citizens shrug their shoulders, the congress bows out, the courts decline judgment. We are at war.

But hold on! The president, we were informed, was not 'declaring war,' he was ensuring protection of 'our interests' in the mideast.

In effect, a multitude will die for oil. And the oil won at the price of blood will, much like the blood, be spilled over land and sea.

But unlike the blood of the innocent, the oil of the guilty and greedy will be poured out to no one's benefit.

The oil is a curse, the curse of Cain. The blood may, in some unforeseeable blessing, be shed to our redemption.

Say it again, Uncle Sam! As it was said bloodily in Grenada and Panama and Vietnam.

We are victims of the worldly word, the word that politicizes all questions, breaks promises, pollutes life with a vile cynicism, commandeers humans, rounds them up like cattle, arms them, commands them to kill and be killed.

It is as though the warriors are marched into a mysterious cave. A sign above the portal reads: Dwelling of the Principalities.

At the door, welcoming the warriors, assuring them as to the rightness of the cause, stands the smiling master of legerdemain.

The cave door closes. Sounds of strife are heard, gunshots, cries of anger and despair. The world waits in fear and trembling. Something sacred is transpiring, out of sight and witness, outside accountability, a war of the titans. Witnesses, judges, reporters? Surely they are inappropriate, as at any sacred liturgy. Forbid them to enter.

JOEL

The cave door opens amid a cloud of fire and smoke. And a sorrowful procession emerges, masked bearers of the dead. They lay the bodies here and there on the ground; groups of huddled mourners clot. A priest moves from one group to another, comforting, reassuring. His word is an ancient one; it has a classical ring.

He lays a hand on the shoulder of this or that survivor; 'dulce et decorum est....,' he intones, 'what a noble thing, and befitting, to give one's life for our country....'

Relief from such times, grant us relief! To know there exists a starkly unequivocal word, a Word that judges all other words, that invites and welcomes and reconciles the living, the warriors and victims, a word that touches hearts, offers a truth that ennobles and elevates the human. And by main and gentle force, unmasks all deceitful, duplicitous and disordered words!

The vocation of the word of God in our world, according to Barth and Stringfellow, is the rebuking and exorcising of the worldly word. The word of God thus stands in combat against the worldly word, against all words uttered with base intent and duplicity, the word that spells death.

And the combat never ends; the word of God is a necessary and inevitable hostility against the word of the imperium.

Thus it is written. The word of God was spoken to Joel and the noble company of prophets. And the same word, if our humanity is to be salvaged, must resonate in ourselves and our world.

❖ ❖ ❖

Let us take up the matter in some detail, the word of God as irreconcilable with the imperial word.

This is the plain scandal of the word. It also implies the dangerous vocation of the one who announces the word.

The prophets, it is clear, must in one way or another, be silenced. History bears this out. Murder upon murder, all the more desperately repeated, from the time of Joel even unto Romero — murder is invoked and multiplied — even as it is shown to be awesomely futile.

Thus the history of empires takes on the bloodshot visage of a Macbeth. And it all goes nowhere.

Nothing, no violence, no suppression, suffices to silence the word of God.

It is as remarkable as it is ignored — this constant harping of the prophets upon one theme — the word of God in combat with the word of the powers.

The combat continues and intensifies in our lifetime as the word of God confronts propaganda, decrees, manifestos, triumphalist liturgies, false promises, empty moralisms, concordats, treaties of 'non-aggression,' S&L deals, declarations of war, economic legerdemain, state of the union nonsense, flags, parades, the orchestration and panoply of deceit.

All manner of questions arise. Is the conflict between the Word of God and the imperial word so striking and constant merely because of this or that unlucky historical circumstance, something easily (or not so easily) remedied? And is it a conflict that occurs now and again when the word of God strikes up against an occasional, exceptional malfeasance of the powers?

Or does conflict arise because the word of God has the ill luck of being spoken, set down, transmitted solely in bad times? Does the word of God conflict with a misadventure of worldly power, sorry or sordid or murderous as may be — but a departure from the decent 'democratic norm,' an episode, a lapse from civic virtue and honor?

Or does the conflict of the Word of God against the word of 'the dwellers on earth' — does this rest upon the nature of empire itself? Let it be understood: the conflict arises as well from the nature of the word of God. That word stands here and now (as in the time of Joel and in every time) as a word of sovereign judgment.

As such, the word of God announces here and now a rehearsal of the end time when the nations will undergo universal judgment. The word is in the world as a witness to the fidelity of God; but the moment for laying down judgment in virtue of that fidelity is not yet. Not yet, but certain to come 'on the day.'

Let us speculate. If there came into being a 'godly empire,' would not the word of God invoke a blessing on it? Did not Paul in fact invoke such a blessing on the empire, implied in his exhortation to civil obedience on the part of Christians? (Rom. 13)

That being so, why all this pessimism, the threat and dire warning and brimstone atmosphere of the prophets?

Or perhaps such pessimism was appropriate solely to their time and circumstance, and no other.

Let us look at another side of the same matter. Can it be true, as Barth and Stringfellow and Ellul and other insist, that the 'godly empire' is simply an illusion — an illusion useful to rulers, hence passionately huckstered by every empire in history?

Put it plain. What worldly power, from Babylon to our own, has been solicitous for the well-being of its poor and unprotected citizens, has repented its wars and warred no more, has honored the just domestically, and mourned their death elsewhere — in sum has stood (or so much as desired to stand) peaceable, modest and forthright in the world?

The conflict of the word of God vis a vis the powers must be regarded as arising from the nature of the word and the nature of empire. The word must be itself, for God is God. And the great powers must be themselves — or not be.

No other Word than a word of judgment could be addressed to the empire at the time of Joel or now — simply because there exists no alternative form of empire — then or now. The opposition is inherent, essential; it proceeds from the purity, justice, moral stature of the Word, as well as from the morbidity, injustice, violence and depravity of imperial power.

The latter being, according to the Word, the prime embodiment of the Fall — to the point that to speak of a 'fallen' empire is a tautology of note.

Thus the book of Revelation derides Babylon, and by strong implication, all imperial constructs and inflations. Babylon is caducic in essence, self-destroying, requiring no external enemy to bring it down, its 'topless towers' have grown top heavy with pride, greed, and the political numbing of its votary-citizens. (Rev. 18)

Indeed we touch here on the essence of the Fall, the heart of that darkness.

Which is to imply several things. In the first instance the conflict in which the Word of God is perpetually embroiled, whether in the Jewish or Christian testament, depends not at all on this or that vicissitude of history, nor on the conduct, outrageous or virtuous as may be, of this or that tyrant or government.

The conflict goes deeper. Simply put, the word of God is appointed to the truth, and this in a world which cannot tolerate the truth.

The virtue of the word of God is a sovereign consistency, in conflict with another sovereign and darkly consistent power.

We speak of 'the nature of things.' The phrase is a pale substitute for the inherent drama, the tragic lot of humankind. John's gospel, as well as Paul and Revelation, convey matters clearly. There is conflict at the heart of reality. Light and darkness, life and death in mortal combat, all creation groaning in hope of liberation; these symbols touch on the truth. The word of God cannot but deny and assail the empery and claim of death.

And thus in Joel also.

All this is by no means to imply that the titanic struggle between the word of God and the powers, engages 'equals.' The victory of God's word is already assured, announced, celebrated.

In life and in death it is the martyrs who announce that audacious word. They live by it, they die for it. For they live by a memory that animates; the imperium of death has failed of its chief assault in history, the indicting, conviction and capital punishment of Christ Jesus, God of Life. Christ is risen. Thus our 'falling away' from life is healed.

And the chief and awesome instrument of that falling away, the one who argues on its behalf, normalizes it, cheapens life and multiplies death.

Alas for death, alleluia for life. Jesus is Lord.

Not every nation will challenge the word of God in equally morbid ways:

sanguinary conflict, murder of the prophets, neglect of the poor, concoction of lies to cover its crimes. Nation states are not all empires (though most aspire to become such if the armies, markets, fleets, land mass and other accoutrements of empire at hand).

But let us listen to the nations and their self-defense.

We are told (above all by our own leaders) that they aspire to an ideal, commonly known as 'democratic.' Our system would be just, invokes something known as 'the rule of law.' A vast legal network, the 'law of the land,' is examined minutely in the law schools.

There exists moreover, an overarching international law governing, as is said, the conduct of the nations and their armed forces, politicians and citizens, especially in circumstances of conflict.

All this. And it all falls short.

Shall we speak of justice, 'equal justice under law'?

We make bold to examine the behavior of these legal savants. And we cannot but note something: the 'justice system' and its appalling malfunctioning throughout the world, the awful prisons, the rigor and racism, the bias and spleen of judges, the capital punishment, the rounding up of political opponents — not to speak of disappearances, torture, and officially-sponsored death squads.

In all such horrific contradictions, Christians have recourse to the reality of the Fall, the incapacity of institutions to attain even a minimal level of compassion and equity, to demand of officials even minimal probity of conduct — such civic virtue in sum, as would bring light to the darkness, the squalid drama of crime and punishment.

Deep in the heart of all, in the heart of institutions, lies the fault. A masked figure, Death, is enthroned there.

Who is to unmask and dethrone that power and crown Life with due honor? The nations are helpless; they can but pay tribute to death. They must wait on an event they can never bring to pass.

Their incapacity stands like bleak Ozymandias in the desert from the time of Joel to the present dark age.

'Wait' is the command of the word of God. "Wait upon Me."

Time is a perpetual advent. On the part of the just, it is a long sussuration and mourning, as justice is perpetually denied, contemned, spurned.

Wait. A strange word indeed, foreign to a culture which teaches its citizens (and would inveigle believers as well) to wait upon — nothing. What meaning can this worshipful, modest, attentive 'reading the signs of the times' bear for such as ourselves? Are we not assured daily, under the dark interregnum of technology, that we can bring to pass whatever we set mind to, whatever project, no matter its cost, no matter its inherent difficulty, no matter its implication (invariably military?), or its moral flagrancy. It can be done; therefore do it! — the first commandment of the cultural decalogue.

The Word of God bears a far different sense of the times. The sense is Joel's for certain, and just as certainly the sense is in conflict with America.

The Word is a great leveler; it stands in judgment on the prideful sense of riding the cockpit of the world. It rebukes worldly time as a false, misleading reading of the times.

It speaks in contrariety of a kind of 'meantime,' a hypothetical, questionable time, a time during which Christians are well-urged to read the clocks differently, to keep their distance — from the times.

To ponder the times, to weigh the times (and inevitably, to find them wanting). To refuse complicity and endorsement, to reject ethos and appetite. To choose in sum, to be judged irrelevant to the times. Even to play the 'guilty bystander,' in Merton's phrase, such a role being preferable to that of the guilty protagonist.

We dwell here on the pastoral aspect of the Word. We are counseled to remain sober and mindful, to regard our times as (for us) a kind of perpetual advent, unfulfilled, partial, falling short of the human ideal proposed by the word.

Implying or commending such attitude and conduct, the Word (and its bearers and believers as well) is declared (and in such a culture as ours with an exact and malign logic) at best beside the point, in all probability dangerous. In the inelegant, even contemptuous phrase, who needs it?

As for those who hearken to the word with all seriousness — let them take care. Their status before the law is unclear, or indeed, all too clear.

In a sense, the Word is thus judged justly. The word of God is indeed in conflict — with America. In conflict with the chief principality of the 'evil times,' with the 'dwellers on earth,' with the 'spirit of the upper air,' the minions and apologists and hucksters of death.

(1:1 ff.) In such times the Word of God is all the more to be invoked and reverenced and obeyed. For survival's sake, if we are to survive in a way recognizably human. And for other reasons as well. Among which one recalls the exorcistic virtue of the Word, the banishing, or at least the setting back of the power of death.

In Joel, that virtue is manifest especially in — grieving.

We are reminded of a very old discipline of the Word, an emotion, a rite that holds large place in the prophetic books.

We recall the grief of Job as his world tumbles about him, the grief of Jeremiah at the fall of the holy city, Isaiah's grief at the waste of nature in servitude to war and greed. And Jesus, weeping at prospect of the destruction of the holy city.

In the Bible there is pure grief and impure, the grief of the innocent and the dark remorse of the complicit. There is the grief of those trapped in a web of brutal power; one thinks of the mourning of the Egyptian mothers as their first-born perish.

There is grief upon grief, consequent upon war after war, a tide of tears and blood drenching the world. The mourning of exiles and refugees, shunted out of sight and mind and a place in history through the grandiloquent cruelty of pharaohs, shahs, juntas, dictators, presidents.

❖ ❖ ❖

The law of the Fall is a law of tears. All must weep; it is the heavy price of existence, as the shadow of death falls on humankind.

❖ ❖ ❖

The world being such, a liturgy of grief must be convoked, Joel announces. Otherwise, deprived of ceremony, drama, music, poetry, a place and time consecrated to groans and tears, words and silence, how are we to survive the thrust of death's blade? It cuts the heart from the living breast.

❖ ❖ ❖

The claim of death lies like a mailed hand on the living. Ideology, oil, land, markets, mammon in sum, are in dispute. Inevitably the innocent fall in the way of the warriors.

War is declared (or the formality is dispensed with). In any case war ensues. On the moment, legitimate claims, whether of soldiers or non-combatants — to their lives, their children's lives, their well-being and future, their homes and villages and livelihood, these are canceled. All are raked by the terrible harrowing — evicted, uprooted, destroyed.

We have seen, we have inflicted it. It is modern war, monstrous, callous beyond imagining. Might defines right; the troops invade; the bombers loom overhead. The disputed area becomes a field of universal carnage.

❖ ❖ ❖

Then one side emerges victorious, we are told. A bloody disputed question, whether of territory, markets, ideological influence, national myth (or perhaps all these) is presumably resolved.

Nothing is, of course, resolved. The war has sown dragons' teeth in the furrow of time. They will spring up and be sown once more, a hellish harvest of armed warriors.

❖ ❖ ❖

Let us follow for a moment the outcome of a given war, any war. The Iraqi war.

The fate of the conquered is written in blood. They will be, at least for a time, a people of vassalage, many among them displaced or exiled, their economy a shambles, their trade disrupted, the necessities of life denied their citizens — whatever vile reduction in sum is decreed by the victors.

Sanctions are in place; children continue to die.

On the anniversary of the invasion of Kuwait, images were shown of a kind of grab-bag of memories of the war: the remains and rubble, the physical shambles, symbols of bitterness and hatred. One improvised monument was shown. It had for foundation war helmets of slain Iraqi soldiers. Another memorial was a Mercedes-Benz, a vehicle which on the day of invasion was struck by a bomb. In it a Kuwaiti prince died. Now the wrecked vehicle is shown, its roof exploded and a giant fist emerging.

And the tyrant, far from being removed or brought to judgment, consolidates his power.

He survives, a symbol of a perennial illness which the war served only to aggravate. For such as him, the war was even welcome.

And the American president, seething with resentment, decreed the sealing of the borders of Iraq: no medical supplies, no food.

And nothing, literally nothing is resolved.

What then of the victors? What has the war (in this instance a declared victory in war, a victory celebrated frantically, fervently) wrought in ourselves?

Does our spiritual estate thrive, our self-knowledge and compassion? Has war brought peace at last, peace to our hearts, peace in the social fabric?

Did we renounce domestic sins of racial and sexual hatred? Did the victors, having learned a harsh lesson (our youths have died too), henceforth renounce the arts of war in favor of equity and justice? Have we beaten our swords into plowshares?

Or is the outcome far different, darker, more sinister? Are the victors grown more intractable, ugly, proud, reliant on and addicted to the profit and booty of war? Are we all the more deeply convinced that war is a good thing (for the victor, to be sure)? Do we continue to produce new and more terrible weapons, to brandish them about the world, to maintain outposts of military and economic might?

JOEL

And more to our point, are there Joels in our midst, crying out, mourning, calling the people to repentance, in the teeth of Mars the victor and his vassal-citizens, the land being blind with flags and guns and cries of unconditional surrender achieved?

Such questions are seldom raised — whether by the victors themselves or the witnessing nations.

But someone, some few, some 'fools for God's sake,' must raise the questions. It is the only mercy we can look to, the only hope for us, the victors.

For the victors are, from every point of view, degraded and deranged and — ultimately the losers.

"The finest arms are an instrument of evil,
A spreading plague,
And the way vital humans are to go,
is not the way of a soldier.
In times of war, those civilized in peace
Turn from their higher to their lower nature.
Arms are an instrument of evil,
No measure for the thoughtful....
Triumph is not beautiful.
The one who thinks triumph beautiful
Is one with a will to kill;
And one with a will to kill
Shall never prevail in the world.

"It is a good sign
when our higher nature comes forward,
A bad sign
when our lower nature comes forward.

"Let retainers take charge
And the master stay back
As in the conduct of a funeral.
The death of a multitude is cause for mourning;

JOEL

Conduct your triumph as a funeral."

(The Way of Life, Lao-tzu)

On behalf of the winners as well as the defeated in war, a liturgy of grief is called for. Thus Joel.

Let us speak of such a communal effort undertaken by the victorious.

It would voice intercession on behalf of those, adversaries as well as friends, who have died. Intercession for those (including ourselves) who have won from war only a sharpened appetite for war. Who, bedeviled and bewildered, beset by warlike propaganda, concealing, justifying this or that incursion, invasion, bombardment from air or sea or land — who must be accounted the true losers, having lost the capacity for love of one another. For love of God.

Intercession also for those in power, who routinely misuse power in the 'national interest.' For those who bomb and discharge guns against the innocent, the aged, the helpless. Those who abuse prisoners — whose hardness of heart allows them no scope for mercy. For those whose fantasies deck them out in the fools' costume of 'freedom fighters' and the like. For those who research and deploy arms and amass wealth, even as the hecatomb of victims rises.

Intercession also for those of the church (ourselves) given over to the crime of silence and collusion. For those among us whose blood stirs darkly as the flag is raised. For us who have never spoken a word or performed an act of resistance against such folly. For us who dispatch our sons, brothers, lovers and friends on murderous errands. For us who dare in our vanity to invoke Christ as national warrior, a holy guerrilla, a figure of parti pris, armed for the fray, taking sides.

We confess such acts, such omissions, one and all. We are indeed progeny of the Fall, subject to judgment — before God and history.

Such sentiments, prayers, hymns, penitence, fasting, reconciling, confessing, are implied in a liturgy of grief.

It is not, alas, the victorious who take seriously the summons of Joel. To the victors belong, not the truth, but something utterly foreign to right reason or scriptural wisdom: the spoils. The booty, the parades, the ecstasy of the blood, the honors bestowed for murderous deeds — all this implied in the hideous achievement of 'unconditional surrender.' Why then should the victors mourn?

Because they have lost something more precious than life itself. Have lost all sense of honor, of the credit of a decent name in the world. Have lost our own humanity.

It is Joel and his like who understand.

And given our circumstances only those who swim counter to the bloody current, who resist war and war preparation — only these it would seem have access to the simple rightness of mourning.

A liturgy of grief.

Let a multitude of hands be raised in a communal gesture. Some of these cut a thread that dangerously holds aloft a damoclean sword. They receive the blade and sheathe it. Then together they lock it away or bury it deep. Better, they beat it into a plowshare. Thus they cancel its threat and sway — over themselves, their politics, their economy; over their children; its sway over their worship.

Such a symbolic act may in time effect the one essential thing. It may draw the sword once for all from the hearts of Christians. In gesture and word and music and dance, the liturgy declares it: I will not take up this sword ever again, nor shall we, nor others in our name. We pray for the victims, that they rest in peace.

And for the living, that we surpass our shame.

Such a service also brings new light to bear on our rightful place in time, biblically understood.

In every culture, the year includes a rhythm of celebrations, memorial days, anniversaries secular and sacred.

But in empires, such meaning as is conveyed by anniversaries is commonly arrogated and conveyed by the empire itself. Independence Day, Memorial Day, Thanksgiving day. Subtly or overtly, the culture sets the tone on behalf of all, including believers; it supplies the text of the drama, its scenery and staging.

Thus America purveys a version of national history, its glories and triumphs. And first and foremost, images of necessary, virtuous wars.

Implied here is something dire. Our response to violence and death, as well as our conception of what constitutes the 'good life,' all becomes subject to the imperium. To the flick of a wrist, to a camera, a sound-bite, to the image of a candidate for public office, to ads and enticements, illusions and distractions.

Also drawn into this vortex, let it be added, is our understanding of religious history and event.

This is terrifying. Shall the state instruct us as to who Jesus is?

An example is close to hand. Months ahead of the day, the economy gears up once more for the orgiastic Christmas festival.

Infant Jesus, creche, gift-giving, feasting, affluent public display, all are urged on us.

The life story of this Child, into what darkness life took Him, what truth he would one day speak to power, what payment would be exacted — such are hardly given notice.

Nearer the original Christmas event, Matthew and Luke offer another version of the event, a version utterly foreign to the culture. Dangerous words and events are recounted; the grief and humiliation of the mother, the helplessness of the holy Trio before Herod's sword and Caesar's claim. Thus early on the challenge is laid down, the contention made plain: between the God of peace and the gods of war there shall be no peace.

Instead of this harsh and driven reality, we are offered a conventional, acculturated 'holiday.' The original event is amortised, cleansed. It is emptied of all adult, political, tragic implication — whether concerning the tyrant, the uprooting of the holy Family, their vulnerability and poverty, the murder of children by Herod.

Crucial is the restoration of the truth of the Event, that the holy Birth be placed in the austere political landscape of its first occurrence, that stock be taken of the forces (alike then and now) that were brought up short by the advent of the Child.

We read that innocent children died by the sword, so that a nascent threat might be removed from the world. We read how heavy deceit lay on the air as Herod sought, by hook and crook, to suborn the magi.

There are implications here, illustrations, beckonings for ourselves. For according to the gospel, Emmanuel is in our midst; the powers of this world are indicted, even as the believers are empowered.

Such gospel reflections are bound to touch ground. Today too Herod's sword is unsheathed; the Child and the world's children are threatened with death by fire and sword. In Iraq, in Bosnia and elsewhere, the children die. And what is to be done?

This is how, among some believers, the Christmas celebration has been observed for some two decades.

Our aim is to reclaim what was stolen from us, to take Christmas back from the imperial larcenists. Simply, His birth is our birthright.

We gather and mourn for the children, the victims. We intercede for the victor nation, which knows nothing of the God of mercy.

As to the locus of such activity, we go to places where church and state are in collusion, where false worship is in progress, worship of Mars and Mammon. At the pentagon or various nuclear installations and laboratories and bunkers and navy ports and air fields, we gather and pray. And invariably, we are arrested.

Thus an old story, in all its glorious and exigent implication, is made new. The Child is born again in our midst, in a world as cruel as Herod's, more skilled than he in murderous ways and means. And we must surround and protect the Child, the children, all the living. Insofar as is possible to, say, a handful of shepherds, a few wise ones. Or a choir of angels.

It should be understood that the empire as such has no capacity for mourning.

By way of contrast, it has much to grieve over, corpses (concentrating only on its own dead) to inter, numerous memorial days to arrange, parades, flags beyond number.

But of mourning it knows nothing; for mourning would bring to the fore words and wordlessness, thoughts too deep for tears, emotions long despised as 'unmanly,' acknowledgment of guilt, the will to reconcile, succor of the victim, gestures of forgiveness, purpose of amendment publicly proclaimed, financial reparations.

Realities in sum, which lie outside the national lexicon.

The burden of mourning lies therefore on the believers, the biblical people.

This is perhaps the deepest meaning of Paul's insistence that we intercede for secular authorities. Radically incapacitated as they are! We do on their behalf what they cannot do for themselves — we approach God in sackcloth and ashes, in prayer and lamentation. Now and again, in highly charged or dangerous circumstances, we don the garb of fools, the guise of the mad — with tears and wailing and gnashing of teeth.

(1:13,14) "Put on sackcloth and weep, you priests who serve at the altar! Go into the temple and mourn all night!.... Give orders for a fast, call an assembly!..... Gather the leaders and all the people ... and cry out to Jawe! The day of the Lord is near."

And in chapter two, verses 16 and 17, the appeal grows in urgency:

"Gather the people together, prepare them for a sacred assembly. Bring the old people, gather the children and the babies too. Even newly married couples must leave their homes and come. The priest serving the Lord ... must weep and pray, 'Have pity on your people, Jawe. Do not let the nations despise us and mock us by saying, Where is your God?'"

Thus the ceremony commended to believers. Through them a stern summons is also issued to the nation — though the citizenry grow radically deaf and blind, themselves casualties of war.

Healing is possible; this is God's hope, and must be our own. The deaf may yet hear, the blind see.

If such wonders come to pass, they will come of mourning.

The nature of this healing merits attention. It is referred to by Joel repeatedly in his reference to 'the Day of Jawe.'

This has been the folly of the nations, that they claimed all days, every day, for themselves. And especially by seizing on the Christian and Jewish holy days as their own, they laid claim to history, including sacred history. Time was, is, shall be, the 'Day of Empire.'

Time is the spoils of the great powers. In the words of one imperial spirit, hot on the spoor of victory in the course of an unspeakable war, that same war brings to pass their 'finest hour.'

To own time is to play God; it is in effect to claim overlordship of human lives. It is to invade the public imagination, to offer images (invariably of war, the memory of war, the prospect of war). To such images many are addicted.

For the images purport to offer a sense of where we stand in time. From the images people take their soundings: 'before the great War,' 'after the Second World War,' 'during the Vietnam Era.' Signposts, as it were, measures laid to the accuracy of memory itself.

Behold, the generals, the politicians are announcing the time. They are like mad guardians of a nursery. The children, they conclude, have not yet learned to tell the time, or they tell it awry. These magniloquent knowledgeable adults must help, must impose their superior wisdom.

Who then is to tell the time aright?

This claim to ownership of time (militarization of the future, the count down) is another form, a more brutal and abrupt one, of an older claim.

We have heard it announced before, in so-called peace-time too. It dictates the terms on which citizens, as well as enemies, are allowed (or forbidden) to live. Those who own the times may at will shorten lives, end lives, extend lives. To penetrate wombs and transplant organs! To stir and rearrange the gene pool of the living! Talk about a promethean conquest of time!

This foolishness implies a grandiose, baroque version of time: Sound Dollar Time, Victory Time, Perpetual Youth Time, Time of the Good

JOEL

Consumer, Armed Services Time, Technological Time, The Thousand Years boast of this or that creaking political calliope. Time in sum conquered and put to service.

Thus every empire proclaims itself as the summing up, the substance of everything time had sought, achieved, tended toward. So we are told, so Joel was told.

We hear of such folly. The day of national revolution, day of unconditional victory, day of the lottery, day of the valiant fatherland, day of the technocrats, the day we walked on the moon, the day....

And then, something else. The word of God, through Joel. A time of mourning, a day of Jawe. Another version of time; time according to Joel.

He puts it this way. The days of the great powers are many, but those days are finally one.

Century upon century rolls up in a scroll. The splendid savage text of power and might is contracted in a phrase. All said and done, the history of empires comes to this: "The day Death prevailed."

For but a day.

In a time named by Joel a 'meantime,' we who ponder scripture, who take our sense of time from the prophets — we mourn for what is surely the mark of our times. The prevailing of death.

Momentary as death is, overbearing as it is.

A rehearsal. A time between, as twilight is between night and day. We move uneasily betwixt and between, holding on to what is yet unborn, letting go what is dying.

We say it, perhaps with a groan. The time of empire, for all its clash and fury, is so to be understood as a mere meantime, an interlude, a twilight hour.

In this too we clash with the powers, and momentously. We take our lead from the likes of Joel, great deflators and deriders all, mocking the emperor as he struts about in his skin.

No matter, or very little, the altitudinous presumptions, the pomp and

JOEL

circumstance, the technique and glitter. The world is a 'silva oscura'; time is the twilight of the gods.

In sum. We are to gather, Joel instructs, to sing and sacrifice and fast and impetrate and shout with one voice, loud and clear, (and perhaps criminally) to the realm and empery of death — our NO!

And this though every billboard and tv screen, every flag, every poll, every weapon, every billionaire, every president, every general, (all but) every citizen, (all but) every believer, every judge and prosecutor and abortionist and warrior and hangman — are shouting, signaling, waving, brandishing a vociferous, all but unanimous Yes!

Thus comes closer — in anticipation and rehearsal, and by dint of us also and our unfailing (but sometimes failing) courage and patience — the Day of Jawe.

On that day, as we firmly (sometimes not so firmly) believe (say it nonetheless, shout it, sing it out!), every presumptuous, contemptuous, larcenous, murderous principality will yield place, be unmasked, be disarmed, be revealed, be judged for what (and who) it was.

The rehearsal of the Day, it needs no repeating, is a painful affair, and more often than not, clumsily performed. This is no stately or majestic ceremony, performed in sanctuaries before the stuporous gaze of the great ones of earth. Nothing of that.

It is a kind of last ditch beseeching. 'All else failing' is the tone. It takes place almost by happenstance, is improvised. Like the liturgy of Joel, it includes 'sackcloth and weeping, fasting and mourning, repentance and sorrow.'

Need one add, they are not well-received, assemblies such as this? They contravene the national mood, the empty ethic, the frenzy of self-congratulation and dark rejoicing that mark the day of victory. Those who mourn in such ways, who recall when others forget, who demand an accounting for bloodshed — they interrupt the show, they are an affront to patriotism and good order.

They confront the lawlessness that suspends civilized conduct and law, the massive spiritual disorder which reigns in the land.

Nor well-received, it goes without saying, by the church.

JOEL

The twilight of the gods yields to an awful darkness.

Then declares Joel, there dawns another day, a final one. An intervention, an act of God. The Day of Jawe. The day of summing up, day of judgment, day of weighing and wanting.

Our eyes shall see it. All history placed on these scales.

(1:15) An ecological disaster is seized upon by Joel as an occasion inductive of a change of heart. (Joel, of course, is not implying that Jawe lets loose the locusts on fields and vineyards, that repentance will bring relief from the disaster, or life thereupon will resume its steady way. Nothing so magical, so simple.)

More is at stake. The plague reaches beyond itself. It offers in fact an image of the Day of Jawe; the confusion, loss, terror, destruction marking that dread event.

Hence the call to repentance is in the nature of a rehearsal of the 'eschaton,' the 'end time,' the 'judgment.'

These are thought to be underway in two aspects at least.

First in the plague which descends upon the world, an apt and terrible symbol of the reign of death.

The locusts bide their time, await their season, obey a genetic clock. They are like a shadow at the back of the mind, the shadow that whispers, "You too will die."

Then they appear in a raging cloud, descend in force, sow eggs in the fields, and move on. It seems for awhile that the worst is over. The larvae hatch; death has broken its egg.

Now it is as though a shadow wielding a vast scythe moved across the fields and vineyards. As though the curved blade were white hot, and wheat and vineyards, row after row, went up in a crescent of fire.

The threat of death, a shadow in nature (in the soul as well) has become a plague of death. The empery of the locusts does not end with the destruction of crops. It aims to cripple, mortify, starve out the community. Even worship is stopped short; there is neither wine nor grain for the altars.

The 'day of Jawe' has commenced. The community assembles, in accord with the instruction of Joel, to mourn the day of the locust. Death must be evicted from the heart as well as from the land.

The community mourns 'that death has undone so many,' not chiefly through the plague, but through the recusancy and sin of the people. For the plague moved on many levels; it devastated the heart and the public institutions as well.

(2:2 ff.) The military imagery of the plague and its application to the Day of Jawe are developed with remarkable skill. The locusts resemble 'a great army.... In front of them, the land is like the garden of Eden, behind them is a barren desert. Nothing escapes them. They run like war horses ... they rattle like chariots ... they line up like a great army ready for battle.... Everyone is terrified.... They attack like warriors, they climb the walls like soldiers. They all keep marching straight ahead and do not change direction or get in each other's way. They swarm through defenses and nothing can stop them....'

We shall hear more in Joel of this rattling of arms.

(2:28-32) The bestowal of the Spirit is abruptly announced. Moreover, the Gift is offered on behalf of all without distinction of age or social condition or sex. Unprecedented!

And the Spirit is offered, be it noted, to a people reeling from a plague; their crops destroyed; their future, to say the least, chancy. Hardly a promising time — or a time for momentous promises!

The bad news mounts in face of the good. It is a time when a harvest of another sort, prophecy itself, is in short supply. And yet the promise is made and met — a superabundant Gift!

The prophecy that the Spirit will be outpoured is itself a work of the Spirit. One thinks of the young and old, the women and men, those who have endured the plague (and the centuries to follow, their plagues of war, exploitation, murder most foul, worldly power gone awry, the terrors and rigors!). In spite of all, women and men and children will learn of the oracle, dream new dreams, see unkillable visions of good things to come.

The Promise and the Gift are one. The Spirit is outpoured.

The word spoken by Joel has been taken into Christian history. The implications of a universal conflagration of love, given our tormented world, still escapes us; it goes without saying.

We wait. In fear and trembling; it goes without saying.

One truth seems fairly certain; it is drawn from the historic circumstance of the promise to Joel. To wit, the coming of the Spirit 'upon all flesh' is radically incompatible with the ethos of the superstate. How can the Spirit of life and love be thought to reign in the hearts of all, while death is the main, indeed universal, medium of exchange among the 'nations'?

Ordinarily, worldly judgments (who is 'inside,' who 'out,' acquire a kind of divine sanction; it must be that God prefers some few above all others, that the Spirit endorses some and rejects others!

From the promise made to Joel to our own day, this is summarily denied. The authentic Gift, it scorns human criteria of 'outsider, insider.' Spirit is the adversary of the chosen few, those whose status before God is presumably based on income, sex, age, yes and this or that religion.

The Spirit invoked by Joel knows nothing of such pseudo-theological blandishments. The Spirit is the Friend of all who are friends one to another. ('Advocate' is Christ's name for His Spirit; we think today of a kind of noble selfless 'Public Defender.')

Centuries later, on a momentous occasion, the text of Joel, like a sleepy fire poked to life, leaps to the tongue of a certain Peter of Galilee. Much like Joel, he has undergone a mysterious inward event. Then, 'emboldened' by the Spirit, he brings it to public notice. (Acts 2:17)

The Spirit first embraces Peter; this is by way of fact and parable. Then, according to Peter, the Spirit embraces 'all flesh,' a carefully chosen phrase, by no means to be equated with the neutral 'all people.' Across the world, barriers, obstacles of all sorts, illnesses of the spirit, hostilities intact for centuries — these must be thought shaken.

Of the great powers, the 'nations,' their armies, their tycoons and oligarchs, their 'ten families,' those who create and maintain and pass on structures of power and control, those against whom the prophets inveigh, under whose heel the 'little ones' languish, generation after generation (unto our generation!) — what is to be said? We read in scripture of the fall of empires, and then we witness the horrors inflicted by imperial structures of violence in our lifetime.

Can the Spirit be thought to prevail, even now? The countdown shortens like a fuse; then we are at war, armies clash, the innocent perish along with the violent.

(But the great ones, the guilty, never die in the conflicts they stir up. Theirs is merely to decide on the ratio between 'collateral damage,' which is to say, the deaths, whether of 'the others' or 'our own,' as computed against appreciable gains — whether these be oil, land, the prevailing of an ideology — always some awesome, unrelinquishable special interest.)

Nonetheless. The Spirit is outpoured 'on all nations.'

Of a certainty not on the powerbrokers, the 'leaders who have become the mis-leaders.' (This 'not' for a start, a kind of clearing of the air.)

In such times as we endure, the Spirit is outpoured on those who say 'No.' A 'no' to the warmaking superstate (the two words forming a redundancy of note).

That monosyllable is the articulate, valiant, pristine, reliable, sane, preferred word of the Spirit.

Worship must echo it, this word of subversion.

To such, the Spirit is offered. To our 'flesh,' as is said.

To that in us — how shall we name it? Whatever is most in need of a healing embrace, whatever in us is fragile, opaque, sterile, withheld, cunning, irascible, cramped, unlovely and unlovable. To that in us which is literally dispirited. To what lurks beyond our control, demoralizing, raw in outbreak, beyond our native power to curb or exorcise; whatever is headlong, violent, taciturn, embroiling; our angers and fears, the conventicle of furies we assemble — the war within.

In effect, the root and upstart and rumble of every war, the unpurged, unloved heart of us. Here embraced, purged, healed, held in honor, beckoned, endowed, sent on mission. Holy Spirit, come.

The prophecy is about — prophecy, renewed and extended.

The vision of Joel takes the form of a promise. A people shall become a visionary people. They shall become dreamers too, and their dreams of utmost consequence. The Spirit confers spirituality. Now a multitude, touched by tongues of fire, will work and pray in prospect of a new creation.

Deprived of the vision, the dream, (we have tasted that death, a politics of contempt and inanition, a spiritless heartless church) the people perish.

As we see day after day, a people perishing. People barely functional, people in despair, inanition, numb, off kilter, spiritually at odds, directionless.

Perishing? Those in charge, those in power, the affluent and assured, those who have 'made it,' who embrace as their own achievement, come war, come misery — the 'filthy rotten system'? (Dorothy Day) Yes. Perishing.

We are ignorant of our own powers, their renewal, their strengthening by the Spirit. We are kept ignorant of these; it is the common political tactic and the tactic of much that goes by the name religion as well.

Thus we come to know only our powerlessness. This is the common taste and sense and inner feel of the times. We hear the news (invariably bad news), the decisions made in our name (decisions, all said, concerning who shall die and who kill), decisions deriding our repute, stealing our income, our native powers and resources, distracting our children unto madness.

And never a word of consultation, never a hearing or public debate.

The charade of an election year. The convention, the delirious delegates, promises voided, protests gone on the wind.

The bad news is contempt, we are a people devalued. Mourning in Babylon is our vocation.

The wasted and wandering lives that meet our horrified gaze each day are a parable all but beyond bearing (dare we say it to our soul?), a parable of our own condition — knowing that we too mourn and suffer and wander in a spiritual wasteland.

And yet we are assured constantly by a metronomic leadership, glib with the magic phrase (a drug named heal-all), that we are citizens favored of heaven, members of the most powerful et cetera on earth, et cetera. So much nonsense, so little substance!

We question: Has the Spirit passed us by entirely?

One must tread lightly here and gaze widely and not be deaf to hints, starts, implications, rhythms that vibrate at fingertips and yield only before silence. 'Non in turbine Deus': God is not in the whirlwind, the irrationality and chaos of public life.

It is not a time of greatness nor a time when great expectations make sense. It is 'a time of leveling,' as Kierkegaard wrote. This is all the more terrible as the level of political life, like a watershed in a time of drought, imperceptibly recedes. No whisper of rain, no relief. And we lose the human norm — we are left with only a hint, a stratum in rock, a memory, a low water mark, a lost measure. If only in such times we were enabled (by the Spirit to be sure) to take an accurate measure of the human, to preserve the measure intact! Alas, the technique of the lie grows more skilled; the subhuman like a dwarf on stilts, totters about boldly, presents itself, voluble, vivid, as — superhuman.

Nevertheless. Let us pay tribute to the people of the Spirit in our midst, the Joels, dreamers and visionaries young and old. Those who hold fast to ideals and noble work, though nothing seems to come of their best efforts; who are not victimized by the cult and fashion of results, proofs, justifications, outcomes, efficiencies. But who simply keep on, hold on, sensible as they are of the goodness and truthfulness of the 'thing to be done.'

Let us be thankful for those who serve, who succor, feed, clothe, hostel and heal the wounds of those commonly considered worthless, expendable. And so doing 'see that it is good.'

Those who resist war and are jailed and 'see that it is good.' Those who harbor endangered and unwanted 'illegal aliens' and 'see that it is good.' Those who resist the aborting of the unborn and 'see that it is good.' Those who counter the tide of vengeance known as capital punishment and 'see that it is good.' Those who cherish life, start to finish, women and men, unborn and aged, loveable and unlovely, and 'see that it is good.'

These are, in the biblical sense, the genetic people. They bear witness to the biophilic Spirit of Life. To them, all honor!

They sense the Spirit; how the 'no' they utter in such pain and effort is of the substance of the 'gift to the nations.'

(2:28,29) Dreams and visions!

Let us dream, let us tell of the vision. The gift of the Spirit surpasses the pedestrian, fact-ridden, banal, self-aggrandizing, self-defeating, tedious version of life peddled by the culture; its gestures and images by turn inert, empty and monstrously agitated.

According to conventional wisdom (then, now), a plague is a plague is a plague. And then we think of Joel; the plague is something more, something incalculable. It is the occasion of the outpouring of the Spirit.

And we think today of — AIDS.

According to one view, the scourge is a scientific puzzle, nothing more. It is received as inexplicable (for the moment), uncontrollable and infuriating. It mocks (for a time only, we are told) the omnipotence of conventional medicine.

Or another kind of unwisdom, this from the churches. Big theological guns are brought to bear against the ill; theories of guilt are fired, heard round the world. AIDS is a curse, a judgment of God launched against sinners in our midst.

But how rarely is AIDS regarded as an occasion for the outpouring of the Spirit named Compassion, Wisdom, Counsel, Fortitude; an occasion for expedient stock taking by all; a reminder of the societal crimes in our midst; a reminder of our scape-goating, our violence against the poor, our racism, our addictions and appetites. An occasion as Joel has insisted, of 'repentance and return.'

JOEL

His is a sequence worth noting: first, dire event, then account of conscience, and finally, prophecy renewed.

As Joel views his scene, throughout the land death is in the saddle, riding hard.

But the vandalous passage is never taken by the prophet as an arbitrary disaster in nature. The locusts, so to speak, are loudly abuzz with a message. It remained for Joel to translate the message, good news together with bad.

Good news ever so slightly surpassing the bad? The plague, he insists, is a spiritual reality as well as a physical; it devastated not only the land, but also the human heart. In consequence 'your broken hearts must show forth your sorrow.'

In Camus' novel *The Plague*, the doctor, a kind of self-deprecating antihero, is asked why so awful a catastrophe, apparently descending from nowhere, without rhyme or reason, is devastating the city.

'Why us, why Oran?' is the cry. The city is much like others of its kind; it contains rich and poor, spouses and children, intellectuals and pleasure-seekers, honest folk and knaves, workers and parasites. It seems in fact rather faceless, uninteresting, comatose under the African sun, lapped by a tepid sea. Why then the disaster?

The doctor, in contrast to the Jesuit in the story, is not given to long speeches nor is he skilled, as is his ecclesiastical counterpart, in the God-talk that numbs. His answer: "They forgot to be modest, that is all."

Thus the plague touched ground, found its victims. The ground, ready and fertile, was a farrago of appetite and ego, of idle minds and nascent greed, lust and boredom. And among the citizenry, Christians and others, little sense of one another.

The doctor makes no claim to superior wisdom. He is quite prepared to be called an unbeliever. He goes about his work, coping with death, healing where he can, mustering what help is available. And he alone touches the heart of the matter; he understands the spiritual reality lurking in the filth and fury, the distempered rodents and foison of corpses. He offers in his laconic way the only prophetic word.

According to Joel, the promise of the Spirit follows on a disaster —

locusts and drought. This too is a parable. The crops are destroyed; the land is sere; the people literally spiritless. And no one (or hardly anyone) can offer meaning or direction. An impasse, marked by fatalism and futility, ensues.

Are humans no more than ciphers in the world, at the mercy of an ill wind that bears in its wake the insect hordes?

Be it understood. Joel himself (though he would make no such claim) is the breakthrough. We are not the playthings of the gods (nor they ours). We are — responsible.

His words are a chief credential; the promise has come true. The disaster of the plague is not opaque, chancy, unanswerable.

This is his honor; the Spirit speaks through him.

The God who knows the human heart, its measure and beat, speaks to the recusant 'people of the swarm.' The words are fearful, devastating.

"It was I who sent this army against you." (2:25)

The locusts descend; the larvae are sown; the soil is ready. In the human community, beset as it is, the inhuman awaits its hour. What is to be born then, what faces are set against life, what voracious appetite and squads numberless — we shall learn more of this in the Valley of Decision.

The name of the plague, all said, is war. And war's seedbed is the human heart, its radical 'immodesty,' its will to play the perilous game called 'Superhuman.'

(3:1 ff.) Joel takes up the theme of a judgment of the nations. The portents are not encouraging to those principalities.

Let us take note that the crimes here enumerated, are finally of one kind. They are the crimes of bellicose tribes of the earth, wrought against the innocent and defenseless. They are crimes of war.

"All the nations are impugned; all have sinned against my heritage."

The crimes are dwelt upon in some detail; the scattering of people in exile, the dividing of illegitimate spoils of conquest, the sparing of no one of the conquered. The moral degradation of the 'victors' is such that a boy is sold in slavery for the price of a prostitute, a girl for a drink.

We have a kind of Yalta scene, or a Versailles. The unconditional victors sit about, cynically casting lots for this or that prize 'including human souls.'

(3:4 ff) The indignation of God is roused against three port cities, where the crimes previously charged have taken an especially heinous form. But the hour of requital is at hand. A theme of judgment is joined to a theme of war.

This is to be understood as a holy enterprise, this scene of judgment. At long last a countervailing voice is heard. It summons to the dock the predators and wreckers who bestrode the centuries. (3:9) 'Sanctify the war!' is the cry of the outraged heart of God.

Let it be said as simply and directly as possible. From the moment Cain struck his brother down, till the last echo of the last illimitable bomb loosed on the world, all wars have been, are, will be, supremely — unjust.

Judgment thus becomes a symbol of the first just war of history — indeed the only one. It is the substance of the end time. The end of history is not only the end of warmaking; it is judgment on the warmakers.

Such is indicated here. Judgment is the harsh and dreadful face of love. The warmakers, imagine it! shall be held accountable.

This 'war' (in the context a curiously apt, indeed shattering word), which is to say this judgment, this accounting, a final one, is to be a public event. It summons those who, contemning all earthly forms and approximations of justice, have wreaked unimaginable havoc — and have purportedly, and for a time, walked free. And who, it must be concluded, have placed themselves cynically beyond — accounting.

The indignation of Jawe takes fire, the metaphors multiply. Let the drama proceed. Let the nations appear in the Valley of Judgment.

(3:9 ff.) The warriors are assembled from all times and places. They are decked out, armed to the teeth, just as in their heyday. One final time they bear the weaponry and accoutrements, the pomp and glory that marked their rakes' progress on earth.

And Jawe wears a mask of cosmic irony, ring Master of this woeful circus: "Even the ill must say, I am a warrior!"

It is nightmarish, and why not? the great powers have turned time and this world, ecology and community, to — nightmare. "One bears ten horns and seven heads ... on each of its heads, is a name insulting to God." (Rev. 13:1)

Human, less than human, superhuman? Such caricatures of the living were never seen on land or sea. One resembled a leopard with feet like a bear and a mouth like a lion's. (Rev. 13:2) Moral grotesquery is mocked, a mishmash, a hellish epiphany; the mighty wear the guise of clowns, charlatans, caricatures. Their cacophony mocks the clear song lines of creation.

They have crossed those lines, trampling all taboos under, obscuring and despising moral clarity. They are killers all. How shall they not shock and repel?

Their history was all a sham, a charade, a false front. Behind it brigands and cowards and killers lurked.

There comes at long last, a moment of truth. According to the vision of Joel, they are captive to a justice they thought in their folly, only to subvert. They stand in the dock of history.

The electorate honored them unduly, a violent public applauded them, generals and tycoons and oligarchs. They were adored and courted and stroked as very godlings. The anti-spirit, the unholy spirit inflated their sails; they worked signs and wonders, they were dazzling, superhuman, subjects of awe and adoration: "The whole world was amazed and followed after the Beast.... They worshipped the Beast, saying, 'Who is like the Beast? Who can resist It?'" (Rev. 13:4)

And be it understood, the assault was a spiritual one, a 'war in heaven.' Which is to say, a challenge laid down against the God of life and love.

And laid down as well against God's witnesses on earth. The Beast throve on the blood of the saints. Its malignant vocation came to this: the making of martyrs. "It was allowed to fight against God's people, and to defeat them." (Rev. 13:7)

And for every martyr who fell, be it known; a signal defeat was struck against the principalities.

But not here, not now.

In verses nine through twelve we are offered something surpassingly strange, a prophecy that reverses prophecy. It is a painful and sardonic word, mocking the conduct of the legions here standing trial.

We imagine God playing an Ionesco, or perhaps a Pirandello, or Wallace Stevens' 'emperor of ice cream.'

Absurdity is enthroned. God reverses the decalogue, stands the commandments on their head: Thou shall kill, shall lie, shall defraud! As though to say: Let us now see what the world looks like, when all and any crime is declared allowable.

Read another way: Let us see the world according to these eminences. In their twisted view, prodigious world shakers as they have been, defendants, alas, as here and now they are. (All and any crime was and is and shall be allowed!)

The paradisiacal word of peace spoken by Isaiah and Micah is reversed. It is like the twist of a blade in an immemorial wound. The wound is war, the supreme crime of the nations.

Do it then, make war! cries the God of irony. "Hammer the points of your plow into swords, and your pruning knives into spears." (3:10)

It befits them, like a sword its scabbard. What else have they ever done, what other skill and will have they shown?

So judgment has sounded, fortunes are reversed, masks stripped away. In order to be healed, our illness must grow worse.

Thus the great nations, each represented by its warriors, appear. Have they learned any office other than war? If so, how comes it that their clothing is military, that they bear their weapons into the court of judgment?

JOEL

A puzzle: does the text speak of the living or of the dead? It scarcely seems to matter; living or dead, they bear arms. In life they made common cause — in murder. It was their only skill.
And as they lived, so they died.

It is as though a catastrophe struck them down in one vast swath. Then they were buried — weapons in hand. One is reminded of the store of ancient— Chinese military images recently discovered. A multitude of set faced warriors, as though awaiting even in eternity a military order or perhaps some stirring of a wind of resurrection.

Resurrection? Hardly. Obsession. War.

Judgment at hand, Joel declares. And the warriors rise. They are — unchanged, unconverted to the gentle uses of peace. Stern-faced clones one of another, resembling and dissembling the world of animals, 'leopards, bears, lions.' Enemy resembling enemy, they assemble in battle array.

Nothing but war! Or so they believe, and so they come, in a grotesque night of the living dead.

But something other than war awaits. It is named judgment.

We are not to miss the awful force of it, the word of Jawe. No doubt the superpowers of history (including our own) have displayed skills other than warmaking. In the book of Revelation, a threnody for great Babylon resounds on the air of eternity. A majestic angel sounds a cry of anguish; a culture grand beyond words has fallen. It was marked by 'riches and splendor ... fine linen, purple and scarlet ... glittering with gold, precious stones and pearls ... the music of harpists and musicians ... workmen at their trade ... the sound of the millstone ... the light of lamps ... the voice of bridegroom and bride....' (Rev. 18:21 ff.)

None of these was offensive to Jawe, quite the contrary. All this cultural glory was honorable; its loss is lovingly mourned.

Likewise in Joel; no cultural achievement, nothing honorable or truly human is here subject to judgment.

And yet, and yet. One must take in account that these grandiose exploits, the evidence of ease and abundance and status gained and kept and wrought, increase by one means — by war.

Someone paid. Many died. The property was theft, the wars were the quintessential form of imperial health. For awhile.

Dare we translate the scene of judgment to our own day? Dare we include in the procession toward the Valley of Decision, not only armed and visored warriors of antiquity, horses and chariots and the like?

The scene cries out for translation. Our time, our day, our superstate.

Caissons roll into the valley, bearing their sleek armageddon missiles. Generals and admirals stand in battle array.

Then something more, a vast white-garbed coterie. Medical personnel, butchers? No. Civilians, scientists, top-seeded researchers, Nobel prize winners, stars of the Star Wars grotesqueries. And then silk-suited and portentous — politicians, ear to the ground, eye to the main chance. Greed oiled their gears. Were their constituencies to be placated and votes won, blood money flowing free? Let it be so.

And the wheelers and dealers are surely there, the arms hucksters, those brought together by the lure and spoor of money, the buyers and sellers of the Arms Bazaars.

And the a-political intellectuals are present, in great number. These are the ethical hair splitters and theological necromancers, those who wrestle interminably with the wrong questions, whose debates are sterile, whose pride is barren, whose epitaph is a simple alas! They have missed the point of both life and death.

Then to one side, segregated in utmost pride, a coven that sets the head spinning, heads of state. Heads of superstates. Of these and their works and pomps, of their interminable roundelay of guile, ferocity, choler, turpitude, cunning, unctuousness, banality, jugglery, atavism, feverishness and faineant, anarchy 'under the law of the land' — of this enough said.

Of the churches enough said also, or nearly so.

Let it only be noted that we too, congregations and leaders, are summoned here. Many among us have absolved this or that warmaker of all guilt and responsibility, excused this or that argument in favor of whatever war (if only it was waged by their nation). Dignum et justum.

To the peacemaking words of Jesus these magniloquent justifiers paid at any time, scant heed, if any.

In time of war (time and again!), something known as the just war theory was summoned. On the moment the theory was canonized once more, as the only moral criterion available.

Rightly applied, we were assured time and again, the theory was designed to place limitations on violence. Or so it was said.

Still, there was a difficulty. Whether the leadership of any party to a given conflict took seriously the casuistic to-fro of a few 'specialists,' or whether in the midst of indiscriminate assault, any lives might be thought precious, and spared — these matters remained much in doubt.

In the heat of war however, something was hideously made clear — the word of God was throttled 'for the duration.'

"Love your enemies? Do good to those who treat you ill?" Such words suffered a dying fall; first of all in the throats of 'religious leaders,' where the words stuck like a bone. These too in their fetching way, turned plowshare into swords, pruning hooks into spears.

No clear word, never a clear word! Not to the soldiers, not to the head of state, generals, not to the weapons makers, not to the politicians. Not from the churches.

Let us place them in the assembly, they too are summoned, the religious leaders. Again and again they betrayed the gospel, declared the Sermon on the Mount — irrelevant. By a blessing carelessly bestowed, by an evasive liturgy, here a mitigating hand aloft, there a shrug; here a compromise, there a stroking.

Let the casuists, the ethicians of just war theory be summoned.

Isaiah, Micah, Jesus, they inferred, taught an unrealizable ideal. Meantime (which they translated 'here and now, this age, this war'), let us be 'realistic'; we propose to rearrange, mitigate, (in fact) explain away the transcendent discomfiting words of the Savior.

Their preachments were both curious and spurious. Some among them spoke feelingly of something known as an 'interim ethic.'

The theory allowed in wartime, if truth were told (but these gentlemen might well have echoed 'But what is truth'?), allowed any and every violation of the word of God.

Warriors, generals, politicians, apolitical intellectuals, church leaders; each of these in his own way heeded the ironic advisement of Jawe. Each placed hand and mind to a like task, each bent the modestly useful into the absolutely lethal, plowshares into swords, pruning knives into spears.

Each thus had part in bending the intellects and hearts of Christians into misshape, tools of frenzy, humans inimical to the gospel.

On those blades and points, swords and spears, humanity itself, time and again was impaled.

To this has war come, and warmakers, at long last: to judgment. Just war and unjust, total war and limited, wars of defense and offense, skirmishes and vast incursions, invasions, surgical strikes, wars declared and ratified, wars of wanton banditry.

The sanguinary grab bag of history is shaken to its seams. "Thousands and thousands are in the Valley of Judgment. It is there that the Day of Jawe will shortly come." (3:14)

The hegemony of Jawe, God of peace, God of the swords to be beaten to plowshares and the spears to pruning hooks, Christ who spoke (and lived in close accord, and died in fidelity to his word) the Sermon on the Mount — all this effortful love, the tears of God, the blood of Christ, the 'hesed' of Jawe — all, time without number scorned, violated, wasted, contemned. Indeed it is as though the history of the nations had no other mark or meaning or calendar or clock. Sober pens are wont to denote each 'Christian' era as the year of this or that war.

But God is not mocked.

Every war is waged 'in heaven', (Rev. 12:7) against the realm of peace, against God.

Here is the mystery. War would dethrone God from heaven, exile God from earth. We speak here of blasphemy, pure and simple.

On to the final act of time's drama.

A double outcome follows on the judgment of the Valley of Decision; first the diminution and desolation of all creation, then an 'emparadising.'

JOEL

(3:18 ff.) Once more the spiritual estate of humans is reflected in metaphors drawn from nature.

Humans, an uneasy amalgam of the criminal and heroic, flourish and then fall away. Read then as you run, how the soul is mirror of the world and vice versa.

Then a dawn. The innocent will dwell 'on that day' amid unimaginable plenty, the glory of creation restored, rendered pristine and peerless. And the wicked will wander disconsolate, sterile, parched, in deserts they themselves have created, within and around.   Dignum et justum.

AMOS

Wasting no moment on preliminaries, mincing no words, Amos is like a torch lit at a burning bush.

He begins by announcing seven oracles. Each is of moment to the principality addressed. He concludes abruptly; each of the seven is simply —criminal.

The culmination? Israel and her crimes.

And some would have it that the Bible is not political! (Or that the prophets have little or no light to shed on the conduct of the 'chosen' — then or today!)

The method of Amos is austere and subtle. Israel, last mentioned, is first and worst chastised. Thus this son of Israel rebukes any attempt to hide out in the folds of God's garment.

The 'chosen,' so often self-anointed with the honorific title, are chastised — and all the more terribly chastised in view of God's favor.

One is reminded of the famous seven unsealings of Revelation.

In Amos, the progression of the oracles is also carefully structured: (1) blame and threat, (2) a particular crime dwelt on, (3) chastisement.

Two ideas dominate. For all the pretentions of the powerful to sit secure in the cockpit of history, they stand under judgment. God is still God. God remains 'unassimilated,' like a holy Jew, like Amos and his kind. (And in a later day, like Heschel or Buber, Zinn, Chomsky and many others.)

Nor is Jawe by any means to be thought of as a popular God, favored in the polls, reigning happily over a favored majority. No, this is an austere God of judgment.

And who is to announce the judgment?

Amos, a veritable nobody, variously described as a shepherd or a scrub farmer. He tells us something of his background, how he hails from a crossroads village, Tekoa, a day's journey from Jerusalem. There he keeps his flocks, alternating between the edges of the desert and the more fruitful valleys at the verge of the Dead Sea.

The people of his town are dirt poor; so, evidently, is he. A meager existence. By all accounts a solitary spirit.

Then one day the God of desert and plains, the God of solitaries, speaks to him. His life will never again be as it was, uncluttered, obscure, of no public moment.

Go to Jerusalem!

He obeys, from day one an outsider to the coterie of royal sycophant-prophets. He speaks in a country brogue, yea and nay, unnuanced, rude and intrepid even; take it or leave.

The mandarins are not amused.

Once more it unfolds, the age old-conflict between the Jerusalem claque — and a kind of bumpkin-prophet, up from the desert or countryside, rude, denouncing, intransigent.

The story of Jesus, to be sure.

Amos and his anger could be borne with; as the saying goes, 'consider after all the source.' But the herdsman goes further. He insists that Jawe too is angry, that in anger indeed Jawe is one with his prophet. That Jawe abominates the rites and ceremonies of the temple, the chants and sacrifices, the entire goings on!

And why, why? Because insists Amos, all this religion is a cover; in the words of a later counterpart and critic, a 'spiritual aroma which we use to make intolerable injustice seem tolerable.' (Marx)

And the response is entirely predictable. Would an Amos of our time fare differently?

A God of stern justice who will restore justice to those unjustly dealt with? And worse: woe, who will avenge the injustice of the powerful? A God who topples the idols of injustice set up in Israel itself?

It comes to this: According to Amos, Jawe is by no means pacified by the rituals, the meaningless sacrifices of the prosperous unjust. Abominations!

It seems wonderful that the shepherd survived to utter so terrible a message. Survive he did. He spoke up, then after a few stormy months in Jerusalem, returned equably to his beloved solitude.

A trouble-making spirit!

No one is spared. Every political, military or economic question, according to Amos, is a properly 'religious' question. Every public structure, no matter how powerful or self-exempt, is grist for the prophetic mill.

Ultimately the connections hold because structures of justice (or injustice) immediately implicate God — Jawe's 'other name' being justice itself.

According to Paul's letter to the Romans, the justice of God is the grace of God in us. This only is our justification: an outpouring of Godly conscience on the world. Grace comes to us, ungifted as we are - 'fallen' is the biblical word. In any case, morally retarded, impaired, disabled, and all too dexterous in works of injustice.

But the grace of God is disencumbered of our knavish behavior. And the same grace may heal us of such behavior.

The infinite One touches, draws forth the poison, cherishes us — bears with us. Thus, and inevitably, grace touches on time and polity, culture and economics.

Through the justice of God a vision of the human is graciously opened.

According to Amos, its first stage is self-knowledge. The Spirit, all light, bears a light into the dark cave of the soul, into the world as well, encompassed in darkness.

The oracles of Amos also speak of sin, and precisely, of sinful politics, sinful religion, sinful war.

And the response? We shall hear much of it in Amos; as indeed a like reaction thundered against the teaching of Christ: resistance, suspicion, fury, overt denial of truth.

Images of truth offered by Amos are all but obsessive. Truth comes to earth like a relentless cleansing fire. The fires devour palaces and great houses, gates and defenses. Down go the walls of Gaza, of Tyre and Rabba.

There is a second image, the disappearance and displacement of the powerful. Indeed a stronger indictment of the crimes of the 'great ones' could hardly be imagined. The loot of the wealthy is snatched away, kings go under, solid thrones tumble like ninepins. Ah Amos, subversive imagination indeed!

The implication for the believing community is both perilous and plain to see. We are called to be a latter day community of Amos, in continuity with the community of Christ. We are also, for weal or woe, citizens of this or that warmaking and radically unjust 'great power.'

Our status is clear; it is a 'status confessionis' with all the implications of that telling phrase, a state of resistance against the sycophants and structures of death.

GOD'S CHOICE IS A HEAVY YOKE. THE YOKE IS JUSTICE. LOOK YOU TO IT

(1:1) The sins of the nations, according to Amos, constitute 'three transgressions and four,' a perfect number seven. Seven circles of hell on earth.

The vortex of death expands, lays claim to creation, to the future, to human institutions. Shall not our world be named hell?

The questioning of empire: this is the task the prophet is summoned to. And not only questioning, but denouncing. The dark side of apparently benign policy — the slaves, victims, larcenies, crimes of war! — Amos raises a mirror before the imperial face.

But the emperors see an altogether different 'seven': the summing up of every human attainment — sophistication, art, wealth, status; also world markets, fleets, booty, political stability; also steles, monuments, tombs, triumphant arches, papyri. All of these, in various ways, bespeak achievement, the splendor of courts, the immortality already conferred.

(1:3) Light up the cave! To begin with, the Syrians — these are a chief instrument of infernal behavior. They wage war against the defenseless, they 'thresh Gilead with threshing sledges of iron.'

Flails into battering rams. Could there be an apter image of the wreckage wrought by war?

And something more, the spiritual degradation implied in beating tools into weapons. An instrument used commonly to thresh the harvest grain is put to horrid misuse; it ravages humans and the land itself.

(1:6) Next, the Philistines fall under scrutiny. They are great displacers of people, they shunt their victims about at whim. These imperialists create the misery we call exile; rootless themselves, they know nothing of familiar horizons, villages, language, custom. They contemn human attachment and affection. The original 'homo economicus,' the Philistines sell their victims in slavery. (2 Ch. 21:16)

(1:9) The Phoenecians next — these are violators of the sworn word. They refuse to dwell at peace under a humane concordat.

Thus their conduct underscores the deceptive, furtive character of warmaking, the saying that 'in war, the first victim is the truth.' This empire has mastered a tactic known as covert action (of which we also have heard much). Greatly given to night raids and headlong incursions, the Phoenecians cross seas and borders and lay hands on multitudes of captives.

(1:11) And the Edomites — of these Amos offers a biblical insight of great moment.

Truly understood, war is defined as the murder of brother by brother. And here Edom (Esau) has 'pursued his own brother (Jacob-Israel) 'with the sword, stifling all pity. And his anger smoldered forever, and his wrath perpetually.'

Which is to say, war is ultimately personal. The blood wantonly shed is the blood of a common line, it runs from a single vein. One kills, another is killed, and the two combatants, no matter nation or race, are — brothers. In denial of all claims — 'virtuous violence,' 'just' causes — war is simply a sanctioned form of fratricide.

And the fire is never quenched; war smolders on in the humiliation of the defeated, in the pride of the victor. Thus the memory of war begets only war, never once peace.

There must be another way, the oracle implies. The spirit of justice, an outraged and outlawed gift (outlawed, as they say, 'for the duration'), that spirit hovers over us. The first urging of the spirit is acknowledgement of our near hopelessness, our helplessness. For the weapons own us; they, not we 'call the shots.'

But for the grace of God, we are stuck; blood on our hands, a bloody history — the human predicament.

As 1991 opened, war lay heavy on the horizon. The warriors on either side were quite prepared to create victims, exiles, displaced persons — corpses. To beat plows into swords, a harrowing of hell.

The ethicians, the moral theologians and, on the wider cultural scene, the scientific entrepreneurs, the political clones and ventriloquists — these have stolen our Christian thunder. Who is prepared to say, 'thou shall not kill'? Who will say, 'love your enemies'?

The larceny was an easy take. For what is thunder without lightning?

No healing memory, Amos implies, no alternatives arise to assuage the wounds of warlike memory. 'There has never been peace' is frozen into a surreal dogma; it governs all the future. "There shall be no peace."

Old scores, open wounds. Brother against brother, then sons against sons. War is generational, the sword is the proudest legacy bequeathed to the unborn. It lies beside the newborn, ready.

(1:13) And on and on the empty parade, the empires coming, horridly flourishing, falling. Did they but know!

They never know. From the unholy seven of Amos to our own day, empires are a clutch of bats in a cave. It is noon outside, midnight within.

Or like a procession of slaves, chained one to the other; thus they pass into the dust of time, the imperial 'dwellers on the earth.'

Now the Ammonites — their 'perfect' crime is warring on the future. In face of their savagery, even the unborn are — expendable. They tear apart the bodies of pregnant women.

Indeed in a later equally awful time, tearing the unborn from the womb has become, not an act of war, but a common medical 'procedure.'

One cannot forebear quoting in this regard, the plain words of a theologian:

" ... I expect little change from Roman Catholic church authorities, and so expect to face that community mainly [as] a prophetic nay-sayer. However, there is a great exception, and a fine indication of why I continue to think of Catholic Christianity as a nonpareil resource for women's full liberation. Inasmuch as we are made for divine life, and not for this-worldly convenience, feminist positions such as the demand for untrammeled rights to abortion seem to me clearly immoral and so impossible politically. I am as sure as it is given to human beings to be, that Christians cannot support such a demand — that it is demented, and runs counter to women's true interests, the common good, the mind of God, and on and on."

(2:1) The Moabites — their crime is both strange and strangely imputed. They have 'burned the bones of the king of Edom.' Such an act, we are told, was the ultimate sacrilege; it condemned the soul of the dead to a tormented afterlife.

But something more is implied in the oracle — an unheard of indictment. The Edomites were the deadly enemy of Israel. It might be concluded that Amos could ignore a crime against his people's enemies. Is not the enemy of my enemy my friend?

Not to Amos. Condemning as he does the crime of the Moabites, his ethic is astonishingly universal. His conscience is limited neither by an enemy border, nor a friendly.

(We omit verses four and five, the oracle against Judah, as being a later addition. In which case, the following oracle against Israel may be thought to include both kingdoms.)

And finally, and at great length, verse six and sixteen: 'the point of the entire passage' (*BJ*), the sins of the people of Amos, the covenant people.

One or another of the crimes adduced lies beyond our ken, even beyond our ingenuity, but most are distressingly close at hand. Of interest here is the change of tone. A far different footing before Jawe is implied.

Imagery of fire, the truth as retribution, the summary removal of tyrants, all such images as governed previous oracles are absent. Now the words are all of gentle (or not so gentle) love — love outraged.

This people know the better, and for all that, do the worse. Their sin is therefore of a different order entirely from that of 'the nations.'

(2:6) There is first of all the matter of justice and justice denied. Justice, Amos charges, is cynically bought and sold. And this among 'God's people.' For a price, a justice of sorts is available to the rich. For the poor? Nothing of the kind — or a justice so grudging, so delayed as to amount only to a mockery.

Crossing the palm, that is the first instinct. Justice has become a mere commodity, a debased transaction like the trading of 'silver coins and a pair of shoes.'

(2:7) The system is by turn violent and duplicitous, as occasion requires. There are many ways at hand to 'trample the head of the poor into the dust of the earth, and make crooked the way of the lowly.' (Revised Standard Version)

The images are awesome, shadowed. Threat of retribution hovers over. It is as though by common will and effort, the poor are shunted to one side, into the dust. As though this is the proper task of 'civilized' institutions — police, armies, courts. Out of the way, out of the way! Forward the march of commerce and consumerism, warriors and arms!

As in the summer of 1992, the streets of New York are 'cleared' of the homeless. The eyes of democratic conventioneers, arriving for fun and games, were not to be offended by the offscouring of the system.

The 'removal' many times repeated, makes a crooked way, a trench or ditch. Into it the poor are shoved, a via lacrymarum, a road of tears. Thus the New York homeless join the history of Amos and his beloved victims, slaves, exiles.

From the time of Amos to our own, an entire social apparatus is contrived, like the noose of a public hangman, to throttle hope. Undesirables (read: the poor, the lowly) seek relief and are lost in a labyrinth of delay, evasion and contempt.

Finally, many disappear or give up. And for all official notice, it is simply a case of good riddance. Indifference toward the living, a shrug of relief toward the dead.

At the same time, declares Amos, among the great ones a cult of pleasure degenerates into a cult of prostitution, male and female. Thus worship 'of My holy name' is profaned.

(2:8) Around the altar other bizarre practices flourish. Pledges of compassion, laws forbidding usury (Ex. 22, 25-26; Dr. 24, 12) are in effect declared dead letters.

Such worship, God says laconically, is of 'their god', not of 'Me'.

(2:9 ff.) It comes to this: if the people have chosen to forget the mighty works of liberation and cherishing, yet God's memory is neither enfeebled nor recusant. Thus Amos.

God remembers. God's memory is a citadel of truth, of event, of benefits outpoured. But God not only remembers. God also beckons the people to grow mindful.

To recall the blessing is to recover that sanity we name a sense of history. Deprived of the memory of past blessing, what shall we say of the tribe?

No ceremony to renew and restore, no star to steer by. No heroes to offer a measure of the human. All bearings are lost.

In verse nine the sticking point, in more ways than one, is the 'destruction of the Amorites,' a terrible verse. (Past it *BJ* tiptoes gingerly: "Amos ... uses the term 'Amorites' to designate all the peoples who occupied Palestine before the Hebrews arrived." Indeed. And is no moral judgment called for?)

According to Amos, Jawe is a warrior god, the god of a warrior tribe. And to that degree, a god whose activity echoes, not the nature of true God, but the instincts and appetites of the tribe.

Need it be added that today we are still encountering, on the long road that leads to the self-naming of God, this violent tribal deity?

Jawe is not yet clearly seen, not yet; is hardly distinguished from the gods, the idols, the 'works of our hands,' the gods who would put a sword in our hands and our blade to a brother's throat.

How far we are from Jawe's "I am who am." How far from the images of Emmanuel: "I am the way, the truth, the life.... I am the door.... I am the good shepherd.... I am the vine."

Barth is of point here: "If we glance at the history of human desire, human assertion about this Being, the first and strongest impression we receive is that of a human skill in invention, active on all sides and taking the most various routes; but also of human waywardness and human violence with this concept, this idea of God. Hence the picture of an infinite variety of possibilities, the picture of a great uncertainty, of great contradictions."

Difficult to untangle — the contradictions. And the violence. They lie here, in a text shot with blood. A scandal to some, a vindication to others.

We read of a God who disowns warmaking people and presents himself as a God of peace. And shortly thereafter, the same God reminds the Israelites: I have utterly destroyed your enemies. I glory in the deed. I remind you of it, this great deed on your behalf.

A dreadful purpose and thoroughness, no one spared, 'fruit above, roots beneath.'

The matter should be put plainly. Unwelcome the text, and unsavory. This is the bloodthirst of the tribe.

This is the god we longed for, and 'honored' in 1991, in the Arabian desert. And before that, the god of war in Grenada, in Panama, in Vietnam. This god we summoned again and again, a warrior to our side. This god ensures military victories, and crowns foul deeds with an infernal blessing.

The scandal is not in God; it is in ourselves. The scandal is our gods.

On biblical violence, Walter Wink is, as usual, helpful and lucid:

"Violence is the most often mentioned activity and central theme of the Hebrew bible. This violence is in part the residue of false ideas about God, carried over from the general human past. It is also however, the beginning of a process of raising the problem of violence to consciousness, so that these projections on God can be withdrawn.

"For in scripture, for the first time in all of human history, God begins to be seen as identified with the victims of violence.

"But these occasional critiques of domination in the Hebrew bible continue to alternate with texts that call on Israel to exterminate its enemies, now or in the last days.

"The problem of violence could not have been discovered in a nonviolent society. It had to be gestated at the very heart of violence, in the most war-ravaged corridor on the globe, by a repeatedly subjugated people, unable to seize and wield power for any length of time.

"The violence of scripture, so embarrassing to us today, became the means by which 'sacred' violence was revealed for what it is; a lie perpetrated against victims, in the name of a God who, through violence, was actually working to expose violence for what it is, and to reveal the divine nature as nonviolent."

(2:10-12) The wonders of forty years, liberation, providential love, are compressed in a verse.

I have sent prophets among you, like Moses, Debora, Samuel, Elijah,

Eliseus (Deut. 18:15-22) and admirably austere spirits (Nazarites) like Sampson, Samuel, and later John Baptist. But you know well how to disencumber yourselves of such troublesome spirits.

You teach the ascetics the art of dolce vita, you silence (in one way or another) the prophets. That accomplished, everyone, morally speaking, resembles everyone else. Everyone agrees implicitly altruism and compassion are 'out,' self-interest and greed 'in.'

Thus the vision languishes, and the truth.

The decline, as always, takes a political form. A commonweal (commonwoe) of acquisition and acquiescence grows apace; a perfectly sound, secular version of empire. And this, be it noted, under the presumed sign of the 'chosen.'

The implications reach far beyond the tribe. Today also.

For example, the 'seven richest powers' meet in perfect amity in Paris. The occasion is billed as an 'economic summit.' An image befitting the occasion is that of an awesome larcenous agape, a celebration of planetary greed. In the course of their deliberations, these tycoons banquet regally.

And what of the have-nots, the nations of the poor? Their table was set apart from the mighty trenchermen. The delegates of the 'poor nations' looked on like children, faces pressed at the window of the 'developed' world and its bounty.

The seven know their constituency well. And the nine points of the 'law' known as possession, holds firm. For awhile.

Memories linger, memories of far different behavior, Amos implies. They tell of courage and free vigorous speech and objections hurled. Alas, the memories grow dim. Nazarites have become good consumers, prophets have gone stale.

(2:13-16) A vivid contrast marks the oracle. Images of retribution leveled against the nations, are altogether lacking here. No fire, no exile.

To this people God says with a kind of contempt — I leave you to yourselves. No more is needed. The harsh outcome is in your hands —

that you become what you are.

The images are all of diminution, exhaustion, loss of nerve. The exultant and warlike, the valiant and speedy, fall by the way. Their hearts fail them.

In the decline of the military, in fact and image, is there not implied a fading away of the military god, as imagined and worshipped? One thinks so.

The chosen have lost the power of choosing. They no longer ratify the covenant in any real way, whether personal or communal.

Where has it vanished, that image of the beloved, bride, companion, friend, partner, image of a people set apart from the nations, a sign of God's hope for all humans, the reign of justice and peace? All such images have vanished. They have no bearing on personal or political life.

To Be Chosen Is To Choose; You Choose Badly

(3:1,2) Now hear this word. The great mercy of history, your release from bondage and exile, has vanished from memory.

In Amos the vexed matter of 'choice' comes up again and again. Invariably, the consequences are badly understood, neglected, ignored. It is all one — awful.

Thus goes the oracle. Once long ago, it is written, the love of God, a love that 'goes before,' sovereign, ignoring every credential, all merit or deserving — that love came to rest on a people. On a motley band of slaves and exiles. A people whose past is a tormenting memory, whose present is humiliated, all but hopeless.

And their future? This is a people of no future.

But the love of Jawe is a hovering eye and heart. It is hardly idle; it is hands too. It strikes like a lightning, healing, liberating, interceding, a mighty compassion and power. It creates a future. A new book, a veritable Genesis, opens.

We lose a sense of the outcome of this, the outrage.

This people turn on God. And inevitably, on one another. Their conduct is deliberate, icy, inhuman. In bizarre fashion, they come to resemble their former oppressors. Enormous changes occur — changes of heart, of politics, of worship. The victims become executioners.

This story Amos tells. The slaves are freed through no act of their own, through the mighty act of their Emancipator.

Is a miracle required to bring them out of bondage? Very well then, they will have a miracle. A septenary of miracles in fact, confounding the oppressors. Come out! I will show you a power surpassing the horses and chariots of the pharaoh.

So the people come out and wander in desert places. They murmur of revolt, this pitiful remnant. And almost as a matter of course, they turn to idols. Nonetheless, they are fed and cared for, yes and harassed as well, by prophets. And finally they are given a code and covenant.

They stand at length, who had crawled the earth. A people. Arrived in the land of promise, they prosper.

A nation takes shape, with borders and laws and armies and the rest. A hegemony, a series of small political entities, knotted together in common memories, the horrid past made bearable by present blessings. And the land, it is theirs.

And a temple, stirring communal memory of the great acts of God. The slavery in Egypt, the exodus, the desert years — all translated, transformed by ritual, a rhythm of life giving memories, healings. To know the past is to walk with God.

No longer a despised scattered tribe. They are — a people of covenant. When they summon identifying images, as they do in worship, these are all of beauty and strength and hope, images of themselves as bride, friend, beloved.

Alas, as they prosper, they forget. As they forget, they lose form and firm sense — of being a people of vocation, worthy of prophets, mindful, grateful. A people of worship, assembling to hear the word that created them, a word of compassion and justice. A worship that creates a just people, this the prophets harped on, irritated, would not let go. A people whose behavior, because they worship, is consistently human. Whose worship recalls, among other great matters, the inhumanity they have undergone, the oppression. Tolle et lege!

They prosper, they forget. Are the two one, inevitably? Recount, recall, dramatize the horror, the deliverance, the 'passing over,' the desert years,

Moses, Sinai. Remember the golden calf, and beware. Remember the manna, and give thanks.

Tell it to the children, tell what was done for you. Eat the bitter herbs, feel the hundredweight on your backs, remember the bricks without straw. Remember too the decree: the death of the first-born and the angel of salvation.

Recount, recall what you have endured, what torment, humiliation, chains, exile, scorn, hunger and thirst.

Remember all this. Lest you repeat it. Lest you inflict it on others.

We forget; it is all but a national pastime. Spectator sports help greatly; so do national forms of hard and software, from VCRs to weaponry. Those 'mighty acts of God.' They are all but forgotten. It is more suitable to forget, more convenient, less of responsibility clings to amnesia than to memory.

Nothing like daily violence, pushed in our faces by media, to induce forgetting of nonviolence, the actual achievements of the biblical 'meek' in a violent world, the magnificent potential for creation of a human order of things.

Violence pays, violence works; this is the tired conventional unwisdom, strenuously peddled worldwide, by those who have most to gain by the proliferation of murder en mass.

In the kingdom of amnesia someone must remember. Amos tells the forgotten story since the priests, along with the rich and powerful, have become a collective tabula rasa.

The story is told also 'for our sakes,' as Paul reminds us. A warning as to the possibilities, the 'pits' (psalmist) into which we too can fall with such ease, such sublime intentions gone for naught. O Desert Storm, the winds blowing back, blinding the warriors!

What crimes we humans are capable of (torture, death squads, oligarchy, silk-suited charlatans huckstering arms in the world).

We would know nothing of that dark side of ourselves, remember nothing, repent of nothing, were not the word of God, its story of divagation and betrayal, of sin and forgiveness of sin — were not the evidence before us. Would know nothing, which is to say, know nothing except distancing, numbness, despair.

Models, ikons, even of sin. Models (even rarer) of forgiveness.

Otherwise, know-nothings. Knowing nothing of ourselves. As though inhuman conduct were both the birthright and legacy of the nations, as well as of that 'family I brought out of Egypt.' Which is to say, a hard saying and needful of the state of Israel today and of 'the nations' at large. As a warning. Corruptio optimi pessima; the direst falling away is that of the best. "Lilies that fester are far worse than weeds." (Shakespeare)

We might have concluded, left on our own, that in the 'normal course of things,' a good people becomes better, a people once summoned responds, a chosen people continues to choose rightly.

This is the 'pride of life' John speaks of; it is capital to an understanding of sin. Those who pride themselves on being special, unique, virtuous, God's own (but in fact, left to their own resources, are poor as all others) — this is how such people (read: citizen-believers) commonly regard themselves and their prospects. And all this with a certain self-satisfaction, a certain self-justification.

Good, and bound to be better. Progressive, initiators of change. Meantime, the flag, the oil interests, the war in the offing, the homeless, the debtor nations, the poor, the 'economic summit.'

Progress, a progressive people? Everything in fact is out of kilter, points to a people dead wrong as to self-knowledge.

Then the assumption, the myth that captivates: we prosper, therefore we are just, indeed justified (which is to say, self-justified.)

God? Who, where is God?

Let it be recalled nonetheless, the 'great act' of God. The liberated according to Amos, seldom recall the truth of God, or they do so cursorily, as a matter of nostalgic form, a debased liturgy.

Nevertheless, God was once a flame in the soul, a cloud of unknowing, a pillar of fire, a giver of manna, a breaker of idols. God touched the prophet's tongue with a fiery coal. God spoke, the people were attentive.

They found occasion to rejoice as well, and frequently, with dancing and timbrels and feasting. There was nothing in the world like this, this God who reversed things, stood with the underdog. Why not then the exhilaration of freedom, free at last, chains cast off, dignity and a sense of justice in the air.

It all changed. Behold the tawdry present. The crimes, indignity, injustice, the utter likeness to those who once sought to destroy them.

Are we hard put to think of analogies today? For a moment, let us consider an unlikely one.

Suppose (it is much more than a supposition) that a community in Central America has suffered for generations under a ruthless oligarch. To such, the peasants are of no account; worse, they are solely of economic account, each a hundredweight or so of slave labor. So things proceed, for centuries, in the main satisfactorily — for a few.

Then, something else. A priest speaks up. Who is this god, he asks ironically, who cherishes the rich and offers a celestial, never-never sop to the poor? No such god exists. He declares with passion that the God of the Bible has taken sides with the underdog.

At such a word these nobodies raise their heads. They become restive, covertly pass hand to hand a subversive book; it tells of a Pharaoh and a Moses. And of an outcome, bizarre, inflammatory.

Swift as gunfire, the reprisal. Certain among the peasants are made examples of, they disappear. Eventually corpses turn up, in the dust or in a garbage dump.

Briefly put, we are to imagine that eventually, the peasants win out. Their Moses appears. They win control of the land. Justice prevails, and they care one for another. A politics of compassion is born; it extends even to the persecutors.

Then other changes. The new leaders, politically astute as they are, also become ambitious. They find the taste of power sweet indeed. Their mandate, apparently from heaven, becomes an irrefutable credential. So they keep in their own hands, or pass to others of like mind, the reins they once snatched from the oppressors. They also accumulate wealth.

Eventually, the handbook of liberation is closed with a thump. We have learned all we need to know, is the implicit conclusion; we have other instructors now. Behold the new oligarchs, new injustice for old, a new power elite lording it over.

Still, we need not go so far afield or summon the unlikely (even the likely) future. If we find the word of Amos hardly to the point, it may well be because the analogies are so terrible, so exact, so near, so firmly lodged within us. Within the Christians, within the Jews. In Palestine, in the United States, in South Africa, elsewhere. Indeed if a map of today's world were to show only those 'chosen ones' who, given time and occasion, choose to betray, it would turn one color: blood red. War, injustice, recusancy, greed, control, disappearance, torture, apartheid.

This is no dark dream, it is plain fact. To betray is the common behavior of 'godly' people, of the 'chosen.' Indeed, betrayal seems an act much favored by those who proclaim: we are the chosen. In political life (as well as in personal), betrayal is simply taken for granted.

Such may be admitted or covert; no matter, one simply betrays, falsely promises, violates his word. All with a heavy touch of cynicism. And small remorse, if any.

Thus, according to Amos, a bitter contention is inevitable. On the one hand, there is the world's estimate of human nature, which the world itself sets out to verify to the letter. Amos takes it in account; indeed he must. It is his field of combat, the disputed territory of the principalities.

All, all are drawn into the vortex, even the most favored. So with Paul: "All sin, and deny the glory of God." (Rm.)

There being another side of things, a contrast and relief. And of this also Amos is witness. It is an only hope.

The love of Jawe is asserted again and again, even as it is violated and scorned, again and again. A love reproving, remembering, rebuking, restoring. Breaking and entering the stronghold of the powerful.

And in the lifetime of Amos, taking sides once more — this time against that quondam underdog who terribly has become the overlord.

(3:1-8) "I have known, of all the families of earth, only you."

And then the terrible 'therefore,' like a bronze door closing on its hinge; "therefore I will come to you, in full knowledge of all your iniquities."

The retribution will be all the more terrible, as the choice and its blessing have been perverted.

Times of holiness, times of blindness and corruption. In the worst times (the times of Amos), prophecy is in effect forbidden. Only the 'career-prophets' (2:12) flourish. Later the prohibition, acid with contempt, falls on Amos himself. (7:12-15)

Meantime, the images of truth proliferate; prophecy is an irresistible calling, there is no turning aside from the summons. It is like a law of nature, a law of gravity, a law that governs the behavior even of the brute beasts. To prophesy is simply to admit that an effect has a cause, a cause an effect.

Amos, like others of his kind, is hard pressed by the servitors and guardians of a wicked status quo. He is much in need of vindication. And it is not long delayed.

In verse seven in effect, Jawe has spoken — spoken through his servants the prophets.

A cardinal point, then and now. Once the prophets are silenced, what is left to us? Law and order, and a dreary regimen of authority, with many a thump of book and swing of the tocsin, proclaims that certain ones only speak for the divine.

The arrogance of the priestly caste and its instinctive distrust of prophets is an old story, never quite done with. Indeed, when a way must be found to suppress the truth, a way is also found to dispose of truthtellers. Some are put to the door. Others are held in ridicule or disenfranchised.

In more abrupt and condign moves, when the discomfiture of a brutal state coincides with the impatience of the church, trouble-makers are simply 'disappeared' or murdered. We have seen it all, we have been complicit in much of it.

(3:9 ff.) One might have anticipated, if an indictment of the recusant people were to be announced, that Amos himself would be summoned as witness for the prosecution. Has he not suffered much at their hands?

Or perhaps the poor and the victims would be hailed forward to tell their story?

Nothing of the kind. In a grand organ burst of indignation, God assembles the pagans, Assyrians and Egyptians, imperial neighbors, all great enemies of Israel. Long judged as they are to be 'outsiders,' morally inferior, spiritually benighted — nonetheless, let these unlikely ones bear witness to 'the disorder, violence and rapine' of Samaria.

The indictment is simply put: 'they know nothing of uprightness.' The like indictment had often been leveled against the pagans. Now the same 'nations' are witnesses for the prosecution. A more scathing irony could scarcely be imagined.

The political situation is appalling, the indictment speaks for itself. A regime is in place; its marks are plunder and plenty for the few, impoverishment for the many. Worship drones on, the priesthood is proud of purse. But quietly or abruptly, by common agreement the sacred has been abolished. Which is to say, justice is exiled, compassion a lost virtue.

Matters of covenant, once looked upon as binding, have become subject to 'review' by the state. To all effect, God is a mere ornament, an item of the decor of empire.

And the outcome, the decision of the court? Moral healing, restitution of spirit, liturgical reform? Nothing of these is mentioned. It is as if the moral illness of the chosen is terminal. God, according to Amos, accepts the situation qua tale; so be it.

The oracle is cast, not precisely as a threat, a thunderbolt from a clear sky. It reads like a flat statement of logic. You have so conducted yourselves — this is the outcome: your decline and fall.

God is by no means the agent of catastrophe. You are. And as for Amos, he is simply a scribe, the recorder of events already underway.

What then of hope in so dire a time, what of that fragile 'youngest daughter of God'? (Peguy) The image is extraordinary.

A lion is devouring a lamb. The shepherd, despite the royal roar and appetite, contrives a last ditch measure; he snatches from the jaws a relic

AMOS

or two, a foot, a shred of ear. Thus he can demonstrate, by these pitiful remains, that he is guiltless of the loss.

Is God the shepherd? We must not press the image dry. The point is — a relic, a remnant, evidence (when facts point ominously in a different direction) that all is not lost.

All is not lost. This is the meaning of hope, as God hopes on, despite all. As God hopes on, in the hope of people.

Amos is the first to speak thus; it is a capital point with him. (5:15 and 9:8) Isaiah will make classic and central the same subject, the hope that resides in the remnant; in those who come out of the furnace, the exile, the cave of lions; in the refusers; in those who hope on against all hope.

Who are these faithful few? What are their resources, how do they survive such times? Amos grants us little or no light on the subject. He makes only a passing reference to the 'anawim' who survive.

It is as though the existence of the remnant, their survival, is his only point. No 'how to,' not even a spiritual regime or discipline, no tactics offered.

By an act of God, behold the remnant, the base community, those snatched from the imperial jaws. Ourselves?

THAT YOU WOULD RETURN TO ME!

(4:4 ff.) The teaching method of God is aimed at conversion of spirit. In Amos the method takes a terrifying form: a septenary of domestic plagues. The image, together with its ironies, is pursued in all bitterness and exactness. As the two kingdoms have aped their pagan neighbors, retribution of an ironic kind is exacted of 'God's own,' a clear recalling of the plagues once leveled on Egypt.

There is yet another implication, equally ironic. Egypt had held the Israelites in bondage and humiliation. Only intense suffering, even to the death of the first born of the realm, loosened the iron bonds.

And now? Among the chosen the covenant is sundered, the enslavement forged anew. And what will serve to liberate?

The sevenfold retribution unfolds, an awesome series of ecological disasters. The series is marked by increasing severity: famine, drought, blight, mildew, locusts, pestilence, death in battle. In a defamatory likeness, Israel is likened to Sodom and Gomorrah!

And finally, a definitive chastisement is threatened, a closure. It is left unnamed, as though it were too terrible to conjure up.

Is there to be a final act, an end time in his own time? Amos seems to indicate something such. But his fulminations fall on stony ears. An eery normalcy prevails around him. No premonition troubles the people or their rulers. Well-oiled, the wheels of empire hum. Bread and circuses, prosperity and euphoria! And a tempest rumbling away, just over the horizon. Its name is Assyria.

Hearkened to, obeyed or not, the prophet must speak. He does so, we are left perplexed as to the outcome. How was the dire word received? Do his oracles bring in their wake a saving remorse? Following a general amendment, was the chastisement averted?

For Amos the matter was simple. The outcome was not his concern. He spoke the word of God, that was his charge and vocation.

Then he returned to his flock, that was also his charge and vocation.

There is a sensible detachment in this simple coming and going. Amos has done what he could to bring relief in an awful time, such relief as only truth can offer. The word must be spoken, into winds favorable or contrary.

Let them blow as they may, one is not in command of the winds. No, the point is to conduct one's self as faithfully. He speaks up. And then adieu! The outcome is in other hands.

It is as though Amos departs with praise on his lips, a mood of celebration most endearing. We see him turn away, he is lighthearted, he sings a doxology of departure, an itinerarium. Such detachment 'from the merit of one's works'!

His final oracle is charged with the terror of truth; he leaves the words there, hovering on the air. Will they gain a hearing from those they threaten most, the powerful and wealthy? Amos does not know, we could almost say (but how wrong we would be) he does not care.

The oracle is a reminder, to Amos himself, to us. Who God is, Who has spoken. Again, Barth:

> "Holy scripture describes a work, and first the work of creation. Alongside, God puts something else, something different from God — namely the creature, without having need of it, in the power of Almightiness, in holy overflowing love.
>
> "Secondly, a covenant is set up between God and creatures. Once more an inconceivable fact; why precisely between God and humans, of whom from the beginning it is narrated that we are unthankful to God, that we are sinners?
>
> "In spite of sin, sovereignly overlooking it, reserving for God its amendment, God surrenders, to become the God of a tiny despised people in Asia minor, Israel...."

This is the God of creation whose mighty works speak for themselves. Creation 'flings out broad its name,' for all but the blind to see, and see beyond; it is a kind of second scripture, inexpressibly noble, various, 'charged with the grandeur of God.'

To God Amos turns in praise. In so doing, he opens another valve of the heart, another rhythm. Praise is beyond utility, free of duty, of tasks and taskmasters, free of the need of action — free even of the burden of the Word, of repeating, underscoring, insisting on the truth of God. No, once was enough. The finger that beckoned him here, beckons elsewhere.

We note too the sequence: first the task, then the liturgy. Task without celebration is a form of slavery; it indentures one to outcome, tactic, success, efficiency, proof of worth — those mechanisms of power that land us, deflated and captive, once more in the worldly systems we thought to cast off.

And what of celebration without task? It is the empty chatter of temple worship deplored by Amos (and Jesus).

Justice? Compassion? The realities become intrusive; they are put to the door. The doxology drones on, empty.

Meantime, the God invoked by priest and caste has escaped the net, is occupied elsewhere. As Amos knows, God treads the streets of Samaria with the poor.

(5:1 ff.) A lamentation, a kind of funeral before the fact. Israel is compared for the first time to a virgin, seized by death before she can taste the joys of marriage. The image is borrowed by Isaiah (1:8; 10:32; 37:22) and Jeremiah (18:13; 31:4,21).

A tender image indeed for an empire on the wane. Lost, but not utterly lost. We have heard it before: a remnant will survive, despite all.

In verses four and six "Seek Me, and live" is twice repeated, as though the tormented human venture itself had grown plain, were reduced to its essence, four words.

Nor is the first admonition, 'seek Me,' to be construed as an urging to more or better worship, to prayer or holy solitude. The guilt of those who refuse to 'seek' is of another order entirely. They and their sin are here identified. Secret decisions and public conduct are held up to judgment; they 'turn justice to wormwood, and cast down righteousness to earth.'

At times it seems as though the story of us humans were one vast net of evasion, cast over, concealing simple home truths. Or more awfully, and in more concentrated form by far, it is as though the history of religions were such.

Still we learn — something of God's view of justice-as-essence, of the human itself, of that designation of the human we call religious. Something also of the meaning of sin.

Of more than passing interest in this regard is a rather strange phenomenon. The churches who evade questions of justice with all their property-ridden might, are much occupied with questions of 'sin.' These entities are driven to an obsessive jotting and tittling of matters sexual, matters cozily domestic, of good order and liturgical nicety. And all the while justice, that seemly health giving florum, is turned to wormwood.

If justice has become wormwood, what cup is lifted to our lips? And equally to the point, what word is offered an unjust world?

One thinks here of words carelessly uttered and lightly flown from the tongue. Words which hardly issue from anguish, from fasting and grieving, in the manner of the word of Amos. Hasty, frivolous, all but absent-minded, how can such words be taken seriously? They are a demonic brew, a diluted wormwood.

Their effect is to dilute conscience; justice, injustice become murky matters in the mind. And ego, greed, pride of life flourish abroad.

Then there is another cup; it is distilled from the plant justice. It enables those who drink to live by the word of God, and if required, to die for its sake.

Amos had drunk of the cup, had offered it to others. We are told that for all the daring of his oracles, he escaped death. For some reason, those who turned sweet justice to poison and passed to the poor a cup of wormwood — they let him go. He survived to return to his flocks.

But survival or death is hardly of point. Amos spoke the word of God and let the chips fall. Beyond doubt he risked his life, even as Isaiah (and Jesus) lost theirs.

In such matters as the integrity of the word of God, there are neither winners nor losers. There is only — vocation and consequence. Amos speaks and takes his chances. Whatever might befall, let be. Then in a gesture of sublime detachment, he turns away, his work finished.

Let be, and God be praised.

God of sweet nature, how gently the doxology of Amos begins. This God cradles the universe at heart. All living beings are like an infant, they fall asleep or waken attuned to the rhythms of day and night, ebb tide and full, starlight and dawn.

And then the whiplash. For every rhythm a counter.

We come now to humans, and what shall God make of us?

We are not to conclude easily that ethical matters follow the gentle pattern of nature. Humans have another side, a dangerous one named freedom. Dread choices are possible, even likely. A spasm of greed and pride — and the florum of justice is turned to wormwood.

Shall God quaff it and wince and be silent? All the while cradling us, morally infantile as we are, in the everlasting arms?

No. This is the God of sweet revenge — of surprise, of tables turned and thrones toppled, of vindication, of the death of false hope and the birth of true hope. The poor, their veins infected with the wormwood of injustice, raise their heads. See the great ones tumble, the strong walls.

"You have to think the way the fellow in psalm 1 thinks; blessed is the one who walketh not in the counsel of the ungodly.

"When I was thinking about this psalm I was praying, and I will tell you how I put the psalm to paper;

"Hallelujah for men and women in Haiti who do not join forces with the malevolent regime.

"Hallelujah for the Haitians who do not enter into the gluttonous pillaging by a band of the bloodthirsty, in whose midst brother sells brother, in whose midst a brother is not his brother's keeper.

"Hallelujah, because the path of those Haitians who reject the regime is a path of righteousness and love, and that is what the Lord requires.

"Where there is beating, breaking and destruction, the righteous are not. The way of the Lord is the way of justice, and justice blooms on the banks of Deliverance."

Amen.   (Fr. Jean-Bertrand Aristide)

An old theme and a constant one. Two extraordinary women take it up as their own. Anna (1 Sam. 2:1-10) and Mary (Luke 1:46-55) thus celebrate the unity of the two covenants.

(5:10-12) We note (God takes note of) the dark side of imperial 'normalcy.' According to the code of palace and temple, it is normal that integrity be despised and just judges be derided (or removed), normal that the weak be crushed and ruinous tithes imposed, normal that oppressors and extortionists flourish.

Therefore, says Amos (says God), let another ironic normalcy be declared. Let it turn imperial normalcy on its head, this new normalcy of the Realm of God!

Hear then: in the new order of things it will be normal that the wealthy are evicted from their mansions of dressed stone. Normal yes, that stolen vineyards and their choice wines be snatched away from them!

A notion dear to the powerful is a sense of spurious diurnity. The throne is strong and shall abide; it is planted firm in nature, a very Gibralter. Kings and great ones prosper. It is normal. They stand outside accountability and conscience, normal.

And then the normal consequences (and always elsewhere): social misery and economic slavery. These are 'the squared blocks of Rome' (Chesterton). They are cornerstones of reality itself. It is beyond imagining that such arrangements will not perdure.

How persuasive it all is, how impermeable! The decor, the wealth and perks and glitter and notoriety, the sycophants, the career prophets and soothsayers, the armies, the booty and slaves, the triumphant processions — what an unassailable case for legitimacy, virtue, staying power!

Fall in line, fall in line!

And then the other side of things. The side no king, no president or junta or shah need take seriously. Those who wait in silence for the glance of God. The tears of the prophet. The outer dark, the circle of misery. The ghetto, the homeless, the slums and favelas. The nameless and disenfranchised, the people of no account, helots, exiles, the landless, the captives and slaves, drawers of water and hewers of wood, builders of pyramids, these too.

And that sinister architecture erected in the shadow of palace and temple, always in the name of law and order: bridges of sighs, interrogation rooms, subterranean cells. People go in, ghosts emerge.

Who shall withstand all this? Who challenge it? The answer, according to the principalities, is implicit in the question. And the question is rife with contempt.

The imperial arrangement is deep founded; it is 'in the nature of things.' No one shall withstand it, and live.

For awhile the powerful prosper, the system is intact; it rides a high-noon of power. The empire rejoices in military victories, the boundaries expand, the loot rolls in.

But watch. Contrary to imperial cunning and might, the stage is set for a literally unimaginable event: the dawning of the Day of Jawe. 'On that day' (a solemn phrase for an ineluctable will, an event that cannot but come to pass), the empire will fall. Socialized terror, like a military tank on the prowl, will be halted in its tracks. A solitary monk sits in its path, wrapt in prayer, impeding.

(5:16-18) And what of the meantime, the time of Amos and ourselves?

God through the likes of Amos, plays the part of — subversion. Every least 'no' brings the Realm closer, every denial, every unmasking, false hopes stood on their head (especially the hopes of those who invoke the Realm as a blessing accorded their crimes).

The Day of God will fall upon the oppressors like a bolt of lightning from a clear sky.

Shockingly, the finger of God points to — Israel. Unlikely, unheard of! The great Coming will hardly be in a form the nations and their sedulous apes have anticipated. They have dreamed of a great light; they will be enveloped in darkness. They will be like someone who flees a lion — and falls prey to a bear. Like someone who enters his own house, a safe place, puts hand out and is stung by a serpent.

Another sign of the immanence of the day — grieving.

Consider the times, we are urged. A time of darkness, such darkness as cannot, it seems, be further deepened. A time of monstrous preparation for war. A time when all talk, all persuasion, all perverse logic, points in one direction — to war.

A million warriors faced off in the Arabian desert. A last minute charade of 'diplomacy' preceded; it was empty, meaningless. Our side, we were told, had taken 'a last feasible step' to avoid the war.

Then the word came down sternly: no negotiations. The United States is 'firmly committed,' strongly backed. Weirdly, this non-negotiator goes to Geneva to sit (to negotiate?) with his opposite number. Only, in fact, to repeat what has been said all along.

It is as though the instructor, after trying patiently to convey a message to a muddled, indeed retarded schoolboy, grew restive. He will try again, but mark you, only once more!

Virtue, just cause is, of course, on one side only. It is so unassailably on the one side, so clearly absent from the other, as logically to make any attempt at peaceful settlement or quid pro quo — out of the question.

The faithful grieve, and keep silent. If they resist, speak up, march, sit in, pour blood, raise an outcry, it is all the same. Grief. Grief for the wasted chances, the wasted lives (and not altogether those of soldiers and non-combatants and exiles, the wasted lives generals too, and of the inert congress and the clever tricky president and the other power brokers).

Grief is a form of emotional sanity. The world at times is too much for bearing. An appalled silence, ashes, fasting, waiting on God, these are the recourse.

In contrast, a bizarre vitality, a feverish restlessness moves in the public atmosphere, a heartless self-satisfaction. We have here the fevers and chills of power, the sense rife among the 'dwellers on the earth' — that their 'mandate' is essentially limitless, that moral codes, from international law to the Sermon on the Mount, are irrelevant scraps of paper, blowing in the wind.

Verses 21 through 26 might be termed a definitive word on false worship.

Such empty incantation proceeds on a double assumption: (1) matters of justice in the world are of only indifferent interest to believers, and (2) God readily approves the current religious arrangements. God, in the manner of an earthly tyrant, is placated by the rigamarole — even as God is unmoved by injustice.

AMOS

The text is capital. Many later prophets will take up the theme: Hosea, Isaiah, Micah, Jeremiah, the Psalmist. So, later still, Luke 11:41; Romans 12:1,2 and especially John 4:21,24.

The key question is not of false gods (though these, in a conjectural text, are mentioned (verse 26). The false gods symbolize the corrupt worship, surely. And the images of the gods eventually are borne along into exile. One does not easily surrender them! Surely an arresting symbol.

What worked at home must work on the road!

Idolatry is thus unwittingly defining itself. Alienation from truth and justice is idolatry. It has polluted worship all along.

Now, a new phase, exile. And better, it is implied, pack up the images, follow their blind lead. Better this than a pretentious temple charade thrust in the face of the God of justice and righteousness.

How Doctor King loved verse 24! With what mellifluous splendor the 'ever flowing stream' of justice 'rolled' from his tongue!

But first and last, from his life.

THE FIVE VISIONS, COMMON WOE, COMMON WEAL

(7:1-3) Prophecy is often a service of intercession. This is a great theme in Genesis, in Exodus repeatedly, as well as in Jeremiah, Ezekial, Daniel, Micah, the Psalms.

Amos too intercedes for the people. Not only is he a truth-teller. Through his access to God he also bears a special burden; he has known the sin of his people. Such knowledge may stop the heart in its beat, but it also impels him to plead for the delinquents.

He knows the sin of the mighty, of those who prosper from sin, whose authority is steeped in sin, who set in place structures of sin, who ensure that sin be the very rule of empire — sin in the sanctuary, sin in the marketplace, sin in the economy, sin in the armed forces.

And through this compounded woe, God through Amos harps on sin, insists on the accountability of sinners. This too is a form of intercession.

And then there are the 'others'; the 'little ones of Jacob.'

AMOS

In verse one, a vision of sorts, a quotidian one, all too familiar to a farming people. The stage is set for a catastrophic famine, just at the time of the first growth. (Presumably, the mighty ones have ensured their own interests; the king's portion is safely harvested. Thus the plague will affect only the poor, the 'little people.') And the eye of God, and of the prophet, rests on the scene.

Not a word so far, no threat. The vision speaks for itself. The next move, Amos, is yours. He makes his move. It is a plea: "How will Jacob survive, he is so small!"

We note that the intercession is somewhat wide the mark. Jacob (Israel) is hardly to be accounted 'small'; it is by all accounts quite a thriving empire!

But the task of the prophet here, like that of any skilled advocate, is to make the strongest case possible for a clients. And after all, it is the poor, the Jacob folk, who are being pled for. It is these who recall a less violent and luxurious time, a time more pleasing to God, the time of desert and covenant and manna and true worship.

The poor, to be sure, are 'always with you.' The mighty, let it be said, ensure that. These latter filled their barns (then, now) to capacity — and the devil may take the others!

The plea is skillfully put. Can God resist the pleading of a shepherd, himself one of the lowest and least, on behalf of subsistence farmers?

(7:4-6) Likewise with the second vision, of wildfire running far and wide. We are in a mythical realm; the fires here threatened have already devoured 'the abyss,' whence waters rise to nourish the earth.

Amos repeats his plea, once more on behalf of the little people. And God attends.

(7:7-17) A longer vision enters upon the vexed matter of religion. And the question rises: Who speaks for God?

The vision opens with deceptive simplicity. A plumb-line lies in someone's hand; it is to be laid against a wall, a wall that is out of kilter.

The wall stands, but barely, wobbly, insecure — Israel. With the strong likelihood that it will shortly crumble.

The image is an announcement of doom. Both the 'high places' of idolatry and the 'sanctuaries of Israel' are to be brought down. Sternly, no distinction is made between the two. God will unsheath the sword against the dynasty of Jeroboam, which is held responsible for the abominations.

There is much here between the lines. Evidently Amos has announced the vision in public. The high priest, quick as a wink, recoils. He senses the danger and hastens to rebut the upstart prophet, to defend his royal patron.

No question whether the word of Amos is genuine, no faith is invoked or even implied. Politics alone governs the scene; the politics of temple worship, the prerogatives of king and priest, equally threatened.

The stage of the conflict is set; priesthood versus prophecy, career versus truth. An old story, and hardly a stale one.

Diplomacy gets underway immediately. The priestly plan is two-pronged. First a message is dispatched to the king: You and I, let us together rid ourselves of this troublemaker, for he prophesies your death by the sword (surely an inaccurate, indeed inflammatory report). More, he fulminates the mere fantasy that our people are to be seized and sent off in exile.

The first message is precautionary. If all else fails, let the king intervene. Meantime, perhaps something less draconian can be contrived. Let us see if matters may not be settled amicably, one to one, as between two 'religionists.'

The chief priest Amasias summons our Amos. The tone of the mighty one is faintly sardonic, not so faintly cynical. Shall you and I not exchange a private wink, he implies, in common cause as we are, and knowing well the source of our livelihood?

Therefore the message: Go please, visionary, and join the career prophets in Judah; your living will be assured there. Here in Bethel, you are, shall we say — inconviencing. You utter unwelcome words, in a setting utterly foreign to such as yourself, indeed a 'royal sanctuary, the king's own temple.'

Could affairs have been put more plainly?

To wit, Church-and-State, as a hyphenated reality, a presumably enduring, sanctioned fait accompli. The worship drones on; the income is satisfactory. What need have we of your kind?

We owe much to a corrupt priest. But for him, Amos would remain a shadowy figure, like a later prophet, John the baptizer, a mere 'voice, crying in a wilderness.' But here, confronting the arrogance of the priest Amasias, Amos takes on flesh and form and stature.

He stands there, four-square, a very Socrates before the bar. He will not be moved, invokes no defenders, disciples, credentials. He speaks for himself. The establishment, rife with contempt, would be rid of him. Amos recoils. The silken tone, the undercurrent of menace, the spleen! He draws a deep breath.

Let us for once have plain talk, let us clear the air.

First of all, as to who I am, in contradiction to your innuendos, I belong to no 'school of prophets,' as you imply. I am a poor shepherd drawn despite myself into the vortex of the divine. Nothing to gain, everything to lose! I came here, I faithfully spoke, and that is all my trouble.

❖ ❖ ❖

There is more to come.

The king's priest has denied a hearing to God's word. So be it.

Far from softening his defense, Amos lets fly a totally offensive oracle. Now hear this. For a start, Amos quotes the priest's blasphemous anti-oracle, his attempt to silence the word of God. Then, like a burning arrow, a new threat is launched straight at the priest himself.

Hear this. God says not one of yours, no possession is to be spared, neither wife nor sons nor lands. And finally you yourself will perish in a foreign land, (an 'impure' land, a land of idols).

So the episode ends. Priests take warning.

(8:1-3) A fourth vision, equally simple, almost quotidian, something of a still life. A basket of ripe fruit appears. So are the people ripe — for disaster. There will be no pardon, since there has been no repentance. The flimsy joy of the temple chant will turn lugubrious. And corpses will lie everywhere, too numerous for burial.

(8:11-14) Among the frightful chastisements to come, this: 'hunger and thirst for the word of God.'

It is passing strange. The plaint of Amos has centered around the stone deafness of Israel toward that word. Who hungers, who thirsts, who could be described as even remotely interested in the rantings of an unknown shepherd?

And yet, cries the shepherd, the day is to come when a people, starving and parched, will 'wander from [Dead] sea to [Mediterranean] sea, from north to east, seeking the word of God.' And worse, 'they will not come on it.'

The image is one of profound alienation, spiritual and ethical incoherence. Imperial religion and captive priesthood — these have lost all meaning. The young and vigorous turn elsewhere, to foreign gods and shrines. False religion abroad, false religion at home. It is all one, all a disaster.

(9:1-4) The fifth vision, by all odds the most terrible, is reserved for the famous sanctuary of Bethel, lofty symbol of imperial impiety. It is from here the high priest issued his fulminations against Amos, bidding him out of sight, out of mind.

Amos sees God, 'standing beside the altar.' The announcement is telegrammatic, bare of detail. It is a shepherd's vision, candid, direct, unadorned. No hint of the splendid theophanies of Moses, Ezekiel and others, no apocalyptic symbolism. One wonders, does the shepherd see — the Good Shepherd, do these two speak a common language?

In any case, the form of the epiphany is hardly the point. As we shortly learn.

Amos is instructed to dramatize the shattering effect of the word of God. Here and now, at this blasphemous shrine.

The vision is thus a drama after the fact. Through Amos, God's word has already rent asunder the fabric of deceit and complicity woven about the sanctuary, the false worship miming true. Now Amos is literally to bring down the temple.

We understand this as a drama of a spiritual struggle, already underway.

The rites of the imperial priests, the solemn feasts, holocausts, sacrifices, canticles — all are stigmatized, swept aside; they are fraudulent, they are null and void. Not Jawe, but the gods of war and the gods of creation — these are being worshipped! (5:26) And meantime, the money flows in, the frivolous charade goes on.

It is all ended, judged and rejected.

The word is relentless. The proud sanctuary is down. More, God pursues those who conducted and profited from the sanctuary of infamy, as well as those who tarried there, and in doing so were corrupted. Cursed be the place and destroyed the votaries! No passage in the book of Amos is so terrible, so detailed and final.

It is helpful to recall that in issuing a curse, prophets are insisting on moral consequence, accountability. Evil deeds, evil institutions, contain within themselves the seeds of retribution. So the 'justice of God' acts to endorse or speed up or fully reveal a process already underway. Thus through a curse God lays down the law, intervenes in the world, and this both in the present age, in our passage, and at the end time.

Ordinarily there are no witnesses to the crimes of power, or the witnesses are corrupted and bought off, or are too fearful to speak. But God, we are told, stands there, through the prophet. God plays the Witness, the One who sees and takes in account. Denounces and judges a crime that is otherwise beyond accountability.

In the Gulf war the supine media yielded before an overbearing president and military (one and the same) and grew silent on the hour. Crimes were perpetrated — no witnesses, no reports, no images.

And who were appointed to act as witnesses uncorrupted and courageous? We were — and to a measure, we did so.

Through the curse God places against worldly power a 'measure.' We have seen the plumb-line, laid against the people. (7:7) A precious gift, a reminder of moral stature and virtue. And this in a time when the measure of the human is all but lost in moral incoherence both social and personal, in a stampede of greed and violence.

So far and no further. The 'taking measure' implies limits, boundaries, taboos. It is exactly such limits that the priests and the king are violating.

It implies also something else, a great hope. For the measure of the human is always, in the eyes of God — godliness. God knows her own, and loves them.

Even as the godly measure sets ethical boundaries, it stretches our sense of the human, beckons us beyond what we had named a limit, whether of endurance or compassion or hope.

The measure also cancels out much that is taught and urged in a given culture — invariably a deceptive, even inhuman measure: selfishness, moral indifference, greed.

It is as though the crimes adduced by Amos, crimes of injustice, pillage, warmaking, rapacity, contempt for the poor — all are resumed in the crime of idolatrous worship.

Such worship serves as cover for the structural crimes, renders them presentable, of little account, normal, 'religiously acceptable' in fact. So goes the reasoning, fostered by the priesthood. Is not our prosperity a sign of divine favor? How then can the worshipful be accounted anything but virtuous? Can public behavior be held reprehensible when it has won our official blessing?

The shepherd becomes for the nonce a very angel of retribution. He brings down the sanctuary (the word of God has already rendered it redundant), the 'worshippers' are scattered.

But they do not escape. God undertakes a kind of search mission, terrifying and relentless. Nothing, no place in creation serves to impede the judgment, to offer a hideaway for the wicked.

(9:5-9) And yet for every curse, a blessing. For all violation of the honor of God, a doxology. This outpouring of praise is heavy with the burden of the preceding judgment. Grief in place of false joy, the earth atremble with rhythms of birth and death. That tiny ray of hope shines once more, a first frail hint of dawn. Not all have been renegade, a few are faithful. In the remnant is the hope.

(9:11-15) Though all seemed lost, squandered, wasted, and the loss is ratified in the strong terms of God's decree, still, all is not lost. The minute cataloguing of crime and retribution is shown as — penultimate.

What then is the final word concerning ourselves, what the outcome of the human venture? The question is tormenting, the facts hardly reassuring, then as now.

The sanctuary of Bethel is level with the dust. But the spirit of Bethel, complicity with imperial crimes, avarice and indifference to suffering — these lie deep in our history, deep as the first pages of Genesis. We are guilty indeed, and according to Amos and his like, we are to be held accountable.

Still, the judgment leveled on us is not to be likened to the workings of human systems. God's is a judgment of love, not punishment. Renegade, boldly intent on evil as we have shown ourselves, still the mystics are right, Amos is right. God is God. No wickedness on our part has turned God aside from love.

Only imagine! The final word (as in Revelation, that book of apocalyptic hope) is given over to 'hesed'; compassion, return, restoration, healing, rapture even, fecundity, recovery of the land.

Standing with the prophet, taking sober account of the worst in us, cataloguing our crimes with surgical exactness. Yet God creates another reality. God imagines the least likely event in creation, that we humans would undergo a change of heart.

Not only does God imagine the event. God brings it about. "I shall do these things." This is the unkillable hope that resides in the heart of God, a hope that proceeds grandly to create what it envisions.

Therefore, so goes the logic of hope, all is not lost. There abide Amos and the remnant, and the truth they announce at such cost. This is the seed sown in the furrow of time, an only hope.

AMOS

Out of the worst times, hope. Electric with surprise, bound with a loving logic that unseats all calculation, even the dark calculus of despair, the book of Amos ends with a series of bountiful and unlikely events. The people, we are told, return from exile to a land grown intoxicatingly fruitful, a paradise, a garden of innocence restored.

Memory itself is healed. Such wonders contradict and cancel the horror that has preceded.

All is transformed to — alleluia. At the word of God, 'that day' will dawn, the much abused human, like a florum long trampled under, will bloom again.

OBADIAH

A distillation of tears and gall.
The shortest and beyond doubt the bitterest oracle of the Jewish testament.
A work of vast complications and large ambivalences — and this in some twenty-one verses!

The bitterness of the prophet is off-putting. Until perhaps we are led to reflect that we too live in a time when bitterness of heart is the commonest of ills.
We measure time's passage as post-war or pre-war; surely not the most uplifting or heartening of measures. Have we finished with a war, closed accounts, proven our valor? Made our point? Or must we undertake another invasion?
Those, for example, who applauded the Gulf War were urged to bolster their bellicose spirit with hatred for the 'enemy.' Those opposing, if not careful, could draw on a contrary source of ill feeling — hatred, alienation toward domestic leadership.
In either case, one and the same illness. Dare we call it prophetic?

How difficult it is to live one's life in a good spirit, without rancor either toward the 'evil one,' Hussein, or 'the evil one,' Bush! How easy on the other hand, to identify our own 'Edomite,' personally demonized — as does our prophet here — once and for all tag the adversary, curse the unchosen one out of existence!

Not to be missed, and so easily missed in such times, are the words of consolation and hope implied between the lines of this bitter little manifesto. To wit, we do not live by vengeance alone. Can the vengeful spirit ever be rightly thought of as life-giving?

Did the prophet imagine (could Jawe have imagined) that a people could sustain themselves for long on an emotional diet of hatred? It seems literally unimaginable.

Hate makes waste, makes war — then and now.

And hope, perverted to 'hope in victory,' is no more than a wind inflaming the guts.

Such is the mood of the inflammatory tract of Obadiah. One hears between the lines the sharpening, brandishing, clashing of swords, the appeal to blood and fire — universal solvents of the 'problem' of the enemy!

Alas for the prophet and his fulminations. They are of only indirect help to us. The awful events he must cope with (as a less furious voice than his would remind us) go far deeper than this or that declared enemy.

One must pay heed to a mystery: Evil would take up its dwelling in the hearts of all — the would-be virtuous and the evil opponent; the follies, the perennial rampaging of us sinful humans — no matter the offensive occasion or offending other.

We are great ones for letting off steam, one could say, and the saying lets us off altogether too lightly.

Let us say rather, great ones for letting blood.

The book, it is said in justifying tones, can be taken positively. It speaks of the faith of Obadiah in the justice of God — even as the 'law of talion' is invoked with a vengeance. Thus *BJ*:

"Violent as they appear, the feelings (of the author) are not to be thought merely the narrow views of secular nationalism. The sentiments are rather an expression of Jawist theology concerning the strict justice of God....

"They convey faith in a just judgment; in a God who here and now, must reward the just and punish the wicked. Even, be it added, if awful memories of the sacking of Jerusalem feed a rancor which refuses to lay down arms."

So God is invoked; nonetheless, the difficulty is stubborn, and remains. The sticking point of the theory being, as we've learned since, that 'an eye for an eye' leaves the one who plucks out eyes himself blinded.

Mutual blindness. A better image for the climate of wartime could scarcely be summoned.

This we also witness time and again: the lethal tit for tat named modern war. We see its consequence, the cyclonic spiral that draws men, women, children, conscience, the good earth and its resources into its vortex.

How avoid the blindness?

Let me venture one alternative. Moral clarity remains unimpaired in proportion as one has other projects and concerns in mind than vengeance and violence. And this especially in time of war!

Thus goes both the tactic and spirituality of resistance: loud and clear, saying no; placing one's self deliberately, publicly, at legal jeopardy, outside the ambit of folly.

Another reflection. Using the book of Obadiah as a kind of fulcrum, a vantage point, one might put himself in the position of, say, an Edomite of the period of Obadiah. How is the enemy estimating — the enemy? Does our Edomite take a startlingly different view of Jews — who hold so vengeful a view of Edom?

Or today, do Iraqis (I mean the citizen, parent, wage-earner, those commonly inducted or otherwise victimized in war) do these view Americans differently than we view them?

Manifestly, the Edomites have been guilty of heinous deeds. The crimes are recounted here (as well as per longum et latum in Psalm 137). The Israelites, it would seem, had sound and bitter reason (as worldly logic goes) for setting down in their scripture hair-raising fantasies, dreams, oracles, cries for vengeance, here and elsewhere. Images that even today seem torn from a living throat.

As worldly logic goes, vengeance is mine, says the Lord. So it is said.

But does such prophecy, taken at face value, offer anything more exalted than worldly reasoning? If so, if the world's ethic and the prophet's coincide in this bloody matter of mutual hatred — then we, a later and far more belligerent tribe, are also justified in invoking a God who 'stands with us.'

A God not only on our side, so to speak, after the talionic deed is done. But a God 'before the fact, the bloodletting'; a God who impels and urges and blesses the deed, the vengeance. Not only blessing the armies (awful enough), but provoking them to battle.

So we are left with — a God of battle, a God of vengeance, and this God, beyond all doubt, the true God.

To be distinguished from the gods of the Edomites?

Distinguished, differing — in what?

This God of battle and those gods, all said, strangely appear to resemble one another. They concur in the inciting and inflaming of violent behavior. Whose God then is for real?

We have here a notable dilemma, seemingly beyond resolution (in Obadiah's time as in our own).

It would seem a sound idea to reject all attempts, however well meant, to spiritualize an extremely ugly, purportedly godly, justification of violence. Better, one would think, to call things by their name, however repellant. And then proceed, by way of contrary evidence (for Christians, drawn from the example and words of Christ) — to choose. And so to conduct one's life.

How comes it that Obadiah's screed holds a place of honor in the biblical canon? What is the consonance and continuity of his teaching with the other prophets? And more, what sort of God is acknowledged by those who choose to honor so vengeful a book?

There the book lies, inserted neatly and embarrassingly (but hardly

OBADIAH

peaceably!) in our canon. And questioning us with its flat brevity. Nothing mealy-mouthed or unctuous — implacable the text, ferocious.

Nicely ignoring — not to say despising, among other powerful and contrary voices — the possibility, the foreshadowing of a Christ figure, of some embarrassingly overt teacher (and practitioner) of nonviolence.

A Christ figure? According to splenetic Obadiah, such a one is beyond imagining. More, such a one, even in hypothesis, is devoid of all interest, whether in prospect, hope or ideal.

Here and now and for all time in effect, in this avenging God (whom Obadiah feverishly invokes and quotes) lies our true prospect, hope and ideal. Period.

And if such an event as the Incarnation of God were to come to pass — why, to what point? And if this God were to show among humans, a nonviolent face, what then?

Obadiah offers his own dark vision of the human; we require, he implies, no other instruction. More (or worse, as the case may be), his version holds, he insists, a divine sanction. Jawe approves his version of Jawe.

The implication is — steely. Take up the sword. The sword is the final 'arbiter mundi.' It is also tool and sign of the human itself. Jawe has spoken.

And what of those deprived of the sword, of those who renounce it? They show their true colors; they are somewhat less than human.

Jesus, ('put up the sword') less than human?

Images offered by other prophets regarding the 'One to come' (if such images might be thought to mitigate or reprove the violence of war and its attendant slaughter) — these are darkly ignored.

Meek and mild, and mounted on an ass? A suffering Servant, who answers evil and cruelty with patient goodness? By no means!

In such wise this tiny tome — and the awesome choler of its author — joins (and enjoins) the behavior of multitudes unborn. Through Obadiah

OBADIAH

and others of like mind, the hand of Mars invades the womb.

How then is his message to be thought profitable in light of other (and so different, so conflicting!) biblical words?

Something like this: All but in spite of himself, let Obadiah remind us of a long and bitter history of bellicose folly. How easily, with how light a breath are stirred into flame the worst instincts of us humans!

And how ancient (how contemporary) the attempt, even through sacred oracles, to enlist God to this or that dark cause!

(1:10-12) He has moments of clarity, moments when sanity prevails. The charge against Edom (Esau) can only be termed right and proper; brother is pitted against brother, Esau against Jacob. The charge is hauntingly raised here, with a twist: "Take no joy at the sight of your brother, on his disastrous day."

Who are we, who is our brother? The question is as old as Genesis. Raise the question again and again! And this even though on both sides of the rampart, adversaries hold one another transfixed in gunsights, denying utterly the validity of the question. Denying it in blood.

"Shame will cover you, you will disappear forever."

Shame is the reaction due to acts of shame. Otherwise, one 'disappears'; one's humanity is simply obliterated by shameful acts.

It would almost seem as though the two parts of the prophecy are self-canceling. (Perhaps this is an irony or a koan, and we are to puzzle it out.) If one is 'ashamed' of shameful acts, on what score does one 'disappear forever'? Is shame in itself a kind of disappearing act? Or is the absence of shame?

We are invited to suppose a shameful war. It ends; there follows no show or evidence of shame, but something else entirely. A nation wallows in the glory of its self-proclaimed 'victory.'

In our recent history, no need of suppositions. We have seen it all: yellow ribbons, flags, parades, breast-thumping generals and president.

If such be the case, according to the prophet, the 'disappearance' of an entire people is underway. Any resemblance to civilized behavior, the humanity of the glory-bound, must be thought in utmost jeopardy.

(1:12-14) "You should not have ... you should not have." The judgement is laid down after the horrid fact. War is war is war: 'what you should not have done.'

War is that implacable dark urge, the 'sin' diagnosed by Paul as one horrid evidence, perhaps the chief, of the human propensity to evil.

Among other illnesses, war brings in its foul wake enormous confusion and division of spirit.

The native bent of the soul toward virtue and goodness, this is not so much obliterated by war, as rendered muddy. Whose cause is just, whose wicked? What is goodness, after all? And what evil?

(Rm. 7:15-19) "I do not understand my own actions. For I do not do what I want, but I do the very thing I hate.... I can will what is right, but I cannot do it. For I do not do the good I want, but the evil I do not want, is what I do."

The collective 'I'? In war, most of all in the permanent warmaking state, the 'evil within' is socialized; it takes outward form, infects and claims institutions: pentagon, research laboratories, bases and bunkers and air fields. These form the inner circle of infection; from them the disease seeps into the body politic. No one, nothing is left untouched.

A bizarre 'welfare generation' of the high and mighty, a feverish prosperity-austerity economy trickling down like an acid on the national conscience is thus created and ever expanded.

We have seen it: the bemedaled generals writing their enormously profitable 'memoirs,' the entrepreneurs and weapons hucksters and researchers, the scientists and engineers, the vast armed forces, trigger at the ready, and finally, a vast work force at the mercy of international terror and hostility.

And the arrangement is all absolutely useless; it offers nothing useful, nothing good or serviceable. An international cartel, joining with domestic imperial policy, is given over to the works of death, their socializing and normalizing.

OBADIAH

A dialogue between an eighteenth century African king, Chaka Zulu, and a British official:

"In your country, are you masters of your lives, or is your king?"

"In England, each of us is the ruler of his own life.."

"Can your king order you to war?"

"Yes."

"Can he order you to die?"

"Yes, he can."

"Then you are no longer masters of your lives."

Let us suppose that an international crisis has arisen; the possibility, then the probability of war.

Special, altogether urgent interests are now involved and converge. The trough is filled; the appetites are voracious. A huge investment of money and talent has been mounted in view of (indeed if truth were told, in hope of) one contingency: war.

No need to underscore the provocation offered by prior, mostly secret arrangements; all those weapons, all those soldiers (otherwise unemployed and possibly dangerous to law and order), all those weapons experts. Get things moving! Test the weapons, prove the sound nature of the permanent war economy in a 'dangerous world.'

(1:11-14) Let us take to heart the indictment of Obadiah. He has forgotten for the moment, his 'godly' vengeance. Now, with infinite tenderness and fury, he speaks on behalf of the defeated — to the victors.

And he speaks not as an outsider, but as one of the defeated and victimized.

(How hard it is, how unlikely it has become, for us to step over this line, to join the defeated, speak for them, suffer with them! And more, from that vantage, denounce the crimes of the victors!

And yet, in the Witness for Peace presence in Salvador and Nicaragua, in the Honduran and Mexican refugee camps, in the Peace Encampment in the Iraqi desert, in the Nevada Witness against nuclear testing, in domestic courts and jail upon jail — in many ways important to victims [and unheralded by the media], exactly this has occurred. The truth has been spoken and dramatized, the consequences embraced.)

As I write, these are among the multitude of the Companions of Obadiah, those who refuse the demonology of the victors and who stand with the victims.

All honor to them!

Louella Bassett; Frances Bond; Elizabeth Walters, IHM; Ardeth Platte, OP; Peter Dougherty — for reentry trespass at Wurtsmith Air Force Base.

Kieth Kioller; Peter Lumsdaine — for disarmament action damaging NAVSTAR sattelites.

Fr. Frank Cordaro — for reentry trespass at Strategic (nuclear) Command headquarters.

Fr. Karl Kabat — for disarmament action at Missouri (and later at a North Dakota) nuclear missile silo.

Mark Davis — for malicious destruction [sic] of property [sic].

Margaret Millett — for aiding and abetting in the above.

Helen Woodson — for disarmament action of Missouri nuclear missile.

Leonard Peltier (Native American political prisoner).

Fr. Ray Bourgeois — for protest against American training of Salvadoran military.

Gregory Boertje; Philip Berrigan; James Reale — for protest at the White House on behalf of Iraqi children.

To all of these our thanks, and a muted Alleluia!

Of any war in history, the words would be true, though Obadiah speaks of a war of his lifetime. (1:10) "You robbed and killed your brothers." You robbed, you killed. The killing was a monstrous larceny, the most atrocious of all, the taking of — a life.

(1:11) Nor are the so called 'allies' spared in the indictment.

(What an old story! The excuse of 1991 was: We proceed with the war under the approval of the United Nations. We were not 'making war' at all in any commonly understood sense; we were part of a vast peace-making, peace-keeping force!)

But read Obadiah; he translates with fearful symmetry, our situation:

OBADIAH

"Your allies were co-conspirators in your crimes. They stood guard while you pulverized Baghdad. In consequence they were as responsible as you."

("Strangers carried off the wealth... and divided it among themselves...." Let us speak of markets and oil and military alliances forged, as well as a harsh lesson delivered to potential troublemakers anywhere.)

(1:12-14) There follows a series of 'should nots.' After the fact, after the crime.

After the technology was aimed and discharged, after it had been put in place, long after it had been blueprinted and developed and tested.

In the beginning, at the jump start of the infamy, something like this occurred: To minds rendered icy by cold war obsessions — a question, a tease, a problem occurred. It was a mere tic in the mind, a spark that exploded an inferno. It whispered, 'Why not?'

One (otherwise unendowed) scientific genius, sotto voce, as it were, said to a colleague (likewise unburdened by conscience), "I believe it can be done." And the second whispered back, "Yes." And the two chorused, "Therefore it should be done." And the world shuddered.

Behold then the 'should' of this scientific malpractice, an awesome principality, a very Goliath, bulging with credentials (nine points of the law in its favor, up and up and up, the supreme court in the pocket of its butcher's apron).

Do it.

And then our lad, a David, and his stern faced 'should not' — Obadiah and his like.

Who prevails? In this matter we require no instruction.

The prevailing is for a time only, let it be added. For a 'meantime,' and no more.

The 'should not' of the prophet is the precious moral core of the minority consciences named above. Of them and of others of their like.

Need one add that the same prohibition is virtually a lost word in the populace, in the 'just war churches,' all but beyond retrieving in the public authority?

Thus the 'should not' loses out to a brutal assault of the kingdom of necessity on the Promise, the realm of God.

"You should not have gloated... have been glad... have laughed at them...."

Thus is forbidden all public and private rejoicing over war, all religious services celebrating a 'god on our side,' all obscene joy in a 'victory' whose devastation and human cost are thereby ignored. Too bad for the enemy, too bad for the earth!

Thus is forbidden and biblically indicted, in effect, the unholy and gleeful events, religious and secular, that in America followed on the Iraqi carnage.

Thus also are defended and honored — by implication — all those who observed the 'should not' of the word of God. Those who interrupted parades, displayed signs and symbols of mourning, stood vigil at military and government headquarters, poured blood, blocked official passage.

(1:14) It is as though the prophetic bones of Obadiah shuddered in horror at the imperial behavior of his time.

The Edomites, for their part, committed two enormous crimes: they 'posted themselves at crossroads, to exterminate those trying to escape.'

(And our forces [we learned only after the carnage] pursued the fleeing Iraqi soldiers and buried multitudes of them, alive, in the desert.)

The Edomites delivered Israelite refugees to the merciless hands of the Babylonians.

(And we, withdrawing after the conflict, delivered in effect the fleeing Kurds to the hands of Hussein.)

(1:15) Obadiah's God is indeed vengeful. But with the prophet's insistence that judgment awaits the victor, we can have no possible argument. A clearer statement of accountability and consequence could hardly be conceived.

Obadiah thus underscores once more an ancient understanding. (And ironically and invariably, the great ones of every age choose to ignore it.) "What you have done will be done to you. Your actions will judge you."

Call it Buddhist or Hindu or Jewish, as here — or Christian. The traditions come to the same thing: what goes around comes around.

And the warning is violated or ignored, so constantly, so blindly one could well conclude that such a prohibition had never been uttered!

It is as though imperial authority were quite simply, at the time of the prophet and through the ensuing centuries, genetically mad.

We have here a clue, not only to the moral estate of war criminals, but, more importantly, to the secure confidence of the just who resist them.

The ethos of those who say no, who endure consequences under a corrupt 'law of the land,' includes a sense of the 'day of Jawe.'

Everything in the social and political and military scheme of things, all that is trumpeted and puffed, as standing beyond critique or judgment — all is here declared by the prophet to be provisory. Wickedness and its celebration is tolerated, allowed a limited swath and scope in plain view and prospect of judgment — of 'the day.'

The resisters and the principalities!

The powers are unassailable; they bask in a kind of full noon, the full bloom of empire. In that intense light, they see reflected their own glory. No shadows, no hint of sunset, decline, the onset of darkness.

Their sense of prevailing and perdurance is far off kilter. In effect, the prophets insist — even as the mighty sing their own glories — their regimes are tottering, altogether vulnerable.

And then there are those 'others'; those who fall afoul of a foul system of 'law.' These could hardly be said to bask in high noon; to the contrary, they pass their days in a kind of twilight. Their good name, legal status, fortune in this world, all are placed in question.

One thinks of the meager light falling upon a prisoner in his cell. It may be a twilight or a dawn, hard to say which. The prisoner is helpless.

He can do little or nothing by way of mitigation, correction, connection with loved ones, further resistance, homilizing, organizing. The time of all that is simply past. No way seems open to bring the truth to bear, that truth for which he pays so heavily.

His former life has come to a halt. In his solitude, if he ponders the past, it may appear efficacious, even a certain satisfaction. But only in a bitter way.

His activity surely accomplished something: It set him afoul of the law. He was heard; he 'made his point,' as judges are fond of intoning in avuncular fashion — just before they strike.

The law strikes hard.

Thus it was that conscience brought him to this place, this impasse and helplessness.

He marks the day on the wall of his cell. The date? Whatever it be, one might think of it as the day before the Day.

We ponder Obadiah and his indictment of high crime. We think of wars, then and now, and of conscientious refusers.

Everything that once seemed ethically clear has been tumbled 'for the duration,' head over heels. Murder is no longer murder; it is now legitimate and honorable. Women and children and the aged and enemy soldiers alike, stand in the gunsights. Criminals ride high and mighty; the innocent are in lockup. Propaganda rants on, loud, self-confident, for the most part prevailing: 'all is well in the empire.'

All is not well. We stand with, pray with the prisoners. And more, because of them we take heart. The bread is rising. On the day of Jawe we and the 'enemy' will break bread — and no bread of affliction at that.

(1:17 ff.) Other images of God, of Israel, of the future, of vindication (even bloody vindication), of the vast and final victory of the just — these occupy the latter part of the oracle. We need not linger overmuch on the themes.

One thinks of such verses as an outcry of the oppressed — who have become, in their long-suffering, a people obsessed.

Victims have their dreams — as, of course, do victors.

Dangerous, those dreams of the victimized, herewith indulged, indeed in a sense canonized by Obadiah!

The danger is this: Reality is much altered by a bloody filter. The suffering community, by a kind of slow attrition, comes to resemble its persecutors. Like images, like ideology and, in consequence, like behavior.

(Even the ever cautious *BJ* has this mildly dissembling note on what follows: "We have here an imaginary, ideal version of the future. One is not to press such matters literally.")

That famous interplay of imagery and conduct continues, one thinks, to this day.

Does not contemporary Israel dream of being one 'among the nations,' a clone of the USA, both mini and mighty, credentials secure, secret, intact — summed up in 'nuclear capability'?

The first image Obadiah offers, by way of reciprocal punishment-vindication, is that of a cup. The wine is bitter. Edom has held it to the lips of the vanquished people; perforce they have drunk it to the lees. But now the same cup is passed to 'the nations.' And on quaffing it, they simply disappear.

The vanishing of great worldly entities is thus foretold.

Empires, as we know, are not greatly given to imagining their own demise.

To speak of Edom, there was no prior thought that so dire a happening was in prospect. No images, certainly no images circulating in the nation, whether around or within, prepared for it. Everything pointed in a totally other direction — that of perdurance, earthly immortality, glory unfazed and unfading.

Then those other images, the Obadiahan ones.

They arise in those who have tasted the bitter lees, the dark chalice of power, and who have seen the fallibility and ignorance well masked, the mortality denied in murderous battle. The Obadiahs have tasted death in its many guises and analogies, undergone the guile and ferocity of the law, seen the self-deception of the godlings, their preposterous muscle-flexing claims.

Truthful and deflating, the images are spoken, written, seen by prisoners and their like — the exiles, the disappeared and tortured, 'lives of no value.'

Those truth tellers! 'For the duration' they are put to silence. And in silence, even the enforced and final silence of death, they yet are heard.

OBADIAH

The truth passes on; it undergoes a sea change; others become the truth keepers, the custodians of the biblical word, their dignity and vindication.

We ponder Obadiah. Perhaps we will see him bent over his text. He shakes his head in regretful denial here and there. For he must know it: A greater than he has come among us. That other, to whom he paid no honor, forms the soul of the believer.

Even the wise, 'even great Homer,' nod, fall short. The wise too may grow wiser. I see Obadiah pondering, urging, blessing the counter text of Jesus. "Love your enemies, do good to those who persecute you...."

Our resisters and martyrs! This is the text they have by heart, the counter they offer, all so gently, to the imagery of conquest, vindication, vengeance.

Obadiah, like most of us, is in great need of Bible study.

He has God all wrong, a God cut to his own cloth, his proclivity to ire, his lacerating need of a vindication that borders on vengeance.

And then his strength. He knows the principality of empire, and its hardly fetching ways, so accurately, truthfully!

Shall we say of him — part prophet, part darkness?

JONAH

A Cautionary Tale

Into our bible
self-willed, blustering,
dissembling, unresembling
the line of holy soothsayers -

Comes this unseemly
malcontent prophet,
out of step with
hallowed ones, martyrs,
pages flickering
with tongues of fire
& fiery haloes

Fretful, muttering
No I Won't,
You Can't Make Me,
he light with big hands
hell fire of the mind -
when
all around (Jeremiah,
Isaiah, Daniel, Ezekiel) -
tongues of fire -
Yes I Will!

Jonah's game; all said,
to play in minor mode -
(jut jawed, dead set
comical, farcical) -
to outplay, outwit
creator Jawe!

'I could make me
yes, in half a week's time
a better world
than this teeming
massa damnata,
good & evil
grimacing, groaning
false faces all -
no line demarcating
saved / bedamned -
the holy decalogue
annulled, dishonored -
the sanctuaries
bellowing with false Baals!'

Jonah
could you, could I
give ear to the plea
Augustine
at wits' end uttered;
'noverim te, noverim me!' -
O grant for all follies
delusions, inflations,

JONAH

feints, false starts,
a penetrating wisdom -
that You
mammoth Icthys
swallow me whole,
and I
wound, bound in your womb -
in stupendous
eructation
emerge,
(evicting
the 'body of this death')
into
imagine! -
birth, rebirth.'

In despite of all
(so goes the story)
reneging, tergiversating,
matter & man
came together -
truculent will
in wild water,
grew creaturely, calm -
mammoth, the billows
slid him under,
Then, a Something
swallowed him whole!

Jawe as Icythus!
that monstrous fluke
that maw all mercy -
sings
like a deep sea
harp of high heaven -

'Someone inside me
like the universe!
Not much of a man
homunculus Jonah
unlikely seer -
seeing what?
so near
zer-
o
as to mick-mock
my dearest fairest
Ninevehan
beasts & flora
infants & crones

Never the less!
Of this the least
my mothering nights
will mightily make
at length - a man!

JONAH

❖ ❖ ❖

We note in the book of Jonah, how the heart of God turns and turns about.

Ironically, spontaneously, mercy is offered the great ones of Nineveh, lost in idolatry and yet much beloved — this to the scandal of conventional religion and its practitioners, including Jonah. The prophet has grown callous, cynical, yes conventional, arbitrary. God and the prophet have become a scandal one to the other.

❖ ❖ ❖

God the wily is in effect staging a play within the play.
Will generations read, hear the text aright?
Will the church? Will the system, the powers? Maybe, maybe not.

❖ ❖ ❖

We have a book of the Bible which might with good reason begin, 'Once upon a time...' or 'Once there was a man named Jonah; to him God spoke....'

Intriguing questions to start with: How strange that (1) the book contains no overt moral instruction, in the manner of the other prophets. And (2) who is the author of the book, anyway?

Since we don't know, we may as well presume and on our own, take sides. To wit, the author is Jonah himself. In which case, his humility befits the outcome of the book, rather than its unpromising start. Jonah is in effect offering 'a mordant, ironic commentary on his own character.' *(BJ)* Delicious.

We know him, we are meant to know him. He lives in our skin.

❖ ❖ ❖

Let us call his book a kind of extended parable. And let us be wary! We have in hand no conventional tale to be told or heard in an idle hour. Like the stories of Jesus, the book of Jonah subverts 'normal' expectation. How does a prophet behave? Is he not always obedient to the voice of God — passionately so? We shall see.

❖ ❖ ❖

The spiritual ancestors of Jonah, as well as those who follow him, leave a consistent trail of heroism, obedience, sublime poetry and rhetoric, fulminations and comforts drawn from the heart of Jawe.

JONAH

And from this one? Something else, something unheard of: grumbling, low spirits, absence of prayer, self-will, stonewalling.

Something of ourselves? The point of it all? Let us see.

In another view, the book is one of those immortal children's stories, serious by implication, much fun in the telling. Nothing more delightful than a tale around which 'children' of all ages can gather, and at the end, capture the point of it — piquant, elegant.

Jonah much resembles a character in a story concerning a certain Samaritan, and outsider, a pariah, we would say. Of him little was expected. But eventually, all such expectation was turned on its head, made to look ridiculous. (Lk. 10:30)

And both stories end with a question.

The question in each case, be it noted, contains its own answer. Should not God show compassion to people and beasts? And who showed himself to be a friend, despite all, to the man in the ditch?

Much has been gained, if the reader, grown attentive, puts herself in the stance of the originals — Jonah and the nameless one who comes forward to question Jesus.

We stand there, in their skin. The eyes of the heart are opened. In the Jonah story, as to insight into the compassion of God; a compassion which is strictly scandalous to the conventional believer — strangely enough, in this instance the prophet himself, Jonah.

As to the Jesus story, much is implied concerning who stands inside the orbit of God's favor, and who outside — whether in God's view such boundaries exist at all, then and now, or whether the 'line in the sand' is not drawn there by our ill will.

In any case, both the Samaritan and Jonah are to be accounted, in a sense, as — outsiders. Each, regarded through the eyes of surrounding culture, is an unlikely protagonist.

Also perhaps, unlikely in the eyes of those who themselves have been called — unlikely.

Imperceptibly that is, we come to accept a kind of mirror view of ourselves, second rate, first rate; this in accord with the multiple mirrors of friends, family, even adversaries, flashing in our direction their morse code. "This is what, who, I see when my gaze falls in your direction."

The conduct of Jonah would seem to indicate something of this: I've no followers to speak of; no one wants to hear from the likes of me, even Jawe is so at odds with my sense of things and people, sin and virtue, my will, God's will, my word, God's word.... So. Just watch. I'll play prophet in my own way!

Jonah and the nameless Samaritan — what good can come of these? Such are ordinarily regarded as — ordinary at best, faintly suspect or foolish, out of step. In any case, by no means to be emulated. See the priest and Levite gingerly passing by.

We take note of other prophets (the majestic character of an Isaiah or Jeremiah) and of a striking contrast to our author-protagonist.

And yet they and he stand side by side in our Bible, we are to learn from each of these, in highly different degree to be sure. Say it: Jonah, prophet 'malgre lui!'

Jonah and the anonymous Samaritan. Can we add, the resemblance between these two dissolves the 'insider, outsider' lines often drawn, and sedulously guarded, by the godly?

Jonah, be it noted, is not at all adverse to drawing the line himself, hard and fast. In certain ways, he embodies the worst in a stiff-necked covenantal people. We Jews inside, they of Nineveh outside!

And the Samaritan. Ironically and quietly, in selfless compassion, he goes about the affairs, unfinished or neglected as may be, of the self-styled 'people of God.' While their their 'godly' personages pass by the wounded man. Other affairs, other directions!

Something gets in the way of seeing in these two — a possibility, a stubborn, hard-won, unfinished greatness. There is a fault in the eye, a mote or a plank; and it impedes other eyes than Jonah's, or for that matter, the mysterious Samaritan.

No fault, be it added, in the eye of Jesus.

JONAH

In the later tale, as we know, Jesus plucks a nameless one from the shadows. Ancient prejudices, a mix of bad religion and worse culture, have set him apart — aside from a history called by the insiders, 'sacred.' Which is to say, ours and not theirs. Noble spirit, nameless one. Out of sight the Samaritan, out of mind, is the implication. He belongs — elsewhere.

A poison is at work; a social healing is badly overdue. Jesus sets about it. He will dare make of this nebbish the compassionate hero of a story. A shocker! "I shall deflate the racism, the virtuous pretentions of the inside players."

In Jonah's story too, popular expectation is set on its head.

Let us tell of a prophet, yes a prophet, with little or nothing of value to say. Godly insights announced with authority? Of these, nothing.

Stubborn, wrong-headed.

A prophet moreover who prays not, or seldom.

Disobedient. Rancorous, sour, chauvinistic.

In whom prejudice ages long, festers.

A religious man? He makes of 'Assyria, Nineveh,' dirty words indeed, laden with generational hatred. It is lodged in him, a stone in the guts, festering away. The memory of the oppressed.

A long fuse is sputtering.

"One must recall here the place of Assyria in Israelite and in ancient history; it was the first great imperial power, a bloody, aggressive and plundering nation....'

'This is the city which the author represents as the object of a prophetic mission from Yawheh; and Yawheh receives the repentance of Assyria. Clearly, ...compassion and forgiveness can go no further." (McKenzie)

(Consult also the book of Nahum on Jewish attitudes toward Assyria — a book that runs close to exultation over the ruin visited on an ancient enemy.)

Memories of old wrongs, forced exile, pillaging of the temple, enslavement, these constantly fed by resentment, oppress Jonah. No one, we note, is harming or threatening him. Sour memory is his burden; and in this he stands surrogate for the temper of his people and times.

Sour memory or liberating memory. We have a clue, an important one, as to the deep source of behavior, good and evil.

Something else of note. The task of this prophet, as he sees it, is in no way directed toward vindicating Jawe's holiness among the nations. Jonah's needs are simple. He wants the abomination destroyed.

(Much subsequent 'religion' has conducted its affairs in the world in a similar way. A passion for a paramilitary 'solution' to remove the 'irreligious.' A strong preference: the destruction of the enemy rather than his conversion.)

We might be inclined to think of I Corinthians 13:1 as written with the likes of Jonah in mind — not to speak of ourselves. Without love, we lose it. Jonah nearly lost it.

There came, so the story goes, a first command issued by God to Jonah: Go to Nineveh. And our drama is underway.

But what is Jawe to do, when Jawe's 'prophet' refuses, in effect despises and flees from, the errand assigned him?

Must God become the adversary of His own prophet if the lost are to be salvaged?

So afflicted, our Jonah. And here we are offered a clue as to his covert, even shocking flight. He sniffs the wind, he is wily as a hound on a short tether. And how is he to cut the leash?

Or shall he obey and proceed to Nineveh with a word implying — salvation? It goes against the grain, against supposition strong as death, the death of the heart. Jonah's religion kills the heart.

Who 'we' are, who 'they' are (so he might be thought to mutter in his beard) has long been public knowledge; the knowledge is set in stone.

Jonah, it must be said, knows his scripture.

This sudden outburst of mercy on the part of Jawe contradicts previous oracles of great moment, denunciations of the Assyrians and other mighty 'dwellers on the earth.' Ezekiel had promulgated them, a divine warrant issued against tyrants and their benighted peoples.

Did not a great one among the prophets say Jawe said: They are damned, I shall destroy them?

❖ ❖ ❖

Therefore, Jonah: This going to Nineveh can come to no good. Intolerable. I shall disobey until the mood of Jawe passes. He will come to his senses and know that I was of more sensible mind than He. That I was, shall we say — obedient to a higher law.

We have here a species of religion that assures the votaries, to their immense satisfaction: you are inside, chosen, covenantal. Then keep the circle tight and close.

The god of such worshipful folk speaks thus: Behold, I draw the line; it is for you to guard it.

Thus a purported vocation becomes an obsession. The inner circle of the saved tightens into a noose. And who is caught there?

❖ ❖ ❖

The temple of God, the temple of God! Psychologically, the insider devotes much attention to locks and bolts, their installation and upkeep. Which is to say, security, orthodoxy.

There is, of course, a price attached; the air of the holy place grows stale. So do its ceremonies and, above all, its ideas.

In time, the insider's self-understanding is reduced to this: there is — surely there must be — an outsider.

The temple, and the worshippers therein, honor the true God. They and they only.

This rigorous orthodoxy must be insisted on, mimed, made the subject of litanies and mantras. Night and day, watchmen must guard and forfend. For renegades and heretics lurk just outside the portal.

A hardened theology develops. Its purpose is to justify the inside-outside obsession.

❖ ❖ ❖

In the mind of Jonah, Jerusalem is a walled city under siege. It is the holy city, only if over and against it, there exists a Nineveh. The elect require the sinners.

Christianity has had no great trouble with this.

❖ ❖ ❖

(Mt. 7:3-5) "You hypocrite, take the log out of your own eye, then you will see clearly to take the speck out of your neighbor's eye."

JONAH

The text would seem to apply to Jonah, an early form of 'projection.' The 'speck' in the neighbor's eye, as Walter Wink says, is actually a 'chip' from the log in one's own eye.

Does Jonah need the 'enemy' to be 'himself' (a self, so to speak, unto himself, a false self, dare one say a 'religious' self)? Is the command to go to Nineveh to be understood as a mercy, a summons to 'face' himself? Is his flight from Nineveh a flight from — himself?

An ancient story that has withstood the frictions of time.

Draw Jonah in primary colors, in two dimensions.

A cutout image perhaps. Or carved in very slight relief, hardly issuing from the background.

Or he is wound up like a toy for flight.

But this resolve of his implies no great strength of spirit, nor does his haste proceed from immanent soul or self-command. Dread and anger shake him. It is as though Jawe were to shout angrily to a frail shy animal. (Only Jonah is not shy or frail; it is only that he loves his life beyond measure.)

He has no nuances. A weathered look, a rolling eye and set jaw, denoting it may be, a deep thoughtfulness. But more likely a deep willfulness.

Only later does the face soften and gain many moods, as though he were seen through a rain-blinded window. Or as though his eyes were blind with tears. A prelude it may be, to a joy he has never known.

He becomes human in the dark with no one to see, as is fitting: "When you pray, go to your room, close the door and invoke your God."

(There is something of a Jonah mood on us in these days. We have endured of late the suicide of a dear friend, a man of fame, of immense energy and surpassing talent. For years he gave himself to the needs of the homeless in our cities. He accomplished much and paid up.

He lived among the destitute and became their champion. He tested himself against the jagged edges of life in a great city, fasted for improbable lengths of days, on winter nights slept with the homeless in the streets. So living his life, he laid down a challenge to churches and secular authorities alike. A challenge to his friends as well; and we were brought to know how seldom we measured up.

Granted, he was heroic, for years. But he lost the human measure. He lost us too, for whatever we could offer. He cast some of us aside, for we could not match him.

More, many among us never wanted to; winners, losers, first or last place, hero or common run; this was simply not our game.

He was of the stature of a Jeremiah, we conceded it readily; and we were — Jonahs. No emulation in our bones, only — friendship.

So he dared the fates, ventured to the edge of life, the verge of the world that veers off dizzyingly into — a void.

There at land's end, at friendship's end, the voice he heard was a Berserker. He plunged over.

"Too long a sacrifice can make a stone of the heart."

Wherefore we pray. Deliver us from the single way, the only way, from obsessive heroism. Deliver us to the common life. Deliver us from presumption, from the despair that bears a double face — that of peacemaker and pacesetter. Instruct us in the many steps of the dance. Show us the multiple ways to become human.

And may our friend know the peace which his tumultuous heart denied him in this world. Amen.)

Jonah is an anti-hero. In this he matches our mood — both rather dark of mind, melancholic, on the down side.

And we're strangely grateful for this.

We see him, by hook or crook of fate (or providence) perversely taking the long way round; Tarshish for Nineveh. And then astonishing — he lands in our Bible!

Grateful for this less-than-hero. Heroes? Popular ikons, generals, politicos, they merit a second look, a skeptical one. They tend toward the bully, the greedy and violent.

They seem to grant no middle ground. They create losers in the process of winning.

We long for something else: steadfastness, courage to face the day, and (above all else) decent treatment of others.

Camus created perhaps the classic anti-hero in his novel *The Plague*. The doctor goes about his work in the stricken city, assuaging the afflicted, saving whom he can, simply keeping on. He regards himself as agnostic.

JONAH

When he is questioned as to why the city lies under the siege of death, his response is laconic, but it touches the heart of the matter: "They forgot to be modest, that is all."

The Jesuit on the other hand, a noted preacher, is rife with answers, a kind of theological windbag. One has the impression as the story proceeds, that the preacher of salvation is much in need of salvation himself. The sorrows of the dying and the survivors touch him lightly if at all. He announces only sin and punishment, those ancient themes of the heartless.

But there is hope, even for him, and eventually he undergoes a change of heart.

Contrast, opposition, light and darkness. Let it be suggested also that Jonah is a kind of opposite foil to Moses. It's of interest to trace the call of Jawe to each, the response (on Moses' part) of a gradually dawning obedience and understanding (Ex. 3-4).

And then the dodge of Jonah.

We have also in Jonah a peculiar double mind, enervating to true purpose. On the one hand, he is presented (and presents himself) as God's man, charged with a holy errand and word. And, on the other hand, the overt denial of vocation.

Astounding. The story of this little man (who quite possibly never existed) is taken up by Jesus, a fiction truer than truth. (Mt. 12:39-40) "As Jonah was three days in the belly of the whale, so will the son of Man be three days in the earth."

The least among us, we are reminded, is to be held in honor.

We have no psychologizing or agonizing as Jonah flees the summons. A simple story, a simple outcome. A little man who might have been a greater, but for a certain impeding, wizening influence.

He is like a November apple on a failing tree, a fruit that unaccountably failed to mature. Perhaps a branch faced too strongly northward. In any case, late autumn has arrived, and our apple is somewhat hard and green and out of complexion with the season.

JONAH

What to do? He and his like (for a good story involves many, though told of one) require a thorough shakedown, a ripening environment. Thus the story.

He springs from a people who according to their own prophets, are afflicted with a grave stiffness about the neck. The trouble has invaded the genes, so to speak, and by the time of Jonah, is strongly hereditary.

We cannot but take note of his stance, upright, head on high as though impaled on a ramrod. He will do what he will do, come Jawe or high water. And by the same token, he will not do what — which brings us once again to chapter one.

Not many words are recorded of our purported hero. Yet we adduce something that can hardly be missed. On the list of items to be salvaged from life's not better moments, his own skin ranks first.

Yield before Jawe, obey, depart on the moment for Nineveh?

His religion forbids it.

An epic? Perhaps, but if so, a kind of epical put-down. Strong elements of satire, even on Jawe's part a gentle buffoonery, needling, testing.

The note is struck early; Jonah's is the pedestrian way. Jawe simply speaks to him, no such epiphany occurs as terrified Ezekiel and struck him down (Ezk. 2:1). Or as descended on Daniel where he stood by the river, and fell prone, unconscious (Dn. 10: 4 - 10).

So we start with a rather conventional instruction from on high. Jonah is told to go to a foreign city. Once arrived, he is to announce that the wickedness of its citizens has reached the attention of Jawe.

But what is this? The command issued, our hero (of sorts) wastes not a moment; he all but scuttles off the page.

This purported prophet has quickly become an anti-prophet. Not for him the lofty way.

We almost had no book of Jonah at all! We almost had no more than a smoke, a passage, tracks on a road, a disappearance. Thus early on, we note a not entirely subtle deriding of the protagonist.

In light of the stringent command of Jawe, how short Jonah falls! Kierkegaard writes:

"And this is a pitiful thing to one who contemplates human life, that so many live on in a quiet state of perdition. They outlive themselves, not in the sense that the content of life is successively unfolding, and is now possessed in an expanded state. But they live their lives, as it were, outside themselves. They vanish like shadows, their immortal soul is blown away.... They are already in a state of dissolution before they die."

Jonah's soul may not be laved in grand virtue, granted. Nonetheless, our man knows a few things.

One, he's heard a voice sending him on a questionable errand; on behalf of a folk (goys) Jonah can summon no great affection for.

Jawe may, in his present mood, hold the spiritual well-being of Ninevehans as an urgent item.

But Jawe is Jawe, and Jonah is — well, we shall see.

Second, the long and short of it — he's not going.

A prophet, and a determined refuser? Unheard of!

Told to go north, he flees south, and fast!

Jonah calls to mind the story of the two sons (Mt. 21:28-32) who are, possibly, in a physical sense, one, but of double mind.

To each, we are told, a command is issued by the father: to work in the vineyard. One responded obediently. Of course he would do it — and then did nothing of the sort. The other was cheeky. He said — facing off with his father — no. And then went and did as told.

Go to the goys, says Jawe, tell them they also are included in the orbit of mercy. Tell them to shape up.

This most unsettling Jawe!

JONAH

Let us not hesitate to invoke current realities: the wickedness of New York or Bejing or Tel Aviv. Let us imagine a Jonah, sent to a great contemporary city. It is infected through and through with injustice and violence. And the messenger is instructed to deliver therein, a stern warning.

God is forever shocking the gods.

In such ways as this: A people despised as furthest removed from grace, beyond the pale — these may come to surpass those commonly regarding themselves as snugly within the orbit of grace.

Nineveh, according to the true believers, is Sin City. The appellation may or may not be correctly conferred. Up to a point, Jawe seems to agree that such alas, is the case.

But then, we are told, something happens. The Ninevehans, one and all, are wondrously, instantly converted.

Caution as to intemperate judgment is therefore advised. God delights in judging the judges.

There is the matter of divine threats to be taken in account. The fulminations lie like unspent thunders in the texts of the prophets; the pages all but mutter as they turn. Jawe frets at the backsliding of humans; prophets are instructed to bring sinners, whether domestic or foreign, to heel. Or, failing that, to spell out in fierce detail the impending alternatives: Armageddons, earthquakes, plagues, droughts.

What is one to make of such threats — especially since, more often than not, they are simply aborted? One expert offers a subtle comment:

"The divine threats, even the most categorical, are hardly to be taken as the expression of blind destiny. They rather express the will of a God who is merciful.... The threats attain their purpose exactly — when they need not be executed." (L. Gautier)

Deep waters here.

One of Jonah's least attractive qualities, call it envy, ire, spleen, is presented as a kind of dramatic warning. Take heed; our prophet speaks for all who grow impatient at the patience of God — who so react when rare items like borrowed time, hope, promise of mercy are offered those of quite different ilk, age, skin, nation, ideology, religious attachment, sexual proclivity.

Nineveh thus stands surrogate for all who are declared by insiders to be outside. Nevertheless, the citizens of Nineveh are to be shown compassion, to be sent a message: "You too count for much, to you I offer the dignity of accountability...."

Threats are uttered; they hang on the air, then shortly are dissipated.

The religion of Jonah is ruled by what might be thought of as a showdown mentality. Something like this: Jawe is for us only if He is against others. (The male pronoun seems peculiarly appropriate here).

What of the 'day of Jawe.' And when will it come to pass?

(And strongly implied: When shall we ourselves be vindicated, our holiness, integrity, be manifested to all?)

Our story turns ominous too, it has strange twists and turns. Jonah is a slow burning fuse of petulance. He stands for many of his compatriots; he echoes their sense that 'Jawe owes us much,' and this 'much' implies that 'Jawe owes the pagans not a whit.'

Why then should I, Jonah, extend myself in a thankless errand? "What we have undergone from the likes of these pagans!" "And was it not all endured for his honor?"

(1:14 ff.) Jonah, we are told, went down and down; first down to the port of Joppa, then down into a ship, then down into the hold. It is like a vain attempt to recapture childhood, then infancy, a return to a 'safe place,' a womb.

He will shortly descend further.

A mighty storm arises.

Tempests are a favored device of every story-teller since the Flood, a source of excitement. (We are after all wrapt in the story, we too are recapturing something of childhood.) Also a device to bring on a crisis, in view of an eventual triumph, to show how courage may prevail over brute nature.

Storms disrupt normal routines and timetables. They set ships and lives off course, delay arrivals. Disputes may break out on board, mutinies even. Decisions must be made in the teeth of disaster.

Voyagers, for the most part sure of themselves, people of substance on errands of state or economy or R & R, parsimonious as to time allotted this or that — such find themselves now and again tumbled ashore in strange, even bizarre places.

Perhaps even worse transpires, as they are brought low, tumbled overboard, reduced to ragged castaways.

And then, of course, God makes use of storms. As we shall shortly see, and Jonah shall see, and to no great credit of his.

Our story-teller is a master of paradox and the subtleties thereof. A storm rages. The crew turn to their gods in near despair.

And Jonah, the purported true believer, sleeps below decks.

Mum's the word. Not a syllable has he revealed concerning a certain recent event, his flight from duty — though his dereliction might be thought highly pertinent to the disaster befalling.

A prophet?

The storm worsens. Shortly Jonah's slumbers are shaken by the furious captain; that official names him in contempt, 'the sleeper.'

It is brought to Jonah's attention rather brusquely that while he takes his ease, the crew are toiling and sweating against their unsteady fate.

A truthful image: sleeper. With regard to true awakening, mindfulness, he sleeps life through. He is half-comatose, half-conscious — of himself, of Jawe, of his vocation. He lives like a sleepwalker whose only driving force is a nightmare.

Jonah reminds us of those other sleepers, the three disciples in Gethsemane (Mt. 26:36 ff.)

Such sleep is a kind of moral befuddlement, a numbing of soul. Too much grief to be borne!

JONAH

We tread softly here. We know our limit; we look with compassion on such sleepers and the relief they seek. Only a valiant soul remains conscious, alive to the summons of a terrible hour. Being conscious may even exact blood. (Lk. 22:44) "And being in agony.... His sweat became like drops of blood, falling down upon the ground."

Once awakened, Jonah is questioned closely by the captain. (1:6) In effect, how can this be — that when all are endangered, you neglect to invoke your god, even as we call upon ours?

We have in the scene a repeated implication of the story-teller. To wit, the faith of the pagans is admirable, the faith of the believer woefully wanting.

There, as the storm gathers force, our reluctant prophet grows suddenly articulate.

The faith he refused to offer the people of Nineveh he now declares in the bedraggled circle on the heaving deck.

The formula might be thought to roll trippingly from his tongue: "It is Jawe I worship, the God of heaven who created the sea and the dry land."

The confession is a kind of classic stereotype. Jawe is spoken about rather than addressed; a majestic being surely, but absent or at least distant. A gesture of fealty, no passionate commitment.

Jonah strikes one as an academician, a theologian.

In the hearts of the sailors dwells another reality entirely: a faith stirred mightily by the threat of death. A somewhat muddy mix of superstition and hope — these, and a courage that looks fate in the eye and dares its worst.

They decide to cast lots, to discover who, so to speak, is the Jonah in their midst. (An ancient device, we are told, by Roman savants, Cicero and Horace, designed to break the cover of the guilty.)

The dice roll.

(1:12) Jonah's reaction is typically curious. "Cast me in the sea, and the

JONAH

storm will calm."

How, we ask, does he know? Is the prophet so in touch with the divine will that he connects the calming of a storm with a human sacrifice?

Is this proffer of self-immolation an evidence of despair?

The lots fall to Jonah.

Meantime, the sailors, a minim of the Nineveh to come, turn spontaneously to prayer.

The sequence is is quite unsettling. The believer has slept through the storm, indifferent to the danger he has occasioned.

And the sailors? They are greatly distressed by the outcome of the lots. They renew their efforts, bend anew to rowing, hoping to reach land and save their sorry guest.

All in vain, the storm grows more fierce by the moment.

The sailors fall to prayer. We might range the world and come on no nobler 'pagans' than our present crew.

(1:15) Nothing avails, over it goes with Jonah!

The waves receive him, the turgid waters grow calm on the moment. And the sailors, we are told, offer sacrifice, and make their vows to the holy One.

Jawe, it appears, is everywhere to be reckoned with. On sea or land, it is nigh impossible that Jonah claim the last word for his own, the argument won.

Whether the sins of Nineveh be in question — or our fleet footed prophet — no matter the pretention, pride, self-justification, any or all of these are — penultimate. From Jawe the last word.

Period. God punctuates, then terminates the argument. Alpha, Omega, in My beginning is My end. The last shall in a wondrous sense, be first. A 'great fish,' otherwise unidentified as to provenance, becomes the vast vehicle of Jaweian ingenuity.

This creature, a noble leviathan of the deep, is dispatched by the divinity on an errand. As to the language of the instruction, or of the piscine consent, we know little or nothing. Whatever the word, Jawe spoke or hummed or whispered or thundered. And the fish, in contrast with the sorry prophet, obeyed on the instant.

We imagine the majestic regent of the deep speeding like an arrow over the pathless waters.

Then our man, thrashing about in the sea, is scooped up like a mawful of plankton. Gently he tumbles down and down the piscine gullet; finally to be deposited, oily but intact, in those spongy depths.

Nothing for it, there for a time he must abide — meditatively.

Engulfed he is in that cushiony darkness, ignorant as the unborn or the newly dead, of the outcome of this stupendous event, knowing nothing of direction, path, port of call. Loss of control. All considerations of moment, in the hands of — another.

And of time, neither dawn nor high noon nor sunset nor night nor day does he know. He is stripped to the bone of existence, dry bones. Ignorance and helplessness are his name. Credentials, proofs, self-justification — done with.

Jonah is at the end of whatever resources he could once summon. No more fleeing, no more self-justifying, no more evasion.

He is at the mercy of — Mercy.

He has been an image of folly, scheming, self-serving, tantrum and mood, pathetic childishness, grandiloquent emptiness. He schemed and equivocated and fled his vocation. And lost.

He drops his hands, empty. And he shines there in the darkness, all alight, a man made of St. Elmo's fire.

And Jawe is silent, like His own great sea angel. Jawe upbears and cherishes. All in the darkness of unknowing.

The poet Rilke is both comforting and disturbing:

"We have no reason to mistrust our world, for it is not against us. Has it terrors, they are our terrors; has it abysses, those abysses belong to us; are dangers at hand, we must try to love them.

"And if we only arrange our life according to that principle which counsels us that we must always hold to the difficult, then that which now seems to us the most alien, will become what we most trust and find most faithful.

"How should we forget those ancient myths that are at the beginning of all peoples?.....

"Perhaps everything terrible is at the deepest being, something helpless that wants help from us."

In his fishy hostel, Jonah sets himself to prayer.

This, be it noted, for the first time in the course of the story. It will be recalled that the pagan sailors pled for their lives in the eye of the storm.

But Jonah? Up to this moment, is he not a prophet without a message — dare we say, a prophet without God?

In the belly of the great fish, with no likely egress to the land of the living, Jonah has touched — bottom.

He went down to Joppa, thence down to a ship, then down into the lower deck. Now, captive in the great maw, he scarcely abides in this world.

At last I have him, says Jawe to himself (and the tone, it must be granted, hints at a measure of satisfaction, as of a fisherman holding aloft a catch). Let him dangle here.

For it may be, continues Jawe ruminatively, that our man will yet, despite all, come on a dark wisdom. Truly he has need of it.

It is an apt moment to recall again how the imagination of Jesus was suffused with the tale of Jonah. Jonah, persnickety and tardive — and Jesus, hastening toward Jerusalem — a likeness between the two? Indeed one would not have thought so.

And yet the likeness is insisted on, both with respect to the death-resurrection theme, and the theme of judgment.

To the latter first. Jesus draws upon the broadly implied irony of the Jonah story. Something strange happened on the way to Nineveh. Or in a later and more tragic and actual event, on the road to Jerusalem. The believers, the chosen, the covenantal people — all those words and names and evidences of a special sense of being in the world, of credentials and privileges — these are shaken out, emptied. (Mt. 12:41; Lk. 11:32) "At the judgment, the people of Nineveh will rise against this generation and condemn it, because they repented at the preaching of Jonah...."

It staggers the mind. Nineveh proves more believing, trusting, loving, penitential, apt for conversion — than all those true believers, the chosen ones of temple and Torah.

The analogy becomes a bitter pill indeed. The erstwhile pagans become witnesses for the prosecution, against the chosen. The neat scheme of salvation is unraveled, the sigil is reversed, truth is stranger than illusion.

The chosen have overdrawn their account; they are bankrupt on the day of Jawe. The beneficiaries, heirs, are the formerly despised, the goys.

As to Jesus' reference to 'the sign of Jonah,' there is an apparent difficulty. (Mt. 12:40) "Just as Jonah was in the belly of the whale three days and three nights, so will the Human One be in the heart of the earth three days and three nights."

The imagination of Jesus! He summons the ancient stories, draws them boldly to his use.

But if the story of Jonah is fictive and the story of Jesus factual, how can the latter call up the fiction as analogy? Deep waters here.

To His way of seeing, there are truths truer than fact. His imagination embraces the improbable and lo, all is changed.

How else approach the resurrection, except by imagining It? There is no reasoning can touch that outcome, no earthly logic. But there is rhyme to it, His morning-beyond-death.

Therefore we imagine. In a stupendous ruction, Jesus and Jonah are cast forth from the maw of death. Then they meet, unlikely brothers, face to face, the one a mirror image summoned by the Other. There they stand, delivered, on the firm ground of a new existence.

JONAH

We listen to Jesus, who insists on the likeness. Not, to be sure, that his temperament in the least resembles Jonah's. The likeness is in the drama of death, the 'going down' of Jonah eventually revealed at its truest; an image of the death of Jesus.

And a further stage. The death of Jesus, as Paul will take up the theme, is cosmic in scope — our death and coming forth as well. Jonah and Jesus - and ourselves.

In Merton's phrase, (along with Merton himself) abiding 'in the belly of a paradox.'

The paradox being; what seemed to be (and indeed was) the monstrous final claim of death, this is turned about, becomes the occasion of the plucking forth.

By a providential hand, Jonah is extruded from the belly of the sea beast, chastened indeed, and safe. And, of import to our analogy, quite of a new mind.

And Jesus? We name his outcome, for want of a better word, resurrection. Of its prelude we know much, the brutal circumstance that went before. It is as though the witnesses were determined to set down with exactness all the sorry details. No room for doubt! It was a corpse delivered over to a tomb; and the burial place sealed and guarded.

We know enough and more of that prelude we name Holy Week, (except perhaps that it was a prelude). But what of the new life proffered after 'three days and nights in the depths of the earth'? Of this we know next to nothing. The imagination is balked.

But what of ourselves? Paul speaks of this penultimatizing and pushing aside of the shrouded principality — the one who scrawls a graffito 'Final!' on every tomb.

The intervention is certain, period. Of details, hardly a word. The pen drops from his hand.

He must grasp at negatives ('eye has not seen, nor ear heard...'). Before such splendors as await, that magisterial mind is reduced to a stutter.

JONAH

(2:1-10) Rather tardily, Jonah bends to prayer. And one is led to reflect that nothing quite equals a triduum in a Leviathan's guts to bring one to knee.

Quite a transformation! Can we believe our ears? From this artful cantankerous dodger comes an altogether magnificent prayer! It is plangent, self-deprecating to the point of tears, lofty and majestic in its imagery, dwelling on the goodness and providence of Jawe.

His soul grows transparent at last, a lamp in the breathing darkness where he abides. And the prayer of Jonah takes its rightful place among the noblest of the Psalms.

A chant of triumphant deliverance.

We note the ironies implicit in the words.

The sailors on board Jonah's voyage of escape, we recall, fell to a prayer both seemly and timely. (Indeed Jonah seems to have taken a cue from them; or so the author would hint. The sailors' prayer and his, especially in their conclusion, echo one another.)

He seeks divine help at last, this stiff-necked prophet who once spurned the call of Jawe. A prayer of last resort; preceding it, what could only be named his eccentric wayward way to God.

What understanding at long last has come to him, what light in darkness!

Up to his present plight, he has been an adult (of sorts), caught up in a cautionary children's' tale. And how will he extricate himself?

His prayer takes its start from — the unlikely place where he languishes and lingers — from darkness and dead end, the manifest absurdity of his predicament.

Nothing previously from his mouth, of such words as he comes on now: 'distress,' 'outcry,' 'outcast' (indeed one had thought him rather in the nature of renegade), 'the pit,' 'soul fainting within,' and a promise — 'what I have vowed I will pay.' And finally a renunciation of self-will and stoicism: "deliverance is of the Lord."

A strange equilibrium is at least possible. He had placed himself, as he imagined, at the farthest remove from the eye of Jawe, had run to the end of the world. And at length, he reached only the end of a tether. It tightened and held.

JONAH

But Jonah is hardly to be thought a species of stiff doll, to be turned about this way and that by a guiding hand. Self-will! We have seen him in action, intransigent and much given to moodiness. Such as he will not easily be set right.

He fled and learned nothing in the fleeing; how then was he to be instructed?

The flight was outrageous; one issue only drove him, his own well-being. Let us see then, over what terrain and waters he must be drawn back, what losses he must endure, what altitudinous pride be tumbled, before he stands in the light.

It is all in his prayer, the way he will be drawn. By way of chaos, the belly of sheol, the deep, the heart of the seas, the flood, waves and billows, weeds, the roots of creation, the pit.

A long way home, and parlous beyond telling!

He speaks of idols (2:9); one thinks it a puzzling intervention. He thinks perhaps of Nineveh, and the work he shied from. If they are idolaters, so is he. Better, so has he been, no less 'serving vanities,' no less prodigal of 'grace.' Serving — himself, to no good purpose and no one's benefit, least of all his own.

And finally he offers 'sacrifice and vows.' (And perhaps he learned the gesture from the beleaguered sailors?)

He confesses that 'deliverance belongs to Jawe.' Much has he changed and all to the good.

The gain being — his letting go.

Nineveh, that far and fabled point of light, awaits. He is fit now for the world and the neglected task.

(3:1 ff.) So he obeys, an arrow straightened in flight. Goes, be it noted, because so commanded.

And still — he is given no message to deliver. Except the message to himself: Go.

As for the rest, "Announce there the words that I shall tell you."

It is like a droll tour de force, every word tells. There is a rather exact repetition of the first command: "Go to Nineveh." Then an entirely contrasting response.

What our prophet has lost in ego, he has gained in elan; he obeys on the moment.

Shall we call him transformed?

We approach Nineveh at the side of Jonah. We see the great city through the eyes of popular legend.

It is as though a tale of New York were bruited abroad, its grandeurs intact, indeed inflated, its shame and violence and greed vacated. And the tale, let us imagine, reached the ears of a remote Amazonian tribe.

Something like this: the word would filter down and down. "A divinely great city, three days' journey in breadth!"

We consider also Jonah's plight. He is a foreigner newly arrived, and from a people long at enmity with the inhabiting people. Worse, his message is hardly apt to render such an audience benign. It is an unlikely, even preposterous threat Jawe has entrusted to him. "Yet forty days, and Nineveh shall be destroyed!"

(We remember, centuries later, with what derision the words of Paul were received, in a strangely reminiscent scene in Athens [Acts 17:16 ff.]. And the apostle's was no such inflammatory message as Jonah's! Paul walked softly as an Indian scout, beginning with praise of Athenian achievements, on to his point: resurrection. And they turned away.)

Undoubtedly destruction is not the entire message of Jonah. Nonetheless, his words sounded like a drum of doom.

And on the instant — what? An effect out of all conceivable proportion to the cause!

The words of this stranger are launched on the urban air. We imagine a small fire, no larger than a match flare, starting up. The flames pass, as though the very air had grown combustible. Jonah is heard, by one or two, by a few, by a multitude.

It is astonishing, beyond all logic or experience.

Beyond — hope?

JONAH

Shall we venture something? The episode is an image of the wild, improbable hope of God?

Questions vex, trouble the heart, grant us no peace. The troubles of our time! The wars, the insuperable hold on imagination and energy; of violence, fear, greed, idolatry of death. Will there ever come relief, an end to our plight?

And then this image: the instantaneous conversion of Nineveh. It is improbable, impossible. It never happened, it never could.

Image, promise, vision. There it stands. In the (eventual) obedience of Jonah and its miraculous outcome, we see as though in a sublime elixir, a concentrate held to the light — a hint of meaning. Jonah, no longer playing a surrogate god, takes his measure at last. He grows modest.

And our implacable gross history comes alight, grows transparent. Nineveh is an image of all peoples and all time and of the end of time. Direction, outcome, non-absurdity, time and ourselves (God the chance taker!) — behold us, as such a God would have time and ourselves one day, one impossible day, to become, to be.

If we humans were capable of hearing, the miracle of Nineveh would 'come true' in the classical sense of the words. Only imagine! Beyond brute facts, beyond the yawning boredom of Athenians and the distempered leaders of Jesus' time and the colossal blindness of most of us, stands the longing heart of God. Scheming, providing, preempting even.

How shall Jawe open on our behalf a less tragic course than we blunder along, a less awful ending to the human adventure than we madly pursue?

Behold Nineveh, the change of heart, of structures, of the fabric, the very soul of people and things. A vast tidal wave sweeps filth and debris into a sea of mercy!

The heart of Nineveh beating to the rhythm of the heart of God.

Ourselves, as shall be.

Even through such unlikelies as Jonah, even through such as ourselves. This the Nineveh story provides: a glimpse, more — a promise.

What might be; more, what shall be.

Thus the dynamic of the story, so long delayed by the intransigence of — a prophet. Then, the whirlwind, the firestorm of the Spirit sweeping all before.

Wrought by a Word which had been denied, delayed, grudged — and at long last uttered by a notable refuser.

With such mad hope awakened by our story, shall we relegate the tale to a dustbin of myth?

We have never grasped the hope of God.

We are Jonah. We fear hope.

For what happened in Nineveh must first happen in Jonah, the letting go, the non-attachment. Detachment even to death.

The power of the story perdures. Jesus, as we are reminded, pondered it, claimed it, referred to it passionately.

To think of it breaks the heart. Jesus encounters a people by turns adamant, irascible, vengeful. The times are evil, the outcome ominous. For consolation, he draws on the wondrous conversion of the Ninevites and is thereby consoled and strengthened.

And more; for the story implies a heavy judgment against the religious leaders who are bent on destroying Him.

Jonah, we are told, went only 'a third of the way' into the great city. There, somewhere in a suburb, he had but to raise his voice. And it was as though a portent appeared in the heavens. The entire city, its commerce, pleasure, routine, came to a halt.

And Jesus? No Jonah, no evader of God's will, He dwelt among his own for years, reconciling, healing, sowing hope. Nothing of these, nor the sublime sum of these, sufficed.

Under the brusque threat uttered by Jonah, the pagans turned to Jawe.

No such outcome with the religionists of Jesus' time. We sense the heartbreak: "And behold, a greater than Jonah is here" (Mt. 12:41).

(3:6-9) The conversion cuts a wide swath; from low to high, slave to royalty the word of Jawe passes. Finally a kingly proclamation is issued: "Neither human nor beast, herd or flock, shall taste food or drink water." All the living are enlisted in the laborious work.

The herds and flocks are one with the great whale, the ravens of Elijah and the ass of Balaam. These too are messengers of Jawe (more prompt and obedient by far, than Jonah!). They too enable salvation.

JONAH

(3:10) And seeing this stupendous moral upheaval (someone has described the conversion of Nineveh as a first and greater pentecost) God undergoes a munificent change of heart. Change on earth, change in heaven!

There is in fact a long and striking tradition which tells of Jawe 'repenting of the ills threatened.' We know from prophets who went before, from Jeremiah and Ezekiel and on to the episode of Nineveh, that divine threats, no matter how explosively put, yield before tears, fasting, sackcloth, prayer. And this without regard to the prior status of malfeasance, whether of a covenantal people or others.

(4:1-11) Now (sigh) another turnabout. The mercy of Jawe lodges like a bone in the throat of Jonah.

So goes this strange reasoner; granted, he himself has been the subject of a great mercy. But was this not meet and just; is he not the Lord's anointed?

It is mercy for others, the outsiders, he cannot stomach.

A perverse will, we conclude ruefully, is easily come by, and is eradicated, like a bone in the throat, only with trouble.

The great city is converted.
And the event brings no joy to the prophet, only gloom.
Jonah withdraws.
He stations himself on a hill outside the great city.
One cannot help conjuring a kind of dour, brooding bird of prey.

His behavior sends a message, and not the most reassuring. Jonah is in fact playing armageddonist.

Quite an irony, a certified prophet in close theological combat with Jawe.

Jonah has no peace in God.

He is a primary heretic; and he dwells within the house.

Like a post runner finishing his stage, he hands something forward into history, tossing his burden to an oncoming rider (the message not yet delivered).

It is an astonishing word on his tongue, (hardly to be thought the word of Jawe!) a formidable armature of opposition, against this God of non-taliation and mercy.

God may have restored him to favor. But what of that?

Jonah thinks this a small matter, for is he not in the nature of a special case? Only dignum et justum then, that he be elevated to the status of spiritual satrap over the pagans.

And if required (to his splenetic mind it is certainly required) that he play executioner-by-proxy of 'those others,' dwellers outside the pale — why, so be it!

Small matter also that God has ordered the pale filled in; that God takes good pleasure in those who pass over, to and fro, and shake the hand of the adversary, declaring bloody matters ended once for all.

Jonah will have none of it. Brooding there, the mercy of God turns his heart to stone. His conduct is a testimony, preposterous, by turns voluble and wordless, to a truth. God, alone among gods or humans, is named He Who Suffers Fools.

Not gladly, but suffers them nonetheless.

This God, thinks Jonah, how is he to be borne? He changes plans without once consulting with his prophet. A courtesy to be sure, and long due. He bends low, lends ear to humans and their lunatic behavior.

Now behold, the former strenuous sinners are sinful no longer. They are wrapped in sackcloth, wailing out their pleas for pardon.

Is not Jawe tracing a zig-zag course in the dust of history?

And what does it all portend, concerning the people of status and their sworn spokesman?

Who, pray tell, are now to be accounted the chosen?

Jonah inflates like a blowfish with righteous indignation.

JONAH

He and his kind, all said, wear a kind of stale outmoded air. They are solipsists, stuck in their tracks, out of time and its tumultuous events.

Not at all, they counter. They would worship God; they are religious folk. Skillfully they weave a concatenation of texts that drum their cause.

God is their trouble.

What are they to make of this God, admissive and permissive at once of the laborious human ascent, deigning to bless, to watch over and cheer us on? And now and then to wipe the brow of poor Sisyphus, burdened with his rocklike conscience. Up he struggles, down the burden tumbles, no end of it, no outcome.

That climb of ours, so halted and slowed, celebrated and rejected and derided by the poets and philosophers, from the primitive myth- makers on to Camus and ourselves! They have brought hell to earth. Their only word for us humans is — pity; that, and a carefully veiled derision.

The human venture is essentially absurd.

Jonah's trouble is related, but other. He too is addicted to absurdity, another kind to be sure, than the Sisyphean.

It comes to this: He would have humans resemble his god, which is to say himself, in respect to punishment, retribution, unforgiveness. On this scale are they to be accounted 'chosen.' Or to be damned.

As for Jawe, Jonah would have Him in agreement, or....

Something amiss, something lacking? Of softness, of nuance — of the feminine. We sense in him (and in his god) a dire imbalance, lack of such qualities, such possibility of joy within!

In a former episode Jonah has sat, solitary and helpless in the belly of the whale.

There, as we have seen, he learned to pray, to wait in hope.

But these can be unlearned as well.

Here he unlearns them.

Above the city he frets and chews his beard.

And below him, under his jaundiced sight life goes on.

Dawn to dark, an uninterrupted rhythm, peaceable and chaotic, leisure,

JONAH

labor, converse, travel, commerce. Children, adults, the aged, birth and death, conflict and high culture; all the vagaries and variations of a great city hum away like a hive.

It is all as usual.

To our solitary, it is nothing short of outrageous.

The last day canceled, no catastrophe, no fire and brimstone?

His irascible spirit is demoralized.

Jawe's delight is in altering the course of things, turning creation counter.

Let us astonish them, is his thought. Stand them on their heads. Let us see, good-humored and serious at once, what will occur if night is exchanged for day, north for south pole.

We shall show ourselves merciful to the goys and scandalous to the true believers.

And then, we shall set ourselves a harder task: mercy toward Jonah.

And God sighs and shakes his head.

How difficult to love one's own!

The conversion of Jonah is more daunting than Nineveh!

The outpouring of 'hesed' that salvaged the city is concentrated with enormous patience on this despondent and vengeful one.

On God's part, the exchange is lightsome and immensely moving.

It is as though a prince set to work transforming a troll.

Self-justification above all!

Let sweet logic and sweeter poetry fly afar. Let paradox, compunction, brio, glee, benevolence, vanish from the earth.

Jonah, one cannot but note, has a highly selective memory at his disposal; he summons it.

Why, he declares, he knew from the start how dignum et justum was his first refusal to go to Nineveh!

It astonishes, the sophistic twist.

He addresses Jawe. The tone is one of injured innocence. His very virtue has been called in question.

JONAH

"Did I not say before I left my country, that this is what you would do?"
"This is why I did my best to flee to Tarsis."

And then the wonderful climax. We rub our eyes, we can hardly believe it. "I knew that you are a loving and merciful God, always patient, always kind, always ready to cancel your threats."

It is ourselves, fretting and frittering away our lives, perched on a very Everest (if Everest were a muttering volcano) of illogic.

We require the lesson, as Jonah plays out before us our own ferocious folly. As he underscores witlessly our emptiness, ignored and repressed.

How shall we taste, savor the sweetness of God?

Jonah is no freak. How many speak in his dour tones! How our universe is set muttering against mercy, how we summon instead to our side the gods of iron and havoc!

They are around us, they would be within us, a vocal plague on the air.

God is on our side! Let the Ninevehans be like us: obtuse, perverse, childish, punishing, vengeful, — or be not!

The voices speak from media and government and pentagon and war industry. They would even instruct us from pulpits.

They set alight the avenging fires of hell, we become brands and torches in a world made combustible. The world will end in fire! God wills it!

Thus Jonah on the hilltop, biding his time, ill hope against worse.

He is not alone. And Jawe is not his only interlocutor.

Jonah has history on his side. He is both patron and progenitor of an attitude, a religion, a version of God.

He and his version of reality (which are one, and inseparable) must prevail!

It is, all said, a war cry.
God reproves it, and tenderly.
(4:4) "Do you do well to be angry?"

JONAH

How shall God teach Jonah a better voice?
He will not be taught.
His anger, would be righteous, self-justified, is a wildfire. It takes hold. Multitudinous armies twitch into action, wars and more wars, retribution, hatred, murder.
The anger legitimates and blesses any outrage, any crime.
(For nothing in creation so makes of murder a virtuous thing, as a cross or crescent traced upon the sword) — God wills it!

Does God too grow angry? We are assured so.
But in God, 'hesed' overcomes anger; God is ultimately the tender One.
We, for our part, have taken the anger of God for very God. We preach sin and neglect forgiveness.
We fear mightily we cannot stomach the God who forfends, forgets, reconciles, takes to heart.

Thus a few artless sentences exchanged on an ancient hilltop bear an enormous weight of truth.
So simple, they are a blazing revelation of God — from God.

(4:3) How easy for us at the same time, to dismiss with a kind of superior contempt — maladroit, fractious, self-pitying Jonah!
We have in him, among other wonders, a very genius at seizing texts to his own advantage.
A great text suffers a kind of spiritual larceny: "Now then, let me die. I am better off dead than alive."
The citation is from a noble source, the prophet Elijah, as he flees the wicked and wearies of life on the run (I Kings 19:4).
To claim the words as applicable to himself, as Jonah does, is an exercise in theatre of the ridiculous.
And yet, and yet. Shall we grant him a grudging tribute — that of sincerity (albeit it an altogether wrongheaded one)?

A weird anarchic logic, if there be such a thing, lurks in his mind.
If God indeed is the God of the living, the One who restores, regenerates,

never entirely gives up on the broken work of Her hands — if all this is true, and if Jonah has been awry in thought and understanding, if he (except for his brief sojourn at the bottom of the world) has never made peace with the God of peace, if a word of vengeance must be declared native to God and a word of mercy foreign — why then it must be that creation is the very empery (and we the progeny) of death.

If if if.

If the Jonahs of the world are to prevail, we are indeed doomed.

Death to the Ninevehans! has been his cry.

Now, death to himself!

For who, dwelling in the maw and empery of death, would seek life, love life, give all for life?

We concentrate on Jonah and perhaps not wisely.

It is Jawe we need a glimpse of, an epiphany.

Jonah we know well, perhaps too well for our own benefit.

Before Jonah there have, of course, been many prophetic wrestlings between God and lofty souls. Many among the great obeisants have resisted the terror of height to which they were beckoned.

In such dramas, whether involving Jeremiah, Ezekiel, Job, Daniel, we catch glimpses, salutary and precious, of Jawe.

The method, the near madness.

Issuing from great conflicts come our ikons, exemplars, saints, martyrs. Our poetry, our tragic theater. From Job to Aeschylus to the stupendous 'terrible sonnets' of Hopkins.

Jonah is another matter entirely.

He is like a midget in a giant's costume.

His cause is puny, his language inflated.

And God is — patient.

In the scene on the hillside, the transcendent One enters in conflict with

JONAH

a prophet. The event has a history. Invariably such encounters are beneficial at third remove, to ourselves. They instruct us in the stormy nature of faith. Serious questions are raised. Little light is granted. We hear much of darkness, of walking therein.

Here, we have something utterly new, something previously unheard of.

The transcendent One lays aside all splendor, taking on a guise of the maternal, the patient, the gratuitous lover — unrequited, all but absurd.

Thus Jawe vis a vis Jonah.

How does God cope with a fractious child?

This would seem to be by far the more difficult task and test.

And it is not in any case the outcome that is at issue, as for instance that Jonah acknowledge his peevishness, learn to laugh at himself — simply grow up.

Does the pedagogy of Jawe succeed, does a more bearable or malleable prophet emerge?

Of the outcome we are told nothing.

Outcome is not to the point of this extraordinary tale.

The greatness of God is measured in this way: in conflict with Jonah and his kind. Ourselves.

The drama, it must be admitted, is hardly remarkable as to the quality of its human protagonist.

His part is in fact clumsily conceived and spoken, unelevating. Hardly is Jonah to be thought of as a Sophoclean or Shakespearian protagonist!

And yet, for some reason, touching on matters such as human pertinacity, what might be thought of as the Jonah in us — the drama plays and plays on. Time is the forbearance of God, in a world that has become a kind of perpetual and perverse nursery.

Let us take a close look at this tribe, squabbling and squalling — changelings and orphans and crybabies.

One would hazard a guess that they have been dealt with abusively. What is certain is that they are most abusive of others.

Their minds are cruelly inventive, edged with dangerous anger. Their weapons are at the ready.

These children are prometheans; they wield stolen fire.

They have drawn secret maps and concealed them here and there, diagrams of conquest, of earth and sea and air and space beyond.

This tribe allows for no peace.

How shall God bear with us?

Here is the testing ground, the threshing floor, the wine press of the holy.

Here also is the heart of the story of Jonah: our own drama, neither remarkable nor heroic. Staged, enacted again and again. The story of the God who hopes on, despite all. Who hopes that on some distant day, in some eon to come, by an outcome we are helpless to bring to pass, we will shed the skin of Jonah, a skin very like a shroud, for a better.

Well, there sits the prophet, hardly content or flourishing in spirit. And below him the great city, whose people have come upon a better way. Nineveh is converted, in spirit touched by grace, transformed, unharmed.

And all in Jonah's despite and spleen.

He flourishes only in the ruinous prospect of others.

One more lovely and lighthearted episode, and then we are done.

He sits there; day succeeds night. The heat of the sun beats intensely upon our vigiler.

And God makes a tender plant to grow and offer shade.

Shortly a worm (it is all done in syncopated time, this sweet confabulation) at God's instruction, appears. The worm, as worms will, turns; it consumes the sheltering plant.

Then more trouble: God sends an east wind that plays havoc with Jonah's unprotected poll. And his plaints are loud: "I am better off dead than alive."

In words both cunning, benevolent and provoking, the story is summed up by Jawe.

Jonah's grief for the plant's demise is off kilter. He is ecologically obsessed in one direction only, and that hardly a human one.

JONAH

While to Jawe a shady plant is a plant is a plant: 'it grows up in one night and disappears in the next.'

But what, asks God, what of the 120,000 infants of Nineveh, helpless sucklings and bawlers and mewers, who 'do not know their right hand from their left'?

(What, the heart cries out today, what of the children of Iraq?)

And then, as a tender afterthought, what of 'those many animals'?

The questions are, of course, unanswerable. By Jonah or ourselves.

And with this we leave our unlikely protagonist to his gloomy hilltop ruminations.

And Jawe? The last word belongs to Him. It concerns children and animals, which is to say, the future of living things. Whose well being, one concludes, was of small concern to Jonah.

But as to how this last word of God's tenderness was received, what change it wrought, where it beckoned our hero?

Perhaps more to the point, where it beckons ourselves?

For 'a Greater than Jonah is here.'

MICAH

THE TRUTH WILL OUT

A wild book, surely! True of the other prophets, doubly true of Micah, a torrid, icy mix of threat and promise.

Threat indeed, and given the folly and wickedness that seem endemic to us humans, fitting. Or so we think in contrite mood.

But promise? Dwelling as we do in the kingdom of betrayal, all promises are off. Or so we think, as near despair threatens, cozened, sold short as we so often are.

And yet, and yet. The promise abides, the promise of Jawe to be sure — and not the tattered and bartered excuses that in our lives, pass for the real thing.

Promises kept; the prophet's delight.

Praise cannot mount too high for the precious document that lies in our hands. Without cavil or excuse, Micah conveys a sense of the dire reality of his times; awful times, harsh and deviant and rife with division and injustice, a realm of darkness.

What is to be done?

In the first instance, we are urged to face our predicament squarely. Let us not fall into the pit of 'normalcy,' from which few issue again into the light. Let us take to heart the painful honesty of Micah and his noble companions. Let us walk after as they have walked before.

MICAH

One ponders the text, hardly knowing whether to laugh or weep. Recognitions! How consistently awful is the behavior of the great nations! Stone blind they stand before the criminal evidence of their predecessors — even as they rush to repeat the crimes, rush to ruin!

And then the absolute need, if we are not all to be driven mad, of prophetic thunders, breaking on the polluted air! Deprived of such outcry and witness, what could life offer?

A kind of 'second death.' And on earth, hell. No relief for the victims, no judgment upon the wicked.

1991. I open the book of Micah in a time of war. In church and state, a mad debate is in progress as to the justice or injustice of the slaughter. And the war goes on; international law is contemned, voices of conscience spurned.

Daily, women and children are slain. One feels to the bone the shame that hovers like a foul smog over the land. The military families (mostly poor and non-white) are deceived and benighted by blare and blah; the young soldiers, their lives hardly underway, led off like baaing sheep to the slaughter.

And the unspeakable crimes of the air force!

Day after day one seeks a measure of sanity, pondering Micah. There is a God who witnesses.

Let it be said, let it be hammered home: Despite all, the trump of judgment and accountability sounds against the empire and its follies. Thus it is written, thus I believe.

Micah much resembles another valiant spirit, Amos. Each is sprung from a country people, each is rugged and stern and lucid in conscience, dramatic and to the point in speech. Each inveighs against the power brokers who converge like a cloud of locusts on the great cities, from Samaria to Jerusalem.

(1:1:16)   Micah begins in medias res, a mood of 'take it or leave.'
He sees in vision a theophany, a Great Descent of Jawe from a kind of

MICAH

celestial temple. One notes that the vision is not granted for the prophet's own sake; the vision is unlike the personal ecstasies of Isaiah or Ezekiel.

Here, Micah is rather in the nature of a passionate onlooker, a kind of court reporter, a third person witnessing a judgment.

A social judgment to be sure, and hardly against the nations! If we are alert, we are astounded. His lightnings are loosed against the 'holy cities,' Samaria and Jerusalem.

All nature is shaken. The ecology of earth reflects the human tremors of this momentous event.

Why then the tremors, the shaking of foundations?

Shall we simply say the empires were, and remain to this day, deaf as the stones of the road?

They careen through time and this world; they write at pleasure, their version of history. Lackeys are summoned, artists, architects, pseudo-prophets. Whether in word or work, the resultant fiction tells of virtue, glory and valor, of just causes and conquests, of the splendor and intelligence of rulers, the huzzahs and adulation of subject peoples.

Micah is hardly impressed. Let us (we all but hear him) open a crack in this adamantine wall of — nonsense. Let us hear rather, and speak on behalf of, the foot soldiers and their families, the hoplites, the slaves who built the mammoth tombs, the captives, the tortured and disappeared. Let us make our own history, and tell our story — from below.

Thus the prophets, and their indispensable vocation. Precious as it is, and across the range of ancient literatures, absolutely unique. In no other land or culture have the likes of Micah appeared, pricking the conscience of the king. Nowhere such oracles, fierce and utterly fearless, denouncing the powerful, defending the poor and powerless, offering a vision of human alternatives. Dangerous, exhilarating!

And then those other court 'prophets.' Indeed our great ones often refer to them and always with contempt — a motley crowd of hangers on, drawn like parasites to a rot, pupating, multiplying their kind, even as the kingdom is more and more strongly drawn to imperial ways and means.

O prophet peremptory! These others are contemptible mercenaries of the word. They wither under the hot sun of his scorn. (3:5-9) "For you, night and no vision; for you, darkness and no divination."

We have in Micah both prelude and promise.

He begins with a noble biblical cliche: Jawe is not indifferent or absent; Jawe is a 'hidden God.' Jawe 'will come.'

The statement is consequential. The behavior of mortals occurs in time and this world, never in a void.

Protestation, prosperity, polls, pomp, successful routs and wars — together with the justifications masking the crimes — the eye of Jawe rests on all. All are accountable, especially those who consider themselves beyond accountability. This is the terror of judgment and the hope of the martyrs.

So here, Jawe 'descends.' Judgment is immanent.

The judges themselves, among others, are to be judged. As the Talmud later declared: "A judge should always imagine that a sword was pointed at his heart and Gehenna yawned at his feet."

And again: (Ps. 82:1) "A judge who administers justice equably causes the Shekinah to alight upon Israel; as it is said, 'He judges among the judges.'"

(Ps. 12:5) "And a judge who does not administer justice equably causes the Shekinah to depart from Israel; as it is said, 'For the spoiling of the poor, for the sighing of the needy, now will I arise, saith the Lord.'"
And again: (Is. 1:25 ff.) "The holy One, blessed be he, does not cause the Shekinah to alight upon Israel until the evil judges and officials are removed from Israel. As it is said, 'I will turn my hand upon thee and thoroughly purge away thy dross, and will take away thy alloy. And I will restore thy judges as at the first, and thy counselors as at the beginning. Afterward thou shall be called the city or righteousness, the faithful city.'"

So are the rulers hailed before the bar, superior though they consider themselves to law of nations or conscience; grandiose, contemptuous, self-

MICAH

deceived.

How unpleasant, untimely, impolitic, maladroit, extreme, truculent, is this upstart Micah, inflicting on the mighty his 'message from on high.' Is he not a mere unknown — graceless, judgmental, daring to instruct others as to God's way and will — defaming God's chosen ones?

It is invariably painful for the self-justified to be accounted — unjust.

Let us pity then, those great ones whose estimate of themselves is skewed in their own favor. For suddenly the likes of Micah appear. One jolt and the world has gone mad. The good opinion of the great ones, so dearly bought, is upended. Willy nilly they are judged, found wanting, convicted. And the entire process claims a divine warrant!

Micah cuts to the bone. His has the detachment of a surgeon — or a saint. He will, for good cause, let blood.

Did his words win a hearing, was he honored and hearkened to?

We close the book as we opened it, not greatly informed as to the outcome of such diatribes.

No matter, it is implied. There they stand.

Micah and his like exist in our scripture as a puzzling epiphany. They are worlds apart from our longing for neat, satisfactory endings. Unappetative egos as they are, we may take them or leave. They are sent simply to speak the truth. They utter it, and that is all. The outcome is in other hands.

As to another savorless matter, Micah, God help us, is — judgmental. He stands before great or lowly, as a surrogate judge, ferocious, incandescent with indignation and fury.

He is possessed by the hot anger of the just. But his spirit is complex; a tender, even plaintive note is also raised. Attention to this is crucial, if we are to see him whole. (1:8)

Like a Jeremiah or a Job, he is stricken by the ills of the world, by injustice and recourseless suffering. He loses control, lays his soul bare: "I lament and wail, go barefoot and naked; I utter lamentation like the jackals, mourn like the ostriches."

MICAH

And he knows that he too stands under the fierce light of the judgment he invokes on others. (But for the most part, this is implied; it is as though his stance before God were once and for all taken for granted).

(1:6-7) Actions here and elsewhere attributed to Jawe ('I will make Samaria a ruin'; 'I will lay bare her foundations'; 'I will break her idols in pieces...') — these can be thought of in two ways.

According to the first, the 'threats' are to be taken as simply natural outcomes. Judgment and accountability are expressions of the moral structure of the universe, the laws of nature. To act in the moral realm is willy-nilly, to accept consequence.

'What goes around, comes around,' is the expression.

It could hardly be illustrated more clearly than in verse seven. The idols were paid for with the salaries of harlots, themselves symbols of the prostitution of the land — to mammon.

The idols will come down, the ill-gotten gain all a waste.

In another sense, the ruin wrought against the natural world by us mortals is to be taken parabolically. Images of downfall and destruction, as 'laying foundations bare,' 'breaking idols,' are mirror images of the human condition, of the break-up of community, of moral chaos.

(1:10-16) In the Hebrew, play on words abounds, we are told, as Micah names the catastrophe immanent to the towns of Israel.

In a parallel way, we might think of American cities and the claim implicit in their names, to 'newness': New York, New Canaan, New London, New Brunswick, Newton, Newburgh, New Haven and so forth. A boast implied, a departure, a fresh start. No more the crimes of the old world cities!

And yet, and yet. How speedily the claims are canceled, the boast proven empty, the tired, repetitive, stereotypes that emerge in these 'new' settings!

We venture on the streets of any 'new town' in the land. Crimes abound, socialized indifference and numbing, homelessness, evictions, political chicanery and greed, racism. Original, ironically made new, newer forms of cruelty and injustice. And yet the crimes are old as those denounced

MICAH

by Micah.

(1:16) The vision of lurking ruin all but drives the prophet mad. In desolation and anguish for 'the children whom you cherish,' he literally urges his hearers to pluck out the hair of their heads.

Thus also today, the all but insupportable anguish, the wars, the wars, bewildering, haunting.

There have occurred to this month of 1991, three self-immolations in protest. May these tormented souls find peace at last!

Others of us, grieving for the dead, keep at what little we can offer, seemingly fruitless as it is, day after day.

And for a multitude of others, whom the media victimizes and fixates, there remains only a kind of functional despair.

(2:1-5) Seizure of lands, interestingly enough, is first in the list of social sins. Cheating the poor of their holdings, evicting them for payment of debts, brings its own revenge.

God mocks these heartless ones; they will lose their loot to foreign enemies. The losses will be irrevocable.

(2:6-11) But who lends ear to Micah, this forecaster of doom and gloom?

Protests mount against him. And the prophet's riposte is mockery: "'Stop preaching at us,' they cry, 'stop preaching such things!'" Stop pouring out on us this flagon of God's wrath!

Predictably, they invoke the covenant, that universal solvent and savior and credential — whose glory Micah would forsooth, strip from the chosen! "Are God's words not benign toward God's own people?"

Micah is adamant, yields not an inch. To compromise is to lose all.

So he renews the assault. He sees works of injustice teeming like maggots under a flimsy cover, purported favor from on high. "It is you who prove to be enemies of the people!"

These parasitical hangers-on! They seek out others who will echo their debased language, flattering, cozening the great ones. (Clerics, preachers, bishops flitting about the corridors of power, even in the midst of a horrid war, offering warrant and cover on behalf of mass murder!)

If only Micah could be persuaded to join in the ruse of power, to bestow a blessing on shady matters, ensure a solid return for vicious undertakings!

Scorn and bitterness beyond measure! They consider themselves enlightened? To him, they are simply drunk; power, ego, greed have turned their heads awry. Mockery again: "If only there were an inspired one who would forge this lie: 'For prophecy I pour you wine and strong drink'" — there, cries Micah, "would be a prophet after their own hearts!"

(2:12-13) And yet, after much contention and bickering and reproof, on behalf of the demoralized and humiliated remnant, (and their betraying mouthpieces as well) there remains — the promise, intact. The theme is an ancient one: restoration and return. "I will surely gather all of you, will gather the remnant...."

One is hard put today to take the promise to heart. Wars unending, and we helpless to assuage the suffering inflicted by violent authorities; wayward, arrogant, numb.

And yet there it stands on the page: the word of Jawe. What to make of it? Do the prophets serve us only promises, illusions rosily indefinite, so long delayed as to have no bearing on present horrid event?

How dampened our spirit, how little remains of combustible hope!

We pray for an act of God to restore our humanity, to lift the yoke of pharaohs from our souls. "A noisy multitude, they shall burst open the gate and go out through it!"

(3:1-4) For the leaders, renewed contempt, fury, denunciation.

Many play the game according to accepted rules. Shall Micah then hang upon their words, accept their bribes, observe a covert, complicit silence?

Not for a moment. Face to face he addresses them: "Is it not your duty to know what is right?"

They have sworn to uphold the pact, the covenant. Instead, they have grown utterly reprehensible, 'enemies of the good, lovers of evil.'

Plain talk, scalding, truthful.

The imagery that follows, the horrid details! Such officials are at the same time maitres d's, chefs and guests at an orgy. They prepare, cook and feed on human flesh.

And these are purportedly religious men. One imagines them concluding their calamitous feast and turning with blood on their hands — in prayer to Jawe. And God turns away, sickened.

A like surreal imagery, we note, is offered in Revelation. Images veer between battlefield and banquet hall. What emerges is a composite horror, an image of war. War is a wanton feast of carrion: 'the flesh of kings, flesh of military officers, flesh of warriors, flesh of horses and their riders, the flesh of all, free and slave, small and great.'

And a supreme irony: the guest are summoned to the 'banquet of God' by an angel. (Rev. 19:17-19)

Total war, lubricous banquet.

Thus is unmasked the truth of imperial criminality. The crimes are perennial; they are ideologically justified (religiously justified), concealed, evaded, explained away. Are not the wars of empires invariably just?

And the churches nodding 'yes' with supine gravity, as though they spoke for any god but Mars.

"They eat the flesh of my people ... like flesh in a cauldron, like meat in a kettle."

"You who abhor what is just and pervert all that is right, who build up [America] with bloodshed, and [Washington] with wickedness...."

Let it be said plain. The indictment is laid afresh, against Mr. Bush, his warriors and necromancers, the officers of the U.S. Air Force, the weapons' makers, the Congress, the Supreme Court.

The crime, among others: the incineration of hundreds of women and men and children in a Baghdad air raid shelter in February of 1991.

"God shall hide his face from them at that time, because of the evil they have done."

The indictment also must include certain religious eminences, tainted with thinly masked, usurious greed. These puppets will proclaim 'Peace!' (translate: 'just war!') for a price, for a place in the sun of lordly favor (Cardinal Law, Mr. Graham et al., take note).

MICAH

Concerning the crimes of war, such as these have nothing to say. And their silence is blasphemous, for it implies the approval of Jawe. "The sun shall go down upon the prophets, and day shall be dark for them.... They shall cover their lips, all of them, because there is no answer from God."

For these, according to Micah, the bright sun has sunk; only night around and within. That, and the scornful silence of God.

And what of Micah himself?

'The breath of Jawe' burns in him; he has become a very furnace of justice. A fierce joy lights his bones.

The fire consumes, but his spirit doubles its stature. In awful purification, he gains 'strength, justice, courage,' he grows incandescent with self-knowledge. And with political wisdom as well. It is given him to know the truth, that he may 'declare to Jacob his crimes, to Israel his sins.'

(3:9-12) No other prophet, not even Isaiah, equals Micah in the furious denunciation loosed upon chiefs of temple and state.

He has endured the regime of those who 'render justice for a bribe,' of a priesthood who 'give decisions for a salary,' of prophets who 'divine for money.'

A hundred years later, the prophecy of the destruction of the temple was quoted by the Judeans who defended Jeremiah. (Jr. 26:18-19)

Yet despite all their efforts, Jeremiah was condemned out of hand. It is clear that Micah too risks his life at the hands of the temple coterie.

"Yet they lean upon the Lord and say, 'Is not Jawe in the midst of us? No evil shall come upon us.'"

The ploy is at once ancient and new. The authorities stand in a safe place, do they not? What need then of argument or defense? An age old hermetic apparatus of church and state must be thought to speak for itself.

Of what import such resources as we control, power and money and prestige, if not that we and no others (let alone this solitary undocumented alien) stand as very oracles of God?

Thus faith degenerates into bad faith. Priest, prophet, secular leaders, all join in a chorus of self-justification. Are we not sons of the covenant? Is not God on our side? And this being true, what evil can touch us?

MICAH

Against these Micah wastes not a word. No refutation of their sordid claim. It is long since canceled by their behavior.

And this silence of his is also a parable, and useful for the future. Claims, counter-claims — and who speaks for God? Here and in the future, in Micah's time and our own, let the contest of the prophets, face-to-face, proceed.

For Micah the matter is a simple one. Hearken to the word by all means, hearken and obey. But look also to the conduct. The one who speaks for Jawe does the works of Jawe in the world, works of justice and peace.

And if in the lords of earth, word and work do not concur, look elsewhere for the will of Jawe.

Look, he dares imply, to me, Micah.

Lo, a cunning apparatus of civility and salvation has ground to a halt, and this exactly when the arrangement is most skillfully dovetailed with self-interest, highly touted, prosperous, securely in place. Bribes, fat salaries, mammon — a vile surrogate for the justice of Jawe.

Micah is granted to see the all but invisible hairline fissures opening, to hear under semblance and show, the rumblings of a quake.

He sees something else. Concurrently and inevitably, while the few are prospering unjustly, a multitude is dissolving in misery. Injustice stalks the land and haunts the temple. It wears the gaunt face of the victim.

Is all well in the land, are the coffers filled, the priests complacent, church and state humming their tune in harmony? Micah hearkens to another voice, a grave, measured diapason.

Like a vast outgoing tide it draws along the singers and their tedious harmonics of 'all is well.'

Out they go. Beyond their depth, and drowning.

The soul of Micah is like the soul of a shoreless sea. He orchestrates the sublime rhythms of moral consequence.

There is a hint here, and more than a hint, to be attended to. The text reaches like a living pointing hand, in our direction.

These notes are set down in March of '91:

A spasm of military glory erupts in the land. We have prevailed yet once more over our enemies. Indeed, thanks to a weaponry of awesome and indiscriminate power, victory has come quick and cheap.

An immense victory! The Vietnam syndrome scotched, once for all! Veni, vidi, vici; presto, a mere snap of the giant's fingers, and the thing is done!

If one were to trust the media (and only a foolish head would do so), never on land or sea has there been so clean a war, except perhaps in the fictions of hi-sci films. The images presented to the public (after a meticulous screening by the military, to be sure) were unprecedented; the war was no more than a bloodless 'surgical operation.'

It was as though the land of the enemy were a kind of hospital operating room. A few mysterious masked figures, neat and bustling and skilled as surgeons, bent above a winking console and screen, pressing this button or that.

The screen showed a land unpopulated as the moon, pocked only with military installations. Which our 'smart' missiles proceeded handily to remove from the earth, with no damage (as far as could be seen) to (merely hypothetical) humans.

That multitudes died, and horribly — soldiers, women and children and the aged and ill — the bloodshot fact was simply excised from the scenario.

Regarding the bombing of the Amariyah shelter:

"This reporter viewed the unedited Baghdad 'feeds....' They showed scenes of incredible carnage. Nearly all the bodies were charred into blackness; in some cases the heat had been so great that entire limbs were burned off. Among the corpses were those of at least six babies and ten children, most of them so severely burned that their gender could not be determined. Rescue workers collapsed in grief, dropping corpses; some rescuers vomited from the stench of the still-smoldering bodies."

(Columbia Journalism Review, May-June 1991)

"The shelter housed 500 Triple decker-beds. Gulf Peace Team interviews with neighborhood residents revealed it was very crowded

that night. February 13 was an Islamic holiday; occupants of the shelter held a celebration. Some of the 17 survivors were people who had slept in a hallway because of overcrowding.
(*The Fire This Time*, Ramsey Clark)

Not to be wondered that our leaders were obscenely jubilant. Not at all wonderful that the churches, feebly objecting as they did before the war, were cowed by the speedy outcome.

There was no mood to bring judgment crashing down like the gavel of Jawe upon the perpetrators of mass murder.

Indeed in most sanctuaries, quite the contrary; president and priest each in his own sphere, makes common cause, whether by silence, inertia, or open and criminal rejoicing. And for the moment, political prospering.

Nevertheless. Come Micah, shout it aloud:

"Therefore because of you, your land shall be plowed up like a field, your proud cities reduced to rubble, your temples overthrown and overgrown."

(4:1-14) So we come to one of the high points of the Jewish testament, a triumph of the believing imagination; noble imagery, a light struck in the darkness of centuries.

Swords into plowshares! I give thanks for the text, for all it has meant to the peacemakers, always and everywhere.

In 1980, gathering in prayer and discussion regarding the nuclear arms race, eight Christians discovered the text anew. Thus was undertaken the first of the Plowshares actions, in nuclear arms factories, air bases, submarine bases. A hundred of us, Americans, Europeans, Australians, to this day have endured both trial and prison in a nonviolent effort to preserve life — to preserve a reality even more endangered — hope.

Our text is in a sense, nobly redundant. It is found whole cloth in Isaiah also.

We need not linger over a critical discussion as to the why and wherefore

MICAH

of the repetition. One is simply grateful. How remarkable that words of capital import, expressive of so unlikely and wild a hope, should be the common pronouncement, word-for-word, of two prophets.

It is as though one such proclamation simply would not do. The nations converted to the ways of peace? Come now, be sensible; the nations are the nations are the nations. Their very health is war!

So mad a hope, stated in contrariety to the plain evidence before commonsensical eyes, in face of the usual violence of street and home, of economy and military, of courthouse and jail, of church and state, of our history and experience, the banality and blatancy of it — how easily driven offstage is such an unheard of hope!

Nonetheless, it must be insisted on, underscored. The eye must discover it, wild with surprise, amazement, delight, twice incised on the heart and mind of great spirits, an absolutely central text of our bloodshot history, a fierce contradiction of millennial misbehavior, a momentous turnabout — witness of two visions.

The image is bathed in a serene light of hope. There is first of all the image of the 'mountain of Jawe.' It rises majestically in the dawning sun, as though shouldering aside the surrounding hills. On its summit rests the temple.

And we have at once perspective, eminence, a noble center, pride of place — and more, a clear summons. To this nub of a longing creation come 'the nations.' The message is unmistakable: The mountain and its crown jewel, the temple, are a political as well as a spiritual reality. The two are at length one.

Something momentous, it is implied, has transpired in the world at large. It had its start on the holy mountain; it can be described only as an act of God.

We grow lightheaded with the glory of it; we scarcely credit our eyes, resting on so astonishing a text. The image flies in the face of worldly wisdom; it is daily declared null and void, as wars deface and debase our fair creation.

What are we to make of it, fated as we are year after year, to mourn the crimes of our nation? What make of the promise, buried out of sight, out of mind, our only history that of wars abroad and domestic attrition — with more of same, we can be sure, in the making?

How came it to be, such an oracle? It declares that the nations have shed their armor and cast away their weapons. In effect, they have ceased to be — themselves: incurably, addictively, perennially violent.

They, which is to say we, no longer need bear the shame of war, worship the idols of war. At long last the nations submit before the God of peace. Their people stream toward the temple, approach the heart of creation, to bear witness, to worship in spirit and truth.

Equally astonishing, the interior change. The people search their hearts;they discover a different way of existing in the world. Against all prospect, against the brutal derangement of our humanity wrought by war upon war, they discover — the ways of peace.

(4:2) "Come, let us go up to the mountain of God." A song beats on the air as the people stream toward the temple, a psalm of pro-gress. It has also elements of exorcism; it places on their lips the new reality that dwells in their hearts. The words are of penitence and chastened hope and mutuality. No distinctions of rank or place; all, high and low, are intent on song and pilgrimage.

Citizens of empire and neo-believers, they (we) have much to unlearn; even more to learn.

The pilgrimage is also a parable. It is as though, in the course of coming to believe, step by laborious step, the people are being stripped, disrobed. Had we put on the national flag for a cloak? Was this our prideful vesture, our utterly false and banal identity?

Mysterious hands are casting aside the filthy rags of the past, the 'ways of the nations.'

From unfaith to faith, which is to say, from violence to a renewed heart and mind. The venture is chancy, fleshly, gradual, consequential, political. It is also beyond our deserving or capacity, a matter touching the heart and nerve and marrow, a matter of a 'new creation' in place of an old.

Which is to say (as Paul will declare centuries later) the new creation is to the old, the believer is to the 'dweller on the earth' — a nothing, a voice, a zero.

What we once were, what we are called to be. Our vocation, honor, hope, at long last the 'why' of our place in the world.

"That God may teach us God's ways, and we may walk in God's paths."

Each generation must translate the text anew, bring it to ground. What are godly ways, and God's paths, where do they lead?

Are we teachable at all? At best, slow learners!

We have known in the world, to our utmost despite, little beside ungodly ways. Who among us is not wounded in our humanity, lied to, cozened, subject to a moribund leadership, all but broken under the winds of war?

God's ways. Which is to say, and for this generation, the ways and skills and works of peace.

Despite all. Despite the wars, the preparations for war, the enduring irreformable ways of war — in Vietnam, and Panama, and Iraq.

"That God may teach us..." since we discover to our confusion of spirit, that it seems beyond our powers to teach one another or to learn from one another ways which are godly and to that degree, truly human.

A hard lesson this, and never entirely learned: that we learn to behave humanly in a world which is manifestly and virulently inhuman.

(4:4) And at length, at long length. "They shall sit under vine and fig tree, and none shall make them afraid."

The gentle promise is in the nature of an oath solemnly struck. "The mouth of God has spoken."

Can we walk with that promise?

(4:5) And the people round off the ancient oracle with a liturgical verse. It bespeaks (or invokes) a notable clarity; in effect, it is in knowing God that we come to know who we are.

And further: knowing God, naming and worshipping God, we are also enabled to name the idols. In more senses than one, behold the wisdom implied in the gift of faith.

Elsewhere, confusion thrice compounded. A weird mixture and interpenetration, god talk, banalities of loyalty and patriotism, a religion

MICAH

wrapped round in flags and ribbons, a religion dead and wound about in a shroud.

A religion of the sword. A religion of the dollar. A religion of free enterprise and unfettered appetite.

(4:6-7) 'The lame... those driven off... the afflicted... the remnant....' This is a strange and strong language, the stubborn preference of this regnant Jawe.

And not merely a preference, but an unmistakable choice-in-favor. God chooses, then creates a new reality. Making much of little — Jawe's delight. The disabled and wounded become God's own flock, the 'remnant' of which we have heard much, from Exodus onward. Of the travail of these exhausted and wayworn ones, a powerful people will emerge.

(4:9-13) Two ineluctable events, one following pell-mell on the other. First, exile, mourning, loss of all. Then, restoration and return.

It is the most ancient and terrible of rhythms — and who has not, in one fashion or another known it? Summed up for Christians with finality (and yet not final at all) in the death-resurrection of Jesus.

The rhythms are played out, surely in minor key, but nonetheless surely, in the lives of the faithful.

And here and there in our lifetime, in no minor key at all; a passionate, immediate, literal playing out of the original; in torture, seizure of land, rape, violent death, disappearance.

And the heartlessness, the void. Those who inflict, those who evict, refuse, deny, betray — these under cover of authority and guns are guilty of prodigious crimes.

(4:12) For such, the judgment is final and abrupt, a summation, a dismissal: "But they do not know the thoughts of God, they do not understand his plan, that He has gathered [those others] as sheaves to the threshing floor."

That preference of Jawe once more. And more than implied, stated flatly; the rejection of ruinous authority. Indeed such as these, the 'many nations,' contrive plan upon plan, military, economic, educational, (religious to be sure); five year plans, war on poverty plans, national recovery plans, 'new world order' plans. It is all fiction, delusion. It issues from contempt, the will to control and enslave.

For this reason they fail. The nations have lost (or rather, despised and spurned) the center, the human, the direction — as defined, bestowed, revealed by God.

Of every plan of this tainted ilk, two things may be predicted. Each, despite all disclaimers and sweet-tonguing, is a form of warfare against our humanity. Our souls will be diminished, their fires extinguished, in proportion as we fall in, willy-nilly becoming another factor, integer of the 'plan.'

We have here repeated an ancient biblical insight: The faith of the 'remnant' does not go unchallenged.

This must be accounted both tragedy and triumph; on the one hand, that so feeble a community should be regarded as so great a threat. And on the other, that so great suffering be wrung from the faithful, simply because they choose to utter their 'no' to the almighty mongers.

The plans of the nations, as is plainly in view here, push hard against another plan. 'The many nations are assembled against you'; you, that is, the 'remnant,' the 'wounded,' those to whom the plan of Jawe is made manifest. Who are indeed the heart and pith of that plan, in whom God's plan both lives and is dramatized — like it or not, reject it or not — is made known to the nations at large.

Each and every imperial contriving, without exception, will come to naught. This is a simple matter, though attention to it is much neglected.

The confabulations of the nations are hailed, promulgated, set in place with fanfare. And one after another, the plans totter and waver and fall of their own weight and ineptitude, houses of cards. For the nations know not the plan of God.

The game goes on. 'Not-knowing' is both inheritance and legacy of the nations. It is their self-definition: literally to know it all.

Need it be added that the nation has a plan for the faithful, as for everyone else? The faithful, like everyone else, are to become - faithless.

MICAH

True believers, yes, but with a difference. One's being Christian or Jewish or Buddhist will become an adjectival matter, a modifier at most, of the main and central noun.

In day-to-day practice, calculation, speech, choice, one is to be American first — this together with all baleful implications, whether in political or economic or military sectors, that follow.

In practice, by the same token, one's faith will shortly become — a former faith, moribund, banal, a dead letter. The kingdom of God 'within' is bartered away for a mess of pottage.

One has joined the know-nothings.

(5:1-5) The messianic hope: a Someone, otherwise unidentified, will snatch us from ruin.

That perennial cry, echoing down the centuries! An exalted hope and a degraded one. Again and again among Jews and Christians, Marxists and confirmed capitalists, it is declared: he nears! Or in despair: he is still afar!

The hope is seized on by our gospel. Both Matthew (2:6) and John (7:42) incorporate it, drawing upon our text, daring to bestow on the hope a local habitation, Bethlehem, and a Name — Jesus the Christ.

Frequently the hope is secularized, a messianic mess of conventional promise. In America, every four years or so, like a fish with no memory, cultural optimism rises once more to the stale bait, named 'free elections.' The fisher-citizens are transfixed or inflamed, as the line bobs mysteriously in the water.

Then lo! the reel spins and the fish is taken.

And, alas, must be cast back, rejected! It is either poisoned or undersize. In any case, nothing gained.

(5:5-15) There follows a complex interplay: forces old and new, complementary and antagonistic, divine and all too human.

We had best take the passage in globo, for a start.

We begin with a quotation (5:5-6). It is as though Micah were reporting on the pretentions of his own people, the Judeans. They make a large boast, these lilliputian folk; or perhaps they see themselves as a valiant David standing up to the gigantic Goliath named Assyria. "Just let them dare invade us!" "We'll show them!"

Not only will they utterly repel any attempt at invasion, they will counter by invading and occupying Assyria!

Thus a great chatter of tongues and clatter of weaponry, as Micah hears it in street and market. The challenge, from a worldly point of view is pathetic, the roar of a mouse.

But there is a deeper issue. Such talk indicates the death of trust in Jawe, for Micah the nub of the matter. Bellicose, irresponsible, mocked by Micah, the people of the pact are themselves being transformed and hardly for the better. To all intents, Judea sees itself as a kind of mini-Assyria.

And the awful declension, as Micah realized to his dismay, turns about a simple, utterly crucial matter: militarism vs the oath of covenant. Are the people sworn to nonviolent trust in a nonviolent God? If so, verses 10-15 must be verified.

(5:7-8) Meantime, the 'remnant,' the faithful ones, are to attain a sense of themselves drawn from images presented by Jawe. As here.

And yet once more, the stark contrasts implicit in the texts urge us to proceed with caution. Who are these peculiar people, how do they behave in the world?

They are first of all, gentle as 'dew... as showers upon the grass...'

Then they are something else; the contrast bursts on the page like a roar from a leonine throat. 'Like a lion... like a young lion... treads under, tears in pieces, and none to deliver.'

This is the sensibility they will take on. Perhaps we make too much of the violence implied here. Perhaps the word merely pays tribute to the contrasts and complexities of a people marked by a union of opposites, of strength and tenderness.

Resembling their God? They are created 'in the image of God.'

In any case, the great 'prevailing promise' of verse nine, as is stated plainly, depends upon — disarmament.

Nationally, personally, in fact and symbol, in spirit and truth. Put aside the weapons — and the will — to destroy. Lay down your arms, change your lives.

(5:10-15) The details follow. They go to the heart of the matter.

MICAH

The word of God declares it. Weaponry and war are not merely to be regarded as a human aberration. Something more is at stake: a mystery of unutterable evil.

Strange at first blush (5:11) 'cities' are 'cut off,...' 'strongholds' 'thrown down.' For the evil of violence has been entrenched, socialized. It is one with the economy, the politics, the thrust of diplomacy. And all such structures must be shaken to their foundation.

These are matters of sensible observation. For all but the functionally insane.

And something else. It is as though behind the scenes, the headlines, the media 'hype,' two secret events were proceeding.

As though the advisors, diplomats, strategists, policy-makers, power brokers, generals, were working a kind of vile magic; 'sorcerers, soothsayers.'

They walk the dark side of the moon of creation; they cast the awful shadow that dogs our days.

All who make war stand as surrogates and guardians of the empery of death. They keep a universe that is a house of death; 'swept clean,' plausible.

These are the caretakers of fallen creation. They dramatize that veering and reeling of our nature noted by Dante in the 'Inferno,' away from 'the Good,' off kilter, in favor of, in tribute to death, — whether socialized or personal. The infliction of death, to be sure, and never its undergoing!

For such a base clan, Micah, like Isaiah, has only contempt. Once and for all, Isaiah has summed them up in an image of withering scorn (Is. 19): 'like drunks, staggering in their vomit.'

Secondly, the magic men function as a kind of debased priesthood. They are the instigators of a demonic cult and worship. Their magic takes form and focus, shrines arise, sanctuaries, 'images... pillars.'

Such places are, to be sure, strictly off limits to such refusers as would challenge the vaunts of these artisans of death, their precincts posted with a dire message: 'lethal force against trespassers is in effect.'

In such places the worship of death proceeds. But the obscene proceedings are also frequently, courageously, brilliantly interrupted; and this is our hope.

MICAH

One is at a loss, groping about for images.

It is as though the necromancers had melted down and recast all the guns of the predatory 'nations' into a monstrous image of Mars.

Thus the prophetic understanding of warmaking as the dominant idol, the most pernicious of all 'works of your hands.'

Verses 10-15 offer words to be savored in dismal hours and days.

If we but believed! (If I but believed!)

The great promise is uttered. Then another rhythm, running fiercely counter. A threat follows: destruction of the disobedient nations.

But the catastrophe need not be. The threat is spoken; it hangs ominously on the air, a dark shekinah — but only as an occasion of conversion. For God's part, we are to know that the grand promise stands. Its signatory is Christ; the covenant is signed in His blood — 'given for you.'

And yet, and yet. The hope of the God of peace is endangered; it must confront the slings and arrows of arrogant, intransigent 'nations.'

A stalemate. As then, as here and now.

God the maker of peace, it must be conceded, is hemmed in by an atrocious freedom. The peace pact is delayed, limited, even declared null and void by the 'nations that do not obey.' (And what of the church that does not obey?)

(6:1-16) Mountains are invoked, all but personified. And no wonder, these are places of moral as well as physical elevation. Up and up our aspiration mounts; from their lofty vantage, one presumably sees further (and deeper). On the peaks prophets received their charge; covenants were struck or renewed.

And here on an unnamed mountain, a vast trial is called to order; an entire people stands in the dock.

The image is a prelude of a final judgment.

Thus the present scene acts as a sharp warning, especially aimed at authorities, secular and religious. Beware, mend your ways! The 'last day'

MICAH

is to be dramatized, here and now. Though the powers of this world find perennial ways and means to evade accountability, here and now judgment is underway.

Such a scene as Micah describes is properly and uniquely prophetic. (We note the parallels in Isaiah, 3:13-15; 5:3-4 and Osee, 4:1-5.)

Indeed 'describe' hardly does justice to Micah's passion. Of another ilk than an 'objective' scribe, he takes sides, initiates the process, acting as God's surrogate.

Can it be imagined for instance, that the Pharaohs or rulers of Assyria or Babylon would be summarily hailed into a transcendent court to account for their crimes? Unthinkable. The gods are chary of offending the godlings.

"Arise, plead your case before the mountains, let the hills hear your voice." The mountains, we recall, are favored sites of divine intervention in both Jewish and Christian testaments. One thinks of Sinai (giving of the law), of Nebo (the traditional site of Moses' view of Canaan and of his death [Dt. 32:49]), of Garizim and Ebal (mountains opposite one another, east of Nablus, scenes of the blessing and curse, respectively, part of the ritual of covenant renewal), of Ramah (where Saul pursued David, met the prophets and fell into frenzy). In the Christian testament, Ramah becomes Arimathaea, home of Joseph who buried Jesus (Mt. 27:57). Likewise we think of Carmel (scene of the ordeal of Elijah and the priests of the Baal [I K. 18:19]).

Also in the Christian testament we recall the Mount of Beatitudes, Mount of Transfiguration, Mount of Olives, Mount Calvary, Mount of Ascension.

(6:2) The 'enduring foundations of the earth' are to lend an ear, as God outlines the case for the prosecution.

One is hard put to express it with even minimal accuracy, let alone with the passion implied in the text. But something like this: justice, the quest for justice, the unveiling of truth long concealed, the mysterious hand tracing on a wall the crimes of the sceptred delinquent, the prophet facing off the king. "You are the one!" — these are of the essence of whatever sanity we preserve, the vindication of divine law, of reality itself.

The above denied, little sense can be made of us moral surrealists in our mad careening through time and this world. Can this or that ruler, citizen, soldier, taxpayer, church-goer murder and raven and amass and defraud and play the predator (or be silent before all this) and still walk free and feckless in the world?

Not if there is a God. We hear God's word — a saving unmistakable No!

(6:3) The plaint of God, the heart of God in travail: "O my people, what have I done to you, in what have I wearied you?"

And the grand acts of God on our behalf are recalled, one after another. It is like the unrolling of a splendid and storied carpet; the people have trodden it, gently, safely, through awful places.

They were well advised to remember as they walk. That long and prodigious memory of Jawe!

The storied carpet is centuries long. It unrolls; now Jesus walks it.

Nothing daunted, the plaint of God upon our lips, logical and breathtaking at once, we Christians intone the heartbroken reproaches of Jawe.

We dare place them to the tongue of Jesus as He undergoes His agony.

For Jawe's Son is named Jesus, and the mercies of Jawe culminate in an act all but beyond imagining — the passion and death of the Beloved.

Good Friday comes round, the ancient reproaches must take new realities in account. Detail by detail, Jawe's Son mourns the unbearable ironies, folly against mercy, cruelty against gentleness. A sign of ineluctable mercy, and then a bloodshot countersign, are raised on high: "What I have done for you, what you have done to Me."

❖ ❖ ❖

JESUS SPEAKS

Is this the botch they make of it,
the world I made?
          round it was
and round and round, a roundelay
and all in sweet accord —
                beginning,

     interweaving,
      ending —
tears that fall, memory's
mere asperges
    falling unfailing —
beginning, end, the circle drawn.

Then this befell, the fall of worlds.
Beyond the pale
    pillar to post
they drive me like a dog.

 Now
  illimitable
   stops
    the heart of all.

(6:5) '....that you may know the "justices" (lit.) of Jawe.'
"I say more, the just man justices, acts in God's eyes what in God's eyes he is; Christ." (Hopkins).

1) Acts on God's part, of 'justice:' i.e., God's side of the bargain stands intact. Promises kept, no matter what, no matter our renegade estate.

The fidelity of God issues in blood and water, from the Heart of Christ. O my people!

2) On our part, we are issued a summons to remembrance of this: spontaneity, response, responsibility.

(6:6) And the prophet responds.

What form is the response to take? Surely a yes, a thank-you of admiration and praise.

And let us include the most primitive, atrocious and exigent of gifts: human sacrifice, 'the first born of my body' (as in Gen. 22 and Ex. 22: 28). Is this to satisfy for the 'sin of my soul'?

The vexing question is raised and must be, then, now — perennially: What gesture gives good pleasure to the Creator?

With Micah, we pour out the lees of the cup, a wine gone rancid. The older sacrifices and sin-offerings fall to ground. And along with those,

MICAH

the hundredweight of obsessive guilt.

With Micah we are done with all that. Fill the vessel with new wine! We bear the cup into the holy of holies, where a God who is 'spirit and truth' awaits our worship. A community imagining and honoring Him. A community created in His image.

"Do justice, love kindness, walk humbly before your God." Micah has learned from the grand trio who went before him, the triple urging he so nobly states. Borrows, better: from Amos (5:24, etc.), from Osee (6:6, etc.), from Isaiah (2:9-19; 7:9; 30:15, etc.)

This is how the just imagine God, the images that arise. 'You have been told,' or 'God has shown you' — 'your true good.'

Need it be added, as Karl Barth and Ellul and Stringfellow have somberly reminded us, that apart from the divine instruction, we are powerless to imagine God (or for that matter) — to imagine true worship. Thus Stringfellow:

"....the liturgy as sacrament is inherently different from religious ritualism, in which the propriety of the ritual practice itself is all that matters....

"Notice too that the liturgy as sacrament appropriates as its ingredient symbols, among others, the ordinary things of the common existence of the world — bread, wine, water, money, cloth, color, music, words, or whatever else is readily at hand. Sacramentally, we have in the liturgy a meal which is basically a real meal and which nourishes those who partake of it as a meal. At the same time, this meal portrays ... an image of the Last Supper, of which Christ Himself was host, and is also a foretaste of the eschatalogical banquet in which Christ is finally recognized as the host of all humanity.

"The liturgy therefore, wherever it has substance in the Gospel, is a living, political event. The very example of salvation, it is the festival of life which foretells the fulfillment and maturity of all of life for all of time in this time. The liturgy is social action because it is the characteristic style of life for human beings in this world."

Apart from God whispering his name, the name of lover and friend, there can be no knowledge of God. Until that moment of secrecy and utmost altruism, we are lost in the predawn of the tribe. In our nostrils is the stench of animal blood. Or more horribly, the stench of human sacrifice.

Apart from God. Paul knew that dizzying hiatus, that soul-fault in creation. He wrote of it; it is as though his pen were dipped in gall. The predawn of the tribe, he implies, perdures in our refusals. Upon the lost, who make of their plight a perverse virtue, no sun can rise. (Rm. 3:23) They 'have fallen short of the glory of God.'

Therefore. We are hardly free of the stench of human sacrifice; it continues to mock the hope of God. War upon war. A perennial inhuman predawn, and the works of darkness.

War: a contrary, twisted version — atrocious, implacable, choleric, sanguinary — of 'the good.' War is the health of the state, the mortal illness of citizens.

And what of believers and the war-making state? Jawe or no, those who don the uniform have resolved to work injustice, to hate with impunity, to walk in arrogance.

Waging war, complicit in war, we are powerless to imagine, summon, conjure up, the truth of our own humanity (powerless, in consequence, to worship 'in truth').

'Noi siam venuti al loco ov' io ho detto
che tu vedrai le genti doloroso
c'hanno perduto il ben dell' intelletto.'

('We are come to the place where I told you
you would see the sorrowful people
who have lost the good of the intellect.')
            (Dante, *Inferno*, canto 3)

Is the image of hell, or of hell on earth?

(6:8) And one wonders: Is the 'command' triple, or one? In any case, it would seem that the grand design of 'doing justice' includes both tenderness and humility.

And the command, issuing as it does from the heart of God, is also a clue and key — to the heart of God. Is this not the God who from Micah

MICAH

to Jesus to Paul to ourselves, again and again, despite all, does multiple 'justices,' loves tenderly, walks in humility the human way?

(6:9 ff.) Let us not, Micah warns austerely, succumb to enervation and illusion. Do we have eyes to see? Can it be presumed, for instance, that the preceding command is largely observed — either in his world or our own? Let us see. Let us return to the city.

Sin City to be sure. There, the old game goes on, a sweaty stew, a bear pit of greed, venery, duplicity and violence.

In verses 9-12, as in Amos (8:5), much attention is paid to the greed and attendant fraud of the merchants.

And a note of black humor, a sardonic smile on the face of Micah — the chicanery comes to no gain, but only loss.

Summer, 1992. We are seeing greed and fraud elevated explicitly to national virtue of the highest order. The operative word is 'explicit.' Greed and fraud have always been high on the list of national virtues; but the fallout, so to speak, as to guilt and consequence, usually was spread among many. These fetching ways of bankers and high rollers were not yet embodied in one: a single Jovian entity, a god who summed and surpassed the gods.

Now however, an image is cast in gold and unveiled for our homage. A billionaire presents himself and his project. Single-handed he will purchase the presidency.

What could be simpler, more utilitarian, more saving of dispersed effort, more — American? It must be conceded that the gentleman has removed from the electoral game a clumsy complexity.

Perennially we witnessed a given scene; by presumption, it was thought to perdure. Every four years a coterie of sycophants pupated, pooled their resources, and declared their man. Bought and sold! Designated, delivered!

But this year, a feisty independista requires no minion-millionaires. When the almighty appears, how the mighty fall back!

Purchaser extraordinary, consummate consumer, world auctioneer, he designates and delivers — himself.

(6:13-16) Stinging, subversive, implacable. One hears the laughter of the gods — the gods who being so sedulously served, turn on their adorers.

And the mordant irony of Jawe! Despised and scorned, He does not laugh, not once; He weeps rather, or grows enraged, or with a kind of last ditch persistence, issues instruction through his beloved Micah.

And knows alas that in all probability the lesson (greed, fraud, consequence) will fall on ears of stone. Knows that generations come and go, and the lesson is unlearned, the stone hardened to adamant. Unto this day.

Some lessons, some words, reproaches, threats, outcomes, simply hang on the air or sit the page. This is their fate, the fate of the word of God. Micah may rail and fume as it pleases him. And so may Jawe. But those who fuel the world's machine have other words to speak, other projects, other means and ends.

And these, be it admitted, prevail. These all but invalidate the 'other word.' The worldly word wins. It renders impractical, irrelevant, to no point, the word of God.

Such things, bitter as they are, must be said. They are matters of experience today also, for whoever would take seriously a vocation such as Micah's. Taking for granted the denial, denigration, mocking of the word of God is, let us say, a working hypothesis — of those who take seriously the same word.

Given our world, the word of God is a loser.

As in the verses at hand, clashing as they do with the noise of God's word in conflict with the worldly word. As though in hand-to-hand combat, shield were struck against sword.

On the one hand, eating, amassing, sowing and the like, curiously good, normal activities. But in context, too much, too much. Wanting it all, at whatever cost to whomever, and the devil take the hindmost. Behold the works of the world, conducted according to the 'rules of Omri and Ahab.'

Rules, that is to say, of the capitalists, the consumers, the free marketeers. Rules of the millionaires and the military (undeniably a redundancy).

And then, the intervention of God, the downfalling, the unmasking, the bringing to naught.

Behold the Subverter extraordinary, the Derider, the Contemner, the Desolator in action.

MICAH

(7:1-20) The human predicament! What we have made and unmade, of ourselves, body and soul and community, what we have made and unmade of creation! The words burn there on the page. They twist in their own fires; they blind the eyes — or they open the eyes.

One turns to Jesus and Paul — for relief or denial or mitigation? Hardly. For verifying of Micah. There one finds a like indictment, incandescent and furious. Indeed, Jesus borrows from Micah to express for his generation the atrocious divisions that fall upon families, when under one and the same roof, the gospel is heard by some and despised by others (Mt. 10:35-36; Lk. 12:13).

And Paul (Rm. 1,2) underscores our predicament — and our hope. It is as though the story of Kafka, 'The Penal Colony,' had become part of our biblical canon. Across the page of his own flesh is written the biography of the race, of blundering humans fallen on inhuman ways, the story of our crime, punishment — and despite it all, our salvation.

Micah sees no hope for us; rather, no hope in us. Which is by no means to say, no hope.

He is like the surgeon of T.S. Eliot's Four Quartets: "In order to be healed, our illness must grow worse." So in these awful verses, our mortal illness is revealed.

Or Micah seems a guardian angel or an incubus, his spirit redivivus in Karl Barth or Ellul or Stringfellow or the like. All those biblical opponents of witless, predatory, temerarious religion; opponents of the proponents of so banal and lethal a 'product.' Religion Made In America!

Grief for a start. The world invading his guts, Micah mourns deep in his soul for what his eyes light on abroad, what he must cope with at home. Must judge, must resist and rail against. The vocation that makes of him a pariah, loser, a man apart. Burdened, cursed with — vision. In the kingdom of the blind he is criminal, for he sees.

It is as though he composed a prelude of the 'terrible sonnets' of Hopkins: "I wake, and feel the fell of dark, not day.... That night, that year of now done dark, I wretch lay wrestling with (my God!) my God...."

Then a most endearing image. Micah is like a harvester, a gleaner, one who scanning the signs of the season, looks to a good outcome of his labors.

Rightly so, we agree.

And then, unable to credit his eyes, he walks through the orchard, the vineyard — and not a grape, not a fig!

(7:4) Retaining the image: 'those accounted the best are like briers, the upright like a thorn hedge.'

There is a season, say the wise, and a time for everything.

But the times have gone awry; the faithful, the just, have vanished from the land.

Normal relationships are sundered; brother turns against brother, son against father, daughter against mother. Violence rules and ravens; it invades table and couch.

The high and mighty construe the law as they will. The judges are rotten with bribery.

(7:5) Given the breakdown of the social contract, Micah has ironic advice to offer. To wit: trust no one, neither friend, neighbor, spouse! Thus one's behavior serves to mirror the evil and reinforce it. Thus too, though much diminished, one will survive.

Is he serious? Dead serious.

With a deadly word, he mocks the mockers of the living word.

There follows, we are told, in the final songs of hope, a redaction from a later period. A people chastened by exile writes a sublime postscript, a mysterious endorsement of the message of Micah. They have suffered and pondered, and at length they have come to understand. His sublime, difficult words are signed, sealed and delivered. They bear now the plea and endorsement of the unborn.

MICAH

So another generation writes a hopeful word; it soars from the page, up and up, in despite of gravity and the terror of life. It is all quite simple: a saving God stands at our side.

(7:8) There are enemies to be sure. How could it be otherwise, when Micah and the faithful remnant as well have relentlessly summoned the guilty to judgment?

(7:9) There is also a lively sense of personal sin — surely a capital point, and a puzzling one as well. One asks in perplexity, in what could this tireless, courageous, even ferocious man of God, have fallen short?

One sees no inconsistency here. Whether we think of the admission as recorded by Micah or his people, the truth is the same. Godliness exacts its price. They have stood too near the fires; they are all but consumed by blazing holiness.

So they must wait, must be patient. 'Until, until.... In that day, in that day....' (7:11-12). It is a veritable litany of hope, uttered in a time of despair.

Patient they must be: with themselves, with the delinquents, the unjust judges, the extortionists, the oppressors. With vile forms of power that obdurately hold on, resistant to compunction or conversion.

Little can be done. Very well, let us do that little. Let us at very least, not accept that we are abandoned, not yield before the thin margin of an awful present, as though no breakthrough were prom-ised. Let us repeat for mantra: the promise, the promise!

For those who yield to the common despair, hand over their soul; they march to the whip; they are forced recruits in an army of darkness.

"Though I dwell in darkness, Jawe is my light." Who, given such times as we endure (such times as Micah and his people endured), who could forebear echoing the cry? Life grows stygian; darkness forbids the dawn. The terrible social indictment of judges and rulers, great ones and small, is unrolled again, verified century after century, to the letter. Paul will echo the somber assessment as verified in his generation also.

In ours as well, the truth of our times.

Still, another reality. "Jawe is my light."

(7:11 ff.) Now we have something more than the legacy of Micah; a noble reality emerges, a common voice — the legacy of the people of Micah.

Their prayer grows expansive; indeed it is less a prayer of petition, than a growing confidence. It is as though the people were granted a third eye and saw the hope that dwelt in their ancestry, here and now embodied before them, flesh and bones.

Enlarge the boundaries of hope! It hardly matters whether the verses refer to the return of the dispersed or the inclusion of the gentiles or both. It is all one and the same; it bespeaks, invokes, beckons a time when the hope of Jawe, 'that all may be one,' is verified in open arms of welcome and inclusion.

(7:14-15) A prayer, a parable. The words tell of a time of return and restoration — the former beyond doubt; the latter, still partial and chancy.

For the people must dwell and survive as best they might in a semi desert area surrounding Jerusalem. The land is a parched skull. And how in such a place shall a tribe of shepherds and their flocks prosper?

And yet they have memories to draw upon, memories that all but rise from the dead. They take the force of a promise never abrogated. If the past was glorious, what shall be the present?

If our memories tell of the mighty works of God, will not the miracles that once saved us be granted once more? "As in the days when You came out of Egypt, show us your marvelous deeds!"

(The reading 'You came out' is remarkable; it is also disputed. I follow [BJ]).

(7:16-17) And what of the great powers? The prophecy turns first on the relief of the promised people, from the semi-bondage of bare survival.

In the nature of things, and from many angles, the 'nations' must be included in the same world view. How are they to be contained, how (far more difficult) converted?

A bickering and bellicose lot, they pose a constant threat against the survival of our minority tribe. And yet, and yet. The mighty deeds of God include them also. They too are granted a vocation, promise, covenant.

But first, a painful prelude.

MICAH

For the nations are eons distant from the truth of things. Who are they in the world, how does God view their ethos, behavior? It must be seen that their view of themselves ('power', 'ramparts') is totally at odds with God's view.

Let it be said plain; indeed Micah puts it 'plain' (a notable understatement!): 'Confounded... hand to mouth.... ears grown deaf... licking the dust like a serpent... crawling the earth....'

A minority opinion to be sure. How often must one seek out the underdog to gain insight into the powerful!

The implication of Micah is plain. With all their might and main, the powerful offer such staples of the culture as awe, respect, loyalty, good citizenship, presumption of truth telling and virtue, crimes reduced to mere peccadillos, etc.

The faith is a mighty hammer; the images must be broken to shards. Micah breaks them. In Jawe's eyes the 'nations' are, for all their huffing-and-puffing, despicable, criminal. They merit not a whit of respect — not to speak of infatuation or awe or fealty. Their ethos is hollow, their cause bankrupt. Therefore judgment.

Paul is another, later Micah. He summons to judgment the preeminent 'nation' of his time (Rm. 1:28 - 32).

"And since they did not see fit to acknowledge God, God gave them up to a base mind and to improper conduct. They were filled with all manner of wickedness, evil, covetousness, malice. Full of envy, murder, strife, deceit, malignity, they are gossips, slanderers, haters of God, insolent, haughty, boastful, inventors of evil, disobedient.... foolish, faithless, heartless, ruthless.

"Though they know God's decree that those who do such things deserve to die, they not only do them, but approve those who practice them."

What are we to make of this fierce biblical assault against an authority it does not hesitate to call illegitimate? What make of this toppling of the awesome principalities?

MICAH

Is our life in the empire to be marred by a kind of creeping acculturation and passivity, cynicism, silent scorn, questioning, skepticism — or refusal, non-conformity, nonviolent resistance?

And can we not argue in circular fashion something like this? If the behavior of authorities, as observed, (as suffered), falls under the indictment of Micah-Paul, (no matter its religious claims or the benison granted it by a certain species of religion) — then the authority in fact is to be named as Micah-Paul name it: illegitimate, inhuman — godless.

And to be resisted, at whatever cost.

(7:18-20) And so we conclude, on a far different note, a note of plaintive innocent impetration.

No matter now the 'nations.'

Of little account also, the sins of those who though summoned, have defaulted. Ourselves.

Let us accept for the moment (surely a moment of truth) — the truth: Mercy has accepted us, ourselves, our wounds and warts and would-be's and are-not's.

A prayer of the faithful. A prayer akin to the prayer of WH Auden, simple, final, yes audacious:

> I will never be
> different. Love me.

NAHUM

The book at hand is not, by all odds, the subject of intense scrutiny, whether on the part of scholars or faithful. Brief as it is, even brutally to the point — perhaps too much for finicky taste!

Nonetheless, Nahum stands in a corner of the mind — just as his few verses capture brilliantly a corner of history. Our corner?

At least in regard to anonymity, Nahum resembles the great line, the majors. We know nothing of him, or so near nothing as to count for little. Ancestors or progeny? Nothing. Friends, adversaries? Of these we have only the barest implications. (Certain we may be that in the life of such as he, both adversaries and friends abound!)

Thus isolated, the word of Nahum stands of itself, an emanation on the air of this world, intact, sovereign, transcendent to the speaker.

It resembles that word celebrated in the psalm: the word that goes forth, 'My word' embracing the universe, and returning inviolate, God's own.

We are told that the lifetime of Nahum saw the destruction of Nineveh and thus the end of the power of Assyria, an outcome brought about by Babylonians and Medes, and so on and so on.

And who pays heed? The names, the empires, their follies and grandeur, their rising and falling — are written in desert sand. The winds pass over, the great steles and tombs are lost to sight. The inscriptions grow dim; experts may translate, but the words, dates, names hold little or no meaning for us. Dust and ashes, the emperors mingle with the dust and ashes of their votaries and victims.

And what of their crimes? They are noted only through the judgment of these by no means minor voices.

This little book of somewhat less than 50 verses is like a flag of warning raised. No liberation, he would remind us, is final; the realm of God is not yet.

In his time a wild joy greeted the overthrow of the tyrant of Nineveh. Such joy was entirely befitting; according to Nahum it was also dangerous. It could easily yield before an ideology of final arrival, self-justification, the old exclusive sense of being chosen above all others.

Following on the victory came a new political arrangement. It was hastily improvised; inevitably it proved somewhat less than perfect. The dark side of the new leadership emerged. Slowly, awfully, cynically, a new tyranny replaced the old. Then what a loss of nerve! Despair seized on those whose expectations were so shockingly thwarted.

And a reflection occurs. Could such intemperate hopes as flared up from the ashes, have been met by any political regime, no matter how enlightened or humane? Experience is a good teacher, though a harsh one. Under any and all forms of authority, one had best harbor a measure of skepticism. Go slow, go slow; the realm of justice and peace is not yet.

Nahum is minatory in this regard.

We are entitled, of course, to a modest, befitting political expectation; in America too we look for a measure of decency on the part of authorities. Unmet, scorned for years and years, such expectations die; in their place rises a deadly cynicism or inertia.

How to live humanly amid the debris, the decline and fall of empire? There must be a better way than giving up, a longer endurance apt to cope with the vandalizing of hope, the lies and concealment, the secret deals, the pervasive greed and violence that pollute our days.

What is it then, that 'other way'? The question became acute, as so short a time ago, we endured the terrible days and nights of the 'countdown to war,' then the war itself.

That other way, if it exists and can be summoned, touches on one's conception of the human, the political, the meaning of history itself (or the utter meaninglessness, reality battered out of shape by awful daily event).

Nahum offers a clue. The empire, for all its chariots and warriors and gold and silver, is strictly provisional before God. It rises, flourishes, declines and falls.

Meantime, it stands under judgment. That is the first fact of all. In consequence, the eye of faith rests on such an entity — its claims, rhetoric, ideology — warily.

And if the empire fall, and is replaced? The rise of a new political system, whatever its form and apparent flourishing, is hardly to be equated with the onset of the realm of God.

One questions the new, as one questioned the old. Does the present regime promote justice, succor the poor, eschew wars, speak truthfully to the citizenry, itself observe the law it promulgates? If so, rejoice — but be mindful, be wary.

Under old regime or new, the critique continues, accountability is invoked.

Whatever the proclamations or pretentions or rhetoric or promises, one keeps a sharp eye on crucial matters, unfinished or neglected as they inevitably remain — matters of justice above all.

Does a distracted, hectic, feverish mood arise? Are there flags everywhere, all but blotting out the sun? Do the polls show an overwhelming enthusiasm for 'the leader'? Do all walk to a common drum (or a whip)?

We are not to be victimized. We stand under no earthly banner, except perhaps a flag of warning.

Thus Nahum — and others of his kind.

Nahum, we note, has won much disfavor from one school of commentators. He is too wrathful by far, we are informed. Advocating as he does a kind of emotional and political golden mean, a chastening of temporal and political hope — still he violates his own norm. He is hateful toward the oppressor, incurably nationalistic. So he is written off as a 'temple prophet,' and to that degree, an adversary of Jeremiah.

Under close examination of the text, it all seems rather too much, this critical barrage.

Yet perhaps the objections offer a service of sorts. They force us to reflect seriously on the vocation, so often thankless and ignored, of the prophet. Especially the chancy work of denunciation and judgment, a thunder which, then as now, often falls on heedless or itching ears.

We would like a softer voice on the air. (Something known among critics as well, as a 'balanced view.')

To pursue briefly the metaphor of 'balance.'

One might conclude that the huge weight placed in the scales, on the pan opposite the prophetic, is in small danger of being out-weighted. Balance of influence?

The image, like the reality, is a worldly one. Which is to say, the weight placed in opposition to the prophetic is all but overwhelming. It is the weight, the huge gravitational pull of the Fall. The argument, if there be one, is loaded. So are the scales.

The empire's huge resources of propaganda, the applause of citizenry, the conformity, empathy, self-aggrandizement, perquisites and so on, the plain moral numbing that follows — these are a massive weight indeed.

And over against it — what? A puny voice, often solitary, more often than not muffled, drowned out, derided.

Add to the above inequity a crushing weight of resources, altogether in service to violence — war, invasion, seizure of lands and peoples, duplicity, contempt for the poor. And almost everyone approving, applauding — or at least silent, non-voting.

Poor prophet, what a light weight he exerts!

Another image for such as Nahum. One thinks of him, and rightly, as a species of court fool. He derides, he mocks and mimes the foolish greatness that, apart from him, wins slavish approval on every side. Whatever strength he summons is strangely compounded with weakness; he has no personal gain or dividend to be drawn from access to the king. Seeking counsel in serious matters, the royal ear bends in another direction than a holy fool's.

Still, Nahum has more than a passing interest in court events — especially those concluded behind closed doors.

For (and here our image lags) he senses that something odoriferous is transpiring in Denmark. He must say what no one dares say: that crime is in progress, and betrayal of hope, duplicity, greed in the air. And worst of all, war and war-planning.

To survive, to speak up, he must walk a thin line indeed. For his presence in court rests on a double (if truth were known, contradictory) supposition, vulnerable to royal whim.

By royal pleasure, he is present to entertain, to spin tales, to offer oracles of an essentially harmless, non-interfering kind. A court prophet, on the royal payroll.

And then, in his own mind, something else. He knows beyond doubt that he stands under a deadly serious — vocation. To prick the conscience of the king. To offer, now and again at great risk, radically 'other' images than those the royal pleasure spins for itself. Images of the truth, of crime and accountability.

Nahum must be serious; he is speaking for Jawe. And he must be patient, for he is not taken seriously.

And if he is taken seriously? Then he must be steady of soul; the risks attendant on royal wrath are considerable. The prophet-fool may become the prophet-martyr.

(1:1 ff.) No prelude, immediately Nahum announces a common theme of the prophets: the anger of Jawe.

And not of Jawe only, for only an angry prophet could have spoken such verses, alight as they are with fierce combustion.

God, angry? The passage is an invitation, a kind of open season for psychologizing. To wit, Nahum and his kind create a god to their own image. They have 'problems' with the world around them; so they project their fury on a purported angry God. And so on and so on.

Or a metaphysical approach, a natural theology. God angry? Surely no more than a poetic metaphor. For God is a Being infinitely above human emotion, above the world and its ways. This is the divine One whose existence human reason can touch, the Repose of the mind's seeking, the One to whose existence the famous 'quinque viae' of Aquinas lead.

Must one not speak here of the 'taming' of the wild One, the replacing of such a One with a respectable divinity of our own? (Our own, in more senses than one!)

Indeed, speculation gets us not very far. The text is too plain for comfort. According to Nahum, Jawe is not only angry; the holy One is variously 'jealous, avenging, wrathful... will not clear the guilty....' is subject to 'indignation.... heat of anger.... will pursue his enemies into darkness.... will take vengeance twice on his foes....'

Such fury, so wild a weathervane of mood! And the words are not Nahum's alone; they are consistent with Isaiah, Jeremiah, Ezekiel, the Psalmist, Hosea, Zephaniah.

A further scandal. God's wrath is aimed first of all at the people of covenant. They must pay and pay double — for crimes of injustice, false worship, neglect of their sworn word.

In the exile, the divine anger reaches its apogee; Israel is destroyed as a nation.

To speak more nearly of ourselves, what are we to make of the anger of Jesus recounted in the gospels? It is as though the so-called 'anthropomorphism' of the Jewish testament came to rest, like a cloak of Elijah out of thin air, on Christ. Provoked, the incarnate One resembles uncannily the Jawe of the prophets. Confronted with the hypocrisy of the religious establishment, his anger blazes up. (Mt. 5:1-9) Again, infuriated by the venality of the temple coterie, He evicts the sellers and money changers from the holy precinct. (Mt. 21:12-13)

How indeed, witnessing the befouling of fair creation, shall God not be kindled to anger, not be wrathful against the destroyers? The prophets answer — resoundingly. There is fury in celestial places.

And what of ourselves and anger? Is justice to be delayed, and we supine before the reign of injustice — when God grows furious at a like spectacle?

Let it be said that the earth were a far more barren planet, a moral moonscape, were it emptied of the anger of the just.

Let us make place in the lexicon of virtue for the righteousness of just anger. Make place also in the lexicon of vice for the unholiness of conformity and cowardice.

The anger of God, we are reminded by Paul, resembles a combustible material, heaped up against a 'day to come.' It implies judgment; it points to an end time. (Rm. 2:5)

And what of the present time? We dwell, as the prophets from Nahum to Paul remind us, in a 'meantime.' It is a time of ignorance, darkness, blindness. For believers, a time of patient waiting.

Still, a warning is implied: we are not to preempt a judgment that is 'not yet,' as though conversion of heart, even on the part of the unlikeliest of humans (ourselves?) were impossible.

We are to be patient. As some have pointed out and (experience indeed indicates), this to be accounted the hardest of disciplines. What to do, where to turn? We feel at times like indentured slaves of time, put to useless, feckless tasks.

Perhaps it comes to this: In face of an evil that all but stops the heart — it may be there is nothing to be done.

Nothing? Deny it, with all your heart!

The gospel disallows this 'nothing.'

One is to remain alert, to wait on God. To be patient. This for 'a time, twice time, half a time,' as we are told in Revelation. (12:14)

Something indeed to be done.

We have inklings of this from the prisoners, the disabled, the discarded street people, those pushed to the edge, those to whom the world allows no place.

They are witnesses; their long-sufferance, at times their babbling and fury, are God's judgment on our sorry incoherent inhuman mess.

God's anger is aimed at the amnesia of humankind. How easy, how convenient to forget! How enticing to summon technique, manipulation of the helpless, love of money and prestige, military might (this above all) — as the credentials of justification!

Then how are we to retain and renew our memory, how restore, how 're-mind'? It is almost as though God, for our sanity's sake, must summon up through Nahum two historic acts. Each is all but forgotten, shunted aside by the recusant memory of humankind.

(1:4) The act of creation first. Jawe has 'rebuked the sea and made it dry up.' Creation is seen as a conquest of watery chaos. Thus the earth is gently, providentially fitted for human dwellers.

And then, something of greater import. God recalls the great saving acts of a later age, especially the Red Sea crossing and the epiphany of Sinai. The sublime events are ikons of providence.

Also through the anger of God and the coming judgment, in a strange but real sense the dignity of humankind (even of the basest in our midst) is vindicated. Nahum and his like shout it aloud: you, and you and you, are to be held accountable! It is like the thunderous voice of God.

In Nahum and Isaiah and others, creation itself gives voice to the anger of God, 'in whirlwind and storm.... the mountains quake.... Bashan and Carmel wither.... the bloom of Lebanon fades....'

We need no instruction concerning the linkage here insisted on. The times force it home. Between the sound or befouled state of the natural world and our own moral uprightness or perfidy an unbreakable link is forged.

Assaulted by the criminality of humans, creation arises in a tumultuous death throe, an outcry. It is like the shriek of a lorn mother in the art of Kathe Kollwitz.

We commonly stop short. It is as though we could love and cherish creation, even as we cling to our myths of technique and mastery, our version of the universe as a 'closed system,' guarded, dominated, dispensed or held fast according to whim.

Not so. Wondrous this organism — breathing, pristine, benevolent, forebearing — to a point. Like a Buddha, all being and inwardness, a thousand arms extended in welcome and giving. To a point.

Then arising. Angry, recoiling, bespeaking in metaphor and catastrophic event, the fury of the Creator.

But anger is not God's name. (Nor is anger all the emotional store of Christ.) God's anger is — a mood. In Nahum, a contrary emotion keeps breaking through. Thunderbolts and earthquakes? For a time, a time of correction and reproof. No more.

(1:7) It is astonishing and heartening; in the midst of thunderous threats — a flower cracks through stone. We have been told repeatedly, we can scarce credit it. The wrath of God is not forever, the benignity of God keeps breaking through. "The Lord is good, a stronghold in the day of trouble; the Lord knows those who take refuge in him."

(1:8) And then, 'But....' Another threat, a dark mood returning, a reminder! "But with an overflowing flood, Jawe will make an end of his adversaries, will pursue his enemies into darkness."

For our part, this angry God is somewhat less than palatable. We would much prefer a more malleable even-tempered, predictable — even, truth told, somewhat sophistical God. Let us say, a God whose conduct resembled that of the enemies of Socrates, skilled 'in making the worse appear the better cause....'

Especially that supremely 'worse cause' known as empire.

It is nothing short of astonishing; in spite of the constant tirades of the prophets against imperial hegemonies, imperial behavior continues to seduce believers. A benign empire, benign, beneficent, our own!

Thus the worse, appearing the better cause! Invasions, murder on a mass

NAHUM

scale, greed, misuse of the earth — all seen as good, necessary, virtuous even. The myth perdures.

The empire is — a god. Let us say it plain. The empire is an awesome entity; and it offers (or purports to offer) a god-like gift. It justifies its true believers.

Blasphemously — in a way that makes mockery of Paul and the prophets, who announce a God 'who raises the dead, who makes of that which was not, a new creation.'

The empire justifies — our injustice. Worse, it turns injustice on its crowned head; in an Orwellian nightmare, it calls war 'peace,' duplicity 'truth,' murder 'collateral damage,' and so on.

A friend supplied a few examples, culled from a pentagonal orgy of obfuscation:

Bullets are 'kinetic energy penetrators.'

Combat is 'violence process.'

Peace is 'permanent pre-hostility.'

The invasion of Grenada was thus described: 'pre-dawn vertical insertion.'

And in Lebanon we 'backloaded augmentation personnel.'

Let us digress for the moment. There are two bases on which the Jawe of Nahum is to be held — unacceptable.

This God holds us accountable (as above). And God forgives us.

We have other notions of properly divine behavior. Other preferences. All said, we much value guilt above forgiveness.

We know it too well and cringe from the knowledge; God's forgiveness implies a stern condition: forgive us our trespasses as we forgive those who trespass against us.

Is a new start possible, has a lesson been learned? The prophet insists so.

But guilt pursues us like a coven of furies. In our own estimate unforgiven, we refuse to forgive.

Unredeemed, the memory of evildoing allows for no access to the God of mercy. Unrelieved by tears of contrition, every prior folly induces another. Vietnam impels Grenada. Grenada spills-over in fire and blood into Panama. Then the spirit of no-forgiveness lashes us into Iraq.

Will it never end, never be exorcised, this demon of retribution?

NAHUM

Words concerning Jawe: 'pursuit, enmity, destruction, anger, fury, jealousy, vengeance, punishment.' A heavy dose indeed!

And then interspersed, other words: 'slow to anger, goodness, citadel on the day of distress.' And to ourselves, a commendation: 'Jawe knows those who trust....'

We are invited to take to heart the shocking contrariety, and so grow thoughtful.

Only in balance, one mood set off against the other, each modifying the other, do we gain a clue, a hint, access to the Mystery. The Bible too has its koans!

Nahum says it again and again. Jawe is not subject to our images of life and behavior. Jawe judges, here and now. The present thus becomes an image of the final days.

And another caveat: Divine judgment is not invariably a form of condemnation. It is a rigorous, austere mercy, a corrective, the abrupt epiphany of a better way.

Woe to the one, and alleluia to the one upon whom the light breaks. That one will be unhorsed and blinded for a time.

'Hesed' is a hot breath.

(1:9-15) An unusual form — a monologue. It is all but surreal; two audiences are envisioned.

Back and forth Jawe turns. First a kind of 'session of comfort' is in progress; Jawe speaks to the 'little people' of Judah.

Then immediately, a far different mood sets in. A trial is concluded; summary judgment is rendered against the great ones of Assyria.

Two forms of providence, radically in contrast!

In a minor mode, the 'little ones' are comforted by a promise of relief and rehabilitation. But this is almost an aside.

The major theme, whether addressed to God's people or their oppressor, is the downfall of the Assyrian tyrant. (And by implication, the downfall of every tyranny, every principality of every age and place. Let us take note of this, as frenzies assert once more the untruth of imperial omnipotence.)

Appalling, inevitable! "Like a tangle of thorns they are consumed, like a stubble...." And again, like the thump of clay on a coffin lid: "I will make your grave, for you are vile."

(1:9) For start, a question to God's people: "What is your idea of Jawe?"

A challenge is laid down. The circumstance, we are told, is a heavy one. Assyria rides the saddle of the world. Judah shudders in helplessness.

Every reason in the lexicon for doubting the power of God. Then or now, a like loss of nerve! Nothing so raises and multiplies such doubts, to the point of quenching all light as the illusion of irresistible imperial power. The citizens shrug and raise their eyes and go about their business. "What else can one do?" A light goes out, illusion rides the whirlwind.

Something else occurs. The power of big guns becomes a warrant, a credential of God's favor. The weapon takes aim, a debased religion guarantees the outcome. God on our side!

Henceforth, God and the imperium (no matter the prophets and their fulminations, no matter odious wars and idolatrous co-options) — these are partners in a single enterprise. The war is blessed of God; and who shall withstand it?

A God of no violence? A God who, to all evidence, is helpless as his people? A God who, in the shadow of an exterminating threat, commends to believers only the purifying of mind and heart, which is to say, renunciation of impure means?

"What is your idea of Jawe?" Another translation, "What do you plot against Jawe?" One suspects that either translation comes to the same thing. Which is to say, your despair, your itch toward counter-violence, the temptation to adopt the tactic of the enemy — this amounts to a 'plot,' a betrayal.

Such dark speculation implies that your 'idea of Jawe' is utterly at odds with the reality of Jawe.

But Jawe reads the mind. There in darkness lurk prevailing images of the gods. And Jawe reads the heart, where dark designs fester.

There are two modes of faith suggested in the Bible. One, the faith of

Job, questions God. In another, as here, it is God who questions.

The difference between the two tends to meld in the fire of experience. In both examples, of Job and Nahum, the believers are under heavy stress — misfortune, the threat of misfortune. Faith is in the balance. Will God come through?

Perhaps, perhaps not. Amid the troubles, myriad questions buzz about. At that point it were best to confess that one knows — nothing.

(And in any case, the faith whether questioned or declared, must not be made to depend on a happy outcome; that were base magic.)

The faith declared, however feebly or inadequately (or the God questioned, it is the same thing), is a loving quest for the God questioned and questioning.

Nothing else weighs here, no benefit of grace or merit, no worldly or heavenly advantage. Nor, be it insisted, longing for vindication or deliverance from the powers of this world.

This is all too easily said. But it is a naked faith, as Job declares: "Even though He should kill me, yet will I believe."

A multitude of martyrs testify to the terror (but also the genuineness) of such faith. They indeed were killed — and yet they believed.

Ancient history or modern, it is one testimony. No magic sought, no conditions laid down! The faith is the faith is the faith.

The community of resisters in the book of Daniel have an equivalent message for the king, who has demanded of them a blasphemous tribute. The stalwart believers respond: Even should our God not spare us, still we will not adore your gods.

The faith of the murdered Jesuits of El Salvador was of comparable grandeur. For years their university was bombed, they were threatened with death and ordered to leave the country. They remained. Not, to be sure, because their faith rested on assurance that all would turn out to their advantage.

Such a hope would have been vain in any case, unsustainable in the long bitter haul, as each day brought only a deeper darkness.

And then, and then — there was in fact an outcome. They were murdered. No more can be said, or should.

NAHUM

It should perhaps be stressed that the question of verse nine is addressed to Judah, to the believers. (It would, of course, make little sense so to question Assyria, steeped in its idolatries. God probes the faith of the faithful.)

There follows a promise to the afflicted. It concerns their liberation, perhaps near at hand, perhaps not. No hint of timing is offered.

But the purport of the promise, as we learn after the fact, is fearsome. The promise was fulfilled, we are told, in short order. The savage oppressor was removed: "Like tangled thorns consumed, like dry straw."

Near at hand or far in the future, no matter; the prophecies are true. So they come true. The time is not the point; the truthfulness is. Which is to say, judgment is thereby announced.)

Need it be said? The empire casts its net far and wide. Distant peoples suffer hugely at the hands of those whose lust is all for control and oppression.

But not only they suffer, those distant ones who in one way or another are victimized. Domestically too, we are beleaguered and tossed about by the fevers and chills, the violence and duplicity of our leaders. We, like everyone else, are lied to, robbed of income by 'elected' charlatans and thieves. Sons, daughters, spouses, friends, are rounded up to 'serve' in the mighty armed forces, sent on abrupt notice across the world, to die or kill for something referred to with awe as 'our way of life.'

We are in effect a tiny latter day Judah, a remnant dwelling in the midst of an empire mightier by far than Assyria. And much in need of the word of a Nahum! Oppressed indeed!

We are not to doubt the word of God. It is for us to stand firm amid the debris of decline and fall. God is faithful. The outcome is sure.

"Go ahead and wait." (Dorothy Day)

(1:11) It is for God to unmask the idols, only Jawe can know them for what they are and so reveal them.

Thus once more, a wisdom that unmasks an evil, buried so deep as to

NAHUM

lie beyond scope or skill of human discovery; the spirit of death, Belial. "From you (Assyria) has that spirit gone forth, plotting evil against Jawe." This is an understanding of empire that far surpasses the conventional.

What indeed serves to explain the motive of imperial behavior, the scorched earth policies, the ruthless inhumanity? The forces that move the gargantuan machinery are summed up in 'Belial.' The word is frequent in the Bible; it hints at several meanings that finally converge in one.

One reference is to the emperor, Sennacherib: "One came forth from you (Assyria) who plotted evil against Jawe according to the plan of Belial." The king's earlier assault on the holy city remained a terrible memory at the time of Nahum. In 'Belial' the powers of death are also implied, the idols of Babylon. And always, the Adversary of the God of life.

The term, wherever invoked, bears heavy overtones of contempt; etymologically we have in Belial 'the worthless one.'

(1:12) Again, a word to Judah.

The word speaks of the promise. Judah is to live by the promise.

The times of Nahum, we recall, were turbulent in the extreme, the national mood like a chart of fevers and chills.

First came a great oppression, the Assyrian. Then through Josiah, relief was offered, (as promised in the present oracle). A very explosion of joy ensued; Nahum and his stricken community saw the promise of Jawe verified.

How brief it was, that paradisal moment! After the Assyrians, a far worse tyranny fell on the little people — that of the pharaoh.

Thus the circumstance of the present oracle — and its promise — is enlarged. The promise expands beyond our imagining; it becomes cosmic, eschatological. It includes every eon, the centuries of all the living. The promise touches on seasons, years, centuries, thrones and principalities, on each and every conquest, glory, succession.

Who sits the throne, who is elected, who parleys war or peace, who invades, who surrenders? Who persecutes, makes disappear, tortures? Who gives no heed to God or to God's little people? Who appears invincible?

Who plays Rameses, Nebuchadnessor, Phalasar, Sennacherib, Assurbanipal, Shamash Shamukin, Nabopolassar?

Let the great ones, each and all, (then and now!) attend to the oracle, and tremble. The truth strikes terror in the ear of the mighty. And it bears a credential stronger by far than the plaudits of sycophants, than multitudes of 'chariots and horses.' It is — the truth.

The oracle embraces the times of Nahum as well the end of history, the 'last days.' Assyrian, Egyptian, Babylonian, Roman, and so on and so on; the names we know, the tyrannies, the vaunts and pretentions. Each and all, empires that shook the earth are unmasked, revealed in the light. The light is merciless, it is judgment.

Each and all, the emperors wear no clothing.
Each and all, they have violated the human measure.
Each and all, (dare say it, Nahum so dares!) the empires have no future.
Each and all, their fate is — to be overthrown.
And at the end, as shall appear, the saints will overcome!

Thus that 'meantime,' that 'little moment' of liberation, fragile and temporary as it is, like the passing glory of a summer day, has become an image, a hint, a metaphor. Above all, and most poignantly of all, a promise. There will come a time (thus Jesus also prophesies) when the 'little people,' the meek, will indeed possess the earth. Once and for all.

No longer this or that paltry concession wrung from the powerful, concessions designed only to pacify and weaken the will; bread here, circuses there.

The 'little people' might be granted a kind of breathing space, if they consent to huddle out of sight, to labor like beasts of burden (and never to their own gain), to be victimized, be nothing, be silent. And thus be complicit, like sheep led dumb to the slaughter — when required.

This comprises their approved conduct in so called 'times of peace.'
Until they are drummed up peremptorily, to kill and die in war.

They (we) are to know it and tremble and take heart. In the mad cacophony that goes by the name worldly or imperial order, one thing is certain. There will always be a next war. The next war is as certain in prospect as the last war is in history.

What is one to name it — a law of empire, a curse laid on the empire? War is taken for granted; its occurrence is viewed as simply a law of empire, of the prospering of empire — (and of decline as well, if empires but knew, or heeded).

Thus the next war is built into the present war or the war immediately past (or the war remotely past).

But in our national history every war is immediately past. Decades once passed between wars, then a few years between wars, now months between wars. Each war-to-come presses hard upon the present. Win the headlines, run up the flag! It is as though the veterans of the last war tripped over the heels of the warriors newly called up.

The next war is built into history or human nature or fate or the will of the gods. The Bible says so; the evidence is millennia long. It is built in, as mortar and rock are built into an impregnable wall, and the wall goes up and up, stone on stone. It is the wall of Babel, it mocks the heavens.

A wall? Behind the wall, as is told in the holy myth, is a garden; in its light and color, in the play of its beauty, our humanity might be thought to flourish.

But we stand outside, and sweat, and slave, building the wall. Wilfully or blindly, or both.

Or the 'next war' is based on a law, whether of economics or sociology or history or mass psychology or the pathology of power — or perhaps all of these converging. A law understood biblically (and rarely elsewhere) as the law of Gog and Magog.

Thus, inevitably, such oracles as are here recorded by Nahum are launched on empty air (better, into the teeth of contrary winds).

The words are all of contravention, refusal, anarchy, resistance, subversion. It is as though a code word was passed in the midst of a small beleaguered people. It is a dangerous word, and secret. It bespeaks relief, and more. It tolls like a passing bell, the end, the 'cutoff, the passing away.'

The oracle not only heartens the victimized. Ignored or derided by the powerful, the oracle casts a long shadow, a nay-saying doubt, over the throne and its occupant.

Let besotted throngs nod approval, a metronomic 'yes' to the will of the mighty. The oracle speaks another word: 'No.' It raises questions where none are allowed. Like a blade plunged through an arras, it cuts through the official 'line,' cuts to the heart.

It also breaks an evil spell, a blind destiny. It dares summon and enliven the imagination of the victims. Is the present intolerable, inhuman? Say so! Only imagine! Another future, a break in the lock step.

Such a word summons, creates, brings to pass — another future than the one unshakably (so we are told from on high and have all but believed) in place.

("Believe me, trust me, read my lips, no war, no higher taxes, no recession. More troops, war possible, war probable, war as last resort, war as preemptive strike. No troop rotation. War for jobs, war not at all for oil. War against naked tyranny....")

"And now I will break his yoke from about you; and will burst your bonds asunder."

(1:14) To the king of great Nineveh, 'here is a command.'

It seems rather in the nature of a bare announcement: "No race shall bear your name." Whether 'your name' refers to the king or the entire realm is undisclosed. Either way, the threat is a terrible one.

A contradiction, a denial of imperial presumption. The 'name,' implying as it does continuity of power and glory, is to be annihilated.

The king (imagine!) will survive in another way than he conjured: in the annals of a scripture that defied and denied him — that finally judged him.

He is to be brought low. His only interest for future generations will be a warning, the example of a 'caveat,' a 'thou shall not.'

He is thus stripped of his glory, buried alive. His official biographers and chroniclers are rebuked. Despite all splendid evidence to the contrary, all pomp and circumstance, he is a corpse, he lies already head to foot with his ancestors. In a mausoleum embossed it may be, with tyrannical cliches, encomia, the forced tributes of the conquered. Like to alike, ancestor to progeny, dust to dust.

NAHUM

Only his spirit lives on. It is the spirit of death. There will be other tyrants, while time lasts; and their gods as well, always their gods. But the terrible decree announced against each, continues in force against all. It shadows every pretention — while time lasts.

And what of the king's temple and his idols? They too are to come down, 'sculpted images and molten.' Jawe brooks no rivals.

But the conflict is not to be understood as a war of tribal gods with Jawe, so to speak, prevailing — or not. This may have once been the primitive understanding of the tribe; but this was before God formed a people, before covenant.

But not after. And more to the point, not after Jesus. This must be said, and pondered, and taken to heart again and again. God is not one among the gods, superior to them, acknowledged above them. God is — God. No gods before Me.

And this in view of the ever newer gods, the ever renewed tyrannies, the ongoing slaughter of the innocent, the new technological empires, the worship of Mammon, the greed, the duplicity. True. Say it, tell your heart, strengthen your arm.

In spite of the latest war — and hardly the last.

For centuries we have had in our possession (and we have it not, rejected and ignored as is the word of God) an instruction known as the Sermon on the Mount.

And on the other hand, nuclear and 'conventional' weapons, plaguing the earth, overshadowing creation with their threat of annihilation. An impasse.

And what of Jesus and his teaching? Pondered, taken in account?

Alas. It will bear painful recalling: The Iraqi war was immanent and the word from the churches was no more than a Constantinian recourse, a confabulation; something like 'the American actions fall (or do not fall) within the limits of just war theory.'

Suppose one were to counter this, as clearly and simply as possible, in the following way: Jesus has instructed us to love our enemies, to do good to those who would harm us. And in consequence, Christians are not allowed to kill others or to be complicit in such killing.

No such word was issued. Instead, there was much prating of 'just war theory.' The argument for such reasoning being, one supposes, the necessity of being 'relevant' to the times and their insanity.

The scandal, let it be understood, is not that the empire is playing out its immemorial game of violence, threat, carnage. Such behavior is as old as the Assyria of Nahum, and older. The scandal is that the church is unwilling or unable to speak abroad, loud and clear, the plain teaching of Christ.

In time of war (is it ever not a time of war?) the question for the church is a question of true or false worship.

'For the duration' as is said, it is as though one image must be removed from the temples and others installed. The unbearable image is that of peacemaking Christ on the cross. The new ikons are those of the gods of 'just war.'

Idols, 'graven and molten,' are installed in the holy place.

At the same time, the priestcraft is circumspect; not every idol is admissible. Those win entrance and veneration whose spirit allows for murder, but only for 'just murder.'

These authorities are discriminating. There are, after all, limits as to 'just war', so too 'just idolatry.'

And in conclusion: "I will dig your grave, for you are vile." Or another translation: "I will make of your grave an ignominy."

This talk of death and graves, from the mouth of the God of life! We had not heard it before, this stunning irony.

By implication, the king is already given over to death. Death was his declared method of engaging conflict. Death was the common fate he apportioned to his victims, the poor, the 'enemy.' Beyond dispute, beyond serious cavil, taken quite coldly for granted in the circle of his counselors — was the decree, the solution; the death of many. (Does it all sound distressingly domestic and contemporary?)

NAHUM

To what end, we ask, at wits' end, this obsession with death?

Why, it is all quite simple. For land, for treasure, for oil, for the bloodline, for honor, for freedom, for 'our way of life,' for glory, for the fatherland. The debate, the calculus, the to-fro weighing of cost and gain is resolved in these terms: many must die if the empire is to flourish.

But what of the king and his inner circle?

This, a promise — flimsy, besotted, fictional, obsessive — that they will not die.

In their own mind, under the mendacious tutelage of their gods, they are exempt from the death they inflict so broadly and brutally. They can imagine, calculate, decree the death of others, multitudes of 'others'; but not their own. That they too lie under the common fate is literally unimaginable.

Thus we encounter two contrary words concerning life and death. They are beyond reconciling.

There is the word of Jawe and the word of the king. The king: We, our empire, our bloodline, our ideology, our flag, our free enterprise system, our control of world markets, our spanking arms sales — these are immortal.

And then Jawe, like the ghost of Banquo unaccountably standing at the orgy of the tyrant: You will die, your line will be annihilated, your realm scattered.

The truth at last! Had the king ever, lifelong, heard the truth concerning himself? He had not. He heard only praise, abject, fawning, serving this or that interest. And from his subjects, lying low in fear, likewise: praise, thanksgiving. And from his own machinery of propaganda, the same.

He had access to the truth only from — someone named Nahum, a nobody, an outsider. One perhaps to be judged insane, perhaps not. Harmless, in any case. Presuming, like any vagrant madman, to speak in the name of Jawe. A vainglorious one daring to mouth purported quotes of his God: 'I shall do this....'

Nahum beyond doubt goes unheeded; he can be dismissed with a wave of the hand — irrelevant. If lucky, he is let be.

NAHUM

This small non-descript figure (so we imagine him) is as irrelevant as Jesus and his unheeded command: love your enemies. Indeed as we saw the engines of war move toward a terrible hour, a generous sentiment could be felt in both church and state:

"'Love your enemies?' Let the saying be, it can do no harm. It has never seriously impeded us or our forebears."

"Let us then simply ignore it; let the chaplains ignore it, the Christian soldiers, the enemy, the weapons' makers, the preachers on both sides. Let us concentrate our minds' powers. The war is on."

(1:15) The changes of mood, this volcanic Jawe! From the announcement of the death of the immortal one, we turn to a veritable explosion of hope.

The king and his idols are toppled, we are told. Where once there proudly stood both temple and palace, there remains only a hecatomb, dusty, twilit.

And then, a runner arrives! Someone bears good news for the 'little people.' It is as though the messenger of peace must tread on the grave of the mighty, in order to deliver his word: salvation!

The gods, their spell broken, are overthrown. Their name has become a term of contempt. Jawe has named them, that great primal Refuser and Derider. First the idol is set to naught: 'Belial, the despised, the worthless, the wicked.' And the king who paid them homage is likened to them: 'vile.'

Now the religious rites can be resumed after the long horrid hiatus of idolatry and persecution.

In an image dear also to Isaiah, Ezekiel and the Psalmist, Nahum celebrates the vine of Jawe, long plundered and uprooted. Despite all, it survives in its 'remnant.' It will be planted anew, and flourish.

(2:1-14) The transition is subtle but unmistakable. In chapter one Assyria was addressed in words of doom-saying. Now, as to the fate of Nineveh. That empire too will come to the same end it brought to the 'little people.'

And the prophet's tongue is free; he breaks into extraordinary, seemingly spontaneous poetry. He sees, as though with a third eye, the battle joined.

Augustin George praises:

"...the skillful developing of metaphors, the concision and firmness, tonality and dramatic movement of the images.... By violent transitions and fierce rhythms, (Nahum) brings us face to face with the scenes he describes; we commune with his profound emotion. No poet of Israel has surpassed this extraordinary evocative power."

We are reminded of parallel descriptions of battle in Isaiah (5:25 ff.) and Jeremiah. (4:5-7)

It must be conceded that for skill in conveying the chaos, anguish, pity and terror raging through the doomed city, Nahum surpasses both.

The crime of crimes: war!

As a matter of course, with hardly a second thought (certainly without remorse), the great powers undertake war — in this instance against one another.

It is literally impossible (and perhaps fruitless as well) to weigh on the scales of liability which of the combatants is the worse.

A war between criminals is branded in simple truth, for what it is: criminal war.

It is the law of empire, the law of the jungle. There cannot be two empires, two kings of the beasts. Not for long. Like two besotted lions in heat, each faces off, seeking domination of the same pride.

The war is declared criminal. It is as though the repugnance of Jawe can be conveyed only by this extreme example, an assault in which no party can claim innocence.

But what of the innocent, the non-combatants, the defenseless? They are (then and now) cowering, victimized, expendable.

On their behalf, newly widowed and orphaned as they are, the outcry of Jawe!

And for their sake, the eye of Nahum rests with austere tenderness, even on Nineveh, persecutor of his people — he sees that monstrous world encompassing entity, sacked and burned to ash. Medes and Babylonians at the gate! Corpses of innocent and guilty alike piled on a single hecatomb! Pity and terror and no winners!

How different the spirit of Nahum from that of recalcitrant Jonah, refusing to believe that Jawe can love even Nineveh. Refusing to believe that the love of Jawe can be patient even with — Jonah.

Great of heart, Nahum is the inspired onlooker, the witness. The last ditch battle is underway. Contention, voices blaring: Halt, halt! Then: Grab the silver, seize the gold!

No denunciation, let the horror speak for itself. Nahum neither glories nor condemns; this is the genius of the magnificent threnody. His words move in nervous rhythms, a swift, surreal passage from feverish light to dark, the senselessness and panic, warriors glorying in the most debased conduct; rapine, wanton destruction.

Nothing is spared, no one. Total war, an old story indeed!

(1:7) A poignant detail: in the midst of the bloodletting, the 'Lady,' otherwise unidentified, is stripped and led off in exile. With her go her ladies-in-waiting, 'lamenting, moaning like doves, striking their breasts.'

Perhaps, we are told, the reference is to the image of the goddess Ishtar, or to an actual queen. In either case the implication is clear; nothing is sacred, neither human nor ikon.

In a deeper, all but metaphysical sense, the war cuts asunder the human itself. The feminine and the warrior cannot be reconciled. Therefore the hideous logic of force: let all images of tenderness and compassion, whether living or ikonic, be stripped, humiliated, exiled. For the duration and beyond.

The war is total. It also rages within; a war in which the warrior must throttle the voice of his own heart.

When all are inducted, all in lock step — what then of the feminine, the Lady? She is banished, her images pulled down.

The chief god of Assyria, we are told, was a curious deity named Ashur. The god had no consort; he was pure warrior, naked male, so predatory and heartless as to be thought a monster. He was in fact the embodiment and deification of empire itself.

What need had he of the voice of the heart? He required only a steady will, no second thoughts, a sword in hand.

From John McKenzie:

"Politically the Assyrians were the first to realize the world state. Had they developed an administrative machinery to compare with their military machine, it would have endured longer. They did not... and had to hold the empire together by force. A part of this force was the calculated frightfulness of their conquests, which we learn from their own records. They intended to weaken resistance and discourage revolt by making horrible examples of rebels and persistent enemies.

"Hence whole cities were entirely destroyed, kings and their officers were flayed or impaled, whole armies were decapitated and whole populations enslaved....

" The ideal of a world state, that people would attain maximum peace and security under a single government, likewise passed to Alexander and from him to Rome. Thence it lived on in such ideals as the Holy Roman Empire, 'Christendom,' and all subsequent efforts to achieve over a continental area what the Assyrians did...."

(2:11-13) Then the famous image of the lion of Assyria is summoned. The image is wonderfully apt; it combines majesty and horror:

"The hunting of lions was a favorite sport of Assyrian kings; when there were no wild lions, they were released from cages to afford sport for the king." (McKenzie)

The 'cave' and 'den' images are provocative. The empire is predatory and yet is captive to its own nature. It ranges and prowls abroad; it returns dragging its prey, to lioness and whelps. But 'where now is the cave, the den of the young lions'?

Grand palace, lofty temple? Does Nahum envision a cave — or a kingdom? He sees both. "(Assyria) filled his cave with prey and his dens with torn flesh."

And yet, and yet. Judgment is at hand; it is definitive: "I am against you, says the Lord of hosts."

An apocalypse follows. The assault on the city stirs a nightmare brew of surreal images: "I will burn your chariots to a smoke and the sword shall devour your young lions."

(2:8-11) Warmaking is a bloody to-fro, a tit-for-tat. As you have done to Thebes, so is it done to you. Are you then stronger than Thebes (which you sacked) though the Nile, together with powerful neighbors, Libya, Ethiopia, Egypt, formed a seemingly impregnable wall of defense?

Take note of the fate of Thebes; it is to be your own. Exile, massacre of children, the high and mighty led off in chains.

Victor, vanquished. Human communality (for the duration) is divided in two, as though by a sword. A horrid reminder of the common loss of humanity that afflicts the warmakers. No one emerges unscathed; the victors least of all.

In 1991 the American armies prepared for a quick 'surgical' strike and a quick victory against Iraq. A multitude of 'the enemy,' including women, children, the aged and ill, perished.

The death of many was soberly taken in account.

And one wonders: do not the victors, having won the war through massive 'smart' bombing of Iraqi cities, emerge more arrogant than before, less contained, more apt for war, as first rather than last resort?

We shall see; the prognosis is dire.

And who in such circumstances as beset us is to play Nahum? Who will renounce status, self-interest, power, and bring to royal attention certain lost truths?

Who but a lonely figure with no access to power (indeed with no stomach for such access)? Who will undertake so thankless a task?

The king, as is told here and elsewhere, is ill-served by his 'wise ones.' He is distracted and deceived with promises of a war that will cost little and bring vast returns of booty and glory.

No ruler, whatever the provocation or virtue of the cause, goes to war with the expectation of losing. No one senses that the horrors he lets loose on the enemy will be visited on his own people. That unwelcome truth is left to Nahum to utter. "You also, you will be encircled and oppressed;

you too will seek a refuge from the enemy."
The itch, the temptation, the fever, the illusion!

In the flush of national victory, Nahum lets loose his images of futility and defeat. Intolerable, unwelcome, troublemaking, weakening the common purpose, this prophet of ill account!

His cry: Someone must lose, take heed. The victor stands to lose most of all.

The argument in favor of war, any war, begins with a disclaimer of truly disarming candor.

"Let us grant for argument's sake, the premise of domestic and foreign critics alike. Let us concede that in the past our country has undertaken wars that in retrospect seem somewhat (let us be generous, more than somewhat) questionable as to ideology and behavior. We concede this, we are chastened."

"But now, but now! We have at hand an absolutely irrefutable argument for war. We have at length a good war, a virtuous war, an absolutely necessary war!"

"A war whose just cause even the most morally jaundiced in our midst must grant!"

"We enter this war with a will unsullied — with the sole motive of repelling aggression on the part of an implacable enemy."

"Let us therefore utter without prejudice a warning. Such doubters and nay-sayers as raise an outcry against the national effort are in error; they will be dealt with."

(3:1-19) The utterances of the Nahum and his like are a form of poetic deflation, mockery. Deflate, mock, unmask. The oracles thus act as a remedy, a healing; they aim to assuage the illness of the royal imagination, as in verses 12 and following:

You, our leaders, speak at some length of military strength, the number and skill of troops, fortresses, impregnable defenses. Since the truth is in question, let me offer a contrary image. Your redoubtable strengths are no more than — ripe figs, free for the plucking. "Shake the trees, the fruit falls to the mouth."

NAHUM

Deflate, mock, unmask. No better way to convey the unpalatable truth. Who knows, the truth may penetrate even a crowned skull!

Nahum proceeds.

I see your troops weak, falling back, those unscalable gates of yours gaping wide to the enemy.

Dream your fantasies then, concoct your victories in prospect. Set the royal economy on a war basis. In your mind's eye, inflamed with termagancy, multiply cohorts and accountants like a cloud of locusts, your entrepreneurs like the stars of heaven!

Let them chirp and buzz their mad counsel. At sunup, all fly away, no one can rightly say where — or cares.

Intolerable, this Nahum. Figs, locusts — how relentlessly he chooses his images, as though only to degrade the dignity of empire!

And then that jibe of his against the princes and entrepreneurs of world commerce, against gross national income, 'merchants more numerous than stars in the sky.'

As though such matters as greed bore an inevitable connection with war!

Exactly: the prophetic method. The truth, the king unclad.

(2:18-19) And worse, and more.

For conclusion, tell the king of death. Mock the immortal one. Sing threnodies, compose songs of death. Let death hang like a hook, piercing the king's gullet. And this, though his gaze lights only on liveliness, motion, bustle, fire and sword prevailing, a very fever of prescient victory, bearing all before.

Do second thoughts now and again intrude, does the hook twitch in the living throat?

Is the king drawn the length of an inch toward the bitter truth? It must be so. It is called — salvation. And even a king (most of all a king?) must needs be saved.

Nahum stirs it up incontinently, that brew of second thoughts. Like

Daniel he reads the king's nightmares, shouts them aloud.

There is otherwise no hope. For the locusts and grasshoppers have only one string, one tune to sing. It is silly, enervating, an enchantment.

But what happens to a people who go to war, win or lose? Win or lose, what happens to their leaders?

As to the people, Nahum offers images of dispersion. "Your people are scattered on the mountains, there is no one to gather them."

Let us go back and back to the beginning of days.

This people, all people, were created in love, in view of a vocation of love one for another.

A people of covenant, which is to say an orbit of love in which enemies have place. This is spoken of, daringly and insistently. In this covenant, enemies occupy an altogether special place, a pride of place.

It comes to this: the word 'enemy' and the terrible reality (a reality of sin) for which it stands is hereby erased.

'Enemy' is a prior word, a prehuman word, a word on the tongue of the fallen.

'Enemy' is a word of sin, a word to be transformed.

In virtue of covenant, it is declared null and void.

The covenant cancels all enmities; more, sternly forbids them. Love your enemies! Banish the word, from your heart and polity.

Instead of the dream, a perennial nightmare.

Our world, a world of sin on rampage.

The first explosive launched in war bursts in the souls of the people at war. At that moment they have lost the nub of things, lost their center, soul, bearings. They no longer know the simple primal 'one another,' the mark of virtuous (which is to say communal) existence.

This is a truth both terrible and crucial — and all but obliterated in the fire and smoke. The simple phrase 'one another' is banished. The hand extended palm up in comity and compassion has tightened to a fist. The fist bears a sword, the 'one another' has become — the armed other, enemy, ogre, monster, satan.

NAHUM

There is now declared a far different vocation in the world for hand, eye, heart — for the human itself. 'For the duration' (that awful phrase, signifying the canceling of compassion, commensality, civility, likewise the canceling of taboo, warning, prohibition, law) the 'one another' is a struck phrase.

The 'one' is now a warrior, the 'another' an enemy. Comity is in shambles. Contestation, perfidy of every sort, murder of children, suspension of civilized norms of conduct — these are allowed, honored, held up as ideal, the order of the day.

Nahum also offers images of the great ones; the images are extraordinarily contemptuous. (They are also, it goes without saying, in stark contrast with royal self-understanding.)

In the prophets, (and not only in Nahum), it must be admitted that respect for a certain kind of authority is notably absent.

Lilliputians he makes of 'the princes, merchants, officials' — and far less. 'Locusts' they are. The image evokes destructive appetite, mindless instinct, anonymity. The insects are voracious, short-lived, expendable. They flock, multiply, buzz about awhile. And at sunup they vanish, this cloud and conventicle. It is as though such as they could flourish only in darkness, as though light and warmth were beyond bearing.

All this is a kind of death. Nahum senses it before the fact. The odor of death sits heavy on temple and palace; a religion of death, a diplomacy of death. A 'second death,' worse than the first.

And then war. Religion and diplomacy enlisted and on the march, 'for the duration.'

Tell the truth to the king, Nahum. The war kills your elite troops, it scatters your people like a chaff: their souls, their social cohesion, their love and compassion. War is a wound beyond healing.

And what, O king, of the conquered peoples?

Secretly, since they dare say nothing aloud, those who have tasted your cruelty, with a single voice celebrate your downfall.

HABAKKUK

So brief an oracle, and from a prophet whose name is all but unpronounceable, like a stutter of the tongue!

And as for himself, he is all but lost in history, an unknown. All but slips off the page. Yet so moving a message is here offered — irony and resistance, cries of distress, of hope, of abandonment, of near despair.

It reminds one of music; portions of the little oracle could be set to music.

We have before us a briefer, intensely concentrated Jeremiah; a seer tormented by the void that opens when moral evil rides high and mighty, and justice is all but made to disappear.

It is the story of his people; and in accord with the compassion and empathy of a great heart, his own story.

The prophets, major and minor, are obsessed with like themes. Victims languish under the heel of an oppressor, in the present instance, the Babylonians, a constant nemesis of the just. The oppressor like a dark shadow dogs the human condition. It is a persistent mystery: how can it be that a God of goodness tolerates a criminal world?

But is there not also a mystery of goodness?

And is it not the office of goodness to resist evil, and thereby make evil bearable? And more, to reveal evil as precisely evil — an office forever as would seem, beyond the capacities or indeed the will of the wicked!

Habakkuk testifies to the persistence of goodness, standing eye-to-eye with evil, naming wickedness for what it is and does.

His is an absolutely crucial task; for his time, for all time. How else in a world quite literally fallen from grace, could grace prevail?

In gracious God, the graced, the just, prevail. Let that much be conceded, and no more. For the space of a dark 'meantime,' their very survival, their persistence, their refusal to buckle under — this must be accounted their prevailing.

The epiphany, the vindication will come later. So it is promised.

Still, all said, there is a unique line of thought in Habakkuk, left unexplored by the prophets who went before him. Others had interpreted the victory of the 'goyim' over the just as a purification imposed by Jawe. God's patience, it was taught, was exhausted by the sins of the 'little people.' When covenant was violated, a storm broke.

Habakkuk takes another tack. He is not seriously interested in linking the suffering of the just with their moral lapses. Judgment is not his point. His plaint is closer to the spirit of Job; or in our testament, to the lament of the martyrs in Revelation (6:9).

He looks steadily at the criminality of the oppressor. And he asks plainly, painfully: How can it be that crime proceeds and criminals prosper, under the eye of a providential God? Must faith be blind — or has the all seeing One been struck blind? Can faith in a nonviolent God survive, when violence has assumed a godlike, preternatural eminence, a spurious normalcy? When the 'chosen' are taken like animals, tortured, scorned, made to disappear — in such a world what is one to make of the divine 'choice?' Has it simply been reneged on?

The terror raging in the moral universe is the theme of the older prophets. They are guardians of national survival and mourners of the lapsed integrity of the faithful.

In Habakkuk, something else. The larger fate of the believing community is concentrated like a sacred elixir, in the suffering of a single servant of Jawe — in the prophet himself.

HABAKKUK

In this special sense (the one implicit in the all), Habakkuk calls to mind two great moderns, Kierkegaard and Dostoyevsky. Their anguish of spirit is his. The world seems no more than a demented, slovenly inn, crowded with every sort of idler, loser, criminal.

He is introspective, mordantly brilliant in his quest for truth; even though the truth suppurates in his spirit, a wound untended.

He pursues the hidden One like a hound, casts his questions like a spell into the dark corners of existence. There the questions abide, mute and sleepless.

Such anguish as his is lifelong and unassuaged; fidelity serves only to intensify it. His moral greatness burns and abides.

One longs to offer relief to this tormented spirit. (Comfort the prophet? But we had thought it his office to comfort us!)

Let be, let be, we cry!. At odds with the times, he cannot. Life itself, which must of necessity include the life of faith, is twisted; it takes the tormented form of a question mark. The scandal is 'the world, the way it goes,' and no God impeding.

He is ancestor of the Hopkins of the 'terrible sonnets':

"I cast for comfort I can no more get
By groping round my comfortless, than blind
Eyes in their dark can day or thirst can find
Thirst's all-in-all in all a world of wet."

(1:1-17) "The oracle which Habakkuk the prophet saw in a vision" (*BJ*). And the plaint is underway.

Strange at first blush! This questioning of God, this acute even intemperate probing of God's goodness (a goodness tenaciously presumed), is the fruit of a vision of God. 'Vision of God' — at least in the sense that the vision is granted by God.

Let us venture this: Bereft of a 'vision,' at least in the sense of a light struck amid encompassing darkness, a small flare alight against all odds in the dark winds of predicament — we lose all grounding.

We lose heart, lose inclination. Shall we turn to a God whose existence, suddenly or slowly, but in any case surely, has become irrelevant to our plight?

Deprived of that small crucial light, we are lost.

Giving up, yielding before injustice becomes the very shape (misshape) of our lives.

Let us grant (for the sake of argument, as they say) the existence of a 'God.' Let us be generous, and bestow on so shadowy a Being a capital letter. Let us go further; dare an intemperate, even absurd leap in the dark.

All this done, all conceded, we ask: are things thereby ameliorated in the world? Has humankind been suddenly rendered fraternal, simply because we have come to believe?

Nothing of this. God or no God, the world is still — itself.

We have here the modern (and ancient) scandal, the dilemma proposed by those who indict faith as bad faith, alienation, cowardice, refusing to 'face things as they are.'

Still, foolish or heroic (or both, since the faith of Habakkuk includes a measure of both foolishness and heroism), the dialogue between Jawe and the suffering servant is underway. It begins moreover, with God approving the near effrontery of the prophet's quest. A painful proceeding, one thinks, on both sides!

One is hard put to imagine that in such times as his or our own, faith could take a form other than this; an outcry, a deep groaning of the guts.

The words are only part of the corporal gesture; the cry of 'how long?' rises, twisting from a deep pit. The times are literally beyond words, madly blind, blindly exterminating. Lucifer is at large.

And God? At small?

The point, the value of this, the faith of a prophet, is not merely that questions are raised. Much more is implied.

The point, the hope even, is — a conversation is underway. Two beings are doing their utmost, to hear and be heard. They shout to one another across the clamor, the lunar terrain of the world, the trenches and guns and corpses, the ghettoes and alleys and dead ends, the skyscrapers and hovels, the vessels aloft in space, the ships at sea.

The two are by turns weeping and raging.

And this hot tempered, dramatic, even dudgenous shouting match, we are told, is — faith, on the receiving and conferring end, both.

We have here in the plain text no fiction, however noble or elevated. No, believe or not (and Habakkuk believes, despite all) — Another, an Opposite, an Adversary, a hidden One, a Lover — Someone, unnamed, unnameable, is near, engaged, hearkens, objects, rages, flares up, sings a love song.

The text is a veil, beyond which stands — an event. Surrounding Habakkuk and his questioning is no void of absurdity. No mythic character is proposed as partner to the dialogue. An Existence stands, a Being, an 'I AM,' independent of the prophet, independent of ecstatic or literary genius, of the bias of scribe or witness.

Something else. Someone. One who acts in the world, or refuses to act, who intervenes, or refuses to intervene. Sovereign. Hidden. Not to be cajoled (though surely to be impetrated, questioned, objected to, denounced even).

Perhaps, all said, the closest we can come to It — to the God of Habakkuk — is the God of Moses, the Being in the Bush, the 'I am Who Am.'

Or the One written of by the evangelist: "God is love."

The prophet cries out. And it is as though a dark Epiphany flared from the heart of Mystery. Someone hearkens and responds.

In a sense, the prophet is offering a circular argument; one believes or not, one stands within the circle or outside. If outside, the text is little more than a literary exercise, noble, tinged perhaps with a hint of pathos or regret or loss.

And if one stands inside? Let it be admitted, the circle is no refuge, it

HABAKKUK

is more like a circle of fire. Its consolations are largely negative, a mere hint, an implication (in more senses than one), a beckoning: Come, the pain and horror of the world await you.

At least this can be adduced in favor of standing there, inside. The queries of the prophet go somewhere, like an arrow into the darkness. And then — Someone cries out; the shaft has struck home.

The words are not lost on the winds of hell (which of a certainty are loosed on the world.)

Not lost. For in this gospel according to Habakkuk, God Is.

And yet, and yet — this God is so silent, so beyond comprehension, so unavailing. 'Ac si non esset' — God is as though God were not. A strange device on the banner.

But not total silence. Can it be that the response, and the cold comfort implied, also issues from a suffering Servant? Is the eloquence of God stifled; is providence reduced to a groan, under the universal swath of death, the wickedness in high places, the wars? Do the tears of God, as well as the tears of the prophet, fall on a mad world? Commingled, are they the elixir of redemption?

Who questions God, who speaks for the victim today?

And who today are the 'Babylonians?' Nothing is more crucial to biblical understanding than to assign, as it were, 'speaking parts' in our drama.

We have a clue in the person of Habakkuk. The questioner has a strange, even cruel credential: he is a suffering servant of Jawe, a victim.

And we are impelled to think of our lifetime, of the base communities languishing under the heel of oligarchs and armies. And at home, the resisters against war in jail, on trial (my brother Philip in jail as I write), the resisters against perpetual war, war as first, not last recourse and option, war threatened and launched, wanton waste and spending for war.

The resisters! They go patiently about their task, intent on an improbable vision: the beating of swords into plowshares.

HABAKKUK

And we think as well of the dead; as Revelation (chapter 6) reminds us shockingly, they continue to question God. 'Under the altar' disquiet reigns, the tongues of the unquiet martyrs ululate.

We summon the nameless dead of Panama, who perished under the monstrous pummeling of the barrios by the Stealth bomber. They were shoveled like debris into mass graves. Who more honorably entitled to question God?

And those Iranian villagers, children, women, the aged, who died in the hideous chemical warfare of Hussein — shall they not question God with pure and remorseless tongues?

And the Vietnamese, and the Nicaraguans, and the Salvadorans, and the South Africans, and the ....

The 'Babylonians'? Best to be precise in assigning — not so much guilt as responsibility.

We recall that other prophets stressed the sins of the 'little people,' their own people, as bringing on themselves condign suffering, exile, near extinction. Which is to suggest that we cannot easily dispense with the constant prophetic drumbeat; God's judgment begins at home, with the reneging people of the promise, not with the pagans and goys.

So be it. As I set down these notes, the world held its breath. The vast armies, spoiling for combat, squared off in the Arabian moonscape. The United Nations, founded on a perennial vision of peacemaking, set about rattling a great sword; it was forged in the perverse fires of a common, twisted will. War, which has served no good cause in recorded history, is again summoned; a good cause and just!

An ultimatum is issued to Hussein: out of Kuwait by the new year, or else.

We have here, in spite of the hurling of epithets back and forth, a Babylonian spirit on rampage — in both camps. It is important to stress the truth; there is no 'good cause.'

The words spoken by Habakkuk against the wicked regimes of his lifetime, fall from his tongue like spurts of inextinguishable fire. And today the same words light up the conduct and ethos of Americans and Iraqis alike: (1:1-4) 'violence ... wrongs ... trouble ... destruction ... strife ... contention.'

To haul onstage the creaking decor of the just war theory is to confabulate a mad mirage. Just? A war? Any war? Habakkuk insists, the stark opposite is true; justice itself is the first victim of war (1:4).

The concealment, duplicity, propaganda, demonizing, avail nothing. If sanity is to be held to, someone must say as directly as possible, there is nothing to choose between the contenders. Each side is simply criminal in the eyes of God.

The Iraqis have murdered the innocent and are quite determined to continue doing so. And the Americans are under judgment as well; an iron-bound will to initiate the war implies the worst form of bad faith. With the blood of Grenada, Panama, Vietnam, Cambodia, Laos on our hands, we would once more make of mass killing a necessary, even a virtuous act. What vile foolishness!

What then is the biblical response to such crimes? Where are we to stand?

We must summon to our side those whose lives and deaths are their sole credential; the great 'cloud of witnesses' who at enormous cost have earned the right, if one may so speak, to question God. Including Habakkuk.

(1:5 ff.) The God of the Bible is well-known for supplying (as here) no direct answers to questions put. Quite the opposite! Nothing but non-answers, or at best, highly unsatisfactory answers.

Jawe it seems, will not be cornered, even by the saints.

We had best not soften or explain away the plain sense of the words. We have here, in reply (but not really) to the anguished outburst of Habakkuk, a brief, even brutal recourse to something known as the 'long view.'

Jawe begins by claiming an insight which in the nature of things is wanting to us humans. The war, the invasion, the consequent misery are, plainly put, Jawe's doing. "I am doing a work in your days which you would not believe if told...." (Indeed!) "For lo, I am arousing the Babylonians...."

This is an apocalyptic admission; we see it repeated centuries later in Revelation. The unsealing of the four scrolls (Rev. 6:1-8) releases a series of mounted rampagers.

The empires, that is to say, are invited, goaded, spurred on, by Jawe. 'Do your worst' is implied. If evil is in question (with the empires of history, it is the only question), let evil be loosed, be itself, let it have its day. Out in the open, a text plain to read! Let it be manifest at last. No sealed orders, no secret deals, no history fabricated in darkness!

This is a word of pure terror. Indeed the answer offered, such as it is, is more terrible than the questioner had dared imagine. Is ours then a kind of 'showdown God?'

Only in the sense, it would appear, that God would have evil at length unmasked — this is the plain sense of what we have called the 'non-answer.' It is unsatisfactory at best, whether to Habakkuk or ourselves. He, and we, had other expectations; and with sound reason, we think. We hoped to hear a word of comfort, of mitigation, a 'religious' word.

We long to hear that the reign of terror (our lifetime!) is to be lifted at last.

Nothing of that, no end of it; terror seeps into our dwellings, our hearts, like a trail of blood under a closed door.

Which is surely not to say there is no judgment upon the murderers. The judgment is here explicitly handed down (1:11) — but is not necessarily executed.

Today that pall, that shadow, that judgment, lies on the monstrous desert protagonists — as well, be it insisted, on the highly respectable officials of both sides; on the dictator and the president, the politicians, the judges, the weapons makers and researchers, on the vast inert citizenry — on all who by default or decision, have set the chariots of Mars in motion.

Let them quake where they stand, where they hurl imprecations and rattle muskets, where they create refugees, take hostages, proliferate want and misery, wreck the earth, contemn the poor. Where they walk away from the carnage, untouched, unaccountable — into headlines, parades, honors.

Let them quake where they stand, justifying all this, each side 'making the worse appear the better argument.'

To no avail. The judgment is handed down.

It is not yet executed, alas. Habakkuk and ourselves are rife with dismay. Is ours a God of interminable delay? Is patience commended to us, again and again, unto the end of our lives, as the chief virtue of the times?

Yes, it would seem, on both counts.

(1:6-11) The mood of Jawe regarding the invaders, must be accounted a sovereign mix of awe and hot fury. Never on land or sea, such an agglomerate of destruction as is here assembled!

The parallel is haunting, uncanny. Word for word, taking in account the murderous technological huff and bluff of our own time, one scans the words as though they were composed this day.

It is as though ancient war machines were resurrected from the debris of the centuries, were cloned, geared up, perfected, then multiplied and immensely enlarged as to omniviolence — then were lined up, itching for the 'all systems go,' eye-to-eye in the Arabian sands. New techniques for the progeny of ancestor Cain!

Jawe might be thought to speak today:

"I am rousing the Iraqis and the Americans, alike they are, bitter and intemperate people."

"They march about the earth, seizing lands not their own."

"Dread and terrible are they; their law, their grandeur lie only in force."

"Their phalanxes are swifter than leopards, more fierce than wolves at evening."

"Their bombers come from afar to possess the sky, they fly like eagles swift to devour."

"All, all assemble only for violence."

"Terror precedes them."

"Their hostages, refugees, captives are numerous as the desert sands."

HABAKKUK

"They scoff at the law of nations, they overwhelm and devour."
"They swoop down like a hurricane - and are gone."
"Criminal they are, one and all."
"Force is their only god."

Where a more acute analysis of imperial character and conduct? The passage, be it noted, has the advantage of a 'view from beneath'; the victim knows the executioner.

Justice, dignity? Perversity lurks in the human frame. It urges only injustice and pillage. "Darkness, be thou my light.' It is as though history had taught nothing to the perpetually retrograde, as though inhumanity were the thorny crown of the human.

An epiphany flares up. In the lurid light of war the warriors see their true face. It is as though all faces were fused in one. And that final form is self-justified. The blood of the victim is its credential. They let blood, and wickedly rejoice.

Thus we are plunged in primordial darkness. The planet flips over, noon is turned to midnight.

It is as though God had yet to say: let there be light. Or as though the demons had decreed: let there be only darkness.

And yet — it is all under judgment . "Criminal they are, who make of violence their god!"

(1:12 ff.) The prophet pursues his dolorous course.

What shall we call this astonishing encounter, this facing off with Jawe? All said, all left unsaid, we are left with — Thou and I. The words have the audacity of a reproof, the trust of a child affronted, confused; but despite all, knowing itself cherished.

Let us for a start, says Habakkuk, call to mind those ancient names of Yours, coined in the fire of love. You are the God of Liberation and of the Promise. You are my God, my holy One. You cannot know death.

And now? You have mounted against us this great adversary, for judgment and chastisement.

All this the prophet grants; and yet it rubs faith raw, and hope as well.

"You whose eyes cannot bear sight of perfidy and oppression, how can you keep silent as the impious swallow the righteous?"

The indictment continues; it is terrible.

The God of justice is confronted here, not by the wicked (their bad faith and self-justification are easily answered), but by God's chosen and just. A sense of indignation and wounding lies on the air; Habakkuk has had enough of such a world (of such a God?).

The images he dredges up! The hook and net of the wicked are busy; Jawe has made of the just a fishy harvest. Evil hands haul in the just, exulting.

There are hints of a kind of perverse orgy; the just are the piece de resistance in the banquet of the wicked.

And yet another mysterious image: "You make humans like crawling things, without mastery." Again, the just? Under so cruel a 'providence,' they are brought low, scarcely to be accounted among the living. They are like eyeless worms.

Bitter, indignant words, an arrow aimed at the heart of God. One is in wonderment; what suffering compounded such poison as tips this arrow?

The image, the wicked fisherman, ends in — idolatry. His catch secured, the warrior-fisher falls to knee before his seine and net (before his sword and shield, before his Stealth bomber and Mohawk missile?).

There is even a scent of incense in the air.

The image goes to the heart of the matter. Unaccountable crime, evil that is even rendered virtuous 'for reasons of state,' (crimes of war that is, liable as they are in principle to international law, but falling cunningly through the interstices of the net) — such crimes biblically understood, invariably imply — idolatry.

The false worship, be it understood, is one with the action that preceded it. What more natural, more godly, (more American) after say, the pulverizing of a Panamanian barrio, than that the warriors of the upper air retire to 'the church of their choice'? That they there give thanks for the efficiency of their 'net and seine'? That the worship be void of regret for the 'collateral damage' done against the flesh of the poor? That flesh which is both expendable, and regrettably combustible.

True worship offered true God?
In search of a more fitting geography, the charade might aptly proceed on the tarmac of the air base, the warrior-fishers in hot flush of their catch, 'offering sacrifice to their net and burning incense to their seine.'
And the motive of all this? The image of Habakkuk is relentless; let us dare apply it.
For the sake of the economy, we are told, for American jobs, for oil — for these the criminality of war is annulled, indeed the slaughter is rendered dignum et justum. So the war must proceed; 'for by these (their catch) they live in luxury and their food is rich.'

And the prophet ends with a cry, the cry of Job, of the martyrs of Revelation: How long O Lord? Is the fisher to fill his net forever, pitiless and engorged?

(2:1-20) The prophet has taken heart once more, and resumed his task. In this instance, under the imagery of a vigiler or sentinel. Is it the nightwatch he assumes?
In any case, night is a fierce, demanding time to stand watch. Darkness covers the the earth, deep as the maw of hell. Who knows what horrors lurk?

He sees himself as a kind of surrogate providence. Has Jawe abandoned the innocent, the just, favoring instead the wicked harvest of the fishers? So be it. If Jawe sleeps, the prophet will not.
Habakkuk's imagery is an implied reproof. Perhaps Jawe is not slumbering, perhaps the eye of God has turned elsewhere. Then the eye

of Habakkuk will be steady in compassion. He will protect the innocent, doubly vulnerable as they are — without recourse and asleep in their houses.

But he remains awake, 'mindful' as the buddhists would have it. He summons to mind's eye the children. And he awaits nightlong a signal from God, a word responding to his 'complaint.'

(2:2) Jawe awakens, turns to the prophet. The response begins with an instruction. "Write down the vision." It must be graven deep and writ large, on stone or bronze or wood or lead, for its subject is — patience.

Write it down! The word signifies a difficult virtue, so hard of apprehension, so rare in act; it cannot simply be passed mouth to ear and thus be thought to enter the heart.

The oracle that follows is a matter of 'remembering the future.' Hence the command: write it down. Indeed, remembrance of the command will determine the very substance of the future.

This crucial matter of memory and its awful opposite, forgetting, amnesia.

We have seen in our lifetime, the assault on the power of memory, a culture that flourishes like a witless Queen of Lotusland, inducing a sweet amnesiac slumber in its citizen-victims.

The penalty of foraging on the cultural lotus is plain to see. Forget Vietnam, proceed as though sleepwalking, into Grenada and Panama, Salvador and Nicaragua. Forget these, prepare a vast plague of war in the Persian desert.

The amnesiacs are biblically illiterate; no oracles engraved on tablets 'easy to read.' The memory of most is a tabula rasa. Its nearest image is a blank television screen, awaiting the next instantaneous flickering to engage wayward attention — for a moment.

T.S. Eliot has described us in a phrase: "Distracted from distraction by distraction."

(2:3) "The vision awaits its time; it aspires to its end, it will not deceive. If it seems slow, wait for it. It will surely come true, it will not delay."

We have as yet no inkling of the content of the 'vision.' There are only generic words teasing us forward — first 'vision' itself, then 'it.'

Thus the grammar itself bespeaks a mystery, says 'wait'; the 'vision' unfolds at the end of the oracle. It is as though the word of God were finally to be revealed only at the end time.

But what of the vision? What is being said to us? Wait, wait on it. The vision is granted only to the patient. Attention to the word of God, an unsatisfactory, indeed anti-cultural matter — patience.

The virtue it is implied, stands as a metaphor — for a biblical sense of the times, (of our own supremely impatient times).

In patience we read the planets differently, in their conjunction and passing. Their tyranny is broken, their hold over us, birth and death, suffering and ecstasy.

No, our clocks read otherwise. So do our hearts beat to a different drummer.

Patience is an act or a habit — of resistance.

It puts us at odds, sets limits, boundaries, taboos. It declares in effect, we humans are neither gods nor super-humans.

Comes at long last the content of the vision granted.

It seems at first glance — banal. No mighty visual theophany such as laid Daniel prostrate, or wrung from Isaiah a cry of utmost unworthiness. Nothing of this.

In a single verse, a remarkably straight-forward, double assertion. Sinaitic, all but juridical, shall we call it? In any case, laconic, to the point.

To wit. There is right conduct and wrong; the moral life is of import, and will be subject to judgment.

Indeed, 'will be' is too tame; judgment is at hand, it is the content of the vision.

It is as though Jawe had distilled from the whole of human history, an extremely simple conclusion. As though the God of thunders and fulminations also were to assure us: God too has calm moments, in which everything, at least for the nonce, comes together!

We imagine a hand descending from above. It is not now writing upon a wall the doom of tyrants; it is drawing a line in the soil of earth.

Judgment. The line cuts deep.

Then the 'vision' appears — more properly, speaks, or perhaps writes — and Habakkuk, reporting the words, himself is rendered visionary. "The one whose soul is unrighteous will perish; the just one through his fidelity, will live."

The dictum is not included in the moral equipment of empires. It is not, to say the least, commonly embraced by these entities or their sycophants.

They tend to another direction. They act on either of two brutal assumptions.

According to one: might makes right, as in the slaughter of the students in Bejing.

Or in the case of western technocracies: we note the invoking of a kind of hypocritical concocted 'necessity.' Wars, incursions, surprise attacks, 'surgical strikes' are presented as a temporary suspension of diplomatic or democratic process, (for which read 'civilized', etc). Recourse to war, so goes the lunacy, is forced upon the habitually virtuous by the habitually criminal - the 'new Hitler' syndrome.

In the latter tactic, (which has a woefully familiar ring) a furrowed face and a passing nod to religion are of great help.

It is not, so to speak, that an active contempt greets such a 'vision' as that of Habakkuk, quite the contrary.

Since one is the leader of a 'Christian' people, one must by all means be found on the right side of the judgment; one must be found 'just,' 'faithful.' All the more so, more urgently so — as one's conduct is callously unjust and unfaithful.

The task calls for what the psychologists refer to as 'doubling'; Sartre spoke of 'bad faith.' In any case, the maintaining, shoring up, huckstering, of a double standard.

In his searing book *The Wretched of the Earth*, Franz Fanon tells of a French military officer who approached him, an Algerian psychiatrist. The two were in the nature of the situation, at odds; at the time Algeria was brutally occupied by the French.

The officer was seeking help. He professed above all his being 'a good family man,' tender toward wife and children. And yet to his dismay, he found himself yielding on occasion to unbounded fury, lashing out, striking his children. Why?

Fanon inquired as to his military duties. He admitted finally to be engaged in the torture of prisoners. 'Doubling,' one concludes, does not invariably work well for all concerned.

In his book *The Nazi Doctors*, Robert Lifton has parallel stories, interviews with the German medical personnel who presided at Auschwitz. For a number of years, they oversaw the extermination of large numbers of Jews and others. This by day, 'doing their job.' In the evening routine, they turned for relief to their families, to music and other diversions. Lifton was unable to report, some forty years after the mass crimes, evidence of remorse on their part. 'Doubling,' in this horrid instance, seemed to have worked well — for at least some concerned.

There is overt brutality and hypocrisy here. One fancies himself 'decent' in private toward the immediate blood line. A narrow circle is thus drawn; within it, affection (sometimes) flourishes.

And this will make do as a personal translation of biblical 'righteousness.' That decent conduct should extend into public life; that the children of Iraq be held no more expendable than our own; that authorities confront the diatribes of the prophets against imperial crimes — such considerations hardly signify.

In public (especially in public office) one simply 'does one's job' — and the devil take the hindmost.

Such would be the working attitude of the military. No great surprise, no scandal; there, one would expect such.

But hardly would one look for fulsome support of military murder on the part of a theologian of note. Immediately after the Persian Gulf war, one such eminence professed scandal that there exists in the churches, a measure of support for officers who refuse to "serve in Arabia."

Evidently, a youth has options available to conscience, only prior to enlisting; but conscience, like a civilian outfit, is discarded at the gate of the caserne. The military is sacrosanct; any deviation from 'duty' is characterized as plain cowardice.

Theology? Theologian?

And as is argued, is one not summoned to be an obedient citizen? May one not rightfully invoke, on occasion, Romans 13 on the quasi-divine character of civil authority?

Or supposing one is 'commander in chief,' does that one not bear a self-evident, irreproachable credential? He is in charge. Election to the presidency fully justifies (in a foggy unbiblical sense) his enacting the 'lesser evil' — in this case, a hideous war.

His office is also the source of his power to exact obedience of subalterns and citizens alike.

Thus all, high and low, become part of a totally closed system, an illusion more powerful than reality and more seductive by far. All stand within the orbit of a totally spurious 'justice,' all are 'faithful.' The circle is closed.

It is the kingdom of thé blind.

Let those who see take warning: in this land, clear sight, clear speech, is a criminal activity.

That closed circle encompasses what might be called the 'vision from below.' How far below, below the human, below the divine, one trembles to inquire. Its source can be only called demonic.

Its genius is an aping of the vision of Habakkuk, an astonishing simulacrum of the real. Its fruit is dire; the 'second death' of Revelation — parallel, despite all contrary claims and pretention, to the 'failing' or 'succumbing' of the vision of Habakkuk.

❖ ❖ ❖

As to the vision accorded by God. "The righteous shall live by fidelity." We will not quibble. It is said that Paul, following the Septuagint version, makes of 'fidelity,' 'faith'; and proceeds to elaborate a splendid theology of grace.

All to the good. What is of point here, so early in biblical history, is the gratuity of the 'vision.' It is granted, not merited. Indeed it is granted, as anyone can testify, when least deserved. It is an overflow of benignity, into an earthly (empty) vessel.

It is also, at depth, our own story — if indeed we are conscious of life as an uphill trudge, and withal graced with direction, vitality — even at times, with joy in 'all our goings.'

We are greatly loved. We need not haggle our spirit or our neighbor (or our God!) with such witless affairs as the measure of our deserving (or otherwise), with making sure, shoring up, self-justifying. Enough to stand under that Overflow and Torrent.

The above reflection is not offered in a spirit of quietism or cultural frivolity. Rightly (which is to say biblically) understood, 'fidelity' or 'faith,' is a matter at times, of plain endurance (even perhaps of 'durance,' and vile at that). It is hardly to be equated with something presently touted from rooftops, flag poles, crystal cathedrals and White Houses (yes, from pulpits as well) as — 'loyalty.'

Indeed, fidelity to the vision is commended all the more urgently in a visionless empire, our own.

In such circumstance, it is required that one be actively and visibly, and dangerously — disloyal; that one extricate body and soul from the close adhesives of the cultural trap; flags, pledges of allegiance, military oaths, taxpaying, consumerism. And above all, from war.

Faith is 'in us without us.'

Fidelity follows through on the original blessing.

(2:5-20) If faith and fidelity are blessed, what then of unfaith, infidelity? They are quite literally cursed by Jawe.

The curses are instructive. They denounce and abominate and summon misfortune on the criminal (and above all on the social and political criminal). In so doing, the curses offer a timely (and timeless) analysis of the imperial mind and behavior. As then, so now!

In Habakkuk, curses take the form of epigrams and satires. The former are verbal puzzles in the zen manner; the latter, mocking couplets governed by metaphor. We would think today perhaps of cartoons, deflating, down-putting caricatures of political or religious figures.

The prophets abound in such humor. It might be thought of as an art form of the oppressed.

To understand the curses, we must summon the social scene of Habakkuk.

Everything, we are told, tended to the overblown, rancorous and minatory. The law lay heavy, a galling yoke. Reasonable choices were reduced to the vanishing point. People were left with awful alternatives — to become accomplices or victims. The best among them, including our author, were literally at wits' end to make sense of a situation that was inherently and cruelly absurd.

Then such humor — mocking, deflating, cutting, a blade unsheathed — must save reason, save the day.

The humor has a deadly serious element as well. It points to a deeper reality than instruction or law can reach — or be it noted, the collusive pulpit chatter that would have people 'content with their lot.'

We hear on the page, the mocking subversive laughter of a suffering servant. He knows the sufferings of his people. He is also gifted with mysterious access to God.

But he cannot play the liberator Moses; he is told 'not yet,' a difficult patience is urged on him.

This by no means implies that nothing can be done.

Is Habakkuk, in spurious 'godly' fashion, to fall limp before the monstrous Babylonian machine?

By no means.

There is a task at hand. It is known variously as mockery, derision, cursing, denouncing. It cuts the tyrant down to size; it stands against every claim of the superhuman, of super wisdom, supreme holiness, omnipotence, omni-competence. Sotto voce it passes the forbidden word, the truth. A simple 'Not so, the emperor is a fool, and naked.'

Thus the crucial task of resistance is rendered — manageable. The laughter of the people is thunder on the sultry air. It portends lightning and a storm; it shakes the throne.

The series of anathemas must be accounted also a work of political analysis. The people are demoralized by the official 'line.' Truth is a rare commodity; it has all but vanished from the earth. Along with, it must be added, a diminished capacity to apprehend the truth.

Everything the people hear, see, touch, buy and sell, the images and urgings and slogans, come to a monstrous fiction.

It goes like this: the citizenry are free, responsible, cared for, served by enlightened public servants, fortunate above all others on the planet, citizens of the greatest etc.

Does it all sound ominously familiar?

An apt metaphor for the plight of such a people is that of an occupied nation, in more senses than one — in the final, sinister sense of an assault on the soul. It enlists the media, the courts and schools, the churches, the economy, the military — to close the circle (the noose in fact) of conformity, obedience, slavery, silken or splenetic.

It aims at a kind of socialized demonic possession.

Only let war come, the circle closes in an hour.

But suppose for a moment, something else. A people, doubtless a minority, taking their lead from Habakkuk, utter a word, simple, persistent, lucid; a 'no.' This in the face of brutal and contrary winds. The refusal might take a satiric, mocking, denouncing, refusing, even cursing form.

Such Christians would know exactly what is being foisted on them, and why. They pierce the meaning of events, a meaning constantly betrayed, concealed, distorted by the party line, the quickening beat of the war drum.

In sum, such would refuse to kill. They declare that the refusal is the substance of their faith — a matter, as some among them put it, of 'confession.'

For them to take part in the 'national effort,' they declare, would amount to apostasy. For them, non-killing is the very heart of the confession of faith in Jesus Christ.

And this, be it noted, even when the penalties consequent on such faith tighten to a garrote.

Let us summon for a moment a worst case. The entire populace, White House to city slum, is prepared to kill. The nation has become in a flash a vast war machine on hair-trigger. Henceforth, 'for the duration,' citizens will be literally 'dressed to kill,' obliged on command to kill, blessed and rewarded for killing.

The fact of a deadly tit-for-tat, that the enemy also kills, that corpses will shortly arrive home from foreign parts — this is taken quite for granted. We speak, of course, of generals and politicians and the like, for whom times of peace are thin times, and they the sorry victims of —

HABAKKUK

underemployment. They grow bored, they grow dangerous.

Mothers, fathers, lovers? These have no voice in such recondite matters as who shall live, who kill, who die. (And for what stated reasons.) Theirs is a different task, and no puny glory at that: to 'lay such costly sacrifice on the altar of freedom,' as one president had it (undoubtedly a recalling of Abraham's son's near fate — with reference deleted however, to the aborted outcome. Isaac lives!)

Indeed in time of war the dead too will be heard from; another powerful voice, all the more persuasive for being ghostly. The voice urges reprisal and vengeance. Or so we are told by the perfervid leaders, who according to an ancient saying of Isaiah, are to be considered 'fools'; but in wartime are transformed, becoming positively vatic.

Let the wise grow silent, folly rules!

(2:5) This restless prowling the world for booty (for oil, for jobs, for 'standard of living?')! The throat is deep as hell, insatiable as death. Peoples colonized, victimized, recourseless, in bondage!

Shall they not then, in jails, in back alleys, in cellars and dark corners of the land, compose and recite their verses, conundrums, songs, pass hand-to-hand their broad sheets and leaflets — satiric or obscene or derisory — or all of these? Shall they not curse the tyrant, and this in God's name, wishing him with fervor a final day, a toppled throne?

They shall, and Habakkuk at their head. Let them know moreover that God is with them. If they are attentive and courageous, they will hear the mocking laughter of Jawe echoing their own.

(2:6) The curses commence. Against greed, first of all.

What goes around — which is to say, appetite on rampage - comes around. Reality is — surprising, especially to the demigods; parabolic, in more senses than one.

Do the king's minions raven about the world, seizing what is not theirs, creating misery on all sides? Behold them then, on a day to come, stripped to the bone, their debtors become fierce creditors, pay up, pay up!

Those they have insulted and enslaved and plundered stand against them. The blood of the victims condemns them; so (and this in a stroke of mystical insight) does the cry of the devastated earth.

Behold then the emperor and his belikes, naked to the winds of heaven. Enough said on that score.

(2:9) The second curse sees the kingdom as a great house, rising story on story, until at the top, the arrogant regent of all has 'crowned his dwelling with a proud nest.' On high, eagle-eyed, he surveys the realm, vast as the horizon itself. And all his!

And all in vain! All to his shame! By crushing many peoples, he 'has forfeited his life,' or 'sinned against his own soul,' or 'worked against himself.'

Judgement! Habakkuk kept crying it; but the cry was lost on the winds, to royal ears it seemed the nattering of a madman. Did not the realm stand splendid and intact, unassailable, over-weening, immune from death or misfortune?

Then judgment approaches like a coven of furies. Now the mighty one is stricken close, to the marrow, in his very 'soul,' his own 'life.'

And that proud dwelling of his takes voice. The kingdom is transformed, it is like a doomed house of Atreus. At sight of the crimes committed under this roof, the very stones cry out, the beams and wood works respond.

The crimes we note, are not detailed; they are simply taken for granted. In such a house, raised on the blood and tears of the indentured, crime is inevitable; the house itself, its scope, its grandeur, is like a vast mausoleum.

Thus, according Habakkuk, the truth of the times.

Thus, our era as well?

(2:12) The third curse: against the politics of violence. Again, the image is one of worldly splendor and horror, both. The city is 'built on blood, founded on crime.' Therefore in vain. It is as though the proud evidence of conquest and control, imperial architecture, monuments, arches of triumph, palaces, courts and so on, were doomed from the start.

No sooner raised on high, a torch is lit. It is all a — 'nothing.' No soul, no future, a city of the dead.

HABAKKUK

A memory intrudes. I had returned from Hanoi at the height of the bombing of North Vietnam in 1968. I visited Washington to speak with authorities of what I had learned. This struck me, the atmosphere of death pervading the city. It lay heavy on my heart, rang like a dirge in my ear: no soul, a city of the dead. No future, except more of same. More incursions, more bombings, more war.

As has surely come to pass.

It is as though the powers of darkness snatched us out of the hands of the God of life; as though we were forfeited, one and all, to death. As though sentence had been already uttered. As though the grotesque nobility of 'supreme sacrifice in war,' had yielded before 'conviction of crime. Sentence: death.'

A countdown. The world has become a monstrous death row.

Of all the curses uttered by Habakkuk, one offers the sharpest word. And it is a word finally of enormous hope. There is to be another 'city' than the sinister glory of this or that imperial Disneyland.

This city, forever new, shall be and be and be; a consortium of heaven and earth. It will stretch from end to end, of time, of the world.

Borrow the old images to be sure, a 'dwelling,' a 'city'; but all made new, marked at last by the holy stigmata of justice and peace.

Take heart then, in this crepuscular and terrible 'meantime.'

Lift up your eyes, let all your seasons be one: Advent.

Be mindful of the promise. It is all a glory, the glory of Jawe and O wondrous! of ourselves as well.

(2:15-17) The mis en scene of the fourth curse is a banquet hall. An orgy is in progress.

Our imperial host must be accounted an icy cynic. He improves the occasion by urging such drink upon his guests as brings them to stupefaction, their muzzy ears open to obscene suggestion.

There follows, in the relentless image of the prophet, a further degradation, a sexual one. The king's pleasure is 'to look upon them nude.' To put the matter shortly, the guests, all presumably male, are urged to 'flash their foreskins,' as the text would have it plain.

There is an additional shame attached to the curse; for the pagan bibbers are one and all, uncircumcised. Thus 'you will be sated with ignominy, not with glory.'

The image is one of irrational depravity, worked be it noted, not against the conquered, but by one victor against another. It is the inner circle and its dynamism, the favored, the sycophants, the advisers and diplomats who fall under the curse.

Theirs is a sleazy cohesion in evil. And the fraternity functions only in limited fashion, by day, as it were. No bond, whether of affection, admiration, respect, holds firm. Shall they come together in celebration? They will. But in a condominium of contempt, all goes sour.

Under the influence of drink (a frequent biblical image for rampaging authority) things fall apart. Spiritual anarchy, cynicism, mutual shame and humiliation pollute the air.

Thus the rulers stand self-revealed, in more senses than one.

What they have wreaked against others, living beings, creation, this comes home, 'to roost' as the saying goes (2:17). The 'human blood you have shed' fills their cups. And the terrible wine drives them mad.

Another image: the spirits of the 'massacred beasts' invade the banquet hall and set up a terrifying dirge. Judgment is at hand, and martyred spirits the judges.

(2:18-20) The fifth curse is not to be thought of as merely the last in an undifferentiated series. Nor is the sin it denounces, separate from the preceding four.

In point of fact, idolatry sums up and includes all preceding crimes; it is a clue to their deepest spiritual meaning. The kings and their pandering subjects indeed 'adored the works of their hands.' In pursuit of conquest, greed, violence, and pride of life, they fell to worship; all 'turned aside from the glory of Jawe.'

Idolatry: a theme never done with in the prophets.

We of a later more sophisticated era prefer to relegate such 'bowing before a graven image' to dark corners of a dark era; a primitive, even bizarre activity. As if that were all!

According to Habakkuk and his kind, idolatry is not so easily disposed of. It invariably implies political and economic misbehavior, the maltreatment of people, amassing of ill gotten goods, conquest and cruelty and greed. This 'turning aside,' this fascination with power and technique and war, in every generation thumps mysteriously at the heart's portal, seeking entrance: 'ye shall be as gods.'

We do well to take warning, and refuse access with all our might.

What else, one wonders, but a dark fixation upon idols would offer a clue as to the conduct of authority today? The idols indeed are vaingloriously consulted, and they speak. But their word is ambiguous, irrational, incoherent. They cloud the mind, and provoke outrageous and distempered decisions.

One powerful element of the biblical curse, as we have suggested, is its derisive quality. To mock the inflation of the mighty is to bring a measure of sanity to an otherwise bizarre scene. Thus here, the elaborate panoply of temple and court, the ritual, pomp and circumstance, melt away under the glance of Habakkuk. It is all reduced to a solitary mime, as pitiful as it is fruitless.

Come down, come down ye mighty! The figure conjured by the curse is ambiguous, one thinks deliberately so. It could be the king or his high priest or one or another of the court 'prophets,' the 'wise ones,' conjurers and so on; or for that matter, the crowd of sedulous subjects.

Any or all. And whether they are hot on the spoor of power or gold or slaves — or stand in the sanctuary at worship, the 'scene of reduction' is the same, the image conveys the truth of the situation.

The heart becomes what it seeks. "Before a stick of wood they intone: 'Arise!' To a dumb stone: 'Waken from sleep!'"

Let them then multiply the weaponry beyond imagining, let them threaten and throb with virtuous passion as to the justice (or even the 'holiness') of war in the making.

Look within, seek the meaning! Habakkuk mimes the monstrous Martian flexing in a distorting mirror of wit; it is all really quite pitiful, and all in vain.

To what then shall they be compared? They and their works and pomps are like a solitary muttering fool, invoking dumb wood and stone.

Mad they are. Would also they were harmless, that we could simply leave the idolaters to their foolish trade!

For all the verbiage and folderol, the triumphant polls, the irascibility and pride, the half-truths and whole lies.... We hearken to the image evoked by Habakkuk — war as ultimate stupidity. And we take heart.

These are precious matters in a bad time. Uncle Sam wants you! It is not solely or even primarily a call for bodies to 'man' (sic) the vast machinery of death. Modern war is total, in a far worse sense than the conventional amassing of warriors and material.

It is a matter, for biblical folk, of the spiritual induction of the living in works of death; a matter of thoughtless heads nodding, of witless consensus, of the crime of silence, of superficial worship, of heed paid to silly polls — in sum, of yielding before the multiple ways in which humans are reduced to cogs, normalized, adjusted, twisted, inducted — into objective insanity.

(2:20) "'But as for Jawe, God abides in the holy temple." The image bespeaks a transcendent presence, and at the same time an apartness, a withdrawal. Your way, My way; and the difference. Disdain, distaste even. God is God, in wartime also. God of peace. Let humans turn to murder, the God of life has no part in the works of death.

Let us confess it: the word of God is banished, exiled, a closed book — 'for the duration,' as they say.

At the point where mass murder is seriously undertaken or envisioned, the providence of God departs the land. From henceforth, the warriors and their sponsors, the president and his advisers, the politicos and the weapons makers, together with the ministers and priests and rabbis who object not a whit, who raise no questions, express no outrage, unmask no move or motive of their powerful, complicit congregants — these structures and citizens and worshippers are on their own.

HABAKKUK

The absence of God is not to be thought total. It is at least for a few, a painful form of the presence of God. There is the bitter taste, the void, the darkness, the public blindness, the bootless worship, the all but total pursuit of violent means....

And at the same time, acts of resistance; the absolute necessity of saying a (totally unsatisfactory, discomfiting, clumsy, more than perhaps ineffectual) No! Saying it nonetheless.

It is as though, for the duration, the 'yes' one would speak to life, the habitual 'yes' that rejoices, celebrates, cherishes, blesses — all this were banished too, put to silence.

The only 'yes' one can summon in such times takes a dark form; a persistent 'no.' Not much indeed, nor greatly consoling; only utterly crucial.

It follows too that the 'No' uttered in the face of war, ensures the integrity of worship; just as the works of war imply idolatry.

(3:1-19) The prayer that follows is in the mood and tone of lamentation, sorrow, confession of guilt, appeal for divine intervention. (We pray: Be to us, Habakkuk, as you were in the grand times of intervention; for our needs are equally distressing.)

At the start, it is as though the pacific soul of the prophet explodes with fury. He and his people have had enough and more than enough of Babylonian tyranny. The imagery tends toward the bellicose: Jawe, great warrior, descend in wrath, put these upstarts and their ruthless forces utterly to rout!

It is hardly to our taste (though it is to the taste of many among us, and the invocation of Jawe-warrior is by no means a matter of 'primitive religious history'). Have we perhaps had our fill of worldly wars? Is yet another war, however celestially certified as to its outcome, not to be thought bloodily redundant?

One would fervently hope so. Like it or not, the counsels of Jesus 'Love your enemies, do good to those who mistreat you,... these discommode us. So clearly stated they are, as to blind the eyes of generations of warrior-Christians.

(3:3 ff.) Jawe once invoked, arrives. Had He then been absent from the world?

Let us say rather, exiled, declared 'irrelevant.' War, power, loot, conquest are the real issues of life. And if Jawe has no stomach for these, in fact abominates them — why then, let us invoke other gods!

Jawe 'arrives,' the transcendent One, not to be integrated or plowed into worldly systems and times. Jawe arrives. And the earthly scene is suddenly all light and fire, perturbation, even disaster. This is no pantheist deity, but the One who subverts earthly systems and shakes the foundations of things.

Indeed, (3:5) plague and fevers mark Jawe's coming; they are personified in Revelation as the rampageous horsemen, scattering their ruin. They also suggest the divine incompatibility with crime — specifically the crime of war. Since from war arise plague and fevers, then let these flourish!

(3:6) Another theme, one surely of comfort to the victims. "Jawe looked about him, and the nations trembled." We see it now and again (all too rarely!) and stand in awe. Who is the judge, and who the condemned, we ask?

There appears one resister or a few; their very glance withers the 'nations.' The courage of a saint, a martyr, is an irrefutable sign; it reveals in all its vacuity, the braggadocio, the bootless pride of the persecutor.

Nature too is shaken — by the God of nature, who is imagined here, not merely 'walking the eternal hills,' but 'scattering' them.

Nothing in creation that is, suggests the eternal nature of nature itself. And more: nothing in nature suggests the immortality of the empire. Such is pure fantasy. And for all that, constantly indulged in. And it stands in great need of correction.

God disrupts with a stern word. All is contingent, save Jawe, all is mortal, all subject to death.

Eternal, immortal — such are the perennial dreams of the empires. All else will fall to pieces, but not this invincible phalanx. What was Hitler's boast? "The third reich will last for a thousand years!"

Purported immunity from death and decline is clung to in face of all contrary evidence. The claim moreover, is invariably wrung from the death of others. The delusion of immortality exacts a heavy price. Many must perish if the dream is to perdure.

It cannot stand; the prophets say it, stand by it, die in witness to its truth. The glory fades and vanishes, the weaponry rusts by the roadside, Babylon, Chaldea, imperial Egypt are a ruin.

In a striking image from Revelation (chapter 8), Babylon is pictured as falling to decay, not at the hands of enemies, but from within. Too much greed, violence, strife, fear, suspicion, too many wasting wars. Folly is received as wisdom, obsessions all the more sinister for being unexamined, rule the day-by-day decisions, the allocations of money, the pursuit (invariably militaristic) of special interests. There is much diplomatic hustling about the world, shifting for advantage, shoring up of alliances and common fronts against whatever enemy.

And yet nothing of this seems to work well, whether domestically or abroad. Is Baghdad reduced to rubble? But even as the innocent die, the tyrant survives.

The news becomes a persistent nightmare, a many-headed monster. No sooner one crisis resolved, another shows face.

And at home there is discontent and economic misery. The markets dry up, the ecology is a disaster.

When the end comes, according to Revelation, there is not an enemy in sight. The 'topless towers,' so to speak, grow top heavy; the empire collapses like a mass of dough in an icy wind.

(3:7 ff) A double combat of Jawe is envisioned; the imagery of the two is closely joined. Each battle is presented as a conquest over chaos. The first illustrates and prepares for the second.

First comes a highly charged, dramatic account of creation: God must prevail over a contrary, bellicose void. The chaos of pre-creation is presented as a force of resistance, a kind of seething black hole. With all its cosmic might it opposes the gentle calling forth, naming, timing and ordering of things, the week of creation, 'inscape,' the flourishing of the web of life.

Thus from the beginning, death and life, personified, are in contention. Thus too the stage is set for a never ending conflict that according to Christians continues until the resurrection of Christ, and beyond: 'mors et vita duello conflixere mirando'; 'death and life locked in awesome combat.'

Thus too the quasi-military character of the images here: 'wrath ... anger ... indignation ... chariot of victory ... sheath from the bow ... arrows to the string ... glittering spear ...' and so on. They signal the original combat, and presage a later, fierce struggle against a new chaos, that of empire. Let the nations know it: Jawe is a mighty warrior from the beginning!

The 'combat of origins' is by way of illustration. Chaos, disorder and death persist mightily, according to the biblical insight. And the same primordial chaos remains virulently active in history, must be subdued again and again.

The storms of the gods (and their godlings) are pent for a time in the cave of Aeolus. There they wait their moment, the coming of the Messiah.

Then the empire vents its full fury against the Christ.

The second chaos wears an imperial face; it is 'the beast from the land' (Revelation) — highly structured, sophisticated, domestically and internationally alert to the main chance, economically competitive, violent as to first instinct and recourse. Caveas! Not solely to its enemies, its name spells — trouble.

We have seen its face, have known the full force of its violence. The power of myth and propaganda and duplicity protect its image. Impermeable against critique, (even the critique of the martyrs it murders) the empire is unassailably virtuous in its own eyes. Indeed all manner of 'religious leaders' are available to stroke and reassure in this regard.

More: our 'way of life', including its not so hidden agenda of violence, greed and control, these well masked by purported virtues of uprightness and benignity, of which we are told much, unto utter weariness.

There is another side to our behavior, and it is dark and stark indeed.

The empire will have the nations of the world (especially the poor and 'developing' nations) walk to the American drum, arrange their internal affairs in ways acceptable to the overlord. And above all, let them indulge in no effort, whether political or worshipful, tainted with the theme of 'liberation.' This — or else.

The 'or else' now and then wears a velvet glove, more often not.

(3:12 ff.) Thus a 'second chaos' bestrides the world. It is the carrier of the 'second death' of Revelation. Which is to say, the empires are the chief instrument of the prevailing reign of death.

These principalities would hand over the saints into the thrall of death. They are thus the sworn enemy of the God of life, and of those who 'witness to the word of God' (Rev. 1).

Upon this hermetic, self-justifying, inhuman scheme of things, Jawe, we are told, descends — to overcome, to prevail, to unmask. "You bestrode the earth in fury, you trampled the nations in anger."

It is as though Habakkuk has seen it all before, this countervailing anger of God. Hence the past tense, a way of indicating the divine steadfastness, as the drama of history unfolds. For generation upon generation Jawe enters the combat, scattering orb and scepter, as the impertinent symbols are passed from fool to criminal.

The action of God in such circumstances is as often as not, simply letting things take their course. Empires rise and fall, events wickedly conceived cannot but end badly for the perpetrators. Revelation develops the Babylonian outcome in somewhat this way. Greed and ego superabounding, the structures simply fall apart.

But Habakkuk and his like are impelled by a fierce intensity. To them, the decline and fall of empire cannot be understood as a gentle gradual thing. No, it must be seen as fiercely accelerated from on high. God seizes the jeweled orb from its holder, takes it in hand, casts it fiercely aside.

Another is suddenly in charge. God 'descends'; which is to say, the end time, the time of ruin is speeded up, it is all accomplished 'in an hour.' Thus a double rhythm seems indicated. The divine non-intervention of 'normal times' yields before stern judgment.

It comes to this. God cannot indefinitely 'stand by' while the earth is drenched in the blood of martyrs.

(3:13) Whatever the version of God's activity, one matter is beyond dispute. Revelation insists on it again and again: God sets limits against evils that are of their native drive, illimitable.

The crimes stop here. The fury of this or that empire, uninhibited by moral qualm or second thought, incurably grandiose in scope, is permitted to exist, allowed its scope, 'for awhile.'

Whence then the limitation, who is to call a halt, and at what point? This is the perennial plaint of the martyrs. (Rev. 6:9 ff.)

In God's own time, they are told, not before; and in God's own way.

The text of verse 13, we are told, is uncertain. One version goes "You (Jawe) have overthrown the dwelling of the impious, to bedrock the foundations are laid bare." Another, "You crushed the head of the wicked, laying them bare from thigh to neck." Terrible, violent, and in sum, coming to the same thing. The empire is down; the day of imperial pretention finished.

And so with verse 14 — a climax of sorts. Warrior Jawe squares off against the chief warrior of the empire, and bests him once for all.

To the eyes of faith, the combat was never for a moment understood as a contest of equals. Nonetheless, there was indeed a contest; the ways of Jawe could never be made compatible with the ways of 'the nations.'

(3:16-19) So our book ends, a tender dying fall.

The earlier clash of arms, divine vs. human, is heard no more. No more war, war no more; the fury that racked the human family is stilled.

Peace has come at last. And Habakkuk is exhausted, enervated, awed at the spectacle before him. His body trembles, his lips quiver, his steps totter beneath him. He smells rot; it is as though the plague of death had entered his bones.

Peace has come, and acceptance. It is as though he walked, subdued, numbed, upon the battlefields of the world and saw there only corpses, anonymous and known, beloved, unrecognizable, scattered like broken dolls the bodies of his people, and of his people's enemy.

Losers, winners, they have entered alike into the awful anonymity of death.

These, and the charred, ruined landscape. It is ended, that history of blood and fire. Our own.

Habakkuk awaits in peace of heart a 'day of trouble' still to come. He surveys the ruined land (3:17). His account is a long aching threnody, a catalog of loss. The ecology is a shambles; the war, like all wars, has destroyed what it sought to own, spared neither fig nor vine nor olive nor sheep nor cattle. The claim of the 'winners' is a mockery. No winners, only losers.

Let us, he implies, take all this in account. Let our soul taste to the dregs the bitterness of a landscape given over to death.

Death all about; which is to say, also within.

Walk the world today. It is a battlefield sown with mines and corpses. Death from AIDS, death of drug takers. Death in the Persian Gulf. Death of the anonymous and innocent; passim. Death of a culture.

The awful 'second death' of the spirit.

Inflicted death, reprisal, destruction of ancient cities, Stealth bombers, smart bombs. Death and more death; nothing learned, nothing mourned or repented. Death pushing hard, necrophilic, siren.

And yet, something else. Something audacious.

Something that must at all cost not be left out, not disregarded. Something other than death. Something called hope.

It begins here, as darkness covers the face of the earth.

This is a mighty leap. It is possible, we think, only to a valiant spirit like Habakkuk.

And we are wrong. "The scripture is for your instruction." "Write down the vision, lest it be lost."

The leap into hope is possible to us, by grace of Jawe.

"Death shall have no dominion."
"But as for me, I will rejoice in the God of my salvation."

HABAKKUK

Despite all, the final word is of a difficult joy, wrung from a monstrous pain. Death shall not lay claim to the last word, not to the last word of Habakkuk, prophet of the God of life. Though death claims that word as the last and loudest, and reinforces the claim with presumption, muscle and fury.

That 'last word of all' is utterly unexpected.
It is as though the ruined earth had broken in song.
As though the blasted trees were swaying like 'stringed instruments.'
As though the dead issued from their tombs, transfigured.
No more 'as though'!
The word of God, the promise, is on every tongue.
'God is my strength ... my feet like the feet of hinds ... tread on high places.'
Alleluia!

ZEPHANIAH

Rage, Delight, Promise

Take care, you combustible humans,
a spirit of pyrexia shakes the earth -
'Jawe,' cries the prophet, 'sets humans afire!'
(and more!
     clap your ears to -
thunder on the left!)
              'Everything!
'Once for all! I shall wipe clean
the earth's distempered face.'

Creation, destroyed?

I swear it. Yes.
I shall sweep away humans and beasts,
I shall sweep away birds of the air
and fish of the sea!'

But wait; what of that lovely virginal
'everything' of Genesis?
     Did the beasts then offend You?
the tiger burning bright,
     the fog-hued paladin
named elephant?
     the nid-nodding towering giraffe
running effortless as cloud before a wind?
     in what have these offended?

ZEPHANIAH

Did the birds of the air, taking cue
from darkling kites and crows, turn scandalous,
mutter, muster, assassins of your will?

and the swimmers that blush and pale
like rainbow signaling
the flood's recession, the covenant dawning -
did these, speechless as coral, recant their vow?

          Or that archangelic
Leviathan, sped like an arrow from your quiver
in quest of recusant Jonah, did he then
furtive, a vast shadow, conceal
his captive close in gut
for ransom or reprisal?

Come then, will You, obeisant
to a black-browed mood,
unravel
the planetary splendors -
(seasons, moons, the sun's burnished
shield of Achilles,
stars named for heaven's heroes,
the constant planets steering
mariners to a haven) -
will you unravel all
close, cunning, woven in a week?
'Hear my cause, you humans!
        I know who flaunts
the rotten vesture of idols,
who mounts the roof covertly,
falls like a whoreson, worshipful
before the blank gods of heaven.
I know who bows, a metronome
perfunctory to me,
whispering in his sleeve, oaths
to Milkin the idol, to upstart
godling Dagon.
        I know who amid trumpets
fills like a cracked cup

the trumpery palace to brim
with poison, fraud, injustice.
You, merchants of misery
your base calculation
stinks to high heaven.
Witness; I shall
repay you to a farthing on My Day.

   Go, mutter behind your hand -
'Toss the coin, no matter heads or tails,
pro, con, evil, virtue, Jawe cares not a whit!'

'Stiff necked bedizened fools
 - Your Honors, Your Holinesses, Your Lieges -
callous, luxurious in your sensual sty,
on My Day
your blood will run in gutters
as from a staved cask a wine
gone sour as hell's lees.

'On That Day
I will race like Eumenides through Jerusalem
this way, that, corner and alleyway,
my hair a torch, my eyes a burning lamp
searching you out,
simulacra, homunculi
mick-mocks of the human.

That Day
your houses gape tenantless!
A hand crossing a cobweb, I rend
your proud vineyards -
stagnant, sterile, thistle and weed and thorn.

'Sodom, Gomorra I name you!
Nineveh your name!
a rain of ruin!
salt pits,
wreckage choked with weeds.
Dry mouthed as a desert cave,

ZEPHANIAH

owls hooting, fenestration
blank, blind as a midnight moon,
crows befouling, cawing
derision upon your grave -
glory, glory gone to dust.

'Know it, you lords of time -
My Day Nears! it hastens, no delay!
Then from the throats of braggards
what gasps of fear, what warriors' knees
knocking like drumsticks
their dull beat of indenturehood!

'My Day - distress, tribulation
desolation, devastation!
Day of fog and darkness
Day of trumpets, war cries
fortified cities
fallen,
towers
scattered like skittles!

'Jerusalem -
is this my city
sunset kissing the rosy stones,
verdant mountains lording over -

'My city?
absorbed and preening
a peacock on a dust heap
a foolish motto flapping on a flag -
'None such, Be Like, Me, My, Mo'?

      I see
tyranny riding high
your rulers carnivores,
your judges wolfish,
your prophets posturing, treacherous,
your priests blasphemers of the holy.

ZEPHANIAH

'Therefore do I summon
ruin upon ruin!
your proud squares
shall stable wild beasts
passers hastening by, appalled,
fleeing contagion and the curse.

'My Day be night to you!
grope about
bats in high noon
vaulting, defaulting, defecating.

'But then, but then
no respite, no recourse?
have done, my heart!
Grief cancels fury,
tears start,
yearning I turn to you.

'O turn and turn
toward me!
      You humble ones, remnant
of all My hope! my hands
cope you, frail birds
in cage and keep of providence.

'That Day of Mine!
deliverance, dance,
banquet, beatitude!
Mount of Jerusalem
transparent as a glass
holding aloft the wine bright city -
Jawe in your midst,
wild lover, bridegroom,
partner of the dance!'

HAGGAI

We have, for a change, a prophet who has little to say!

In a telegrammatic fragment of less than 40 verses, Haggai, otherwise unknown, summons an atmosphere of longing joy. The great return is at hand, the end of exile. A merciful decree of Darius has been issued. It is like a trumpet announcing and celebrating dawn.

Free at last! Now the people may repair the broken strands of Promise, Covenant and Kingdom.

Or so they conclude, in the first fine flush of 'return.'

A parallel occurs. In 1991, great processions of exiles made their way back to El Salvador. They reclaimed the land, risked their lives to do so. They were determined, despite a murderous oligarchy and its festering military, to live once more where their ancestors set down roots. Where their children too, must live.

We were told of the priests who accompanied the people, accepting like dangers, uncertainties and privations in an admirable 'long march.' Known and respected, the priests offered protection to the anonymous peasants.

Along the way home, as though they followed a way of the cross, they paused for worship. And on the day of return, what joyous celebration!

In Haggai's time too, an altogether unexpected blessing: the people have been set free, the great return is at hand.

But amid the bustle and joy, new questions arise. Who is to claim what portion of the land, and to what use is the new cherished freedom to be put?

And further, in what or whom now, is hope to be placed — the hope of a future far different than the terrible years of exile and slavery?

And yet further — what has exile taught the people? Must it not be confessed that priot conduct had contributed to the catastrophe, the fury of the tyrant that all but consumed an entire generation?

Promise, Covenant, Realm: three columns that held aloft the canopy of hope.

Of Promise and Covenant, we continue to draw sustenance, whether Christians or Jews.

But what of that ambiguous third, whether translated as 'Realm,' 'Kingdom' or 'Empire'?

Let it be said that if we Christians have learned anything from our history, especially and awfully from our 'just' wars, crusades, pogroms, inquisitions — then of alliances with empires, armies, worldly polity and the like, we can hold only the gravest of reservations. Reservations drawn be it insisted, not only from our history, but also from near at hand, our own lifetime.

Whether verified in the 'Christendom complex' or in the modern state of Israel, in theocracies or secular forms, what difference? The empires are a horror, their marks are pressed like stigmata on the bodies of victims. In their fetid midst flourish greed, domination, pride of place, violence of every sort, devastation of the planet, hope crushed, racism, sexism, duplicity.

The Great Return of Haggai's time is both fact and symbol.

As a symbol the Return touches us also, who have never tasted the bitter status of refugee or exile, never been shunted about on the roads of the world, lodged in awful camps or pushed beyond the pale at the whim of reluctant hosts. Ours is a far more comfortable story to tell (and that perhaps our trouble), secure in our dwellings and income and education, moving about the world freely at no one's behest but our own.

And yet, and yet. God calls us too. To undertake a Great Return. A discovery and confession of our inhumanity, of the ways in which an imperial, unutterably debased culture, has seduced us also. A Return to one another, to the victimized at home and abroad. A Return to compassion. To a biblical way of life, all but lost sight of in the welter of war and greed.

Turn and turn about. Return, rebuild the temple.

We have in Haggai symbols of newness, amendment, a fresh start. The word of God commands renunciation of a questionable past, a chastened and modest spirit. The fallen temple is to be rebuilt; which is to say, the failed heart, the broken community. The building blocks have fallen, bound together as they once were with a mortar of tears and blood. But they were sundered and split apart, and the walls fell.

Alienation from God, conformity to this world. What meaning could such a temple hold, or the worship that sounded there? From the point of view of spiritual reality, the temple had become no more than another form of imperial architecture. It fitted neatly with the courts and prisons, it welcomed the tyrants and armies, and blessed them.

The worship had become a kind of imperial symposium, a celebration of power and might. It was worship of the gods of 'the nations.'

Make it new, build it new! No more infesting idols in the sanctuary. No gods of armies and conquest. True God. The Ineffable One who accompanied the people in their long trek through time and this world.

Now the question must be raised; what does such a God look like?

Right understanding demands a temple radically new, every stone that is laid. A new spirit and ethos.

In such a temple as God requires (and the godly people as well) He dwells: the God of exiles, victims, the powerless. The community must take an entirely new situation in account; not only the bare survival of the exile years, not solely the joy of return. But here and now, their own status, uneasy and chancy.

They are not rid of tyranny; they have been granted only a respite. Will they now be permitted to claim the land again, to rebuild, even in a modest way, to flourish? The present seems favorable; Darius is beyond doubt

HAGGAI

an improvement on his predecessors, as such tyrants go. But his moods are unsteady to say the least. And who can predict the temper of whoever will succeed him?

Little wonder then, that the returnees favor a modest temple, and a worship to match. Or that they show a certain willingness to hearken to the likes of Haggai, telling of a God of peace and compassion.

So be it, is the message of faith. Let the chips fall, let Darius and those of like mind go their way. But for the believers, the gods of Solomon are dead, and so is imperial Solomon and his line. Requiescat.

Thus comes the word of Jawe to the prophets of return, Haggai and Zechariah. These two are the great instructors of the post-exilic period.

They are also alas, among the last of the prophets, as the Hebrew bible tells.

They are temple prophets, in the spirit of Ezekiel. Their urging is toward a chastening 'return' — a return to a center long dispersed, lost, even despised. The center, the spirit, had been dissipated long before the exile. The culture languished, in favor of imperial confabulations, fantasies, wayward behavior.

Their urging is (and it cannot be said too often), let us return to true worship — in spirit and truth. Return to the word of God, to our prophets and psalmists.

And a turning away, by the same token, from the deceptive wisdom of the powers of this world.

The scene, the longing, the inward wavering, the outer chaos — how familiar they are! We too, would be believers, stuck alas in a stuck empire, how we long — for something. For worship of another god than Mars. For a church that is lucid, resistant, strong.

Cherishing our longings, keeping alive our hopes, forlorn and deprived and sorrowful as we are — thus we survive the awful times.

I set down these notes. We are at war in the mid-east. The conflict, according even to the meager, censored reports allowed us, grows ever

HAGGAI

more savage. The warriors know nothing of respect for civilians, the aged, children. The media suppression and deception are as massive as the bombing itself.

The war violates all known canons of justice; it is simply an indiscriminate slaughter, waged against 'anyone in the way.' It is waged against the mind, heart, sense of truth and compassion. It is a mighty contest — for souls, ours.

We are thus condemned, as far as our authorities are concerned, to war upon war. We are to be inducted, silenced, lied to. We are perpetually exiled from our true self, our soul, from a politics of compassion, from choices or votes that mean — anything.

Nothing but war, war as metaphor and lurking fact and threat. War as brutal onslaught, when required.

But as to Haggai.

(1:1-2) The word of God comes to the prophet, who immediately passes on the message to officials. According to the oracle, their sense of the times is awry. To them it is of little matter, this task of rebuilding the temple.

There is a kind of flaccid passivity in the air. The people ape their leaders, delay, shrug, glance elsewhere. The will is lacking; the excuse invoked is that means are lacking, or the moment at hand is inopportune.

Nonetheless, we are in the ambit of the word of God. Jawe speaks. Other designs and projects hold pride of place. The people build and maintain their 'comfortable dwellings,' it is charged. And meantime, 'this Dwelling,' the Temple, 'lies in ruins.'

Even this, the Word continues, hardly exhausts the situation, the pride and selfishness, the slovenly neglect. What of those princely houses — and what of their inhabitants? How goes it with them?

There follows a series of metaphors; they indicate the unease of spirit, anxiety, dread, of those who might be thought the fortunate ones. Fortunate?

The temple is in ruins; but the devastation serves neither as reminder nor reproof. Some trudge past, some pause, they might be thought to grow silent with a faint stirring of nostalgia. Not much more.

Haggai insists on it: the public mood of inertia and defeatism is the bitter fruits of exile. And behind the mood, permeating it, is a conviction all unconfessed. Material well-being, whether of one's self or one's family, is the sole issue; one almost said obsession.

Thus the financial sacrifice and labor required to raise a house of worship, and thus restore the community to a sense of prideful achievement — this is hardly a pressing concern.

What follows is scathing. The spiritual illness, the diminution, waste and want of spirit, are unmasked. Much labor, Haggai reminds them, no sparing of time and expense are invested in sowing of crops, eating and drinking and clothing themselves. They labor strenuously — for money, for the things of this world.

Which is to say, life has settled into a comfortable, deadly groove.

Excitement, innovation, imagining a different scheme of things, modest steps in a human direction? These are lost arts. We are where we are where we are where, etc., etc.

All this sweating and scheming and cutting corners and assuring a future — it is vain, wrong-headed, Jawe insists. The harvest, in more senses than one, is meager. People eat and are hungry, drink and are parched. They may be well-clothed, the cold penetrates anyway. And money, precious, adored, desirable above all, hoarded, what of it? It is unaccountably devalued or lost. It is as though universally, pockets had rotted and spilled their hoard.

Thus go those years of return, so long desired, despaired of, imagined so differently in the rosy dawn of freedom. It all comes to — very little. The people pick up the shards of memory and habit, and go on, a rather pitiful level of life in the image of 'the nations.'

It is as though a colony, or an occupied people, were forced in the course of a generation, by combined pressure of convention and example, to take on the ways of the master race. Nothing, be it noted, of the old dynastic drive that once marked them, in the forefront of the same nations.

Now we have a culture of cozy bourgeois shopkeepers or small landholders. No great sin; not great virtue either, but a rather deadly mean, more leaden than golden.

HAGGAI

(1:9-10) These verses sum up the situation, and offer a clue as to the root of the trouble. "You expected much, and it came to little; and what you brought home, I blew away. For what cause?" says the Lord of hosts. "Because my house lies in ruins, while each of you hurries to his own house."

We have it plain, an attribution, a judgment. Our petty bourgeois are strong on 'values' of home and family. But in point of religious understanding and practice, they are unacknowledged, perhaps inarticulate, agnostics.

But who shall speak for that old raving, raging Presence, that thunder-browed One, pillar of fire, cloud of unknowing, adversary and lover, jealous spouse, awful judge? Have insight, driving vision, fled the land?

A fog lies everywhere, a deadly sameness.

The people move about like cast iron figures in a village clock.

Mechanically they note the time, they are all ignorant of the times.

Routine! According to Haggai, they are in great need of a jolt. They pay large tribute to family, property, those cozy idols. But they have lost much of their costly heritage, much of true memory. They are afflicted with a kind of stiff jointed diminishing amnesia.

They have in mind many blueprints, projects, buildings to be raised. Each is more urgently required, more serviceable than a — temple. There are schools to be thought of, and courthouses and jails and hospitals and centers of commerce and pleasure palaces.

Such secular practicality governs the architecture of the 'nations.' And what of this people? What do they believe, and build? Such questions must be raised; the faith must be shaken up, questioned, reviewed.

According to the will of Jawe, a certain property is to be set apart, in the strictest sense. A kind of land trust perhaps. Like the sun, like air and water, this land will belong to no one — and to everyone. It cannot be suborned, speculated on, bequeathed or inherited. It will bring no income; it has in fact no conceivable worldly use.

An image of Jawe! The God who can be put to no human use or

advantage, attached to no one's self-interest.

So the sacred enclosure will question in its very existence, the presumed sacredness of property itself. The temple will simply stand there, rendering all trade, markets, income, wealth — hypothetical, subject to scrutiny, precarious, under judgment.

But where is the serious will to undertake such a project, procure the holding, raise the temple? Alas.

And can the affairs of this people be thought to proceed favorably, when the word of God is put to naught?

We have here an old theme of the prophets, with a notable difference. Jawe, we are told, is angered by this soft revolt, this evasion and delay.

Therefore Jawe stops the throat of nature's cornucopia.

The image is one of a deliberate impoverishing, withholding. A drought follows; it is severe, affecting everything, grain, wine, oil. Everywhere the harvests shrink. It is as though (indeed it is a fact) — nature were mirroring the spiritual condition of the people.

They are no great sinners, neither imperialists, warmakers, abusers of the poor. (One thinks perhaps that they lack occasion!). No, they are puny of spirit, penny pinching, strict account keepers. Their sins are negative; eyes to the main chance, they offend by neglect, refusal, evasive silence. Their gods are routine and rote.

They lack vision, initiative, imagination. They dread greatness, expansive dreams, ecstasy, visions, prophecy. If truth were told (it is seldom told, or heard), they dread the likes of Haggai. Only imagine — that a son or daughter of theirs should be gifted, burdened with the pain of God's word! The terror: one's own flesh and blood turning upon them such a word as Haggai's.

(1:12 ff.) Nonetheless, here and there a change of heart occurs. A minority, a 'remnant' rouses itself, hearkens to Haggai. The temple project gathers force.

What, one asks, would be an equivalent today, of this 'building the temple anew'?

We talk, we dream. At times we rouse ourselves, lay a stone to a wall, lend an effort to something known as the 'realm of God.' Something described by Jesus as 'within,' or 'near at hand'; again as 'not of this world'; at other times, as delayed, deferred, interfered with; even as 'suffering violence.'

We lay a stone to the great edifice. Then we defer, bow out. A low mood prevails. We conclude that the project is no more than a mirage, a fiction.

We know that such an ideal, so momentous an event, so blessed a community as is implied in the Realm — that these are absolutely incompatible with the present 'crooked generation'; with its warmaking, its suspicion, unrest of mind, closure of heart, contempt for the helpless, aged, children. Contempt for life itself. Invocation of and reliance on — death.

In such times, the 'building of the temple' can only be a modest, even humiliated work. Many are idle, disenchanted, recusant. A stone is rarely laid upon a stone. One looks abroad, beckons the able of body and mind — and sees alas little of passion for peace and justice.   Quite the opposite. The world's resources, the best minds, the political authority — all seem bent to the same twisted purpose; to scatter the stones, to crush them to dust. To make sport of such naive images and bent of the human as sane conduct, loving community.

All such is considered out of order, 'for the duration.'

The human in any recognizable sense, is 'on hold,' for the duration.

Meantime, the worst, the despicable, indeed (in less demented times) indictable conduct, is held up for emulation and honor. To kill and maim and destroy, to fan to a firestorm hatred of the enemy, to throttle dissent, to insult the earth witlessly and unaccountably — behold the order of the day — 'for the duration.'

That 'duration' merits a close look. It is a period of time quite deliberately consecrated, given over to the demonic, the antihuman; to the power of death.

Such a time, it goes without saying, implies a far different project than the building of God's temple. Which is to say, an enterprise utterly at odds with the realm of God whose immanence was announced by Jesus.

War is the wreckage, the dismantling of the temple. It implies contempt for even the slightest effort to initiate or repair that temple of God, which Christ identified with his own Body. Contempt for those who assemble for a worship that necessarily includes resistance against war and warmakers.

War raises another form of temple. This one is dedicated to the demons, the spirits of death. The project is immodest, immense in scope. It is pridefully spoken of as total, and it is. Total in its opposition to the hope of God, total in its assault on the the community and ecology.

The warmakers assemble, with one purpose. Alike criminal, blasphemous, they together proceed to destroy. They blast apart the architecture of creation; the earth is reduced to an anteroom of hell.

Can one speak rightfully in time of war, of the temple of creation and community arising apace, of ourselves summoned and responding, the beloved community, bringing the realm of God nearer by day, in our works of justice and peace?

Hardly, 'for the duration.'

(1:13; 2:4) Nevertheless! Let the construction of God's sanctuary proceed; and all the more crucially, let it proceed in the course of the awful 'duration.' The call to build community can hardly be canceled because the nations have gone mad! If the harrowing of hell goes on, let the good work despite all, proceed.

Never is the word of God more stringently to be obeyed, than in the improbable bloody present. "I am with you," is here twice repeated. The saying, laconic, underscored, has the biblical sanction of an oath. God has sworn: the work is of God, it shall prevail.

"I am with you." Which is also to say, though Christians and Moslems alike invoke a God of armies, holy wars, salvation for the warriors, 'I am not with these.'

(2:6) In God's view, there is to be a 'little while,' a 'small delay.' This is the time of imperial peace granted by Darius. The peace, as we have seen, is rickety and chancy; it is based on injustice and enforced by violence.

(2:7) "I will shake the heavens and the earth, the sea and dry land. I will shake all the nations." God has but to leave the nations to their own designs; they will shortly proceed, in heaven and on earth, on sea and land, to wage their conflicts.

And there will follow a time both notorious and ominous; a time of the degradation of the human, 'for the duration.'

Thus is our lifetime summed up; the time of Vietnam, time of Grenada, time of Panama, time of the Gulf War. And as interstices of the times of hot combat; times of cold war. Peace, peace, the incantation of generals and presidents and diplomats — and churches. Peace is promised, peace is dickered over.

But alas, never a time of peace. How we long for even so slight a mitigation as the peace of Darius.

It is as though a people dying of thirst were to conclude in their fevers and chills; there is no such thing as water; water is a mirage, there is only thirst.

Verse seven continues with a stunning image. The seams of the nations are shaken out. Their loot, their gross national product, their larcenous wealth, usuries, fruit of injustice and violence — these accumulate, they are heaped up in the presence of God.

And then all undergoes a sea change, is transformed, exorcised, purified. "Mine is the silver, mine the gold." The wealth is no more stained with crime and blood.

Is this because the nations themselves have undergone a change of heart? It must be so. Otherwise the verse could mean only that a very old ploy was once again proceeding. We have seen it before; the dictator covers his tracks by handing blood money over to a complicit church.

The verse is eschatological. The nations have repented their crime. The goods of the earth, no longer subject to festering greed, cant, pillaging, are at last put to good use, to the building of the temple of God. "I will fill this house with glory."

Jawe grows prodigal. More and yet more is promised; more bounty on God's part, a more bountiful response. "Greater will be the future glory of this house, greater than the former."

"And in this place I will give peace." Which is to say, the shaking of the nations will in no way shake the foundations of the temple.

We have here an image of a space apart, a charmed circle. Within it, the 'shalom' of Jawe, rather than the questionable shaky peace of Darius, will flourish. "My peace I give you, not as the world gives, do I give."

By the gift of God we have stood in that circle, have tasted that peace — in sacrament and prayer, in courts and jails, in the community gathered and the community sent forth.

The temple space is not to be thought of as a mere refuge. Certainly it is a place of relief and refreshment; but the respite it implies is temporary. The temple, as Dr. Martin Luther King declared, is a place 'to go from,' a point of assembly and departure. There the courageous peacemakers 'double the heart's might' with an electric sense of a moment come at last, a moment raised to the rafters in ecstatic unity.

And the temple is a point of departure. There the community sings and prays its heart out — out into the streets, where sheriffs await, their paraphernalia of terror, dogs, clubs, tear gas, cruel and at the ready.

(2:15 ff.) Stone upon stone, the walls of the new temple go up. But the edifice, it is stressed once more, stands by way of image and figure. Its glories, only half revealed, correspond to the prospering of creation itself.

There was a time as we have seen, when the people were indifferent to the honoring of Jawe. (1:6) They were obsessed with amassing property, with familial well-being. No great need (or small) of worship, sabbath, temple.

And in their contempt for the God of harvest, of abundant nature — nature failed them. Grain and wine became scarce: "I struck you with blight, searing wind and hail."

Yet a new era dawns. Its date is exact; the day the foundation stone of the temple is laid. On that day too, it is indicated, hope once more vibrates on the air.

It is like the first bird song of a spring day. A second spring to be sure, and early on. Nothing visible stirs above ground, the season is at the verge, a promise.

The word of Jawe is like a kind of holy tease. People are to be on the qui vive, mindful. What signs?

They will appear in due time, and many at that; for the surest sign of all is already in place, the foundation stone of the temple. That laid, the rest is assured. Spring comes speedily — in nature, in the community. This though 'the seed has not sprouted, nor have the vine, the fig, the pomegranate and the olive tree yet borne.'

No matter. Spring is not autumn. And 'from this day, I will bless.'

(2:20-24) The name invoked here, Zerubbabel, figures large also in the book of Zechariah. He is the hero who despite all, completes at last the fabled temple!

He has large significance also for us Christians. Descended from David, in him hope for the messiah is renewed.

It seems fitting then, that this briefest of books conclude with a word to him alone.

We heard it before from Haggai, and quaked for the hearing.

It seems remarkable that in so short a prophecy an ominous word, a dreadful threat, should be twice uttered.

It comes to this: the implacable enemy of the temple and all it symbolizes, is — the nations. What of newness, what renewal of spirit, what onset of courage and resistance will they not speedily seek to crush — these great vessels of wrath, these blasphemers? The temple, the spirit, indeed the Jawe of peace and justice, these stand in their way, in the path of their 'chariots, riders, horses.'

It comes to this: no coexistence. Their thrones are an affront to the throne of Jawe.

The word of God is apodictic, abrupt. "I will overthrow the thrones. I will destroy the power of the kingdom. I will overthrow the chariots and their riders. The riders with their horses will go down by one

HAGGAI

another's sword."

Thus it happens. But only when the temple is not collusive with the palace, when the worship does not celebrate war, when the ethic is clear and demanding, no prating of 'just war' — in effect, of allowable, unaccountable murder.

When the priests are not purveyors of moral smog.

When the temple is itself! When worship of Jawe blesses, commends, multiplies, strengthens the works of justice and peace.

When worship of Jawe summons the nations to judgment, their crimes signified, summed up in an indictment of crimes of war.

He of the nearly unpronounceable name, Zerubbabel, summons and leads such worship. A vocation to set one trembling!

As such, he bears a dignity beyond measure or praise. He is like a 'signet ring' on the hand of Jawe.

And the Savior will be born of this line.
One day, God's Son will lead our worship, 'in spirit and truth.'
Let us say also, He will lead an era of truth and consequence.

ZECHARIAH

(1:1-17) For once we are well-situated as to the time of the prophecy: the exiles have returned.

And remarkably, at the same period a friend and advocate of Zechariah, Haggai, is addressing the 'remnant.'

Return. Physically, the terrible hiatus, the gap of a history lost among 'the nations' is closed. The exiles stand once more on their own dear and familiar soil.

Would that this were all, or the harsh matter of exile so simply resolved!

But the theme of 'return' is hauntingly, even vexingly symbolic. How can the return be complete if people, in recovering their own place in the world, their native landscape, all that is near to the heart, remain alienated from Jawe, conformed to the nations, divided in ideology and appetite, rent with conflict?

"Return to me, and I will return to you." The contrasting theme of exile-return, Jawe insists, is a double entendre. And the second sense (by no means secondary) Zechariah insists, must be attended to. The returnees, are still at odds with reality. They stand at distance from God. Restored to their land they may be, but only in a factual but dangerously forgetful sense. They are still lost, at sea, amnesiac — as to their God, their ancestry and, in consequence, their future.

Ignorant as they are of the great saving acts of God on their behalf, how are they to live a human life? Where is this new found, intoxicating freedom to take them?

It simply will not do to dwell on the recent liberation solely, as though that, or even the previous horrid enslavement were all their story.

ZECHARIAH

The people come from — Jawe. Can they forget their momentous genesis, the pact concluded in the desert, the 'choosing to be chosen'?

It is one thing, beautiful and long desired, to breathe free, to possess the land once more. It is quite another to remember — Sinai, the desert wandering, the pillar of cloud, the manna. Abraham Heschel writes of the difference:

"'The presence of God is not like the proximity of a mountain or the vicinity of an ocean, the view of which one may relinquish by closing the eyes or removing from the place. Rather is this convergence with God unavoidable, inescapable; like air in space, it is always breathed in, even though one is not always aware of continuous respiration."

The theme of Zechariah is in many ways similar to that of Haggai. It is almost as though the two prophets were speaking in tandem from the same pulpit. The temple must be rebuilt, they insist. This is the divine command, central to self-understanding, to worship, to virtuous conduct in the community.

But from the beginning, the temple theme is treated symbolically as well as factually. Of what use to recoup old worshipful splendors, if the hearts of the worshippers remain unhoused?

The word 'remnant' or 'minority' or 'faithful ones' is pivotal here. These have not only survived the exile, they lie under a command: to keep certain crucial memories alive. They are to remember whence they come.

They 'come from' Jawe — in the literal sense of creation, bloodline, ancestry, beginnings. At one time they knew their story, had it by heart, could recount it. Memories strong as an umbilical joined them to the Creator.

In the beginning they were created. (Gen. 1:27) "And God created them in his own image; male and female he created them."

Then, generations later, to put matters shortly, they were created anew. No longer a scattered tribe, enslaved, exiled, abused; they became a 'temple people' with their own rhythms of worship, their sense and celebration of the seasons, their songs and memories, sacrifices and festivals.

Come from Jawe, born anew — of Jawe. Knowing this, joyful for this, human for this. To locate the remnant more exactly in time and place were impossible.

ZECHARIAH

And knowing whence they come, they know by the same token, whither they were bound. Here and now, in return as in exile, in peace as in awful conflict, they know.

(1:2) Whence they came. Justice is not done to the sublime story by parroting in a communal voice: We came of Jawe. The claim was made of old, and in the beginning it was rich with implication. But in time, it became a mere incantation, grew hollow, mechanical, lax. Told in this way, the story even allowed for much crime.

Thus the holy beginnings were tainted; the story weakened, lost sight of, denied in practice, depleted by sin.

Here and now, according to Zechariah, admission of sin is essential to self-understanding as well as truthfulness. The people must be inwardly prepared for their task: the building of a new temple. For the temple is a stately symbol of a spiritual reality — the rhythm and heartbeat of the community.

And to dare speak of a new and noble place of worship is to undertake as well the exorcising of old crimes.

Be unlike those who went before! Deny that bond of blood, refuse that idolatrous, betraying presumption and resemblance! This is a very old cry of the prophets. And the cry is echoed fiercely by Jesus in his assaults on those who claim 'Abraham for our father.' (Jn. 8:39)

He mocks the empty ancestral claim. Undoubtedly they spring from a holy line, these religious 'experts.' But they are degenerate. They are one with those who from the time of Cain, murdered their brothers. The implication is terrible; the opponents of Jesus are murderers 'from the beginning'; they will destroy Him.

From the time of Zechariah, from the time of Jesus, and now, our own time, the call is a summons to strike free from a criminal line.

ZECHARIAH

If one may venture, the question is not merely that we cut free from American cultural history, not only a question of renouncing ancestral racism, violence, hatred, fear of human variety.

It is a question of accepting, indeed welcoming a chancy status in the world, as a member of a 'remnant,' a minority voice, in a resisting community.

And following through on the implications of this: freeing ourselves from the bondage of an authority which has proven illegitimate in fact and principle, which claims cynically to speak in our name. And not only to speak; to foster hatreds, to demonize adversaries, to draw the nations into a moral vortex, to proceed with horrid war upon war.

The eight visions that follow (1:7 ff.) are recorded in succession. But as is usual with such apocalyptic images, these stand outside time. They are in fact simultaneous images of the 'end time,' multiple aspects of a single reality, stressing this or that aspect of a mystery-to-come.

An analogy from visual art might be thought helpful. The eight visions are like eight transparencies, laid one upon another. When all are in place, the work (the last days, the 'end time,' the pleroma, the time of judgment) stands before our eyes, complex, rich in implication. And less baffling.

The images also imply a question (not 'When will all this come to pass?' That question is forbidden; according to Jesus, it is God's best kept secret). The question is rather: 'What will the end time look like? What are its signs, its crucial events?'

Time as we know it, and this world as well (the images imply), will have an end. And the end, the 'last days,' will look like this and this and this....

Such symbols are given through the visions as will enable believers (and no one else) to know that we stand at the final stage of the human journey. The end approaches. And in light of that (or darkness of that) believers will stand firm.

To begin then, we have, as in the manner of Ezekiel and others, visions borrowing heavily from cosmologies other than biblical.

ZECHARIAH

An angel, a kind of interlocutor appears, together with four guardian spirits of a creation regarded as four-cornered. The four spirits of earth are mounted. But they are in no wise akin to the destructive horsemen of Revelation. These are rather images of alacrity, intelligence and providential recourse. Their declaration is simple and final. They have patrolled the earth and have found at every point only a reign of peace.

The whole world at peace! The word is astonishing, all but unimaginable.

We learn that for a single month (February) of a single year (519 BCE) in our tormented history, the world knew an uneasy respite. Peace at last!

But wait. The 'peace' was no more than in indrawn breath, short-lived and precarious, the eye of a storm. More, the 'peacemaker' Darius is hardly to be accounted a reassuring figure.

An epitaph of Darius might honor him, but ever so tentatively. He is among the least murderous in the killing fields of empire. For the space of a month, we are told, he succeeded in crushing a series of revolts among his vassals in the Ionian cities.

A short-lived peace followed. But like most of his kind, Darius could hardly be thought to renounce war. Even as he proffered peace on the one hand, he was intent on another campaign, this time against Athens.

And the Athenians would bring him and his armies to ruin at Marathon.

Death before, more death to follow. That month! A short space indeed, a twilight darkening into threnody and foreboding.

The surcease, which might be thought to bring consolation even to the stopped ears of the dead, is strangely disturbing to the living. The angel stands majestically, endearingly even 'among the myrtles whose roots penetrated the deep.' Does not such a one stand at the very root of creation, of reality? In any case, this guardian spirit, despite apparent good news, is strangely distraught and turns to Jawe for reassurance.

The angel knows something. Does he read the human heart? The 'peace' is crepuscular, a false dawn. It is shortly to yield once more to darkness, lawlessness, disorder.

Worse, the peace is deceptive. It raises false hopes, even in the faithful. It goes contrary to the oracle that declares: Catastrophe is the prelude to the onset of God' realm.

Surely we are offered here an irony almost beyond comprehension. Is

ZECHARIAH

not peace of any sort, be it false, temporary, tentative, to be preferred to the carnage of war? And what of this longing for such a 'sign' as surely implies the slaughter of many?

Irony, wisdom, the long view. Let us take note that the worldwide 'peace' reported by the guardian spirits is a tactic, a cold war in place of a torrid. A moratorium is laid for a time, on killing; the interim deceives even as it disarms. Such a 'peace' is akin to that later awful reality known as 'pax Romana'; the imperial sword nonetheless hovers in midair.

The sword remains unsheathed; it is not laid aside. t is most certainly, not for a moment, renounced. Granted the space of a month, the warrior's arm and hand will once again be refreshed and ready.

Everything in the vision at hand leads to this conclusion. The four spirits of God are not bemused or deceived.

The empire of Darius is intact — which is to say, bellicose and appetitive. The announcement of worldwide peace is a statement of fact, but it implies as well a threat.

And of spiritual import of conversion, of the beating of swords into plowshares, not a whit.

We pondered such dire matters in the midst of yet another war, this one in the Gulf.

After feverish days and nights of bombing, a great spirit of bravado put all objection to rout.

The media moguls were shortly enlisted and thereafter jubilant. They were also fairly repentant of their former mood, the reservations, the second and third thoughts that plagued them before war broke out.

With the war came, as it were, a warning. It behooved them to stand with the civilian chief, to press his hand in silent communion. To smile and smile, and be villains all.

For our leader was proving a very Darius of daring! Our forces grew irresistible.

And our ineffable lead warrior will shortly rise to announce to the world, and this by main force of arms, that 'the whole earth is in peace and tranquility!'

ZECHARIAH

We have seldom, if ever, been graced (or cursed) to know the scripture so closely, in jot and tittle, 'this day fulfilled in your midst.'

'Don't hand me another Vietnam,' this eminence is reported to have commanded his subalterns. Which is to say, massive, quick, bring home a victory. By whatever means.

It was not to be denied that on some grounds a quick ending to the war was much to be longed and prayed for. But to name the outcome 'peace'? The word fled like a dove released from the hand of the fowler. With a cry, the dove was shot down in midair.

Peace fled the earth as the swords were poised.

We too were granted our 'month of peace,' a mere cease-fire, a breathing space extending across the world. It will hardly be decreed out of compassion for exiles, victims, the dead.

(1:11-13) A startling contrast! The spirits make their report: The whole world is at peace. 'Peace, peace' — and there is no peace.

As for Jerusalem and its afflicted peoples, what of them? They cower under a hovering sword. Sixty years of exile and humiliation! Is there to be more?

The angel turns to Jawe on the instant, in immediate and tender rapport. Jawe? Hardly deceived by a hot war gone for the moment cold — but for that, no less a war.

There follows a confession. Jawe is somewhat irritated, yes, at the sins of the people of covenant. But the nations! This is another matter entirely. Their conduct, their crimes awaken in the heart of God an unexampled fury.

Two promises follow or perhaps three. The temple will be rebuilt; a measuring line will be laid round about Jerusalem. And in a more general sense, the cities, 'my cities' will again overflow with prosperity.

We have discussed the temple symbol in the book of Haggai.

ZECHARIAH

As to the measuring line, centuries later the symbol is borrowed from Zechariah by the author of Revelation. (Rev. 11:1-2) 'Taking the measure of,' refers in the first place to the setting apart from common use of a given area or building or personage. The measure declares such exempt, holy, belonging to Another.

In a more interior sense, the measure is laid down by way of limit and taboo and boundary. Which is to say, this world, time, possessions, affinities even, friendships, the bloodline — these are not to be clung to as the final form of things, as ours 'for good,' in permanence.

We cannot finally lay claim to the earth as home or destination. Here we shall rest and build great barns for our store? 'You fool' is the scornful word of God. No more are you the wizards of time, to bend it to whatever use or gain or folly. You are mere birds of passage; you belong elsewhere - elsewhen.

Here the image of the 'measure' is applied strikingly to the entire 'holy city.'

The line is laid down. A calculation is made. Jerusalem is thereupon declared holy, just and peaceable. The city stands in contrast to Babylon, that city of shadow, renegade, feverish with violence and greed. And doomed.

We have here the first inkling of the resplendent vision which closes the book of Revelation — an image which closes the Bible itself, implying that God's word is spoken once for all, given over, consummated, henceforth ours — whether for hearing or ignoring (Rev. 21: 2 ff.)

According to this final image of the end time, Jerusalem is not only declared 'holy'; the city has become 'heavenly,' a political, social, religious entity permeated through and through with the spirit of God, a city 'descended from above.' Jerusalem is the embodiment and emblem of the reign of God. The nations stream in its direction; its scope embraces all creation.

In another sense too, the measure of the city is taken. It is an image of the measure of the human itself. Jerusalem, whether 'measuring up' or 'falling short' (and both occur, as we know from history both ancient and subsequent) Jerusalem remains the 'holy city' — even when it falls away woefully, bloodily from vocation and covenant; 'you who murder the prophets....' (Mt. 23:37)

Such a people can never quite escape the 'measuring line' laid against our humanity in all its horror and glory, our dizziness of soul, our veering between murder and compassion.

We know the human, we taste the inhuman — to our woe or weal. Or both.

(2:1-4) The second vision is of four horns and four blacksmiths.

The quaternaty of horns is an old biblical image of power. Here, in the four-cornered creation, the power of 'the nations' encompasses, hems in, claims all. It is as though a valiant bullfighter were surrounded by four monstrous beasts, not one; and had on the instant, to reckon his odds and make his move. Impossible, he is doomed!

But wait. Four figures suddenly appear, surrounding the beleaguered hero, fronting the murderous horns. This is an image original with Zechariah, an image of unconquerable strength in defense of assaulted goodness. Imagine, four angelic blacksmiths!

What could be more delightfully apt and reassuring to our embattled matador? Four angels, in aprons and pantaloons of leather, sleeves rolled up, hammers in hand. The matador raises his head.

The angels utter not a word, their mein speaks volumes. The horns fall back with a great snorting and pawing of ground.

(2:5-9) Yet another angelic measuring of Jerusalem. And with a different emphasis; this time 'to see how wide it is, and how long it is.' Now the line measures the universality, openness of the city toward all comers.

Human variety is the glory of the human itself.

Thus, let us note in passing, is reproved and set back forever the ancient sins of racism, sexism, and the war against creation itself and against the Creator of this immense human rainbow.

It is all quite wonderful. We hear a conversation of angels; one seems better instructed than another. Take the measure by all means, but by no means in order to set holiness apart or to restrict its scope or render one people a godly elite at the expense of the 'outsiders.'

And the prophet witnesses it all and is rendered thoughtful.

ZECHARIAH

We too.

We move closer to the final form of things, the final meaning and scope of the holy city, indeed of holiness itself, of the godly in our midst.

The measure is taken with something unprecedented in mind; let the world know that creation itself has been given a a new name: Jerusalem.

And let all come in! "People will live in Jerusalem as though in open country, because of the multitude of humans and beasts in her midst."

No more the ancient game of insiders/outsiders. No more citizens versus aliens, no more unclean and clean, no more 'illegals' cowering at the gate, no more favorites or pariahs, no one excluded! And if covenant there is to be, let it be universal!

Alas, in our day far different words are loud on the air: exclusion, extinction.

The world, we are told, will be a better place, more to our liking, and the survivors more to our resemblance, when many have been removed from the world. Let us draw a line in the sand and guard it close and exact a password. Or else.

And we succeed only in turning the guns and the immense rockets on ourselves. On our own souls, against our salvation. Against the feminine, childlike, Arabic, the despised, outlawed, expendable. We have condemned ourselves, in a demented absentia, to death.

"All, all come in, all at home, the many be one!" (Navaho chant).

(2:10-17) In two parts (10-13; 14-17) the prophet breaks into ecstatic song, celebrating the visions that have preceded. It is as though Jawe cannot contain herself. Sing it out! The four horns, 'the nations' that have dared threaten our matador are utterly set back; "they become plunder for their slaves." It is the four angels, those wondrous blacksmiths, who will prevail!

Then the them of 'everyone welcome, everyone come in!'

(3:1-10) We have for the fourth vision a court of justice. And for setting,

ZECHARIAH

heaven itself. The implication here (and elsewhere in the Bible) is simple and brutal; no justice exists in this world on behalf of the afflicted, the underdog.

Still, there is immediate consolation, for worldly injustice is noted and rectified elsewhere. It is to that 'elsewhere' the faithful must look in their affliction.

Comes now one Joshua, former exile, priest and companion to Zerubbabel. He is one of the saints. It would seem to follow in the malevolent nature of a fallen world, that all justice has been denied him.

In our vision, he is about to be rehabilitated. More, he is destined to rebuild the temple.

In this heavenly court of justice there are hints of the arrangements that hold firm in earthly courts. There is first of all a 'prosecutor,' a 'satan.'

Like any dog, he will have his day. In this court however, to our relief, he is denied his say.

On earth such an official, bound over to injustice, would beyond doubt succeed in condemning the likes of Joshua.

But that time is ended; the sun of injustice has set, once for all.

Therefore, this 'prosecutor of the saints,' who the book of Revelation tells us, 'stands before Jawe night and day, accusing the saints,' — here is reduced to silence. This day belongs to the angels of Jawe, and to the just one.

Who stands there, we are told, 'in filthy garments.' The description is at the least puzzling. Such clothing befits neither the celestial setting nor the dignity of the defendant. Rags, tatters, in heaven? We shall see.

Let it be recalled that biblical images of heaven seldom speak of a beatitude once and for all achieved. How boring, one might opine, to the holy protagonists! On earth they were all afire with love and its consequence, dire and harsh as these proved.

And will such valiant ones take their rest forever, cradled in the everlasting arms? It is unthinkable.

So the holy scribes, as it were, ransack heaven itself for symbols, glimpses, hints of the truth of resurrection.

And they come upon this; the earthly drama continues, on a different footing to be sure. But the play goes on!

Here, a drama of two acts, each intensely dramatic. The first presents the earthly estate of the just in time, former time, time befouled by injustice. Filth and rags are their lot. The rags are real; they stink of the despised, scorned humanity of the saints.

This is what transpired on earth; like Christ, the holy ones were clothed in scorn, hailed in court, and condemned for the crime of — being human.

As long as time perdured, so denied they were in this matter of justice, so scorned, violated, declared irrelevant, out of order, banished.

Time is named biblically, simply — the era of injustice.

Then, we are told, time passed away.

Do the rags of time cling like serecloth to the frame of Joshua, even in eternity? Not for long; they are shortly to be removed and replaced.

For we are in a new time, if one can speak of time. A great gong sounds; it is like the summons of a new creation, the time of the justice of Jawe.

The biblical name for eternity is — justice, the 'time' of justice restored, vindicated, the justice of Jawe.

Eternity dawns, injustice yields place. Satan, like his earthly counterparts, the prosecutors of the saints, is put to silence. On earth he scorned the just, rode high and mighty; now he is reduced, deflated, a mute symbol of defeat.

And what of just Joshua? He was an exile, a non-person, an illegal alien. He and his like could be rounded up for slave labor, conscripted for foreign wars or domestic. He counted for nothing, as did his people.

What shall we say of his worldly fate and theirs? There is little to say, or nothing. A single zero or a collective, one or a million, multiplied — is still zero.

Joshua stands with the exiles, the disappeared and tortured. If a lesser punishment than death befell him, it was because he was still useful — to an oligarchy, to a government, to the military, to the gigantic gorged mammon, the god named 'economy.'

The 'filthy garments' imply something more. There is also question of the sins of the priesthood, in whose ranks Joshua has stood. "See, I have taken away your guilt." No need to recall the terrible fulminations of Jawe prior to the exile, against the injustice, neglect of the poor, collusion with the powerful, of the priestly caste.

Joshua is stripped. He was often stripped on earth, but this is a noble ceremony, a lost honor restored. He is clothed anew, in the manner of the martyrs of Revelation. His robes are sumptuous, honorific, the habiliments of high office. He is the chief priest of his people. (Woe to those who assume such robes on earth with no prelude of worldly dishonor to make their honor credible!)

Then placed before the new priest is a seven faceted stone, mysteriously 'seven-eyed,' a precious gem. The priests bear the 'eyes' of God; they are carriers, signs of providence.

The jewel awaits its inscription to be engraved by Jawe. For the temple is as yet unfinished.

We are in a time warp. Joshua's credentials are conferred in heaven; but his task, at the time of the events recounted in the book, remains an earthly one. He will survive to rebuild the temple and preside over its ceremonies.

The meaning then of the oracle? It offers the chief priest a guarantee of heaven's favor. That which is wrought on earth, the restoration of true worship, (and of just conduct) is verified in Jawe's own court.

Times of exile, disenfranchisement, the death of the nameless and innocent, times of turmoil, of moral and political incoherence, of confusion of spirit. Time of wars, pursued without end or rationale, their combustive momentum and mindlessness. The present.

Then times of 'return.'

Mark them, observe them. Return to coherence, peace, justice, true worship.

Continue to return — in the midst of exile itself. Return to prayer, discipline, acknowledgment of God, a sense of the human that war had banished — 'for the duration.'

"For the one who ascends never ceases to do so, going from beginning to beginning, through beginnings that have no ends." (Gregory of Nyssa).

(3:8 ff.) The seven-eyed gem and the branch are gifts of Jawe to the new priesthood.

The meaning of the 'branch,' a messianic reference, is to be clarified later. After the exile, we are told, hope for the coming of the messiah is at last free of imperial pretention. All to the good!

The priests are to 'walk in my ways and heed my charge, judge my house and keep my courts.' And in consequence of this fidelity a magnificent gift will be theirs; 'access to these standing here,' that is to the angels and their holy mediation.

The priests too will be oracles of Jawe. In good times and ill.

(4:1-10) It is all surreal, it makes sense only beyond the rational. The prophet 'as one awakened from sleep' sees a great golden lampstand holding seven lamps, all alight. And at right hand and left, two olive trees standing. The 'seven' being the 'eyes' of Jawe, turned in all directions of the earth. And the 'two olive trees' the twin powers, Joshua and Zerubabbel, the spiritual and temporal authorities of the new theocracy.

(The lampstand-olive tree images will be taken up in Revelation Chapter 11 verses 4-13, signs of the presence of the towering figures of the new covenant, Peter and Paul.)

A question haunts us. Will these authorities, thus ratified from on high, govern more justly than the former? For awhile, invariably for awhile.

At least it can be said that two just men are at the helm — for awhile.

ZECHARIAH

Zerubbabel is addressed with three words. They are warnings as to right and wrong use of the temporal arm. First: "Not by an army, not by might, but by my spirit...." And the sentence is left unfinished, hanging there. It requires no ending.

"Not by military or political means ... [is humanity to be achieved, whether in the individual or the community]."

Is this the implied conclusion? Does the unfinished sentence express the longing of Jawe for a community that, after the perennial exile from itself and Her, will at last...?

Is the ending left to us as a way of self-understanding, understanding of Jawe — or of ignorance and blindness, our own? Is history itself unfinished, in the way of the sentence...?

Or trailing off as they do, do the words hint at the uncertain ending of things, as we place all our bets, resources, a vile bond — place even the blood of the innocent, on violent politics...?

"Between January and October of 1990, the police killed more than forty children in the streets of Guatemala City. In 1989, according to Amnesty International, 457 children and adolescents were executed in Rio, Sao Paulo and Recife, the principal cities of Brazil.

> "This does not happen where capitalism is absent, but where it is flourishing. Social injustice and disdain for human life grow with the growth of the economy. In countries where there is no death penalty, the penalty is applied daily in defense of private property."
> (Eduardo Galeano)

And if otherwise, if a change of heart occurs against all chance and the Spirit of God is poured out on humankind, what changes will the Spirit be thought to bring to pass, even in such a world as ours?

Let us confess that up to the present day, the unfinished word of God sticks in our throats.

It is as though the ending, in foreknowledge or foreboding, had stuck in God's throat as well.

In our time, across the world the successors of Zerubbabel have chosen to create armies and consequent politics of a certain well- known kind. Here, there, all but everywhere, a polity of violence has become the invariable bloody rule. And in consequence, the spirit of God is notably and utterly absent from private life and public.

Such a vacuum exists in place of communally honored morals or holy ikons or an accepted tradition, as to make of earth an anteroom of hell, of policy a maelstrom of lies and incoherence, of our political assemblies a praetorian guard, of war a commonplace, of the Bible a book either tightly closed or publicly burned, of Christians mere citizens of empire, victimized and victimizing like the others, of ....

If God cannot finish the sentence, how shall we?

(4:7-10) That temple imagery! Zerubbabel is given no nobler, more specific charge than to rebuild. The command is issued with all urgency.

Is God presented here as a kind of pharaoh, a builder of colossi at whatever cost of slave labor and death and all to his own horrific honor?

We must regard the imagery from where we ourselves stand: a people by and large deprived of the purity and truthfulness of worship.

Ours is a sour history indeed; the corruption of temple precincts and the priesthood itself. Who looks to priests today or to bishops for a clear evangelical word, passionate as Dr. King's diatribes, bitter as aloes on the tongue, fierce as the passion of Jawe for the 'little ones.' Who seeks from such officials, denunciation of the brazen crime of war?

No wonder we take uneasy refuge in bitterness of mood, dwelling, not altogether worthily, on such episodes as the eviction of moneychangers by Jesus. Now there is a scene we clap hands for!

What would it mean to the afflicted Palestinians today if the Jews were to rebuild their temple? Would it imply a new mandate to a new Zerubbabel — that justice so long delayed, be wrought at last?

ZECHARIAH

We are a people perennially at war — the brute fact. Neither ourselves nor the state of Israel can offer large comfort or noble example, whether to the world at large or to the Palestinians, cornered and crushed as they are.

For the Israelis, for Christians in the world, try as we may, there is no returning to innocence. There is only the effort to accept experience, to walk with it, to make the best of a bad history and a worse present.

Which is to say, here, now, to resist war.

(5:1-4) The vision of the flying scroll. Talk about surreality!

The scroll is the word of Jawe. Bird or Word, the being is enormous; this winged Word has the dimensions of the porch of Solomon! (1 Kings 6:3).

This Word of Jawe, like no other ever spoken.

It has the unerring eye and instinct of a predator. A kind of relentless holy Spirit, beaked and clawed. For sake of the truth, the Word is imagined as searching out and bringing to light those hostile to the truth. Those who steal the truth away, those who swear to and take their stand on, the lying wisdom of the world — these are the prey of the Word. It is in this sense that the bird, the Word, hastens to the judgment of 'thieves' and 'perjurers.'

Then the word of Jawe is transformed in flight. To truth-tellers it comes as a Blessing. But to liars and thieves the Blessing of Jawe turns to a Curse.

This is the other side of one truth. The Word of Jawe, violated in the secure, fault-ridden lives of the powerful, must, nonetheless, be vindicated. So this shocking image of the Word, immense in scope and range, premonitory and all-seeing. The Word patrols the world, and judges. And descends like a falcon upon its prey.

The vision conceives of the flying scroll as a wrecker of vile order, dead routine, ill-gotten prosperity, false peace.

On our tongues also, this Word?

Those proud houses of the mighty! The scroll enters them like a whirlwind, a firestorm, and brings them down.

A 'new world order'? Vile persiflage, bombast!

ZECHARIAH

Say rather, old, creaky, callous, world disorder — and shortly, collapse.

The visions continue, strange beyond telling, to first glance unrelated one to another, spontaneous, cramped, offensive to expectation. Dare we say — cockeyed?

What tempestuous spirits he was host to, this Zechariah!

The book is like a gothic novel, the prophet's is a weird dwelling indeed, for all the world like a haunted house on a moor invaded by sixteen winds of creation, no more able to resist them than a loose shuttered window a gale.

(5:5-11) The seventh vision can only be called — objectionable. It draws for its imagery on ancient prejudices consecrated at some length elsewhere, notably and awfully in the book of Hosea. Prejudices, which it must be added, are drawn into the Christian testament as well in the visions of Revelation: imperial Babylon as whore, a defamed and self-defaming woman.

We had best step softly here, and slowly, and with a look askance at our text. Thanks to women scholars of our time, we have learned something of the horrors wrought by such imagery.

The image is cruelly straightforward. There is no hint of a second thought or a third, least of all of a saving shame. The culture of Zechariah, to all appearances, supports the image; it is set down baldly, as though taken for granted.

More and worse, the image is offered by angelic ministry and with the evident approval of God. What an unassailable credential!

And what woman could be thought to object, to rage, to hurl angry rejoinders? What woman, registering her critique of the text, would not be named upstart, unseemly voluble — she being bound by Pauline command, to dwell silent in the church?

But brief, let us be brief.

The image bespeaks sexual and cultic shame. One cannot but think that it arises, a sexual caprice of dominance and control, from the fantasies of

ZECHARIAH

males-in-charge. And it is transmitted, we are told, through the 'angels,' emanations, very messengers of Jawe.

And finally, if one can credit the intent, the same image is to dwell in the imagination and instruct the behavior of a believing community.

Poor women, poor community!

As to the image. A close look reveals the ferocious intent. Victim and victimizer are alike — women. The implication is clear. A woman is first isolated, held to scorn, regarded as 'specimen,' object. Then by one means or another, she is to be removed — if not from the earth, at least from the arena of action, decision, impact.

And underscoring the cruel charade, let the removal of the offensive 'woman' be done by — women.

At the beginning, as in Genesis, one woman concentrates, body and soul, all malice and error in her own person. She leads all others (especially males — male Jawe himself?) astray. This is simply taken for granted.

There is nothing in the present imagery that resembles other heavenly trials. Here, no prosecutor, no vindication of the 'saints.' Guilt is simply assumed. The woman is criminal, condemned, wicked, irreformable. She is contamination, the spirit of paganism. She is 'the nations.' She must be held to scorn, imprisoned, sequestered.

Her place of confinement is especially humiliating. She is kept in a kind of bushel measure.

We are thus invited to imagine her as a small baleful animal, a mink or rattler. She is much diminished in size, a lilliputian in a world of humans.

It is as though the angel is her appointed guard, and Zechariah is to play voyeur of her humiliation.

Why, we ask, does he not protest, why does he not cry out: "This is criminal, this 'vision.' Release her!" Alas, he much resembles his culture — if not his god.

The scene has the horrid 'normalcy' of a nightmare. The imagery, morally outrageous, is simply — there. Make of it what one will.

The angel plays his (male?) part to the hilt, a lackey or hireling. (It would seem unlikely to assign a 'woman' angel to the task of interpreting the scene). The prophet too plays his male part: lackey, hireling.

So, willy-nilly, must the woman play her part.

The actions recounted befit the words. The angel declares that the imprisoned woman stands for 'the iniquity of the nations.' Then the angel pushes the woman further into her 'bushel' and lowers a heavy lid upon her, declaring laconically, "This [she] is Wickedness."

As with the commentators on the demeaning imagery of Hosea, so here. It is known in the trade, one supposes, or should be known, as a species of biblical 'reportage': no taking sides, objectivity above all. *BJ*, for example, flies magisterially above all unpleasantness: "The Hebrew terms translated here as 'iniquity' and 'malice' signify the despising of God and of God's laws.... This 'mepris' is personified...."

Enough said.

Shall we imagine the darkness and despair of solitary confinement? We heard during the Vietnam war of the infamous 'tiger cages,' in which below ground, prisoners were held. Above them was a barred walkway; on it the guards stood or moved about, observing the prisoners. Food was thrown to them from above; so was other less savory matter cast down on them.

There, all but lightless, under cover in the most inhuman sense, the prisoners languished and failed. Many died.

Shall we name this the fate of women, according to the image? It seems ironic. Almost in spite of itself, the Bible offers a commentary on its authors, its culture. On its preferred god.

Two winged women appear and bear the prison and prisoner away. And it is implied, good riddance.

The outrageous allegory goes on, the angel interprets the scene, the airlift of the infamous basket and its inmate. "They are going to build a temple for 'it' in Babylon. When the temple is ready, they will deposit it there in its place."

Thus the infamy, the harlot, the Babylon, the false worship, all are disposed of, by presumption, permanently.

It is as though everyone concerned, the male prophet, Jawe, women, were agreed: the realm of God could not be thought to arrive until one among them, whose spirit threatened and polluted all of them, was removed. They collaborate.

Then the future brightens. Within the confines of Jerusalem, worship of true God proceeds. And, of course, virtuous conduct, peace and justice abounding. No harlotry, no whoring after other gods. No such women-symbols ever again to befoul the holy landscape.

So it is said; no infamy, ever again.

No need of such a symbol, ever again.

And it is all untrue, the horrid opposite comes true.

Shall we not conclude that imagery approving the vilifying and banishing of the feminine carries its own vengeance?

(6:1-15) The final vision rejoins the first. The theme is of four steeds, this time joined to chariots. 'Winds of heaven' they are called, signs of sleepless far-ranging providence. They come from no human landscape, from 'mountains of bronze,' beyond which the Babylonian gods have their dwelling.

The four chariots are sent to range the four corners of the universe. They are to take special care of the 'land of the north,' whence the exiles will return, 'that my spirit may dwell among them.'

And then (6:15 transposed, *BJ*), 'those who come from afar will build the temple of Jawe.'

The theme recurs again and again. It is as though the temple cult will guarantee, like an impregnable sacred enclosure, the flourishing of a godly people.

We have lived long enough in a bloody millennium to know otherwise. To say the least.

There are no guarantees. None, whether in one religion or another, in

ZECHARIAH

one God or the gods.

To speak of Jawe, no guarantees. Or if there are, they are straitly circumscribed by caveats, as here: "And you will know that Jawe of hosts has sent me to you, if you heed carefully the voice of Jawe your God."

Matters could hardly be stated more flatly.

We know, if we know anything, that we do not heed. Not well or willingly, not for long. People of God, people of covenant? We are deaf to that voice as any pharaoh, any pharaoh mummy.

We are on firmer ground when we summon, by way of chastened contrast, another theme entirely.

A related theme and chancy beyond doubt and rife with risk: the community of resistance, the 'remnant,' the exiles, the slaves, the people who have 'gone out,' the desert wanderers.

We know too the trap that awaits these, when at length the land is in their hands, the newcomers.

We think of other arrivals in a 'land of promise,' whatever its geography — Latin and North America, South Africa, Israel.

Accompanying the fanfare of divine favor, exclusive covenant, religious establishment are lines drawn against women, outsiders pushed out or exterminated or enslaved, insiders flagrantly favored, plunder and prospering for a few, misery for the many — behold the settler state, a merciless unjust bellicose theocracy — or as at present — 'secularacy.' Little or no amelioration, a bitter surfeit of injustice, and war upon war.

(6:9-15) Matters cloud. Matters of succession, of who will legitimately claim the title of high priest. The facts are in, the 'crown of gold' signifies not only priesthood, but royalty as well. The crown rests on the head of a certain Joshua.

The change of title holders, we are told, is a concession. A later scribe amends what might be thought of as facts of history. For good or ill, the priestly (and royal) ascendancy is securely in place when the final version of Zechariah's scroll is written. The original power and perquisites have been joined, and passed on.

According to *BJ* (shall we say tongue in cheek?), we have here an example of 'inspired rewriting.' Indeed.

But shall we be permitted another, rather more secular observation? It occurs to one, as the text is jostled and adjusted and finally takes form, that the powerful care mightily for the retention of power, even to the point of rearranging the (purportedly sacred) text.

As to the literary form, what to say? Is the Holy Spirit issuing here an implied warning, rather than a blank check of approval?

(7:1-14) A 'religious' question arises, and a delegation is sent from Bethel to Jerusalem to seek an answer. The questioners are among those recently returned from exile, we are told. They are palpably sincere.

Their question revolves around an ancient rite, a fast to commemorate the destruction of the temple some 70 years before. Now that the rebuilding of the temple is underway, does it make great sense to continue observing the fast?

They could hardly have bargained on the answer they receive, straight as an arrow. Wrong question! It implies an ancient ploy indeed, a fancy verbal footwork.

They are shortly to be enlightened. For their question conceals an effort to substitute 'religious' matters for other, rather more exigent, quotidian, and grievously neglected questions.

Questions, plainly put, of justice.

The attack from on high is wide-ranging.

Let us, says Jawe, speak of fasting; let us also speak of feasting. Of the meaning of both fast and feast, the thrust, the import. Let us speak of detachment, distancing, also of the probing of motives. Let us get to the heart of matters. "When you fasted and mourned these seventy years, was it really for me that you fasted?"

And then as to feasts, let us put them in the opposite pan of the scales. "And when you were eating and drinking, was it not for yourselves that you ate, for yourselves that you drank?"

What is the meaning of this puzzling probe, the 'was it truly for me?' and 'was it not for yourselves'?

The delegation from Bethel (or from New York or from Tel Aviv, or from any clime or time where religion of a certain kind is much in vogue) will have its answer, and then some. An answer, a tone hardly to the satisfaction of the questioners.

Unto yourselves. The eyes of the 'religious' are frozen in their skulls. At center eye they see only sanctuary, observance, merit, self-congratulation. What others see (what Jawe sees) is pharisaism, show, declamation, emptiness, contempt for the underdog, self-justification, inertia, numbing of soul, letter of the law, death of the spirit.

In sum, a scathing indictment of deviant religion.

Need it be added that the illness is pandemic and perennial; or that the 'answer' of Jawe pinks flesh as yet unborn?

And at the side of the eye, what do such priests, levites, lay-folk see? Only enough of reality as to guarantee a sure and safe passage — toward the temple and its rigamarole. Enough to avoid the impediment, the stone of scandal in the road. Enough to step gingerly over or around the wounded one in the ditch.

Thus goes the 'world view' of the all but purblind, the 'religious' of a certain stripe. The impediment, the scandal, the neighbor neglected, these works weirdly to their advantage. It is possible to be inhuman and still be religious.

'For yourselves you fasted.' And by that spurious credential, you flourished, and in ways that call for a close look. And for judgment.

There is a warning here, an historical connection all but severed by a pervasive amnesia. And a question. Why should people of faith require such scalding reminders of the truth? Are there not scrolls, prophets, a yearly rhythm of feast and fast, groaning and laughter, remembrance, mindfulness? Have the exiles not suffered?

Surely there are a multitude of hints, urgings, help-meets. And yet we fall from grace, the feasts meld with the fasts, day with day, year with year. The heart goes out of us; our tongues parch, the living word fades on the old parchment, we grow torpid under regimen and routine. The neighbor counts for nothing.

No temple can excuse or excise the history.

The old temple came down and rightly so; it was an epicenter of scandal.

ZECHARIAH

It excused injustice; worse, it wrought injustice. Its incense clouded minds; its taxes made money bags of human hearts. Larceny, mammon, greed, an unholy trinity.

Shall there then arise a new temple, merely to undertake the old routine, incantation, jot and tittle, fast and feast; to repeat the old sins, to ignore Lazarus at the gate, that beseeching victim the temple clients have both created and contemned?

"The doubtful marriage between supply and demand serves the despotism of the powerful. It punishes the poor and generates an economy of speculation. Production is discouraged, work is seen as worthless, consumption is deified. People are obsessed by the electronic board of the [stock exchange] as much as by the movie screen. People talk about the dollar as though it were a person, or better, the god in which to believe.

"Since the arrival of Columbus, Latin America has suffered the tragedy of capitalism, but as farce. It is the caricature of 'development'; a dwarf pretending to be a child."

(Eduardo Galeano)

Let the religion come down to earth, ground itself like a living being in human soil.

Or if it will not, let the ruins of the old temple stand, for shame, for reproof, no stone laid on a stone.

The warning is for sake of the future; if the future is to be different, the present must be made so.

So we come (one thinks, not a moment too soon) to the pith of God's insistence that the temple be rebuilt.

This is the God who raises unpleasant questions and demands a response! What will be the quality of the worship, what the public consequence of a pact of truth and love? What reverberations will shake, like seismic tremors, the furthest corners of the land; indeed, the four corners of the universe, patrolled by the vigilant steeds of Jawe?

Let us hear once more the ancient instruction. It was all but obliterated

ZECHARIAH

by the believers themselves long before pagan wreckers brought the grand temple down.

Let the words be incised anew in lintel and cornerstone. And more, incised in the flesh of believers. So deep that if need be, blood will run.

Matters of 'true justice, goodness, compassion....'

And then, "Do not oppress the widow and orphan, the stranger and the poor." The scalpel penetrates to the joining place of sinew and bone, this Searcher of heart and reins is relentless: "Do not so much as ponder in your heart any evil against another."

(7:11-14) Here is our history by way of warning. The ancestors 'refused to be mindful.' Literally, they lost their minds.

And this be it noted, even as the temple liturgy droned on — mindlessly.

Indeed, two phenomena cohabited without trouble: religion vacuous with routine and public malfeasance. The temple justified the crimes, contempt of the neighbor sought and found justification in the temple. It was a suave dovetailing of — dual mindlessness.

'De mortuis nil nisi bonum?' According to conventional piety the dead lie beyond critique or judgment. But shall the Jawe of Zechariah be thought in the remotest sense conventional?

Suddenly, a wild storm rises. It is as though stones are toppled, graves emptied. The dead are summoned to judgment.

The phrases Jawe takes to her lips in this scalding, resentful recall! No ancestral hero, no grand repute remains intact. Root and stem, all come down, before the seeds of the future can be sown.

All is mowed under by this merciless scythe. History is radically rewritten.

Here comes the bitter truth of things, the toppling of the ikons, cultural, religious, military, political. Judgment, prelude to a new start. "They refused to listen, they turned a rebellious shoulder and stopped their ears.... They made their hearts hard as diamond."

A few are excepted, the prophets who paid up, and dearly. And it is they who, in consequence, are spared the scornful deflation of the high and mighty.

In an unwieldy sentence freighted with indignation, the prophets are exonerated. They were faithful — even as they were universally ignored. 'so as not to hear the instruction and the message which Jawe has sent by his spirit through the former prophets.'

Is Zechariah to know a better fate?

ZECHARIAH

(7:7-14) He harps on it, and so shall we; the temple must be rebuilt as sign of a new heart and will.

The reasoning goes thus: the past was a moral disaster, so the temple fell. Now the connection between the two, history and event, must be confessed. This for the sake of a new start.

Where had the truth fled? The fault was not with the prophets; they were simply pilloried or thrust to one side in the rush to empire.

The truth, sin, judgment, was grievously neglected — shall we say in view of other interests?

But the truth will out.

Who is to tell our history? Who knows it without bias or declamation? Who are the offended parties, who the friends? Whose is the wisdom that penetrates the fraud and frenzies of the moment?

In the present recounting, God plays another role than usual. We have here not so much the history of the poor and victimized as such, but a people much beloved of Jawe as the prophets testify.

Here is something different; an accountability all but lost sight of. A veritable burial mound of memory is excavated.

The former lords of the earth, imperial Israel and its temple splendors, toppled. The great ones lost everything: riches, dignity, land. They were whipped off like a herd into the bleak unknown. There for generations a cadre of slaves, pressed to the earth, tasted the bitter lees of existence.

But for the tenacious memory of Jawe, they disappeared from the earth, faceless, nameless, kneaded into a mass, the expendables of history. Their history was in effect, a non-history.

It might be thought to favor health of mind that those who underwent such horrors and survived against all odds should erase such memories once for all.

By no means. Jawe stirs it up, the shame, the loss.

From effect, let us consider the cause. The point digs deep, it wounds and heals at once. For the national disaster was by no means arbitrary;

it was a logical, indeed inevitable consequence of national sin.

This is true history. Can it be told?

It must be told. Even though the national memory, even the self-described religious memory, is — a blank.

Then or today, who will say the awful words: Sin? Crime? Who will dare utter such words at times of national frenzy, times of war? Who apply the scalding truths like anti-medals, anti-decorations to the effigies of the national heroes? Who will discard in scorn the military medals on the White House lawn, as war after war scourges the earth, a harrowing of hell?

The 'true history' called crime and consequence begins and ends with an ecological image. In the beginning, the people were 'eating and drinking,' a reference to the hideous normalcy of imperial routine.

Jawe marks the time differently; it is the time of 'the former prophets,' an ominous phrase, an implicit judgment, for the prophets are by common consent, quite ignored. Abroad in the land, a tranquility of sorts reigns. "Jerusalem and the surrounding cities were at peace, ... the Negeb and the foothills were inhabited..." Peace, but not for long.

Everything comes down. The shattering of the temple-empire is swift, 'a whirlwind.' The people are 'scattered ... among all the nations that they did not know.'

And their fate is enfolded in a larger story, the fate of the earth. It comes as a gentle diminuendo, a mere touch upon mournful strings. "Thus the land was left desolate with no one traveling to and fro..." Then terror strikes the strings, a crescendo. "Of a land of delights, they made a desert! They made the pleasant land into a desert."

The disaster implies an ethic violated, an accumulation of guilt, and a final payment. Who or what exacts the payment? Jawe says: I do. Or put it otherwise — reality itself does.

This is the point, unpalatable as it is, again and again brought up by the God of Zechariah. This is the only healing of a history gone awry.

ZECHARIAH

Of a history dismembered rather than remembered, outright distorted, biased, its ill repute burnished, mention of crimes banished.

Accountability is suppressed. Through media manipulation, through false and fawning worship, through the befuddled adulation of the populace, through macho, merciless valor and extravagant public display, a social ego is fabricated. It is both dismal and determined on its task of self-justification.

This is the blindness of empire, and especially (the point here) that empire which flatters itself as 'religious.' Doubly blind.

Indeed how could the empire be thought to remember its past with any semblance of truthfulness? It could not. To remember would be to relinquish, to repent, to cease being — empire.

It is for Zechariah and his like to remember, and this for the sake, not of the empire, but of the people who are stuck in empire, votaries, subjects, parasites, hangers on, victims and victimizers. Other than the solitary story-teller, no access to true memory.

A dead end, the American predicament, whatever the outcome of this or that military misadventure. Citizens are stuck indeed; in the morass of ideology, the war drums beating away like commanding summoners to a common oblivion.

"Come follow me. And the media falling in first, pied pipers all, in lock step."

(8:1-23) Domestic injustice and violence abroad, these are summoned like ghosts from a mass grave. The summons is a hoarse trumpet of judgment. Only thus, accused, found guilty and cleansed, shall the people be enabled to create a different future.

The judgment, one notes, is quite prosaic, literal. It is conveyed coldly, in quasi-legal terms, the language of a criminal court.

But what of the future? For the 'remnant' has returned, the chains are fallen from their limbs.

Also those other, closer bonds, that far more weighty burden of guilt.

O felix culpa! All expunged!

Let us breathe deep and take heart. It is as though we died in a world gone mad, our world. Then we awakened to something utterly different, a Genesis. We drew into our being the silken air of the first week of the world.

Jawe's passion is our own! Love for the emerging human, that birth so long delayed and hindered! Shall this not be God's triumph, the human healed, reborn, its heart and soul given over to compassion?

A vision of grace and beauty opens, a human future at last.

Jawe is shaken with ecstasy and breaks into song.

JAWE IN ECSTASY (Zechariah, chapter 8)

For this people,
ardor and jealousy, both!
anger kindled to flame —
and did they but know it
all in their favor!

Return, return!
my longing
to pitch tent in your midst!

See, I call your cities anew.
New York, imagine! named
New Faithful.
and the mountain range westward
north, south, gigantic reclining —
Holymount!

In New Faithful
summon to eye
old men and women, each
dwelling companionable
in sunny public places;
and the children —
little girls and boys

ZECHARIAH

a multitude, a tumult!
unimpeded romping —

O my people
poor revenants,
remnant
of those dragged forth
a somber chain gang, into slavery —
Tell me,
do I summon the impossible?

In mind's eye, the promise
shall be, shall be.
Jawe has spoken!

Shall it not be?
shall I not prevail?
come now, who was it
plucked you by hair of head,
east to west
from toil and trouble,
set you down gently
in New Faithful?

Enfolding you
heart to heart
I murmur like a mother
my people, my people

You I hear
murmur
like a shell whispering
the to fro tides
of a sleeping sea —
dear God, our God.

Let hands grow strong
slack knees straighten!
tasks ahead
redoubtable, noble!

ZECHARIAH

choked and impeded
temple and square
with wars' detritus —
waste and want
beasts and humans
one slavish horde
peace a lost art
sword bared against sword.

All, all is changed —
sea change, land change
change of heart!
I kiss the vine's fruit, kiss
dawn and its dew.
My spirit broods, brings forth
peace on earth, plenty on earth.

Dear puny remnant,
for every curse
uttered in despite
I pour
from heart's cornucopia —
blessing upon blessing.

Multiply then, increase
like seed corn scattered
right hand and left —
fidelity, justice!
a green sea of corn!

Rejoice my people!
from every horizon
revenants, seekers,
ten times your number
converge!

Come then, what hinders
my holy hegira?
sweet communality
has not God sworn?

I am your God!

(9:1-17) And what is one to make of it, this hodge podge of threat, tenderness, fury, recrimination, beating of the war drum, beating of the peace drum, promise of a peacemaking messiah, grim portent of disaster? It is all here together, tribal confusion and clarity, clouds and fierce sunlight, weapons sheathed and unsheathed.

It is like a single day of changeful weather under northern skies — this page. Mood clashing against mood, vitriol to sweetness. What a God, what a people!

We swallow hard and follow bewildered, making of it what sense we can.

Even allowing for considerable editing of texts and the fusion together of fragments, considerable confusion reigns. Who is this Jawe? Has Zechariah created a God in the image of the people, flushed with the anger and recrimination of those newly sprung from slavery? A terrifying warrior image of God?

More. Is the purpose laid out here, the inclusion of the nations, even by main force, in the ambit of 'true religion' — is this to be thought the will of Jawe? So, it would seem, the puzzling matter is here presented.

Or is this no more than the fantasy of a people in a trauma of release from bondage?

It might be of advantage to pause and reflect on the psychology of exile and return. The history of this people cannot be grasped if one thinks of them merely as 'expatriates' or 'emigres'; if one thinks only of a multitude driven from their land by brigands, or somehow escaping a domestic tyrant. But surviving more or less unscathed.

Something far worse has occurred here. A proud people, whole and entire, were rounded up and transported. For some sixty years every effort, blind, canny, brutal, subtle, was exerted against them. To crush hope and dignity, to destroy every vestige of their religion.

Their plight is referred to by Jawe as that of 'prisoners'; God has plucked them from 'the dungeon' (*New American Bible*), or 'the ditch' (*BJ*).

Nonetheless, against all odds they survived and returned.

Such a people, to all calculation and prospect, are simply stuck in their fate. If some of them survive, it is at the price of enacting despair in mein and behavior, fawning and smiling in the face of villainy.

They are, they will ever be, prisoners of folly and cruelty. It is worth noting that the author has first-hand experience of this.

Allow them then (this is the tactic of the tyrants) their dreams and fantasies, whether of freedom, return, vindication. Harmless. Let them construct castles in the air, plans and projects that may make a kind of feverish sense to them, but of course will go nowhere.

Let them be secretive, let them be vengeful, darkly plan retribution.

It all goes nowhere.

Landing in the world again, free, is quite a different matter. Either the fantasies are swiftly erased by quotidian realities — or they are hotly pursued, airy as they undoubtedly are, ruinous as they might well be.

Thus matters proceeded, one thinks, with the newly liberated people of Zechariah. Free, free at last! Anything seems possible in the heady atmosphere of the great return. All, leaders and people, are intoxicated with great, improbable projects.

Then lines are swiftly drawn. It appears that reality has only two hues. Everything is either/or, dead black or blinding white. We are the virtuous! Think of the evils that we endured, the malice that penetrated us like a cloud of arrows, body and soul, temple and land! And have we not prevailed despite all? Is not this the proof beyond cavil, that God is with us?

(9:3-8) And Jawe goes along with the hotspur times. Or so it is written.

The adversaries of the chosen, let it be said plain, are presented as a pure darkness, beyond the pale, relentlessly wicked. Then name them! Assign their fate, one and all! Tyre, Ashkelon, Gaza, Ekron, the Philistines, the Jebusites!

The names are of small matter to us, but the fate assigned them is a grave matter indeed. Let it be said plain: Zechariah has confected a god according to a vengeful human image.

ZECHARIAH

The chapter is eminently inconsistent. It makes of Zechariah's little book a bewildering handbook of fitful ambiguities: black on white, white on black, God of mercy, God of the sword! And who is to say or choose, which god is true?

Indeed, an even worse case seemed to prevail. At times the prophets themselves yield to a dark tribal passion. As in this passage. Their voices no longer counter or correct the image of Jawe of the sword. The prophetic voices disappear into an ambiguous text (or one that is all too clear!) telling of a god who differs not a whit from the gods of the goys, who bares the sword and wields it with fervor.

And with reference to Jesus, may one interject here a note?

Who but God could speak so clearly, consistently, strongly? And who but God could be so clearly mistaken so fabulously wide the mark? Of necessity, one thinks, the divine must dwell in Him — since He proved so utter a failure in the world. Outrageous, unyielding in this matter of violence! So the world's logic would of necessity decree that: (1) He be disposed of and (2) His words also be disposed of.

Disposed of, set aside, declared irrelevant. The nations (the churches!) go their own way. There is no ease here, no rest for the spirit, no clarity. There is comfort and blessing only for the endless, mindless violence of individuals, of the nations.

Its recent dark epiphany in the Gulf we cowered under for months.

At least there is a species of consolation to report, icy as it is. A once belligerent religious establishment, Protestant and Catholic, took a rather firm stand against the war. Some consolation, a measure of relief from the utter zero of the times.

But it must be said as well, that the plain sense of Jesus' words was largely dispensed with. The source of the church statements opposing the war could hardly be said to be the Sermon on the Mount. Too clear, so clear the words blind the eye!

Instead, we were offered recourse to 'the 1500 year history of the just war theory.' As though there could conceivably, under the canons set down in ancient times or modern, occur a just war. Or less unlikely still, that the war under scrutiny could fall within the hypothetical frame. A just war waged with the weapons of 1991?

ZECHARIAH

We are in a madhouse where morals are made 'by fools like me.'

The history of 'just wars,' a 1500 year history indeed, of a pagan confabulation, designed to 'limit the violence.' Designed also to preserve intact a church-state arrangement of great benefit to each party.

And then alas, prior to that golden Constantianian era — a puny two or three hundred year history of taking seriously and literally the words of the gospel: thou shall not kill, love your enemies, do good to those who do ill to you!

(9:9-10) Contrast these verses with verses 11-17. Talk about an 'interim ethic'!

We are offered in the first two verses a sublime image; Jesus will take it literally to himself, as though he clothed himself in the image, the very vesture of His spirit. Centuries later He enters Jerusalem 'meek and riding on an ass, on a colt, the foal of an ass.'

The spirit is clothed in the conduct. This is no mere gesture of divestment (though it is that also, the renunciation of the pomps of the gentile lords).

It is much more. Soul is one with body. Does He enter the city to take in hand the reins of governance? Yes, but in the same act, He makes Himself vulnerable to rogues in lofty places.

Their eyes are upon Him. 'Do with me what you will' is his only response. He has voyaged across time, has survived the abominations of history, has refused to reject 'the works of His hands.' He arrives in this place, in a style altogether his own, the available servant of the human.

Shall He prevail?

In the time of Zechariah, edicts are promulgated, designed to bring about a universal peace. The northern and southern kingdoms are united; banished are 'horses, chariots, the bows of warriors.' Peace is proclaimed to the nations. And evidently, from the plain text, peace is realized (O all but unbearable irony!) from the Mediterranean to the Persian Gulf, from the Euphrates to the ends of the earth.

The cradle of civilization and the promise.

ZECHARIAH

We can scarcely credit the text. Are we dreaming? We raise our eyes from the page, the confident words, the heartrending images. Then our gaze falls upon another scene entirely: the universal desolation of war. This messiah and his message — a pipe dream then, a cruel fiction now? An immemorial longing, battered about from pillar to post by the boot of Mars?

Yet the promise stands; it is not obliterated by contrary evidence, event, conduct — even by present follies. Far from it; in another time of bloodletting, His own, the savior underscored the promise once more. In the teeth of Roman perfidy and the violence gathering force against Himself, He verifies the prophecy, dramatizes it, embodies it.

Thus 'hope against hope'; thus the hope that 'moves mountains,' that lies so close to despair as to be its truest adversary.

The godly prophecy yields quickly, so quickly as to seem a mirage, a gloss on the text, a footnote. What tasks were we about, we ask fretfully, when this Quixote rode onto the page, distracting us with his own distraction of mind? — Why, we were busy, our gods and ourselves, about our usual business which, given our world, requires no elaborating.

Does Jawe rattle the weapons and rouse the troops to a frenzy? Are we urged to a holy war? So much the better.

We have seen all this before, unto weariness of spirit. The words are in utter contrast to the sweetness of imagery immediately preceding: the man on the donkey, the promise, the magisterial edicts, the atmosphere of calm and clarity, the clean break with a horrid past, the universal sway of peace. At last, at long last.

(It is of interest, and sobering as well, to note that commentators pass over [gingerly or not, one cannot know] the difficulties offered by such juxtapositions as occur here. Juxtapositions and more, seemingly unresolvable contrasts).

Are we offered two beings, beyond reconciling, the peaceable man on the donkey and Martian Jawe? And what of the timing of the era of peace;

does the tranquil realm of the messiah come only at the end? What then of the horridly violent 'meantime,' which seems to engorge time itself into its maw? Must violence ride high as long as time lasts? How long, O lowly man on the donkey?

It would seem that the two, the hankering after a martinet God and a messiah of peace, go together in the mind, in the world, in time. The nations, above all the Christian nations, persist in rattling arms and crying war. War is their meat and drink, their health, surcease, credential. And for the future as well, the like prospect stands, firm planted as a great stele consecrated to Mars.

In this sense the God of war will continue also to be invoked. The nations will know no other God.

And we for our part must forebear with all our strength, to grant such a god a capital letter, contrary as he (sic) stands to the haunting image of the Man on the donkey.

This messianic One gently invades our feverish days and nights, that Man also known as the Human One of Daniel's vision. He and his donkey step gently on the earth. He makes no great argument; certainly he is no match for the blazing thunder of the 'smart' bombs, the smart human brains. The Human One is so easily ignored, disposed of, shunted aside, if need be put to death — as we know. As He surely knows.

But this is all beside the point. Death is beside the point. Through all that He has prevailed.

There remains that presence of His, those words concerning enemies, love, conduct other than retaliatory. He rides abroad, loving his enemies, preferring to walk the thin line of conscience along which he chooses to give his life rather than unsheathe the sword.

Word and deed dovetailing so nicely; this cannot quite be lost, though the world in despite of Him, in contempt of Him, become a vast killing field.

ZECHARIAH

He lives, his words are sown to the winds and lodge here and there in good soil, the hearts and minds of those who undertake other work in the world than murder. And who go about that work, which He named his Father's own.

This image occurs. War is raging. A few women, men, children, make their way with infinite patience and care through a no-person- land.

Let us be absurd for the moment, surreal. These few are mounted on donkeys or are leading donkeys. They are unarmed. They have come to this awful place for a purpose simply told: this is their world too, in it they have a task, a vocation.

Their's is a task of mercy and sanity — to interpose themselves between the armies. Dangerous! They propose to translate, in whatever way may open, the simple directives of the Sermon on the Mount. To assuage and heal.

The battle rages on. There are contesting banners all about, a multitude of corpses, panic, frenzy and fear. One side eventually prevails. The outcry of victory is raised; it is merciless, a demand for unconditional surrender.

And on the other side, the defeated, from the captives and wounded; indeed on the faces of the dead is lodged a fixed look of ineluctable hatred. It is like a hellish fixed mask. The look speaks aloud. Revenge will have its day; the seeds of another war are sown.

You choose your images or are chosen by them. Religion, conventional or thoughtful, deep tradition or the moment's fashion; and then the frenzied national idols summoning, commanding, the drums, the flags and ribbons. The power of images! From these (Jawe wielder of lightnings, the Human One) spring the conduct, the deed, the life; bloodshot or compassionate.

(10:1-12) Yet another omnium-gatherum of images of Jawe. He speaks in his own person or is spoken of.

Verses one and two begin innocently enough, a rather conventional homily. "It is from Jawe rather than from the gods or their votaries and incantations, that good things are to be sought. To do otherwise, to give one's self to idolatrous practice, can only bring great trouble, loss of the

ZECHARIAH

true way."

(10:3-5) Then the tone, the mood grows bellicose, darkens like the brow of Jove. Such anger, such a vengeful spirit! And we are once more far from the Human One and his confounding meekness.

The impression is strong; this people seldom stand far distant from the sweet itch of retaliation. The mood is raw. They (and their prophet) still lack a firm rooting in the new order of things. So the promise of plenty and peace seems no more than a mirage. What is real and pressing is the here and now — unstable and feverish.

They can scarcely grasp the reality — the nightmare is over. So they seize upon images of military grandeur, victory, themselves as God's 'stately war horse,' themselves as 'leader and chief,' of 'warriors and warriors' bow,' of 'battle,' of 'putting the horsemen to rout.' It is all quite understandable and pitiful as well.

And as their mood goes, so Jawe. The old cry is heard once more. It is typical of the defeated as of the victorious. Generations learn it and pass it on. It is immemorial, a monstrous cliche. It justifies — anything.

Jawe raises the national flag on high. Jawe strengthens the arm and sharpens the aim of this contender or that. This at least is the claim, the Christian claim. Which side is righteous, whose cause is just? It makes little difference, this God (sic) is grandly impartial.

It seems that He raises only one moral requirement: that He be not supplanted. The command holds firm.

These are deep waters; they are tinged with blood. Then or now, the killing of one another in monstrous indiscriminate fashion is a hot item in the world market. By many, indeed by a majority, once the carnage is underway, murder is hardly to be thought morally reprehensible. "For Jawe is with them." Or so it is written.

In many instances, we are told, the 'teraphim,' images of the gods of the nation, were borne into battle. The true believers on the other hand, were forbidden to concoct vain images; God was scarcely to be subject to human fantasies.

And yet, and yet. There are images and images. Some are of wood, stone, metal, as Isaiah reminds. They are deaf and dumb, he insists. Their works are dead; those who fall to worshipping them do so in vain.

All granted, all taken in account, this ceaseless war against a certain kind of images, waged by the prophets.

And then, we read of other images, these proffered by the same prophets. Images clinging to the spirit, borne and cherished within. Images of a God who wages war on behalf of His people, awakening, inflaming, blessing dark instincts!

Shall we forget so easily?

We are speaking of such instincts as in a later time, will dispose of the Human One on the donkey.

(11:1-17) A momentous allegory with discomfiting implications for a time of war. (To Zechariah's vision of the evil and good shepherds, Matthew's gospel is also much indebted.)

It is a time of the loss of a human sense, breakup of a human center, the centripetal force of love. And the disaster, according to Zechariah, is occurring abroad as well as domestically.

The pact of humans with the God of peace has been violated. We are given no details, but the implication is strong that domestic injustice is the issue. The poor, 'the widows and orphans,' the very apple of God's eye, are contemned and written off.

Throw away the wedding ring! Let it go, that ancient marriage, that heart of hearts. Once the passionate kiss of Jawe lay on the lips, the embrace went round and round, a dance, a circle of life.

Another image, that of Zechariah: once, the people were branches of a living tree, and Jawe both trunk and root. But the green wood went sere. So the first of two sticks is broken in the hands of the prophet.

ZECHARIAH

'Let be what is to be' is the symbolic message. The breaking of the dead wood is a gesture of honesty in a time of duplicity and fraud, when religion stands dead on its feet, a wooden idol in stale air.

There is nothing to be done, or very little; this is the sense that comes through. The situation is beyond the powers of the keenest conscience. But that 'little' that can still be done is absolutely crucial if some vestige of the human is to be salvaged.

Break the dead stick then; let the simple act illustrate the breaking of bones, the breaking of hearts!

It comes to this perhaps, two tasks given Zechariah. First dramatize the truth of the situation: break the dead wood, cast the fragments to ground. Thus do the people lie in the dust, inert, feckless, of no worth in their own eyes, in the contemptuous eyes of their leaders as well.

It is the dead end of a story whose theme at least for a grand while was all of green, running with the sap of promise. Now, sere wood; cancel the grand theme; no future.

The second task is dismissal of the other 'shepherds.' The allegory proceeds, relentless. A massive societal house cleaning, or temple cleaning, must be undertaken; three venal priests, a trinity of evil governance, must be put to the door. In a single month rid yourself of them.

But how can this be, given the powerlessness of the prophet? These priests, we are told, were securely installed. They were secular as well as sacred personages.

The point of the task is more than a fantasy of liberation. It is a call to inner refusal. It declares ended the spiritual (if not the political and military) domination that bears down unmercifully on human life. Refuse, resist! A call to abandon despair, impotence, moral paralysis. A call to renew one's faith in an unspeakably evil time. A call to stand somewhere, to raise a cry.

Admittedly, a partial liberation since the forces of death remain securely in the saddle, and the killing goes on. Partial, but still of import.

A judgment is spoken against illegitimate power.

Terrible, yet the word expresses a sense of detachment rather than of fatalism. The powerful, betraying their trust, proceed in the direction they have chosen; very well, let them go. And likewise for the people, the 'flock.' The word of Zechariah announces an evenhanded judgment. (11:9) "What is to die, let it die; what is to perish, let it perish. And let those who are left, devour one another's flesh."

Measure has been taken of the situation; at the same time, the prophet takes the measure of his own powers and resources. They are, by any worldly standard, not great.

And by his own standard, he is forbidden to play Jawe. Indeed, 'playing Jawe' could not in any case deflect the wickedness, whether of the mighty or the lowly, of shepherd or flock.

The dry stick of covenant is broken in pieces. The 'sheep merchants' witness the act and know its significance; the dramatic gesture bespeaks a 'word of Jawe.' They are hardly pleased. They too have sucked dry the sap of the living branch.

The allegory continues. We have the prophet now approaching the merchants. Perhaps he assumes the guise of a public official or a civil servant. He seeks remuneration in view of services rendered.

The request evokes only derision.

Does he think to receive payment for services? Very well, let him be paid.

They weigh out the coins, thirty pieces of silver. According to the law, (Ex. 21:32) it is the price due the owner of a gored slave (not due, be it noted, the wounded slave himself!).

The 'payment' is contemptuous; Zechariah, and through him Jawe, are thus sent a message. This is what Jawe too is 'worth'? This is what the covenant is 'worth'? And the law and the prophets?

'Cast it in the temple treasury,' said Jawe, 'that handsome price at which they valued me.' The payment bespeaks the cynical greed of hardened hearts.

❖ ❖ ❖

In Matthew's gospel, the full range of the 'salary' scene will be exploited, as the betrayer of Christ is 'paid.' (Mt. 26:14)

And on the same scales, it is implied, the worth of Christ is weighed — and found not much.

❖ ❖ ❖

(11:14 ff.) "Then I broke the other stick named 'Bonding,' sundering the union between Judah and Israel." This, we are told, is the earliest evidence of the schism between Israelis and Samaritans.

If the first stick is broken, if the covenant 'with all peoples' is held for naught, what can hold firm? War is inevitable. The sound of the stick breaking is like a first salvo of gunfire.

Then the second stick breaks, almost one thinks, of its own accord. An inner law, old as Genesis, is at work.

❖ ❖ ❖

Something like this: when fidelity is despised and rejected, human bonds in the community are sundered.

The law is implied from the beginning. It is consequent to the revolt in Eden that Cain slays his brother.

❖ ❖ ❖

(11:15) What we are left with is — very little.

The next episode demands of Zechariah the most wrenching, indeed senseless gesture of all. Theater of the absurd!

The two sticks are broken. Now he is told to mime a 'shepherd,' to take the part, assume the gear, the costume and manners. To mime in fact a kind of anti-shepherd. Behold in this ambiguous figure, the resources of the tribe, squandered, bankrupt, despised.

❖ ❖ ❖

And what of Jawe, how describe God's role in all this?

Jawe also plays a part, several parts: the 'emperor of ice cream' in Wallace Stevens' phrase, director of 'King of Hearts,' producer of 'The Works And Pomps Of The Anti-Shepherd, Zechariah.'

There is a dark side of things, as well as a luminous. If you rejoice in

ZECHARIAH

the moon and its light, if you think moonlight is all, perhaps you are — moonstruck. Walk for awhile the dark side of the moon. Then you will come to know the geography of the moon and perhaps of your own soul as well.

And you would take the part of shepherd, of a shepherd praised as 'good'? Or perhaps the part of one of the flock? You would know something of leading others truthfully and well? Of being well and wisely led, at least in longing? You seek in those who hold public trust a compassionate and telling heart?

I give you something else. Taste the bitterness of being misled, badly led, blindfolded, befuddled, cozened, lied to, led like a sheep straight toward a bloodied abattoir.

(I give you — the terrain of Iraq and the wild skies above. There young women and men of many nations, together with resources of every sort, money and gear and weaponry, at least some among them gifted with skills of common sense, civility, communality — all wasted, squandered, to no discernable advantage.)

The anti-pastor, the anti-shepherd, the anti-president, the 'filthy rotten system,' as Dorothy Day summed it up. (We note that the mime is undertaken by Zechariah in the midst of a theocracy. In the high priest [shepherd] is also vested the civil authority.)

Whether social reality, 'system,' or individual, the drama is of negation, darkness, betrayal of high office, denial of the good. The manifesto is hellish. The 'no' is blatant and clear, no mistaking its vehemence. Anti-shepherd, anti-human.

Let us see for a start what the refusal implies, in despite of office, noble tradition, saintly predecessors.

(He) 'will take no note of those who perish.'

(Indeed this 'shepherd' will bring about incalculable ruin and loss.)

ZECHARIAH

On those who are 'strays,' the bewildered, those morally at sea, not a tinker's damn of concern. (Worse, contempt for life itself, whether the lives of humans or other creatures.)

"Those who are wounded, he will not heal." (Rather he will open a great wound across the body of the living and the body of the land. War.)

'Nor will he sustain the survivors.' (To the contrary, let the devastation go on, and the devil take the hindmost — whether in Vietnam, Salvador, Nicaragua, Libya, Grenada, Panama, Iraq.)

Thus the situation as imposed by those who concoct a system of hell on earth.

And on the 'positive' side? We are at a loss; the imagery implies that the crimes of conduct are at least as heinous as the crimes of omission.

This is the behavior, the crime, the state of sin, of those who promulgate and promote an awesome principality of death. "He will eat the flesh of the prosperous and tear off their hooves." The image is of an orgy, a cannibal feast. The system is so voracious, so appetitive, it tends toward an ultimate literal consummation. The system eats those who sit at its table. The guests, so to speak, become the menu.

There is a warning here, and a curse uttered.

The implied warning is spoken for the sake of believers. Knowing the renegade character of the 'shepherd,' they are forearmed against blandishment, strengthened against threats.

(11:17) The curse falls like a thunderbolt upon the 'system' and its hucksters, officials, thieves and parasites, weapons-makers, generals, presidents, those who betray life and integrity, all who amass fortunes wrung from human misery, ideologues who command the media and so distort the truth, all who jettison faith in favor of riches and honors, false teachers who neglect needful clear instruction.

The curse, be it noted, is uttered by Jawe. It calls down the wrath of God upon 'arm' and 'eye.' The arm that wields the sword withers on the moment. Disempowered utterly is immoral power. And blindness, a moral affliction from the start, is here both indicted, condemned — and inflicted.

(12:1-14) Let us with a sense of relief, start with verses 10 through 12. They gleam like a jewel inserted in the (usual?) imperial setting of self-congratulation, assurance, military gore and national glory.

(We have heard the themes before, unto weariness; as usual, they are hauled out here, heavy with the credential of Jawe.)

Imperial aspiration, an imperial God above all, favoring the aspirants!

And yet, and yet, something else, unprecedented, unexplained. Someone. Under the baldachin of national glory, a mysterious figure appears. He/she emerges, first as suffering servant, then as victim, dying violently, perhaps ritually.

In a barbaric moment they have run the body of the victim through, we are told; for what cause or offense, we are told nothing.

There issues from the breast of the newly slain not only blood and water, but a mysterious deluge, a stream of hope. "I will pour out on them a spirit of grace and petition."

Then suddenly it seems, the public mood changes, sobers. The people come to their senses. Glory, dreams of glory vanish on the wind.

Lamentation! "They shall mourn for him as one mourns for an on only son, and they shall grieve over him as one grieves over a first-born."

The tide of grief sweeps across tribes and distance. Remorse, contrition, loss, all of these? We know precious little, only that an event both criminal and saving has occurred. The death of the Servant of Jawe has healed, at least for a time, the imperial illness.

Thus a subtle correction is inserted in the text. Is there a vile death scene? Has an innocent perished? Little matter, or none at all. The nation rides high. The mood is in fact akin to that of the surrounding empires, pretentious and self-inflated. (Indeed the text resembles too closely for comfort, imperial inscriptions elsewhere incised on tombs and altars.)

This people have thought to create a god to their own image. Jawe, we are told, speaks. (12:6) "The princes of Judah ... shall devour right and

ZECHARIAH

left the surrounding peoples." All is contention; the most violent among them emerge victorious.

And Jawe, we are informed, assures the sound outcome. (12:9) "On that day I will seek the destruction of all nations that come against Jerusalem."

Then it is as though an ominous writing appeared on a proud wall. Shall this people play no better part in the world than a mime of Atlas, shoulders gored with the weight of the world, groaning or glorying (we know not which) where he stands? A merciless mercy decrees a better part; let go, let go.

That just one, innocent, done to death — have the renegades done with him? Does his ghost both haunt and heal?

Let the readers, believers, citizens, skeptics, political leaders, priests, make of the text and context what they will.

(13:9) It is a hard place we have arrived at: the heart of things — the human heart.

And we discover something else, something terrible: the heart can also become inhuman and hard as adamant. A heart no more. A stone, compounded of contention and falsity, both.

The theme (13:2) is the removal of 'idols ... prophets ... and uncleanness.' The triad is astonishing. Is prophecy, the heart of God's intervention in our midst, to be summarily removed as an evil? Alas, the hearts of prophets (as one among them here declares) have both hardened and rotted, if such a thing can be.

Ezekiel (chapter 13) and Jeremiah (23:9 ff.) treat the same dolorous falling away, and at greater, more scandalous length. The prophets have betrayed their calling, the truth has fled the land. The multifarious tongues, that bloomed like a thousand flowers for a thousand years, are stilled.

This is terrible beyond telling. Is the silence of God to be preferred to false (or at best, equivocal) speech about God, and worse — conduct that mocks lofty words? It would seem so.

The choices are narrowed. The day is coming, says Jawe, when the air grows thick with a pullulation of false prophets. The signs will be plain

ZECHARIAH

to see. As Jeremiah famously said, such renegades will summon religious language, clothing their lies in a stolen mantle. Their crimes can be summed up: "They will cry peace, peace, when there is no peace."

There is no peace. There is only the austere silence of Jawe. And war.

In despite of that scornful silence, as though to mitigate things (in reality to distort and distemper and deceive) the pseudo-prophets intervene.

Thus is God mocked.

The cry is 'peace, peace'; this amid the hurt and horror of war. Which is to say, in an Orwellian nightmare they call war peace.

Prophets? They justify, (whether in silence or speech) as though Jawe could be imagined to justify, crimes of war. The high and mighty they hold unaccountable. They confabulate distinctions that muddle minds. Prophets? They confuse the unwary, even as they pacify the conscience of the king.

Such are accomplices of high crime. And this, at a time when public authorities should by every means be stirred by the thunders of true prophecy to a very tempest of regret and amendment.

Instead of raising a furious outcry, 'Stop the killing!' the prophets justify the killing. 'Just war!' is their cry. It is a betrayal of the heart of Jawe, crying out on behalf of the victims.

(13:3-6) Let it come to this pass, this matter of scandalous prophecy.

Parents will be shamed by the vain divagations of their sons posing as oracles of Jawe. The parents must refute and rebuke.

But all else failing, they are here instructed — to slay their wayward offspring.

Short of such an outcome, let the false prophets repent, cast aside the stolen cloak of Elijah. Let them come down to earth from their presumptuous heights and return, in the manner of Amos, to their roots. Truthful at last.

(13:7-9) End of prophecy? In any case, not yet. In Zechariah, the fire burns clear.

ZECHARIAH

"'Awaken O sword of mine, against my shepherd
against companion and friend.'
Thus Jawe speaks.
'See how I strike the shepherd
see the flock scattered like chaff.
My hand is turned aside
even against the helpless!
In all this land of mine
(oracle of Jawe)
two thirds shall be cut off, and perish
only a third left alive.

And that third!
they shall pass through fire
But I
shall take their hand
lead them through,
purify them
 like silver, test them
like gold.
Then they will invoke my name in truth
and I shall hear, in hell's despite
and say; My own, my people!
and they; You, Jawe, our God!'"

(14:1-21) This is the story of the 'last days,' a concept so dear to our Bible as to accrete over the centuries a multitude of aspects. According to Zechariah, the days will be marked by (in this order) a showdown battle; a victory for Jawe and the believers; and finally, after much turmoil, peace and plenty.

A 'mosaic,' the chapter is called; indeed. Black tesserae, masses of darkness, relieved here and there by livid flashes of lightning. Then, such contrast! A golden hue and nimbus, Jerusalem glorified. Light reigns, dawn to dusk, dusk to dawn, darkness is banished. And over all, like the smile of Jawe, the temperate climate of heaven descends like a breath of perpetual springtime.

But first the battle and the god of battle.

By analogy, the battle rages within the soul as well as in the tormented world. And the Jawe of Zechariah, it would appear, is likewise tormented within, a Prometheus chained.

We have heard much in our lifetime of a god who stirs up Armageddon. Also of the mind induced in humans by such imagery. Much heat, little light, threatening at any moment to blaze into horrid actuality.

An ideology much given to pride, a sense, to be verified in armed warfare whenever required, that we Americans are masters of the earth.

We desire strongly to see our god approve and bless this (literal) undertaking of the end of things. Nothing quite so reassuring to such thinking as the blessing of a complicit god!

Scripture, we are reminded, is for 'our instruction' — and in ways we are seldom prepared for. To plain sense and human prudence the word of God is frequently scandalous. It puts us off balance with a boldly stated, flat statement — concerning ourselves, our most secret and sullied urges.

Why not Armageddon, it suggests? Let us examine the matter so closely, let us so identify ourselves with an armageddonist god, that we fuse our own desires with his.

The showdown god and the showdown people; the one summoning the many to battle, the many blessed in bringing to pass the final breach and fury.

How then could a given war be termed unjust — when plainly, as in this chapter, Jawe decrees it?

Much to the point: (14:2) "Jawe will gather all the nations toward Jerusalem for battle." The scene, the impulse, the beckoning; it is primordial, it reeks of brimstone. And it is simply set down, and the conclusion left to us: make of this what you will. If such is your god, this or that war is indeed blessed.

If on the other hand, this showdown deity does not speak for the true God, if someone named Jesus intemperately intervenes, more, supersedes this god of yours — more, if the present chapter of Zechariah is recorded as a staging ground for far different decisions, attitudes, behaviors in the

ZECHARIAH

world than are here seemingly commended — if a multitude of saints and martyrs declare their non-alliance with the holy warrior from on high, lay down their arms, turn away from the god and his works of war, prefer to undergo death rather than inflict it — what then?

Surely we have in this chapter a strange form of 'instruction,' bristling with obstacles against sane understanding. Shall we give the words of Zechariah, quoting as he does the bellicose words of Jawe, a meticulous, literal reading?

Some will say an unequivocal yes, will underscore this chapter as imperative, final. Taking their stand, so to speak, beside the warrior god, whose 'feet shall rest upon the mount of Olives.'

(14:9) "On that day the Lord shall be the only one, and his name the only one." What a 'one'!

Presented here are the imperial urge and appetite of a people, hypostasized in an enemy. A very old (and very new) attempt in sum, to compose a credential, to nail it in place. The 'place' being, of course, the slain corpses of the enemy.

Some few read the same text and see something far different: a kind of 'deconstruction'; an implied self-mocking portrait of the 'people of Jawe,' an acute psychological glance within.

They read as well a gross caricature of true God, self-revealed elsewhere as compassionate, mothering, cherishing, mourning the lost, hovering 'over the bent world,' promising surcease of pain.

MALACHI

And at length, this one, the last, the unknown.

And brief; take it or leave!

We see a hand, it spreads a scroll and writes.

No face; or a face veiled, invisible.

    We hear, attentive, a voice. Then another voice.

    How many speakers? One.

An actor, a charged drama, life and death contending,

    the text improvised, passionate,

        lightning on the air!

  Presumption?
  (no other has dared it, even the great ones!)

This one eccolo! speaks for God,
    this one speaks for the people.

    "I will tell you (though I die in the telling)

    the Will of the Holy One,
        incandescent, unknowable!

MALACHI

> Thus and thus says Jawe!
>
> and yes,
>
> I will reveal the secrets, seven times buried,
>
> deep, deeper
>
> than the rubble of Thebes -
>
> your incorrigible hearts!"

So we come to the last of the fiery spirits known as the 'minor' prophets.
And his word is by no means a diminuendo. For ourselves, he offers no least 'carrion comfort.'

It seems fitting that the owner of the voice known as 'Malachi' is quite unknown. The great words dwell on the air, anonymous. 'Malachi' means simply 'the messenger,' 'the precursor.' A 'voice crying in the wilderness'?

It is as though he speaks in the name of another, later, equally noble forerunner, John the baptizer.

And worthily, one thinks. Malachi reminds us of that other hero and martyr; there is a hauntingly similar spirit, a like headlong urgency, style, 'take it or leave.' His questions are not so much raised as — hurled. He shouts as though from the lips of a Michangelesque God, into contrary winds.

Then, (such presumption!) 'oracle of Jawe,' Malachi answers his own questions and by no means in accord with the expectation of his auditors. Then or now?

This is the story of his times and travails. It is tragic and brief, as though incised on a Rosetta stone. The best hopes of his predecessors, Zechariah and Haggai, have come to a fruition — of sorts. But the harvest is rotten. An unseasonable autumn has come, and no second spring.

They have rebuilt the temple so long desired and inexplicably delayed. And the enormous work is no sooner accomplished, than once more, yet once more, the worship degenerates.

Did the enterprise lie under a curse? But had not Jawe blessed it, urged it forward?

Were the walls faulty from the start? It is as though on the day of consecration, the vast edifice were rocked by earthquake, tottered and fell.

And lo and alas, we (and Malachi) are back where we started. The 'prophets of return,' those whose blood and tears melded in the mortise of a great hope; who saw in worship the core and heart of just behavior in the world; and who for sake of the justice of Jawe, desired the temple as the very apple of their eye — these, their labors and hopes, are put to naught. Their lives mocked, their bones scattered like a chaff.

Malachi speaks for them, rages and weeps for them.

Nothing for it, one must start over. This is his sorry unsatisfactory word. Must it always be so, must we benighted mortals always start over? Every oracle, from Moses to Malachi, is launched on the air, flourishes awhile, is heard and obeyed, even celebrated. Then the winds of the world bear the word away — winds ferocious, berserk, demoralizing, a hurricane of the inhuman.

The community flourishes awhile; the love of Jawe prevails; justice is in the air. Alas, amnesia sets in. The people grow prosperous and rotten. They fall away as though in a first untimely frost.

Nothing for it. A remnant, a Malachi, a few believers must start over.

So we hear once more the sublime unwearying (but weary too) voice, the echo of the ancestors, the ancient themes. Right worship creates a just people. Period. Bad worship issues in rote and rot, indifference, venality, violence, injustice. Period.

(Do we grow weary too, hearing it all again? Take heed, take care, look within and around. Never more neglected or needed, the ancient holy teaching).

At the start, a great and central statement, as old as Moses and drawn directly from him. (Deut. 7:7) God speaks to this recusant people: "I have

MALACHI

loved you."

The statement, momentous as it is, does not go unchallenged. How could it be thought so? Indifferent perhaps or truculent, mendacious almost certainly, self-appeasing, taking much for granted, quite sure of themselves — this people can take such love — or leave it.

This declaration of love is no news at all, O prophet-of-sorts. Of course we are 'chosen'!

In such ways the worth of love itself, of the love of Jawe — is challenged. The implication is plain to see; such love can be dispensed with. Other loves occupy the heart (and other, expedient hatreds as well.) So the love of God for us is declared — expendable in practice, a surplus baggage, so to speak. It is discarded, put to naught, in a folderol of 'worship' and public misbehavior.

This being the situation, the tongue of Malachi takes fire.

Let us mount a drama. In it, I shall two parts, Jawe's and the peoples'. Then let us see where this socratic dialogue (much more than imaginary!) will lead.

So he takes up his role, a double part. We see him turning two ways, doffing one mask, assuming another, back and forth, give and take.

First he speaks in the character of Jawe. Then he becomes the voice, soul, interpreter of the people. Speaking for them (against them!) he utters the unspeakable, lays bare the secrets, the greed, the base slavery to routine and law.

If he wears their mask, it is for the sake of unmasking — them.

It is a daring tour de force, brilliantly played, and rare.

The opening argument of God, like those to follow, is a plaint. It is curious, and by no means attractive.

We have heard much of it in the prophets, this affair of being 'chosen.'

It would seem that such love as rests on one people chooses them only in despite of others! "I have loved (you, the descendants of) Jacob, but I have hated the descendants of Esau (Edom)."

A cliche, and by no means harmless. It is also happily contradicted by other prophets; by the universal scope and embrace of an Isaiah, for instance.

To wit, no one, no people is chosen while others are abominated, rejected. All are summoned, all are beloved.

MALACHI

If we repeat ourselves here, it is with a sense, somewhat lowering to the spirit, of deja vu. We have seen such views as are here espoused by Malachi presented elsewhere in the Jewish bible. (We have also seen their corrosive, persistent power, promulgated in our own day.)

Do some stand in the light, and alleluia for them? And are others, the Edoms of our world, relegated to exterior darkness, and too bad for them?

One can only retort; if such be the sorry case, if such dualism dwells in our God, too bad for all of us — and perhaps the chosen themselves are most to be pitied. Is there not danger that they grow cocksure, come to look down on, even persecute those 'others'?

Let it be said plain: the version of 'choice' here offered as of divine warrant can only be thought redundant; more, pernicious.

(1:6) Fathers, sons; masters, servants. So according to Malachi, God sees us, sees himself. Related, blood and spirit. We, the strange wayward changeful unpredictable ones, uneasily taking our place amid an otherwise stable creation. Humans. With, for, in, abided by, cherished by God.

And also over against, opposite to, angry with, in contention against God. And alas betraying, declaring of no moment, casting off as superfluous, onerous — God.

'Only connect,' Forster writes at the start of his novel, *Howard's End*. It is as though in such simple words he was offering a clue to his splendid complex web of character and plot.

It is as though Forster had grasped the image of Malachi. "A son honors his father, a servant stands in awe of his master." But honor and awe and the connection that engenders them are by no means the 'ordinary data of experience in the world.' Could there be in this tormented age of ours a wilder understatement?

And yet the connection is insisted on. It makes sense — and it makes no sense at all. Honor and awe, what we might call a religious sense of the world, a sense that arises like a perfume, beyond the senses, through the senses. It is breathed in, confessed, even celebrated, and this in a time of atrocious suffering and loss. And the same sense is derided in the realms of the highminded. A 'religious sense of things'? Come now!

Nevertheless. The 'claim,' the joining of hands, the bond, the insistence! It is constant and clear. It stands there in Malachi and the other seers: fathers, sons, master, servants. Hosea will have it also, and more daringly, in his bridal image: spouses, Jawe and our unlovable selves.

Only connect! Jesus will dwell on it, enlarge on it, push it further. In spite of the dense — pull of gravity, the past, failure and fate — he beckons, raises us bodily one almost says — toward grace.

He summons us, whose 'place' in the world heretofore has been the fields and scullery (and lucky we were to be assigned even there!) — summons us to sit at table with Himself: "Now I call you not servants, but friends."

"If I am father, where then is my honor? And if master, where the awe?"
"It is you, the priests, who dishonor my name."
"And how do we dishonor your name?"
And so on. Malachi and his interior dialogue. It is borrowed from Greek tragedy; stichomythic, headlong, even furious. This is what it means to be a Malachi (or an Isaiah for that matter, or a Daniel.) It is astonishing, he reads hearts. He knows each so well, ourselves and our God.

In this Malachi is honored. He is godly. He resembles that God who is luminous, transparent as a noonday sun, unconsumed, light giving, filled with self-knowledge, with 'hesed,' loving knowledge of creation.

And what of ourselves? The implication is plain to see; the people of Malachi (and ourselves as well) are much in need of such instruction as is here set down (better, shouted aloud!).

For we have grown opaque, we stand in darkness. We glory in darkness, groping and stumbling about, knowing little of ourselves or of God.

The fierce argument continues. It is as though Malachi, standing exposed in some public place, were being torn in two. Schizoid, the seer! He must raise before this recusant people questions they dare not ask. And in so doing, must lay bare their inmost wounds.

These are the 'polluted gifts' they dare place on the altar; gifts questionable, polluted, surrogate for the stinking meat of the heart.

He responds in the role of a prosecutor named Jawe. This, this is the truth of your condition!

Let us (a furious burst of irony!) offer an example. Would you dare bring such second rate offerings — say, to your High Commissioner, this or that secular authority — and anticipate a flourish of the hautboys, signifying a grateful reception?

Absurd. The gifts speak for the heart — closer than you know.

(1:10) A plaint, and a strange one — but everything is strange here, the words all but fail.

"O that there were one among you who would shut the doors, that you might not kindle fire upon my altar in vain!"

A reflection. At the close of the Gulf carnage in the summer of 1991, New York among other cities, prepared for the Roman triumph. (The wicked glee was predictable and occasions no scandal. It was simply the ordinary behavior of empire.)

But one 'religious' response was notable, in a scandalous sense. A great cathedral of the city welcomed to its sanctuary and pulpit the American generals who led the slaughter and the White House vandal who orchestrated it.

The excuse offered by church officials went somewhat in this wise. These were invited in order that they might join with others, to 'pray for the dead of both sides.'

There occurred among a few clergy and layfolk, a furious and immediate response. They 'locked the doors, that the sanctuary candles and torches be not lit in vain.' The night previous to the service, they remained in the cathedral, fasting and vigiling. And the next day they were dragged forth and arrested.

No polluted gifts here, not in their name.

(1:11) It is as though this were the course of the world. God is impelled to taste the spoiled meat of our hearts. Distaste, nausea has been the theme, and will be. Or so it seemed.

MALACHI

Then in the midst of the shambles, a grand symphonic burst is heard from the mouth of Jawe. Malachi has raised his eyes, besmirched by polluted smoke, and seen — something. Far off, unlikely, luminous, and nearing.

"From the rising of the sun to sunset, my Name is great among the nations. And in every place incense is offered my Name, and a pure offering. For my Name is great among the nations, says God."

The vision once spoken, the plaint continues.

A stench is in the air, nothing worse, a heavy cloud of decay of spirit, obfuscation of soul.

And we are left with that. Commonly known on the one hand as the facts of life. And on the other, what? Vision? Breakthrough?

We have seen both. The worldly sanctuary and the pure offering — lives untainted: the resisters, the prisoners of conscience, those who in the words of Revelation, have 'eaten the scroll.'

The image here is awesome. God is witness to a lackadaisical procession winding its way toward the altar; wounded and sick animals are shunted along by the wounded and sick of spirit.

(2:2) "I will curse your blessing."

This affair known as religion can only be accounted dangerous. Well-lit sanctuaries conceal dark corners. Other presences lurk than those summoned by the orotund preachers.

Let the service proceed under an assumption, more or less blind, that its song and dance are agreeable to all — to God as well.

The sermon, let us imagine, is underway. And suddenly, here and there in the congregation, someone's voice is raised in fury. Then one or another arises and departs the place.

Or one by one, an entire group stands in defiance. Something offensive has been said, something desired has not been said. What could be going on? The worshipful citizens in the pews are befuddled; more than a few are enraged.

The priests are canny. A signal is passed. Guards intervene, or the police. A rumpus, then removal of the offenders.

And what of God in all this uproar?

We have little notion, we say — but perhaps a less foggy notion than is commonly confessed.

"I will curse your blessing."

Leave it at that. A word from on high, as though the mouth of Malachi became transparent with fire. No mouth, only a word. The flat statement stands there to be made of what we will.

But it must be admitted that a free and easy supposition (God's in his heaven, all's well with the world!) — that nonsense is broken. God has spoken. Or perhaps not, and Malachi is a species of mental patient?

This was the situation. At the start it seemed unchangeable and secure. More, it was declared valid. Dignum et justum the priests homilized or sang or danced or invoked a blessing or anointed with oil or processed or sprinkled water or lit incense or distributed bread and wine. In any case, they conveyed to the people through many formalities and gestures who God was, what the divine will, where our appointed place and scope in the scheme, the dance.

The priests gently borrowed the 'I' of a God who is beyond our imagining. They borrowed God's word from the mouth of God. They spoke on behalf of that unutterable Other. Hear ye; God's will.

In their mouths the message made good sense.

In sum, and crudely, the message was, 'No problem.'

It dovetailed nicely with our ways in the world. We were blessed in this.

Nothing of the awesome, the fear and trembling. Squared stones underfoot, the feet upon stone, the splendid processions. Upon this rock I will build.

Annie Dillard (*Teaching A Stone To Speak*) comments acidly"

"On the whole, I do not find Christians, outside of the catacombs, sufficiently sensible of conditions. Does anyone have the foggiest idea what sort of power we so blithely invoke? Or, as I suspect, does no one believe a word of it? The churches are children playing on the floor with their chemistry sets, mixing up a batch of TNT to kill a Sunday morning.

"It is madness to wear ladies' straw hats and velvet hats to church; we should all be wearing crash helmets. Ushers should issue life preservers and signal flares; they should lash us to our pews. For

MALACHI

the sleeping god may wake someday and take offense, or the waking god may draw us out to where we can never return."

And then something else, a terror.

The astonishing turnabout announced by Malachi! Our seams and pockets utterly turned out.

It is a scandal we have come upon, a stone in the shoe of a pilgrim. Or a stick of wood thrust in the whirling spokes, upsetting the easy riders. Interruption of business as usual, the mellifluous mindless business and bumbling known as — religion.

A stroke of lightning in a clear sky. A high fever induced; the crisis that breaks the illness. Such images occur.

Worse and worse, as verse 2 continues.

The curse is already in place; the 'blessing' is no more.

And why? "Because there is no one among you who lays this to heart."

Lays what to heart? It is question of 'giving glory to My Name.'

What that means will shortly be made clear — an instruction underscored through the centuries in the blood of prophets and martyrs.

Say it once more, shout it aloud!

Integrity of worship is to be judged by the integrity of social conscience!

The mystery and the public behavior; the sanctuary and the marketplace. Integrity, mutuality. Or if not, the blessing turns to a curse.

It is as though in a season when warm rains fell, the downpour turned to ice. And this in the space of an hour.

Or on a given day, in nothing differing from former days (as far as could be known), an ancient people went about their affairs. Their fair city stood, alas, in the slope of a volcano. And in a single hour, disaster struck. And one and all were buried alive.

This God is physical and furious, comes on like a blinded Sampson, laying about him lustily.

MALACHI

The curse uttered by such a Being could hardly be thought a form of mitigation or good manners. (2:3) No reproving tweak here or light reminding tap on the wrist. No, a very trumpet blast, a bellow of outrage: "I will break your arms, I will cast dung in your faces (the dung of your worship), and I will cast you and it, out of my presence."

Outrageous Malachi! Are we then to allow that our God may arise, to disrupt in such wise — the worship of God?

(2:5) Levi the ancestor entered upon a covenant and kept it inviolate. So he stands as a generational reproof against the corrupt levites of the day.

It was a covenant of 'life and peace' (how beautiful, how long vanished!), and those same gifts, the hallmarks of the pact, "I bestowed on him."

The gifts have been withdrawn; rather, they have been despised, neglected, squandered. In consequence of their loss, all has flattened out, grown stale; life itself, the worship that in the days of Levi was all of 'fear and trembling.'

Dillard tells stories of such days, and such awe:

"One hasidic slaughterer, whose work required invoking the Lord, bade a tearful farewell to his wife and children every morning before he set out for the slaughterhouse. He felt, every morning, that he would never see any of them again. For every day, as he himself stood with the knife in his hand, the words of his prayer carried him into danger. After he called on God, God might notice and destroy him before he had time to utter the rest, 'Have mercy.'

"Another hasid, a rabbi, refused to promise a friend to visit him the next day. 'How can you ask me to make such a promise? This evening I must pray and recite: "Hear, O Israel" When I say these words, my soul goes out to the utmost rim of life.... Perhaps I shall not die this time either, but how can I now promise to do something at a time after the prayer?'"

The verses that follow are in a familiar pattern. God takes the part of an historical prosecutor. Time itself is summoned to the stand, that ancient time when covenant was forged. Then the co-signer Levi appears, progenitor of the line of priests, witness against descendants gone tedious and venal.

Not many eminences have merited such praise as Levi. God speaks of him with a glowing heart:

"True instruction was in his mouth, and no wrong was found on his lips. He walked with Me in peace and uprightness, and turned away from iniquity."

Any saint of any covenant could but rejoice to be so memorialized. But the encomium does not float on empty air; it proceeds toward a vigorous 'true instruction' in favor of latter-day Levites;

"The lips of a priest should guard knowledge, and people should seek instruction from his mouth, for he is the messenger of the Lord of hosts."

And then, self-evident, the woeful unwelcome contrast. How great the ancestor — and how puny and banal the descendants! Those summoned to be ikons of the Holy One have become the scandal.

"But you have turned aside from the way; you have caused many to stumble by your 'instruction.' You have corrupted the covenant of Levi."

And the outcome? It stands self-evident, to their shame: "So you are rendered abased, vile before the people, as you have not kept my ways, but have turned your high office aside, to human advantage."

Idolatry, the old theme recurs. It shadows the human scene, dogged and demoralizing. Fidelity is a lost art; the covenant languishes on the ancient vine.

The drama continues. Malachi dons his masks once more, sums up, witheringly (2:17): "You weary Jawe with your talk, talk. You say, 'How do we weary God?' By saying, 'The evildoer is good in the sight of Jawe; in such as they, God delights.' Or by asking, 'Where is the God of justice?'"

Subtle, relentless, the diagnosis. It has come to this: that evil and good are intermixed in the mind to the point where one appears in the guise of the other, one indistinguishable from the other. And God, it is adduced, connives with this confusion; the evildoer is called good.

In such days as we endure, what are we to make of the national ikons? Generals are feted, warmakers held in high honor, scoundrels and wastrels of the public trust are celebrated.

To have obliterated a Japanese city by atomic means merits a niche in the civil pantheon....

The scandal. Injustice manifest, bold, massive in the world; and the God of justice by no means equally manifest; and yet the two realities cohabiting the universe.

This is indeed a strange turn. Malachi is here reproving, on the face of it, those who wince at the prospering of the wicked. But is not this a great theme of Job (among others), the plaint, the wound, a cicatrix of the soul?

Why then the reproof of a plaint heard elsewhere, repeatedly, raised so movingly by the martyrs of Revelation?

One difficulty must be accounted central. Who, according to Malachi, are here raising the question of God and evil? It is by no means clear.

We presume that either the priests or their votaries are thus questioning God. If so, the questions ride the ground like a subtle smoke, evidence of a wasting fire beneath. The fire is called bad faith, the bad faith of a debased priesthood.

We need not dwell on it; Malachi has reproved the priesthood scorchingly in earlier verses. In sum, those who benefit from injustice are badly employed in reproving God for the scandal of injustice. Theirs is no more than a covert form of the wickedness they purport to protest.

The just on the other hand, have suffered and died at the hands of the wicked. So they have won the title of complaint. They merit their outcry: 'from beneath the altar,' 'how long, O Lord, how long?'

We shall hear more of these. They are the beloved of Malachi and of Jawe as well.

(3:1 ff.) The 'messenger' and the 'angel.' These presences are known only to a few. But the promise stands; they will come.

And in a strange bending of time, future to past, they have come, these two, according to Christian faith. And a question arises: Have such persons and events been plucked from their native soil and time? Are they put to serve uses both foreign and, at the time of their first coming, veiled in a future not yet arrived?

MALACHI

Matthew is calm; in chapter eleven of his gospel, seeking to shed light upon the mysterious archangelic John Baptist, he simply borrows this image of 'messenger' from Malachi.

More, he lends the ancient words a sovereign patina. Now the words issue from the lips of Jesus, as he extols his friend, condemned to Herod's prison. Such praise, and from so exalted a source! Something of sweetness and strength has vaulted the centuries between. Malachi and Matthew, Jawe and Jesus.

This is a new image of the 'coming of Jawe,' the 'day of Jawe.' No thunder, no lightning. God enters the temple; but this is occasion of neither pomp nor circumstance. God comes as a cleansing fire, a purifier of the holy place.

The scene is one of judgment; the witness for the prosecution is — God. And the defendants are not only the priests. The swath of justice swings wide 'against sorcerers, adulterers, perjurers, against those who oppress the wage earners, the widow and orphan, those who thrust aside the wanderers, who [in sum] do not fear Me.'

These are old charges. In the prophets they are constantly being brought forward — even as, so it seems, the same crimes are renewed by each generation. The banality of sin!

One imagines the walls of the temple dissolving; the world itself becomes the courtroom, the conduct of each and all is bared, placed in question before the court.

Wide world and enclosure, forth and back. We are once again in the temple. An austere cleansing follows; the holy precinct so abused by the priesthood (and presumably by the congregants as well) is renewed on the moment. It, and they, take on the sublime lineaments of the days of Levi, 'as in the days of old and in former years.' Levi would own his place once more, and his priests and people.

(3:6) We cannot have enough of the remarkable confession. "I, Jawe, do not change; therefore you, sons of Jacob, are not consumed." The parallelism is exact, even while the logic stops one short. In what (we might ask in the manner of Malachi) does Jawe not change? It would seem,

MALACHI

to put matters mildly, that steadiness of mood is hardly one of the divine attributes. Jawe, as prophet after prophet announces, is perpetually changing the weather of Her soul; from anger to tenderness, from the will to destroy to the will to save, from 'I will leave your land desolate,' to 'I will be your God and you my people.'

But as matters turn out, the threats, we discover, are for the most part words, words. They are seldom carried out; we come to know that there is a truer truth than they. It is the 'great acts' of salvation, and their after shock of care, fretting, benevolence, a prodigious foison — centuries of forbearance, even wonderment and of rapture of mind at contemplation of 'the work of my hands.'

That love does not change; though it be received in tardigrade fashion, its seeds lost, squandered in swamp and storm — still love endures. No reason to it, no logic beyond its own — the nature, the passion, the plain endurance of love, 'a harsh and dreadful thing.'

Moods are one thing, surely Jawe knows a vast orchestration of these — Sophoclean, Beethovian, Shakespearian in scope! But the heart keeps its mysteries, they stand firm beneath, beyond high tide or low. The heart has its reasons; though they be inscribed in flesh, they are more enduring than tablets of stone.

If God were in this essential to change, if Her love were to weary or grow cold, if it stood as austerely stipulated that love and the return of love be totted up, weighed to a nicety, judged — if the pans of the scales must balance, if love were a simply juridical quid pro quo — then surely we had perished on the instant.

In this Jawe shall not change; in love of the loveless. If He were to change in this, we would be 'consumed' (3:6). This is the mystery, the scandal, the very meaning of time — the patient love of God.

(3:7) The Malachian drama resumes, precipitated by a command, an aphorism both splendid and urgent. "Return to Me and I will return to you."

We are brought up short, for the sequence is awry. Shall we call the statement a subtle variant of an ancient truth, reversed here out of a kind of subtle courtesy?

We mortals are invited then, to undertake the first move in the minuet of delight?

It is impossible; our feet are stuck. It is only the orchestra, striking up the cosmic theme, the 'music of the spheres,' that brings the dancers to their feet. The author we know; and the music, its opening bars inviting the 'first movement' of the dance. Come then! the music is heady, it is in the blood. And the dancers find it irresistible.

The music, the divine musician — and ourselves. In that order, the dance.

Or another instance of what might be thought of as the priority of grace, of love. It is adduced by Jesus, in the story of the son who seizes his inheritance, washes hands of brother and father, and proceeds to make a capital fool of himself; with what outcome we know. (Lk10:20-37)

Certainly the son is a prodigal, a wastrel of note; his conduct is markedly contemptuous of those who love him. He squanders his inheritance, talent, young manhood.

But the father might also be termed a prodigal. No talk of boundary or limit, no grievances, even the heaviest, nursed at heart. He runs to embrace the young penitent, limping homeward ashamed. More, the father places his goods and chattels in service of a great celebration. And most moving of all, he defends his prodigal love against the tedious spleen of the older son.

The memory, the bitterness, the contempt implicit, the shrugging off of responsibility, the crude selfishness and sensuality — all are erased. It is as though nothing of the kind had ever transpired, a bad dream. It signified nothing, carries no weight in the heart of the father.

Thus the noblest of fictions is summoned by the imagination of Jesus; and the fiction is both stranger and stronger than truth. Better, it is the deepest truth of all:

"Attend to this. With my father Jawe, sin is as if it had never been. The son, grown renegade, nonetheless comes home. And every futile step of departure is canceled by that chastened return.

"He is for that — yes, even for having left my house — for the return above all, the more closely melded. He is bound with adamant to my heart."

(3:8) "'But,' you say, 'how shall we return?'"

A question which is to imply in a somewhat defensive mood, one thinks: 'Return? From whence? (But we have in nothing departed from you!)'

And quick as the blink of an eye, they (and we) are informed. (Too quick for comfort?) Jawe is clearly Jewish. The answer, such as it is, takes the form of another question.

"Will humans rob God? But you are robbing Me." (I.e., in this you are found prodigal, have seized the inheritance, and 'departed.')

"You say, 'In what are we robbing You?'"

"In your tithes and offerings. You are cursed with a curse, the whole nation of you."

Malachi the peremptory fabulist, the adroit interlocutor of God!

His thundering intuition is this: a larceny is underway against the God of genesis. It is an unprecedented insulting of creation, worked by the greedy, violent and duplicitous, skimming off the very cream of creation in servitude to death (devastating weaponry, wasting war). The sorry story of Malachi's lifetime and of ours.

Injustice toward humans follows inevitably the initial injustice against the ecology. Thus do community and our gentle planet, together languish.

A cable of disaster is woven, spread wide, then tightened to a garrote.

(3:10) "Bring the full tithe into My storehouse, that there may be food in my house. And thereby [astonishingly] put me to the test."

Which is to say, "Make a saving gesture." Right use, stewardship, portions of harvest put aside for the poor. In need the neighbor stands there at one's fingertips, and the fingers set tingling, at a touch. As though one's humanity did not end there, with empty hands, but continued, with the hands' offering and the joining of hands in the rhythmic give and take of the dance!

"Thus am I put to the test, gently, willingly. You will observe whether or not I respond to the simple but so moving gesture I propose to you!"

The test, the outcome, the promise. "For you, for you [twice repeated]... I will open the windows of heaven and pour down an overflowing blessing."

One dares translate (One also wishes that such matters could be put with the telegrammatic brevity of Malachi!):

The moral ecology of the community consists in its vivid, even valiant sense of justice. Period. Just activity is godly. Just action is the irrefutable sign of the flourishing of the human, as injustice, inequity, moral numbness, greed, violence, are portents of decline and fall.

Just, unjust; our behavior is reflected back on us, as though in a merciless mirror, from the estate of the planet, from all living beings, their flourishing or decline and fall.

Observe, and rejoice or mourn. Our fate is written there as in a living text, in bold type; even the blind among us may read as we run.

"All nations will call you blessed; you will be a land of delight, says Jawe." Thus is the curse turned around once more. Behold, a people of delight as well, a delightful people! A people who take joy in one another, for whom no wanton greed creates need, whose habits of life know no victims, who put no one to the door, whether of heart or community.

Whose joy is the rising of a dazzling rainbow over the earth, signifying the blessing bestowed upon human variety.

No, misery is not endemic to the human, neither is moral nausea, nor despair nor fear, nor the demonizing of others, nor the spleen that finds outlet in war. These need not be.

Such awful matters, be it admitted, are superadded to (or perhaps subtracted from) the human. They are burdensome, parasitic, a drag. Call them right, name them openly — sin, structural sin. The sin of injustice, the curse, as Malachi and his like never weary insisting.

The foregoing is a matter of — the promise. Of what might be, and more; of what shall be. For Jawe has spoken.

And yet, and yet. If the promise is to be substantial rather than etherial, vague, fantastic, it must take in account something known crudely as the facts of life. The so called facts, dire as they are; then the promise. Malachi is a great one for keeping us in a sense, off balance, with both vividly in view.

Is this the only method, surprise, astonishment, apt to awaken to slow learners like ourselves?

We ricochet between the present awful situation of our world, the sin, the injustice — and then that unquenchable, unkillable word that continues to reverberate, even in such hearts as cower within us, long inured as we are to catastrophe.

The promise lives in our bones, an incandescence. We will never be finally, truly content with those awful 'facts' (which in a true sense, we are responsible for).

Something in us, something given us, outlasts it all: a voice, a vision, a hope and healing. Something holy. The worst and darkest that dwells in us and around us, that claims to speak for us, that seeks to degrade us, all this horror is unable finally to kill, to eradicate, to cast off the promise of God. It rises like a sun in bleakest night. Listen, 'for you, for you, I will pour out a blessing in abundance.'

Once more to the 'facts', and the inner dialogue of Malachi.

Of import here, Jawe now turns in heeding to the 'little remnant' of the just. They too have their day, their say. Speak up!

And they do, impetuously. It is a harsh word they utter, harsh as the reproach of Job, more harsh by far than the plaint of the martyrs of Revelation.

"Your words are stout against me," says Jawe. "Yet you [the just] say, 'How have we spoken against you?'"

(In this way). "You have said, 'It is vain to serve God.' What is the good of it?... From this moment we declare the arrogant blessed; they put God to the test and they walk away.'"

And we are told, "God took heed, and heard them." And nothing more.

The scene is anticlimactic. The text comes to a close, leaves us there, the plaint, the threnody, the anger hovering on the air, like life itself, unfinished, ragged, jagged. Wickedness, the just cry out, flourishes like a noxious nest of weed. It poisons the earth and air, and ourselves, powerless as we are finally to root it out — from ourselves perhaps least of all.

❖ ❖ ❖

MALACHI

The exchange is strangely and powerfully reminiscent; we have seen it, heard it before. It is akin to the non-response that confounds the holy martyrs 'under the altar,' their plaint all unanswered. (Rev.6:9-11)

We are told here, "God took heed, and heard them."

As in Revelation, ('they were each given a white robe and told to be patient....') a symbolic gesture on God's part. And in Malachi: "A book of remembrance was written before Him, in favor of those who fear God and seek refuge in God's name."

Not much, but something, that book, that 'aid to memory.' The memory of God is long, longer than the eons, the age of humans, more persistent and lucid. Names are set down, surely criminal names among them. But that is hardly the point. The names that live, that all but leap from the page, from the tongue, the names embossed in purest gold, are those of the faithful.

These are the names recorded by the holy amanuensis, no single one to be lost. "They shall be mine," said Jawe, "my special possession on the day I prepare. And I will have compassion on them, as a man compassionates the son who undertakes hard tasks."

What hard tasks they have undertaken, these confessors and martyrs, what lives of labor, what terrible deaths!

And that connection again, in which God glories and discovers, for our sake, glorious meaning!

And a serious implication too. The noble bond of fatherhood and sonship, denied or affirmed, despised or honored, is matter of judgment. "Then once more you will see the difference between the just and the wicked, between those who serve God and those who refuse to serve."

Until — The Day. So simply put, and so final. The Day of all days, The Day to which all days have tended. The Day without which no day of all our centuries, no least hour of the tormented human venture, can claim sense, meaning, direction. Day of vindication, day revealing for the sake of the martyrs, 'the good, the non absurdity of serving God, of keeping the observances of Jawe.'

Day also on which the plaint of the just is answered, once for all. 'The arrogant seem blessed' no longer, 'evildoers prosper' no more.

No more of that. A fiery dawn, 'burning like an oven.' Like a sun terribly come to earth, 'a furnace,' The Day will consume the wicked to ash. Which is to say, in imagery familiar to the prophets, the fire of God's justice will prevail at length, purifying creation and community of all sin. At long last, after long delay.

And the same fiery planet rises for the sake of the just. But with what contrast! It rides its circuit equably, temperately in the heavens, a Sun of Justice 'with healing in its wings.'

So it is written. And so received, with gratitude to Malachi, the great and good — the unknown one.

For our instruction to be sure, and our strengthening.

www.ingramcontent.com/pod-product-compliance
Lightning Source LLC
Chambersburg PA
CBHW071228290426
44108CB00013B/1326